Demography of the
Black Population
in the
United States

Demography of the Black Population in the United States

An Annotated Bibliography with a Review Essay

Jamshid A. Momeni

Foreword by James F. Scott
Preface by Reynolds Farley

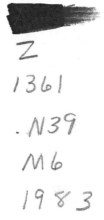

Greenwood Press
Westport, Connecticut • London, England

Library of Congress Cataloging in Publication Data

Momeni, Jamshid A., 1938-
   Demography of the black population in the United
States.

   Bibliography: p.
   Includes index.
   1. Afro-Americans—Population—Bibliography.
I. Title.
Z1361.N39M6   1983   016.3046'08996073   83-5544
[E185.86]
ISBN 0-313-23812-X (lib. bdg.)

Library of Congress Catalog Card Number: 83-5544
ISBN: 0-313-23812-X

First published in 1983

Greenwood Press
A division of Congressional Information Service, Inc.
88 Post Road West
Westport, Connecticut 06881

Printed in the United States of America

10 9 8 7 6 5 4 3 2 1

Copyright Acknowledgment

"The dissertation titles and abstracts contained
here are published with permission of University
Microfilms International, publishers of *Dissertation
Abstracts International* (copyright © 1956-1981 *
by University Microfilms International), and may
not be reproduced without their prior permission."

RR 1-17-86

To My Family

Contents

Figures and Tables

Figures

Tables

Acknowledgments

Without the works of the authors who are cited here, this volume would not have been possible. There is really no way I can adequately acknowledge the great debts I owe to each and every original author named in the index and their respective publishers.

At the level of preparation, I received support and encouragement from Dr. Lorraine A. Williams, Vice President for Academic Affairs, Dr. Edward W. Hawthorne, Dean of the Graduate School of Arts and Sciences, Dr. James F. Scott, Chairman of the Department of Sociology and Anthropology, Dr. Roger D. Estep, Vice President for Development and University Relations, Dr. Avis Y. Pointer, Director of the Department of Federal Affairs, and Dr. Ella E. White, Associate Director of the Department of Federal Affairs at Howard University.

Vice President Williams, by virtue of her intense interest in faculty research activities, most enthusiastically supported this project and helped me find the necessary funds for typing the manuscript. In addition to their encouragement and unequivocal moral support, Dean Hawthorne, Dr. Scott, and Vice President Estep contributed from their budgets toward the cost of the preparation of this manuscript.

Special thanks are due to my teaching assistant, Mr. B. Asadi. During the summer of 1982, when most of the library research for this volume was carried out, Mr. Asadi rendered invaluable assistance in locating many of the references in different libraries in the Washington, D.C. metropolitan area. It also gives me great pleasure to acknowledge the cooperation of the Population Information Program Resource Center at Johns Hopkins University, which in March 1981 carried out a search relative to publications on black population using POPLINE. The material obtained from POPLINE constituted the seed which grew to become this volume. The dissertation titles and abstracts contained here are published with permission of University Microfilms International, the publishers of Dissertation Abstracts International, 300 North Zeeb Road, Ann Arbor, Michigan, 48108. I acknowledge the significant contribution of Dissertation Abstract International to this volume.

I would also like to thank Mrs. Patricia Henriques White, Director of PACE Graphics in Washington, D.C., and her staff—Denise A. Clarke, Bernadette E. Sharperson, Shirley Marable, and Merry P. Phillips—who diligently and patiently labored over the tedious job of typing this work.

Foreword

Some books are written for the express purpose of riveting the attention of readers to several key ideas and thereby providing stimuli to further intellectual discussion and debate. Others seem to grow more out of a recognized yet often unmet need of persons within a particular field of study to have at their disposal a distillation of many ideas that can make direct contributions to research activity. This book by Professor Momeni is one that fits much more comfortably in the second category without in any way denying the importance of the first. Its utility as a research tool will be immediately welcomed by those who have sought to present systematic analysis of the black population in the United States, but often find a bewildering array of demographic works, some of which may or may not have any direct relevance for the particular problem(s) being investigated.

Professor Momeni pulls together in this volume a complete bibliography of demographic works done on blacks in this century, organizes them around major topics in the social life of blacks, and in doing so considerably reduces the expenditure of time and effort future researchers would otherwise devote to accomplishing an exhaustive review of the literature. The organizing theme for the more than 650 entries reflects a thorough knowledge of the demographic literature and a remarkable insight into how the various issues identified impinge on black community life. From consideration of the patterns of fertility among blacks to migration, health, and mortality, one can easily assess the status of our demographic knowledge and determine with equal facility where gaps in our understanding call for further research.

It would, of course, be a mistake to think of Professor Momeni's work as merely another annotated bibliography. Instead, this work goes beyond a conventional bibliography in the sense that it is a compilation of abstracts/summaries/conclusions and findings of most researches done on the black population. Perhaps more appropriately, it could be thought of as being a *Research Handbook on Black Demography* covering works done over a span of about 100 years. Contributing to the overall coherence of the work is an introductory chapter by Momeni which synthesizes the most salient demographic developments in the black community into a readable essay. The systematic care given to the treatment of every phase of the book makes it a unique contribution to the study of blacks in the United States as well as to the demographic literature.

There is no doubt on the part of anyone who has studied some aspects of the black community that understanding the characteristics of the black population is a necessary first step. Yet too often this fundamental phase of analysis of the black community has been neglected. The complexity and diversity of the institutional life of black Americans is made much more difficult to grasp when we fail to appreciate the conditioning influence of demographic factors on social behavior. It is, at the same time, these very intricacies of black community life that give depth and substance to our efforts to gain a comprehensive understanding.

Closely related to our knowledge of black community life must be the concern about bringing such knowledge, whenever possible, to bear on the formulation and implementation of public policies that have an impact on the structure of the black community. Because public policy invariably involves debate and disagreement it is all the more reason to have any consideration of policy carefully supported by as much available evidence as possible. Such evidences have assumed even greater importance in recent years for many policy considerations have arisen in response to changes in the demographic characteristics of the black population. The mass movement of the blacks from rural to urban areas, the changes in the age and sex distributions of the blacks in rural as well as in urban areas—these and other demographic shifts among blacks have had profound impacts on patterns ranging from family and marriage to crime and delinquency, and to various types of institutional participation. Today many of the policies relative to the black community tend to center on various problem areas that are either produced or exacerbated by changes in key demographic variables. It is therefore imperative that these changes in the demographic structure of the black community be accurately documented and their influences properly assessed.

Undoubtedly, this work will not only be a widely sought-after resource for researchers who might wish to examine various facets of black American life, but a reference of inestimable value for those who may seek to have their policy decisions concerning black community be based more firmly on demographic evidence.

James F. Scott
Howard University
November 1982

Preface

Throughout the history of the United States and the colonies which preceded it, racial issues have been among the most important social, economic and political concerns. Quite clearly, demographic aspects of the distribution and status of blacks played an important role in many of the major decisions about how this nation should be governed. The fifth paragraph of the Constitution alludes to this topic when it implies that enslaved blacks are equivalent to only three-fifths of a free person for purposes of apportioning representatives and taxes among the states. The impact of population factors on social issues is well exemplified by the results of the 1840 census when data relative to blacks living outside the slave states were altered to help influence decisions about the continuation and extension of slavery. Even long before the need for a systematic study of population was realized, demographic factors figured heavily in shaping and reshaping many policy issues of major social consequence not only in this country but on a global level.

Scholarly demographic investigations of the black population in this country have a short history of probably less than ninety years. Among the first publications to deal specifically with the birth rates, death rates, age structure and characteristics of blacks was the 1899 publication of W.E.B. Dubois, *The Philadelphia Negro*. Although extremely informative, this study dealt with the demography of the black population of only one city.

For national information about the black population, perhaps the earliest publication was Bulletin 8 from the enumeration of 1900. The Bureau of the Census issued this as *Negroes in the United States* in 1904. An even more impressive compilation of demographic trends concerning blacks throughout the entire span of the nation's history was the Census Bureau's encyclopedic report, *Negro Population: 1790-1915*. An investigation of almost any aspect of the growth, distribution, social or economic status of blacks during the first century and a half of the United States will make use of this volume. In an interesting comment on the racial norms of that time, the director of the Bureau of the Census, in his introduction to this publication, tells us: "It is worthy of note that the tabulations for this report were made by a corps of Negro clerks working under the efficient direction of three men of their own race. . . ." Following the decennial count of 1930, the Census Bureau again issued a massive compilation of statistics concerning demographic rates and trends among blacks.

Before 1940, there were relatively few publications specifically describing the growth of the black population or the social and economic characteristics of the black community. A diligent scholar could track down these publications in a reasonable amount of time. This is no longer the situation. With the urbanization of blacks during World War II and the emergence of an effective civil rights movement in the two decades following that conflict, a growing number of scholars turned their energies to investigating those demographic trends which influence the black population. Not only did they examine contemporary differences in the vital rates and characteristics of blacks and whites but, using new techniques and, sometimes, using new data sources, they were able to reexamine racial trends from the nineteenth century and the early twentieth century. Certainly, it is no longer possible for a scholar to easily locate all the works which describe the demography of blacks. Indeed, the publications are now so numerous that even if you restrict your interest to a specific topic, you will have difficulty finding all relevant studies.

This is why the *Demography of the Black Population in the United States* by Jamshid Momeni will be so extremely valuable. If we wish to learn what has been done about any aspect of the black population, we can now consult this source. We will find not only the definitive list of publications, but we will also learn about the approach and the basic conclusions of the studies. This book will be useful for decades to come. It is probable that, in the future, when anyone begins an investigation of the demography of blacks in the United States, they will first consult this book.

Reynolds Farley
Population Studies Center
University of Michigan
November 1982

Prologue

In this prologue I intend to accomplish two objectives: (a) to offer the rationale for undertaking this project, and (b) to describe the organization and methodology used for compiling this volume.

(a) The Rationale. The twentieth census of the United States was taken in April 1980. Since then some portions of this massive source of data have been published. On the basis of these results, the United States population in general, and the black population in particular, have undergone further significant demographic and socioeconomic changes, most notably in the areas of fertility behavior, sex roles, female role in the workforce, black suburbanization, and family structure.

However, the analysis of the demographic characteristics of minority population in general, and blacks in particular, has lagged behind because fewer researchers have been attracted to undertake the task. This reminds us of a statement made as early as 1969 by Karl E. Taeuber (item 622 in this volume) who called for extensive and substantive research relative to black population, especially in policy related issues. Taeuber pointed out that young and capable researchers must be encouraged by providing incentives or else recruited to do more research on black population because merely waiting for research proposals to come in will not suffice. In retrospect, it is clear that the carrot approach has not and probably will never be employed. Consequently, as predicted by Taeuber, very few researchers have voluntarily concentrated on the study of black population and its impacts on substantive issues such as race relations.

The primary rationale for the present volume is to facilitate and stimulate further research relative to the black population and its social, economic, and political impact on American society. Invariably, funding agencies require a thorough and critical evaluation of the literature concerning the research proposal submitted to them. A successful proposal must demonstrate a thorough review of the current state of knowledge before designing the next research project so that it does not duplicate earlier works. Given that the amount of literature in almost every field has already reached a bewildering level and is expanding almost daily, it is exceedingly difficult for one man to keep up with the existing state of research in any particular field. It may not be an exaggeration to say that many ideas and potential research proposals never get off the ground due to this problem—simply because the time and the resources available to most researchers do not permit a thorough search and synthesis of the literature to enable them to compose a successful research project. This volume presents a synthesis of the state-of-research on the black population by bringing together the results of relevant studies buried in widely dispersed documents. It provides the kind of information that would otherwise have been beyond the limited time, ability, and resources available to many potential researchers. By providing researchers easy access to the existing literature, this book is intended to encourage and promote research in the area of black demography.

In addition to its obvious value as a major source of information and reference, this work also chronicles patterns of change in the black population and closely related topics, such as the black family, from an historical point of view. It also helps nonprofessional demographers, especially politicians and policy-makers, to access a wealth of demographic information under one cover.

(b) *Organization and Methodology.* This work is organized under six chapters: Chapter 1 includes works primarily dealing with black fertility; Chapter 2 deals with the works in the areas of black nuptiality (marriage and divorce) and fertility outside marriage; Chapter 3 includes publications relative to black fertility control—that is, family planning, contraception, abortion, and sterilization; Chapter 4 encompasses publications on black health and mortality; Chapter 5 includes materials on black migration, urbanization, and ecology; Chapter 6 includes works on the rate of growth, composition, spatial distribution, and vital rates for the black population.

Except in a few cases, every publication appears only once. In situations where the heading of a certain publication mentions two or more components of population change, for example, fertility and mortality, the publication will appear in both chapters. I may point out that there was no way of guaranteeing that all materials included, say in Chapter 1, would exclusively deal with fertility—far from it. Almost all entries in a given chapter, in addition to their primary topic, also discuss several other demographic aspects of the black population. As its title suggests, the introductory review essay provides a summary and synthesis of some of the more important demographic developments that have taken place since 1790, when the first U.S. census was conducted.

A conventional annotated bibliography only provides a broad overview of the contents of a particular publication. My intentions were to go beyond the conventional form by providing a compilation of abstracts/summaries/conclusions of major works on the black population. To achieve this objective, and in view of the fact that the authors of many of the entries provide abstracts or summaries, I have provided the annotations. For a whenever possible, the original authors' abstracts/summaries/conclusions. This methodology was used because an abstract or summary written by the original author would be accurate and comprehensive, and thus would best serve my intention. However, in many instances when the authors did not provide abstracts or summaries, I have provided the annotations. For a number of entries, abstracts were taken from the computer database POPLINE jointly produced by the Population Information Program at Johns Hopkins University, the Center for Population and Family Health at Columbia University, and the Office of Population Research at Princeton University. In order to properly credit the sources of annotations, the following symbols have been designated: (1) single asterisk, *, at the end of the annotation means that the annotation is by the original author(s); (2) double asterisks, **, mean that the annotation is by the original author(s) but it has been somewhat modified, mostly shortened; (3) a single star, ☆, indicates that the annotation is from the POPLINE; and, (4) a single full star, ★, indicates that I have provided the annotation. It must also be pointed out that whenever the original authors' summaries consisted of two or more paragraphs, they were pulled together to form a single paragraph.

J.A.M.
November 1982

Demography of the
Black Population
in the
United States

Black Demography: A Review Essay

JAMSHID A. MOMENI

> The Negro race has reached a place in its history when every possible effort should be made to have every Negro child count as a valuable contribution to the future of America. Negro parents, like all parents, must create the next generation from strength, not from weakness; from health, not from despair.
>
> *Margaret Sanger, 1946*

A glance at the front pages of the nation's daily newspapers indicates to everyone the enormity of current social problems facing us today at the national and global levels. These current problems include unemployment, hunger, housing and homelessness, urban plight, racism and segregation, wars or hostilities, and international terrorism. All of these problems demand immediate solutions, but no one seems to have programs ready for solving these problems. Real solutions are not to be found in rhetoric, but in factual knowledge and the process of continuously acquiring and analyzing such knowledge.

One of the most important social problems today, both at the local and global levels, has to do with failure to control reproduction. Just today one could read in the paper that:

I am grateful and indebted to Dr. Conrad Taeuber (former president of the Population Association of America and associate director of the U.S. Bureau of the Census), Professorial Lecturer, Center for Population Research, Georgetown University, and Dr. Larry Long, chief of the Demographic Analysis Staff of the Center for Demographic Studies at the U.S. Bureau of the Census, for their insightful and constructive comments on the original manuscript.

China, whose billion people make up a quarter of the world's population, decreed today that couples can have no more than two children
in the future. "The policy of one couple one child must be advocated,
the birth of second children strictly controlled and more than two pro-
hibited," said a circular issued by the central government, the armed
forces and the Chinese Communist Party. The circular did not say
how authorities would penalize couples violating the ban. . . . The
ban was expected to go into effect almost immediately. A nationwide
propaganda drive on family planning will be launched January first.
. . . Premier Zhao Ziyang said last week the success of the 1980-85
economic plan that calls for a 4 percent annual growth rate and of the
budget plans for the next two years hinges on controlling China's
burgeoning population. Population pressures already are straining
housing, schools and food supplies and draining subsidies for social
services. (*Washington Post*, December 11, 1982, p. A28)

The *Post* article goes on to say that in recent years, couples (family level)
who have had more than two children could not get extra coupons for
rationed food items nor move to a much needed larger home.

Today, these problems are not unique to China. For similar reasons,
India had reportedly attempted to institute compulsory sterilization of
couples after they had a certain number of children. Though doomed to
failure, the very attempt underlines the gravity of the need to do something
about population growth. Many other nations, and groups within nations,
are facing the problems associated with couples having more children than
they can afford.

The question is: Should we allow the situation to deteriorate to a point
when the governments have to issue decrees limiting reproductive behavior
or tell us how many children we should or should not have? Scientists have
repeatedly pointed out that many current human problems are either caused
or exacerbated by the rapid population growth in the present century. In view
of the importance of the population problem, the time has come for every
individual, couple or family, racial or cultural subgroup, and nation to be
concerned about population growth and its tremendous impact on our daily
life.

Most of the 652 entries in this volume deal with some specialized aspect of
black demography. This essay attempts to identify the major demographic
developments and trends in the black community and presents a summary/
synthesis of some of the major research findings. Specifically, it provides an

historical overview of black population growth, regional redistribution, migration and urbanization, changes in the pattern of nuptiality and the family, fertility trends, black health and mortality conditions as compared with the white population during the past several decades and makes suggestions for future research. Such historical overview performs the vital function of providing the user of this volume with a general frame of reference for putting the many specialized studies in perspective. The overall objective of this essay and the bibliography that follows is to promote further interest in research on black population, and thus, to ultimately contribute to population studies.

Rate of Growth

Table 1 shows the United States' total and black population, percent black, and the annual rate of growth of both the U.S. total and the black population between 1790, when the first U.S. census was taken, and 1980, when the twentieth census was conducted. In 1790, of the 3,929,214 U.S. residents, blacks numbered 757,208 (19.3 percent). Despite the relatively rapid increase in absolute numbers, the proportion of the black population declined from a high of 19.3 percent (based on exact numbers) in 1790 to a low of 9.7 percent in 1930. During the depression years of the 1930s the relative proportion of blacks remained stable. The decline in the relative size of the black population was not, however, due to a decline in the rate of natural increase (the balance between the birth rate and the death rate), but was mainly attributed to a differential rate of immigration in favor of whites, especially during the 1900-1910 decade. Between 1840 and 1929 a total of 36.9 million immigrants came to the United States. Of these, 31.6 million (85.8 percent) came from Europe (Bogue, 1969: 807). This extremely high immigration of whites was the major factor contributing to the lowering proportion of blacks whose growth was largely a function of natural increase between 1840 and 1930. The heaviest period of immigration was during 1900-1909 when more than 8.2 million immigrants arrived, followed by the 1910-1919 wave when another 6.4 million came to the U.S. In the 1920s there were 4.3 million immigrants, but the number sharply dropped to 699,375 in the 1930s, and to 856,608 in the 1940s. The 1930s depression coupled with new laws restricting the flow of immigrants into the U.S. are the two main reasons for the sudden reduction of immigration to the U.S. An important element to be noted regarding the percent black is that starting with the 1950s the percent black began an upward trend,

Table 1.   Black and Total Population (in Millions) of the United States, Percent Black, and Annual Rates of Growth: 1790–1980

Year	U.S. Total	Black	Percent Black*	Annual Rate of Growth* U.S.	Annual Rate of Growth* Black
1790	3.9	0.8	20.5	—	—
1800	5.3	1.0	18.9	3.07	2.23
1810	7.2	1.4	19.4	3.06	3.36
1820	9.6	1.8	18.8	2.88	2.51
1830	12.9	2.3	17.8	2.95	2.45
1840	17.1	2.9	17.0	2.82	2.32
1850	23.2	3.6	15.5	3.05	2.16
1860	31.4	4.4	14.0	3.03	2.01
1870**	39.1	5.4	13.8	2.19	2.05
1880	50.2	6.6	13.1	2.32	2.01
1890**	63.2	7.8	12.3	2.30	1.67
1900	76.2	8.8	11.6	1.92	1.60
1910	92.2	9.8	10.6	1.91	1.08
1920	106.0	10.5	9.9	1.39	0.69
1930	123.2	11.9	9.7	1.50	1.25
1940	132.2	12.9	9.7	0.70	0.81
1950	151.3	15.0	9.9	1.35	1.51
1960	179.3	18.9	10.5	1.70	2.31
1970	203.2	22.6	11.1	1.25	1.79
1980	226.5	26.5	11.7	1.08	1.59

* Calculated on the basis of rounded figures shown in the table. Values calculated on the basis of exact figures and/or adjusted figures may differ slightly from these. For example, proportion black would be 19.3 percent if exact figures are used.

** Figures adjusted for census undercount of blacks. For this adjustment see, *Negroes in the United States, 1920-32.* U.S. Bureau of the Census, Washington, D.C.: Government Printing Office, 1935, tables 1 and 4.

Source: U.S. decennial census reports.

reflecting a higher rate of natural increase among blacks. Because of the legal restrictions and the establishment of the quota system, the international migration in recent decades has been at a low ebb, although in recent years refugees and illegal migration may be pushing the total flow into the U.S. to levels attained in the early years of the twentieth century.

All of the fluctuations in the relative proportion of blacks cannot be explained in terms of differential migration in favor of whites. This can best be seen by examining the annual rate of growth. For blacks, this rate (the combined effects of fertility, mortality and migration) was 2.23 percent from 1790 to 1800, rising to 3.36 for the 1800-1810 decade. This increase is explained by the 1808 importation of the last group of slaves from Africa. After 1808 it became illegal to trade slaves. The carry-over effect of the 1808 arrival of the last major group of blacks is also reflected in the relatively higher rate of growth in the 1820s and 1830s when the general declining trend in the growth rate seems to have been initiated. The fluctuations in the annual rate of growth in the late nineteenth and early twentieth century are harder to explain. The sudden decline in the annual rate of growth of the black population in the 1880s is said to have been due to a black undercount in 1890. "However, it is not correct to assume that the fluctuations between the decades of 1900-1910 and 1910-1920 were due entirely to an incomplete enumeration. The influenza epidemic in 1918-1919, together with shifts in Negro population caused by labor conditions, military service in the World War, and the advent of the boll weevil into areas of relatively high density of Negro population, contributed to the decrease in the birth rate, on the one hand, and the noticeable increase in the death rate, on the other" (U.S. Bureau of the Census, 1935: 1). A pattern of sharp increase developed after World War II. The annual rate of growth rose from 0.81 in the 1930s to 1.51 in the 1940s, and 2.31 percent in the 1950s. In the 1960s and 1970s, the annual growth of the black population again resumed its declining trend. The sudden increase in the 1940s, and especially in the 1950s, is attributed to the post World War II baby boom. The declining trend starting with the decade of the 1960s is explained by a drop in the black fertility rate.

Regional Distribution of the Black Population

The original concentration of the black population in the South is as known a fact as is its movement out of the South. Landon (1920) indicates that President Millard Fillmore's signing of the Fugitive Slave Act on September 18, 1850 started a black migration that continued until the start of the Civil War (1861-1865) causing thousands of black people to cross into Canada and others to move from one state to another seeking freedom and safety from their pursuers. Black movement out of the South followed two general directions, first to the North and second, to the West, but despite President Fillmore's action, most blacks continued to live in the South. In 1870, more than 90 percent of all blacks lived in the Southern States, 9.3 percent lived in the North, and only 0.1 percent resided in the West. In the thirty years from 1870 to the turn of the century, there was virtually no change in the regional distribution of the black population in the United States. By 1900, still 89.7 percent resided in the South; one out of every ten blacks lived in the North; and 0.3 percent lived in the West. During the first decade of the twentieth century, there was still very little black movement out of the South, but in the next decade, partly as a result of World War I (1914-1918), a black movement out of the South into the northern urban areas gained momentum. Between 1910 and 1920 the percent of blacks living in the South declined by just under four percentage points, and by the onset of the depression decade (1930s) the percent blacks living in the South had declined to 79 with about 20 percent living in the North, and one percent in the West. By 1940, the percentage of blacks living in the South had declined to 77. The single largest reduction in the black population of the South took place in the 1940s—the World War II era—when the proportion of blacks residing in the South plunged to 68 percent. By 1960, the percent blacks in the South had declined to 60 with a corresponding gain in the proportion blacks in the North and the West—34 percent and 6 percent, respectively. Based on the 1970 census, the movement of blacks out of the South continued into the 1960s. In 1970, only 53 percent of all blacks resided in the South; the proportion of blacks in the North had risen to 39 percent—almost four times the proportion of 1910; and the percent blacks in the West had risen to 8 percent—many times greater than its 1910 black population. Long and DeAre (1981) point out two major transitions characterizing the movement of the black population in the 1970s: (1) After increasing for several decades, the percent blacks in the North fell from 39.5 in 1970 to 38.5 in 1980, and the percent residing in the South remained steady at the 53 percent level. Some other studies indicate that this transition took place mainly during the second half of the 1970s; (2) The proportion of blacks living in the central cities declined. Long and DeAre's findings indicate that the long exodus of blacks from the Southern states into the rest of the country has halted and a new exodus from cities and a counterstream of immigration to the South has begun.

Causes and Consequences of Black Migration

Henderson (1921) in a 117 page essay attempts to interpret the massive 1916-1918 black migration—the first major wave of black outmigration from the South. In sifting out the most salient facts regarding black movements from the mass of literature, he concludes that blacks could not overcome the economic and social barriers of race prejudice in the South causing them to flee to another locality. Henderson also discusses many other motives for black migration, new opportunities, and the problems migrants faced. He further concludes that black migration is not any different from the movements of other human groups, and that like any other group, blacks follow certain economic, political, social, and religious forces operating in the environment of the migrants.

The review of the pertinent literature on migration theory indicates that three basic migration models have been developed in more recent years: (1) the "gravity" or distance model, (2) the "intervening opportunities" model, and (3) "multivariate" models. Irrespective of individual preferences of one model over the other, there is overwhelming evidence that black migration has been a function of a host of socioeconomic and political factors operating at the migration origin and destination in a so-called push-pull relationship. Changes in the social, political, and economic organizations of the rural South and urban structures coupled with technological innovations, wars, and public policies have pulled blacks out of a rural society into an urban environment (Jones, 1978; Lewis, 1971; and Stinner and DeYong, 1969). Lewis (1971), and Stinner and DeYong (1969) point out that the pull factors at the destinations may have been more influential than the push factors at the points of origin. Economic stagnation, and the absence of a strong industrial base in the South, as well as population pressure due to high levels of fertility in the rural area are said to have constituted the most important push factors. Wars and the industrialization of the North which increased the demands for labor, and the technological innovations which have been partly responsible for the breakdown of the agricultural system of the South, and the blacks' perception regarding the relative ease of overcoming racial barriers in the North have acted as the main magnet pulling the black population into the metropolitan and industrial centers. Many researchers cited in this volume have pointed out that the pattern of black migration is not any different from the pattern observed among any other human groups.

The movement of blacks out of the South has not always produced desirable consequences. Observing the heavy black migration to the North during 1916-1917, Scroggs (1917:1043) reviewed the movement of the blacks since 1865 (when the 1863 Emancipation Proclamation decreed by President Lincoln took full effect at the end of the Civil War) and warned against the adverse effects of the heavy black movements. He concluded that: "the mere removal of the Negro to another environment is not the ultimate solution of what we call the 'race problem;' at the most it can only modify the problem. As the European peasant does not escape all his economic ills when he stands for the first time under the Stars and Stripes, so the Negro will still have troubles after crossing the Mason and Dixon line."

As predicted by Scroggs, black movements to the metropolitan area have only modified the problem. Between 1910, when black movement gained momentum, and 1960 the proportion of blacks living in central cities more than doubled; by the 1980 census, 81 percent of all blacks and only 73 percent of whites lived in metropolitan areas. Furthermore, based on the 1980 census figures, more than one third (34 percent) of all blacks were concentrated in the cities of New York, Chicago, Detroit, Philadelphia, District of Columbia, Los Angeles, and Baltimore—mostly in ghettoes, slums, or lower socioeconomic quarters of these cities. These racial and residential shifts have resulted in the formation of black ghettoes and black slums in many large American cities. Hill (1976:231) examining the demographic changes and racial ghettoes asserts that:

> Current civil rights struggles are rooted in three major demographic developments of the American Negro community: accelerated growth, increasing mobility, and rapid urbanization. Almost half of the Negro population now [1966] lives in the North, but the response of American cities to this development has been a vast increase and rigidity in the pattern of residential segregation. Thus, the Negro finds that he has left the Segregated South for the Segregated Northern slums.

Hill also asserts that the violent outbursts in the ghettoes of the American cities (Watts and Harlem, for example) reflect black powerlessness, hopelessness, and despair in their lives. As emphasized by Hill, instituting policies and programs aimed at eliminating ghettoes from American cities *must* constitute a first priority if we are to achieve racial equality. The recent black suburbanization appears to be a partial answer to this important and difficult social problem, but various ecological studies have indicated that the pattern of suburban movement of blacks is not the same as that of whites, for blacks are not evenly distributed in the outer city rings, casting doubts on the effectiveness of black suburbanization as a means of racial integration. Moorhead (1971) analyzing the black suburban migration during 1955-1960, concludes that the suburbanization of Negroes is in fact an outward extension of the Ghetto.

The loss of a black foothold in the Southern agricultural industry is often cited as another major adverse consequence of black migration. Wadley and Lee (1974:283) examining the impacts of black migration on the south concluded that the black farmer "in the United States has nearly disappeared and the black population in the rural farm areas may soon follow." Black farm population declined from 48.7 percent in 1920 to under one percent (0.9 percent) in 1981, while the proportion of white farm population declined from 27.5 percent to 2.9 percent in the same period (U.S. Bureau of the Census, 1982a: 7). Wadley and Lee point to the fact that on the average, the remaining black farms are small and are concentrated in places where cotton and tobacco are still the chief crops. Black farm operators are old, for there is a marked exodus of younger farmers. Wadley and Lee (1974:283) conclude that "farming in the United States will soon be an occupation relegated to whites. Prospects for revival of black farming are very slight."

Black Urbanization

The regional redistribution of the black population not only meant an exodus of blacks from the South, but more significantly, it meant a rapid urbanization of the black population. There are great regional and state differentials in the rate of black (as well as white) urbanization in the United States, but it is beyond the scope of this essay to treat black urbanization in any detail. For the nation as a whole, however, the percent of both black and white urban population based on the decennial censuses are shown in Table 2. Note that in 1790 only 3 percent of the black and 6 percent of the white population were urban. In the years between 1790 and 1860, percent urban blacks remained in single digits. In 1870 when 28 percent of the white population resided in urban areas, only 13 percent of the black population were classified as urban dwellers. By the census of 1900, 43 percent of whites and 23 percent blacks were urban. Percent urban blacks had risen to 27 in 1910. But concurrent with the World War I decade when large scale black migration out of the South started, percent urban blacks increased by seven points to 34 percent in 1920. The 1920s witnessed an additional 10 percentage point increase in black urbanization. Based on the 1930 census figures, 58 percent whites and 44 percent blacks were classified as urban. During the depression decade (1930s) black migration from the rural to urban areas proceeded at a rate one half that of the 1920s. In contrast, the proportion of whites living in urban areas declined from 58 in 1930 to 57 percent in 1940. The proportion blacks during the same period increased from 44 percent in 1930 to 49 percent in 1940. Why blacks continued to urbanize as whites were ruralizing in the 1930s is not readily explained. Price (1969:12)

Table 2. Percent Urban Population of the U.S., by Race: 1790–1980

Year	Percent Urban		Year	Percent Urban	
	Black	White		Black	White
1790	3	6	1890	19	38
1800	5	6	1900	23	43
1810	6	8	1910	27	49
1820	6	7	1920	34	53
1830	7	9	1930	44	58
1840	8	11	1940	49	57
1850	8	17	1950	62	64
1860	8	22	1960	73	68
1870	13	28	1970	81	72
1880	14	30	1980	85	71

Source: U.S. Bureau of the Census, various published reports, and unpublished 1980 Census Data.

explains that "this took place in spite of the depression, or perhaps because of it, since we must consider the possibility of differences in relief programs and the problems of tenant farmers during the period. There was some evidence that 'welfare' was more available in urban areas. Also, the beginnings of crop control, with resultant acreage reductions, forced many tenants out of agriculture," which presumably forced them to move to the cities. As a result of World War II and the social and technological changes that came with it—especially the sharp increase in the demand for industrial labor—the proportion urban among blacks jumped by 13 percentage points in the 1940s. Based on the 1950 census figures, the gap in the percent urban population had narrowed to only 2 percentage points. By 1960 blacks were more urbanized than whites—blacks 73 percent versus whites 68 percent. During the 1960s and 1970s blacks kept up with the pace of urbanization. Based on the 1980 census figures, 85 percent blacks and only 71 percent whites were officially classified as urban.

It is important to note that in a span of 70 years (1910-1980) the proportion urban blacks has increased from 27 to 85 percent. That is, from 73 percent rural in 1910 they have transformed to 15 percent rural in 1980 in a matter of one lifetime. This is one of the highest rates of urbanization, perhaps unprecedented in human history. With it have come numerous problems of adjustment for the black urbanites.

Some of these problems have already been alluded to, but those not previously discussed are the adverse effects of rapid urbanization on black family. For example, residing in the city has increased the number of female-headed households (as discussed later), has brought changes in marital patterns, and even 'abandonment of children.' Pleck (1974) in her study of black migration to Boston concluded that the city did not solve the problem of black migrants but actually extended contact with city created problems unknown to Southern blacks, and offered no escape from conditions of poverty.

Black Fertility

Prior to 1915 no estimates of fertility rates based on vital registration were available. For blacks, such estimates did not exist prior to 1960. Whatever knowledge about fertility patterns and differentials by race available during this time, is based on demographic backward projection techniques, utilizing the census data on age and sex distribution. According to these projections, the total fertility rate (TFR), one of the summary measures of fertility during the entire reproductive years, for black women in the 1850s was estimated to be 7.9 births per woman (Coale and Rives, 1973) as shown in Table 3. This means that if this rate continued to prevail throughout the reproductive life of an average black woman born in the 1850s, she would have 7.9 children. A century later the figure was down to 3.95 births per woman—a 50 percent decline over its 1850 value. Significantly, the 7.9 figure for the 1850s related to a period when fertility rates, both for blacks and whites, were on a declining trend, but the 3.95 births per woman for 1950 related to the post World War II baby boom era when fertility rates were rising. According to the reconstructed estimates shown in Table 3, black fertility, as well as white fertility, continued to decline until it reached a low level during the 1930s depression years. Cutright and Shorter (1979) argue that the declining fertility of blacks before World War II and the increase after the war were primarily due to changes in the health of black women. Estimates indicate a black TFR of 2.80 for the depression decade, 3.95 by 1950 and 4.54 by 1960. By 1975, the TFR for black women fell to an all-time low level of 2.30—a decline of 36 percent as compared to the depression years, and a decline of 49 percent as compared with 1950.

Overall, fluctuations in fertility for blacks have followed the same general trend followed by whites as shown in Figure 1, although the levels of black fertility have always remained substantially above those for white women. By 1980, when rates for both blacks and whites had reached a low

Table 3.   Total Fertility Rates by Race: 1850–1980

Year	Black (B)	White (W)	B/W Ratio
1850	7.90[a]	5.30[a]	1.49
1920	3.52[b]	3.22	1.10
1930	2.80[c]	2.51	1.11
1940	2.83[d]	2.18	1.30
1950	3.95[e]	2.94	1.34
1960	4.10[f]	3.51	1.17
1970	3.10	2.39	1.30
1971	2.90	2.16	1.34
1972	2.60	1.91	1.36
1973	2.40	1.78	1.35
1974	2.30	1.75	1.30
1975	2.24	1.67	1.34
1976	2.19	1.65	1.33
1977	2.25	1.70	1.32
1978	2.22	1.67	1.33
1979	2.26	1.72	1.31
1980	2.27	1.75	1.30

(a) Figure is for 1850-1859; (b) Figure is for 1920-1924; (c) Figure is for 1930-1934; (d) Figure is for 1940-1944; (e) Figure is for 1950-1954; (f) Figure is for 1960-1964.

Source: For blacks, 1850-1960, see Coale and Rives (1973:26); for whites, 1850, see U.S. Bureau of the Census (1980:118), and for whites, 1920 to 1960, see *Trends in Fertility in the United States*, series 21, no. 28, DHEW Publication No. (HRA) 78-1906 (September 1977), Table 13, p. 38. For both black and white rates from 1970 to 1980, see *Advance Report of Final Natality Statistics, 1980*. National Center for Health Statistics: Monthly Vital Statistics Report, vol. 31, no. 8, supplement (November 30, 1982), Table 4, p. 13.

level, the annual TFR for blacks still averaged over 0.5 a child per woman (or 500 children per 1,000 women), higher than that of whites. But the gap between the TFR of the two groups in 1980 was significantly smaller than the gap in 1920. Short-term differentials by race aside, in the long term (1850-1980) black fertility has declined somewhat faster than white fertility. The black total fertility in 1980 was 28.7 percent of its value for 1850; while for whites the 1980 TFR is 33.0 percent of its 1850 value, indicating a slower rate of decline for whites than for blacks. However, short-term comparisons such as that between 1960 and 1980 indicate a lower rate of decline for blacks than whites.

Figure 1. Fertility Rates by Color: 1920–1975

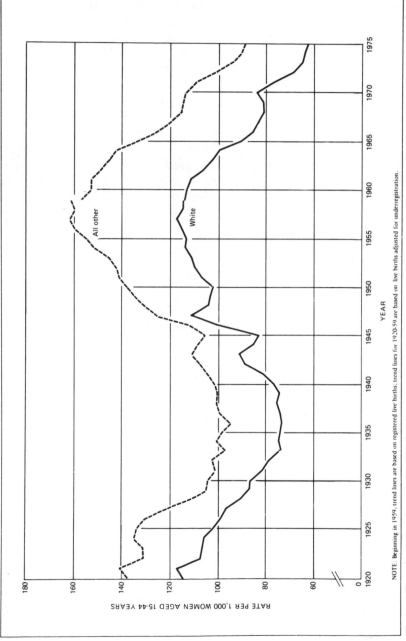

Source: "Trends in Fertility in the United States." National Center for Health Statistics, data from the *National Vital Statistics System*, Series 21, no. 28. DHEW Publication No.(HRA)78-1906, September 1977, p. 3.

Much of the literature on fertility presented in Chapter 1 has focused on the analysis of differentials by race, socioeconomic, and geographic variables. The major conclusion one can draw is that differentials in black fertility are very similar to those observed among whites in the United States. For instance, black women who practice contraception have lower fertility rates than those who do not; black women in the urban areas have lower fertility rates than those in the rural areas; black women with rural background have more children; black women who are married to husbands with white collar jobs tend to have fewer children than women married to husbands with less prestigious jobs; more educated women more often practice contraception, and practice it more effectively than those with less education and consequently bear fewer children than those with little education; black women in the labor force tend to have lower fertility than those not in the labor force; black women of higher socioeconomic status have lower fertility than women from lower socioeconomic levels; blacks marrying at a later age tend to have lower fertility. The socioeconomic characteristics of urban living, and the higher proportion of marital disruptions in urban areas among blacks are said to explain the lower fertility rates of urban women.

As revealed in many of the studies cited in this volume, the higher fertility rate for blacks is associated with their lower socioeconomic status. Farley (1971) emphasizes that in every comparison on the socioeconomic scale blacks are at a disadvantage. Thus, as blacks attain parity with whites the current gap in their fertility rates are expected to diminish. In fact, some studies have shown that at relatively high levels of socioeconomic status blacks have lower fertility than whites. For example, based on a report by the U.S. Bureau of the Census (1980: 129) the number of children ever born per woman 35 to 44 years old ever married, was 1.8 in 1970 and 2.1 in 1975 for blacks with four or more years of college education. The comparable figures for whites are reported to be 2.6 and 2.4 children. Also, several studies (Blair, 1967; Farley, 1970) have shown that despite their higher actual fertility, blacks desire a smaller family size than do whites.

Among theories pertaining to fertility differentials, the so-called "minority status hypothesis" coined by Goldscheider and Uhlenberg (1969: 361) has generated both interest and controversy. Goldscheider and Uhlenberg challenge the view that as assimilation of minority groups proceeds, the fertility of the majority and minority groups will converge. According to Goldscheider and Uhlenberg, difference in fertility of minority and majority groups should not be treated as a temporary phenomenon and must not be interpreted in terms of social, demographic, and economic characteristics of the minorities. "Empirical evidence . . . does not fully support 'characteristics' explanation of Negro, Jewish, Japanese-American, or Catholic fertility. An alternative hypothesis is presented with respect to the *independent effect of minority group status* [emphasis mine] on fertility." Bean and Marcum (1978) have seriously questioned the validity of the minority status theory and have called for further investigation of the topic. In this regard, Bean and Marcum argue that if minority group status affects reproductive behavior in the way proposed by Goldscheider and Uhlenberg, then minority couples of higher socioeconomic status will exhibit lower fertility than majority couples of similar socioeconomic status. Bean and Marcum have also hypothesized that a minority group status effect on fertility is more likely to emerge under conditions of less socioeconomic distance between majority and minority groups.

The strongest criticism of the minority status theory is launched by Johnson (1979). Using the data from the 1970 National Fertility Study, Johnson tested the two opposing explanations—the "characteristics hypothesis" and the "minority status." Johnson's findings support a weak form of the "characteristics hypothesis." The strong form of this hypothesis holds that race itself has no effect on fertility and that differences in black-white fertility arise from varying social, demographic, and economic conditions between the two groups; therefore, as social change equalizes these conditions, fertility differences will disappear. The weak form states that racial differences will disappear, but that distinctive family size will disappear first among the highly educated blacks. On the contrary, the minority status hypothesis states that race itself has an independent effect on fertility and that fertility among educated blacks will continue to be lower than that among whites because blacks must invest more effort than whites in the struggle for success, and child-rearing efforts are to be sacrificed in this struggle. Johnson, using sophisticated statistical techniques of analysis to examine the effects of social, demographic, economic, racial and educational variables, discovered that race did not account for any significant portion of the variation in fertility, thus providing evidence against the minority status hypothesis.

Any individual or group characteristic that is not biologically determined is *learned*, and thus falls in the category of *acquired* as opposed to *innate* social and/or cultural characteristics. What Goldscheider and Uhlenberg refer to as the "minority group status" or sometimes the "independent effect of minority group status" is nothing more than a defense mechanism learned by the minority group in its struggle for success in any society where opportunities are not equally distributed. Given that this defense mechanism is a learned characteristic, it may take different forms in different minority groups. The criticism that must also be directed at the minority status hypothesis is that the authors of this theory seem to imply that there is something racially inherent (as opposed to socially and/or culturally learned) about fertility behavior of minority groups.

Black Fertility Outside Marriage

Traditionally, the birth rate for unmarried black women has been higher than that for white women. Estimated birth rates outside marriage, measured by the number of live births to unmarried women per 1,000 unmarried women, by race for the 1970-1980 period are shown in Table 4. As shown in this table, fertility among blacks outside marriage is significantly higher than that of whites. For example, in 1970 the fertility outside marriage among blacks was 95.5 births per 1,000 unmarried women; the corresponding rate for whites was 13.8. Looking at the black-white ratios of

Table 4.   Birth Rates for Unmarried Women, United States, 1970–1980, by Race

Year	All Races	White (W)	Black (B)	Ratio: B/W
1970	26.4	13.8	95.5	6.9
1971	25.5	12.5	96.1	7.7
1972	24.8	11.9	91.6	7.7
1973	24.3	11.8	88.6	7.5
1974	23.9	11.7	85.5	7.3
1975	24.5	12.4	84.2	6.8
1976	24.3	12.6	81.6	6.5
1977	25.6	13.5	82.6	6.1
1978	25.7	13.7	81.1	5.9
1979	27.2	14.9	83.0	5.6
1980	28.4	16.2	83.4	5.1

Note: Rates are number of live births to unmarried women per 1,000 unmarried women.

Source: Advance Report of Final Natality Statistics, 1980. National Center for Health Statistics: Monthly Vital Statistics Report, vol. 31, no. 8, supplement (November 30, 1982), Table 16, pp. 26-27.

fertility outside marriage, we note that in 1970 the fertility outside marriage among blacks was about seven times greater than that among whites. This ratio rose to 7.7 for 1971 and 1972, but has been on a declining trend since 1973 and by 1980 had fallen to 5.1. That is, in 1980 there were more than five times as many babies born outside marriage per every 1,000 unmarried black women than for their white counterparts.

It is important to study the differences in trends by race. For whites, the rate increased from 13.8 in 1970 to 16.2 in 1980—an increase of 17.4 percent. For blacks, however, the rate declined from 95.5 in 1970 to 83.5 in 1980—a decline of 8.5 percent. This decline is partly explained by a greater acceptance and more effective use of contraceptives among unmarried black women in recent years. The decline in the birth rate outside marriage among blacks is not totally unexpected because the total fertility rate for blacks (Table 3) declined from 3.10 in 1970 to 2.27 in 1980—a decrease of 23.5 percent. In contrast, the increase in the rate for whites is not as easy to explain because during the same period the total fertility rate for whites (Table 3) declined by 26.7 percent from 2.39 in 1970 to 1.75 in 1980.

Despite the rather significant decline in out-of-wedlock child-bearing among blacks, a substantial racial difference persists. Zelnik and Kantner (1970), examining black family formation and out-of-wedlock fertility, explain the out-of-wedlock racial differences in fertility by pointing out that, given comparable socioeconomic background and, holding educational attainment constant, the black female as compared with her white counterpart is more likely to engage in premarital sex, less likely to use contraception, more likely to conceive, less likely to attempt to alter or change that condition (through abortion, falsification of legitimacy records, or marriage), more likely to bear and raise her out-of-wedlock child, less likely to experience any social condemnation for doing so, more likely to experience parental acceptance and assistance together with a more independent status, and better able to feel that her child has as good a chance in life as any other child in her race born into similar economic circumstances. Zelnik and Kantner conclude that these considerations provide the essential clues for the explanation of the phenomenon of high fertility rate outside marriage among blacks in the United States.

Black Nuptiality and the Family

Any discussion of nuptiality and the family involves a distinction between "household" and "family". A household is generally defined as any one or more persons, related or unrelated, who live and dine together under the same roof more than fifty percent of the time. But a family is defined as two or more related (by blood, marriage, or adoption) persons living together. A family is also a household but a household is not necessarily a family. With this distinction in mind, we shall briefly look at some of the demographic features and changes in black households as well as black families in the past several decades.

During the past ninety years there have been significant changes in the structure and the size of black households. Between 1890 and 1975 the number of black households increased from 1,411,000 to 7,262,000—a more than five-fold increase. The number of white households during the same period increased from 11,255,000 to 62,945,000—about a six-fold increase. The size of the black household declined from 5.3 persons in 1890 to 3.3 persons in 1975—a decline of 37.8 percent. Similarly, the average size of the white household declined from 4.9 in 1890 to 2.9 in 1975—a decline of 40.8 percent. The largest decadal increase in the number of black households in recent years occurred in the 1950-60 and 1960-70 decades. While between 1940 and 1950 it increased by 22 percent, the corresponding figures for 1950-60 and 1960-70 were 25 and 29 percent, respectively. After 1970, the rate of increase in the number of black households began to slow down.

Similarly, there have been great changes in the number and the size of black families. Statistics on families became available in 1940. Between 1940 and 1980 the number of black families increased from 2.7 to 6.2 million— 2.3 times. The number of white families increased from 28.7 million in 1940 to 52.2 million in 1980. That is, while the number of black families increased 2.3 times between 1940 and 1980, the number of white families increased by 1.8 times during the same period. Translated into annual rate of growth, between 1940 and 1980, black families grew at an annual rate of 2.07 percent, while white families grew at a rate of 1.50 percent, reflecting a higher rate of growth in the number of black families than that of whites.

Perhaps the most significant indicator of the shift in the structure of the black family is the change in the distribution of families by type: husband-wife, male-headed-no-wife-present, and female-headed-no-husband-present. As shown in Table 5, the proportion of male-headed families declined between 1940 and 1970, but the trend reversed itself in the 1970s. The percent of male-headed families declined from 5.0 in 1940 to 3.7 in 1970, but increased to 4.1 in 1980. The decline in the proportion of husband-wife families has been even more consistent, from 77.1 percent in 1940 to 55.5 in 1980. These declines have meant a significant concurrent increase in the proportion of female-headed black families. As noted in Table 5, the

Table 5. Percent Black and White Families by Type: 1940–1980

	Black			White		
Year	Husband & Wife	Male-Headed	Female-Headed	Husband & Wife	Male-Headed	Female-Headed
1940	77.1	5.0	17.9	85.5	4.4	10.1
1950	77.7	4.7	17.6	88.0	3.5	8.9
1960	74.1	4.1	21.7	89.2	2.7	8.1
1970	68.1	3.7	28.3	88.7	2.3	9.1
1980	55.5	4.1	40.4	85.6	2.8	11.6

Source: For 1940-1970 figures, see U.S. Bureau of the Census (1980:103). The 1980 figures are based on revised, unpublished tabulations by the U.S. Bureau of the Census.

proportion of female-headed families increased from 17.9 percent in 1940 to 40.4 percent in 1980—more than double.

In contrast, the proportion of female-headed families among whites not only did not increase but declined between 1940 and 1960. In the 1960s, this proportion increased by only 1 percent, and by an additional 2.5 percent in the 1970s. Based on the data presented in Table 5, the 1950 percent female-headed families for blacks was about twice as large as that for whites. By 1980, this ratio increased to 3.5 female-headed black families for every one female-headed white family, reflecting the higher degree of structural change in the black than white families during the past few decades. Perhaps the most startling conclusion to be drawn from this analysis is that the increase in the number of female-headed families, the most disadvantaged families, indicates that not only has there been very little gain in racial equality, but there has been no improvement in inequality of sexes. The increase in the proportion of female-headed families may have actually widened the inequality among families.

The marital status distribution (Table 6) is usually affected by the age and sex structure of the population. To minimize these influences, demographers generally restrict the analysis of marital distribution to a certain age group. Glick (1970) recommended that the age group 35-44 is an ideal group for such analysis because it covers a stage in life when the significant majority of those who will ever marry have done so and the incidence of divorce is either at or near its peak. It is for this reason that Table 6 shows

Table 6. Marital Status of the Population 14 Years Old and Over, and 35-44 Years Old, by Sex and Race for Selected Years: 1890–1981

Marital Status	Age 14 and Over							Age 35-44						
	1890	1910	1940	1960	1970	1975	1981	1890	1910	1940	1960	1970	1975	1981
Black Men														
Single	40	36	33	30	36	38	41	11	12	15	11	12	11	15
Married	56	57	61	63	57	53	48	83	80	79	83	81	81	70
Widowed	4	6	6	5	4	4	4	5	7	4	2	2	1	2
Divorced	—	1	1	2	3	4	7	—	1	2	4	5	7	13
Black Women														
Single	30	27	24	22	29	31	34	7	7	8	7	9	8	11
Married	55	57	59	60	53	49	44	75	74	74	80	76	73	66
Widowed	15	15	16	14	13	13	13	17	17	15	7	7	7	5
Divorced	1	1	2	4	5	7	9	1	2	3	6	8	11	18
White Men														
Single	42	39	33	25	28	28	28	15	17	14	8	7	8	8
Married	54	56	61	70	67	66	65	81	79	83	89	89	87	83
Widowed	4	4	4	3	3	2	2	3	3	1	1	1	—	—
Divorced	—	1	1	2	3	3	5	—	1	2	2	3	5	9
White Women														
Single	32	30	26	19	22	22	21	10	12	11	6	5	4	5
Married	57	59	61	67	62	62	60	81	81	82	88	87	86	83
Widowed	11	10	11	12	12	12	12	8	7	5	3	3	2	2
Divorced	—	1	2	3	4	5	7	1	1	3	4	5	7	10

—represents zero exactly or approximately.

Source: For figures relative to 1890-1975 see: U.S. Bureau of the Census (1980: 109-110). For 1980 figures see: *Marital Status and Living Arrangements: March 1981.* Current Population Reports, Series P-20, no. 372 (June 1982) Table 1, pp. 8-9.

the distribution for those in the 35-44 age group in addition to marital status distribution for the population age 14 and over.

As it may be noted from Table 6, in 1890, eleven percent of black men and 7 percent of black women aged 35-44 were reported as single (never married); while 83 percent of the men and 75 percent of the women were reported as married. By 1940, the proportion single had increased to 15 percent for black men and to 8 percent for black women; the percent married had declined to 79 in 1940 for men and 74 for women. During the following 20 years (1940-60), a general shift in marital status distribution is observed, resulting in smaller percent single and larger percent married. In the twenty-one years between 1960 and 1981, the proportion of married black men dropped by about 16 percent, while that for black women aged 35-44 declined by about 18 percent.

In 1981 for black men 35-44 years old, 2 percent were widowed and 13 percent were divorced. The comparable figures for black women were 5 and 18 percent, respectively. The decline in the proportion of widowhood is attributed to a general improvement in life expectancy for black males. In general, divorces have become more common and widowhood less common since 1890, with additional significant changes observed after World War II.

The figures in Table 6 reveal that the changes in the marital status pattern for blacks have roughly followed those for whites. However, in almost every comparison, divorce and widowhood are significantly higher for blacks than for whites. The proportion married in the age group 35-44 for black men from 1910 to 1981 was always less than that of whites; for women the proportion married aged 35-44 was significantly lower than that of their white counterparts during the 1890-1981 period. From 1890 to 1910 percent single for blacks exceeded that of whites, but as a result of the shift in marital status distribution starting in the 1940s, percent single black men exceeded that of whites by a comfortable margin between the years 1940 and 1981. A similar pattern is observed for black women. A larger percent of black men than women have been reported as married in each of the censuses since 1890. The smallest difference in percent married by sex is observed in 1960 (males 80 percent; females 83 percent). This is attributed to the post World War II increase in the number of marriages among black females.

Throughout the past few decades many scholarly studies on the status of the black community in the United States have dealt with the question of the stability/instability of the black family. There are no direct methods of measuring family instability, but some demographic indicators such as percent marital dissolution, remarriage, and matri-centricity may be used for this purpose. Hampton (1979), examining the husband's characteristics and marital disruptions, concludes that husband's age is the strongest bivariate "predictor of marital disruption, husband's income is the most important predictor. A causal model of marital disruption shows that education, employment and age at marriage influence marital disruption through their influence on income. Only age, income and religiousity had a significant direct effect." About 30 percent of all black families in 1970 and 31 percent in 1980 were below poverty level (U.S. Bureau of the Census, 1982b: Table 15). The corresponding figures for whites were 3.6 and 3.5 percent. Again we note that a high level of poverty is not only associated with higher fertility among blacks, but is also regarded as a major contributor to the disruption of the black family. Farley and Hermalin (1971: 1) have observed that "discrimination in the job and housing markets have made it difficult for black men to support their wives and children. As a result desertion occurs commonly." However, in their analysis of black-white differentials in family stability, Farley and Hermalin conclude that some of the recent changes in family status suggest a trend toward greater stability in the black family while other changes indicate an opposite trend.

Black Health and Mortality

A life table is a demographic model that summarizes mortality (and thus health) conditions for a given time period. Mortality levels for a given period may be summarized by the life table which measures longevity in terms of life expectancy at birth or the average number of years a cohort of newly born infants expect to live if they were to experience throughout their lives the same age-sex-specific death rates prevailing at a specified time. The life table may be the most useful model invented by demographers; in addition to measuring longevity, it summarizes the cumulative effects of age, sex, and racial differences in human health and mortality conditions.

This essay cannot cover all aspects of black health and mortality, but it provides an overview of black life expectancy since 1900 as an indicator of changes in black health and mortality conditions.

No data on life expectancy for nonwhites (or for blacks only) are available for the years prior to 1900. However, according to Rao (1973), the life expectancy for whites was estimated to be 40.4 years for males and 42.9 years for white females in 1850.

Table 7 shows life expectancies for whites and nonwhites by sex for selected years between 1900 and 1979. At the beginning of the twentieth century, a white male expected to live 48.2 years, but a nonwhite male expected to live only 32.5 years, 15.7 years less than a white male. In the same year, a white female expected to live 51.5 years, while her nonwhite counterpart expected to live only 35.0 years, 16.1 years less than a white female. During the first decade of the century the gap in the white-nonwhite life expectancy increased from 15.7 years in 1900 to 16.1 years in 1909-1911 for males; the gap for females decreased slightly, from 16.1 in 1900-1902 to 15.9 years in 1909-1911. However, during the 1909-1921 period, there was a significant improvement for nonwhites. The gap was reduced from 16.1 to 9.2

Table 7. Life Expectancy for Blacks and Whites by Sex: 1900–1979

	Life Expectancy				Percent Change in Life Expectancy			
Year	Black Male*	Black Female*	White Male	White Female	Black Male	Black Female	White Male	White Female
1900-02	32.5	35.0	48.2	51.1	—	—	—	—
1909-11	34.1	37.7	50.2	53.6	4.9	7.7	4.1	4.9
1919-21	47.1	46.9	56.3	58.5	38.1	24.4	12.2	9.1
1929-31	47.6	49.5	59.1	62.7	1.0	5.5	5.0	7.2
1939-41	52.3	55.5	62.8	67.3	9.9	12.1	6.6	7.3
1949-51	58.9	62.7	66.3	72.0	12.6	13.0	5.6	7.0
1959-61	61.5	66.5	67.6	74.2	4.4	6.1	2.0	3.0
1969-71	61.0	69.0	67.9	75.5	−0.8	3.8	0.4	1.8
1979	65.5	74.2	70.6	78.2	7.4	7.5	4.0	3.6

*Except for 1979 when the life expectancy values are for blacks-only, the values for the 1900-1971 years relate to nonwhites. However, in view of the fact that blacks constitute more than 90 percent of nonwhites, we have used the term "black", although data are not for blacks-only.

Source: For life expectancy values relative to 1900-1961, see: U.S. Bureau of the Census (1980: 120), and Rao (1973: 409). For 1969-71 values see: Life Tables: Vital Statistics of the United States, 1978, Volume II, Section 5. DHHS Publication No. (PHS) 81-1104, Table 5-A, p. 5-4. For 1979 figures, see Advance Report of Final Mortality Statistics, 1979, National Center for Health Statistics: Monthly Vital Statistics Report, vol. 31, no. 6, Supplement (September 30, 1982), Table 3, pp. 20-22.

years for males, and from 15.9 to 11.6 years for females. The 1920s may be characterized as a decade of setback. During 1921-1931 the gap for males rose from 9.2 in 1921 to 11.5 in 1931; for females it rose from 11.6 years in 1921 to 13.2 years in 1929-1931. From 1931 on, the racial gap in life expectancy for both sexes has consistently declined. By 1979, the gap was reduced to 5.1 years for males and to 4.0 years for females. Overall, the greatest gains in life expectancy for nonwhites occurred during the years from 1910 to 1950. From 1971 to 1979 the gain in life expectancy among males (both whites and nonwhites) has been significantly higher than that of the preceding twenty years (1949-1951 to 1969-1971). Regarding females of both groups, the gain in the first eight years in the 1970s was about 80 percent of the gain during the entire preceding two decades. As pointed out by Rao (1973: 417), three major patterns of historical transition of mortality occurred in the United States: "An initial stage of relative slow gain in expectation of life during 1850-1900, a second stage of accelerated gain during the first half of the present century, and a third stage of slower gains in expectation of life at birth since 1950." Rao's data relate to the years 1850-1968. Despite the significant gains in the 1970s as compared to the previous two decades, Rao's observation is still valid in the sense that in the thirty years since 1950 the rate of gain in life expectancy has been slower than that in the 1910-1950 period.

The major conclusion to be drawn from the analysis of life expectancy is that although there has been significant improvement in all population subgroups between 1900 and 1979, there is still room for improvement in health and mortality conditions of nonwhites in general and blacks in particular. There is still a difference of four or five years, depending on sex, in life expectancy between whites and blacks.

Black Infant Mortality

The infant mortality rate (number of infant deaths under age one per 1,000 live births) affects life expectancy more drastically than mortality in any other age group, and lower life expectancy among blacks is substantially attributed to higher rates of infant mortality among blacks. As shown in Figure 2, there have been significant reductions in the infant mortality rates of both blacks and whites since 1940 when the rate for whites was 43 per 1,000 live births and the rate for blacks was 74. Based on the most recent data available, the infant mortality rate for the United States as a whole declined from 13.8 in 1978 to 13.1 in 1979. For white

Figure 2.   Infant Mortality Rates by Race: United States, 1940-1979

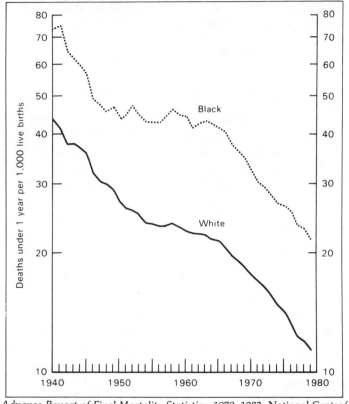

Source: *Advance Report of Final Mortality Statistics, 1979.* 1982. National Center for Health
Statistics: Monthly Vital Statistics Report, vol. 31, no. 6, Supplement, p. 10.

infants it declined from 12.0 in 1978 to 11.4 infant deaths per 1,000 live
births in 1979. For black infants it declined from 23.1 in 1978 to 21.8 in 1979
(National Center for Health Statistics, 1982: 9). As these figures indicate,
significant racial differences in infant mortality still persist despite
improvement in the past forty years. Even in 1979, as it was twenty years
ago, the infant mortality rate for blacks was almost twice that for whites.
Poverty, lack of prenatal care, low birth weight, short gestation periods,
teenage pregnancy, high rates of pregnancy outside marriage, and poor
health of black mothers, to mention just a few, are said to contribute to

higher infant mortality among blacks. Whatever the cause, however, it is evident that improvements in the realm of black infant survival must occupy a top priority in the 1980s.

Suggested Future Research

A number of authors cited in this publication have made specific recommendations for future research. However, before considering any specific areas of study research, it may categorically be stated that substantive research in almost all aspects of black population is needed in view of the fact that black population studies have generally lagged behind those for whites. The following research suggestions are not listed in any order of priorities because all areas are equally important.

1. In the past two to three decades, especially prior to the 1970s, many blacks have come to feel that proliferation of fertility control—contraception, abortion, and sterilization programs in the black communities supported by the government—is an act of genocide in disguise. Many researchers, including some blacks, have called this charge unfounded. In any case, the fact is that the fear has existed and continues to exist (see the section on sterilization and genocide in Chapter 3). The increase in the number of abortions, sterilizations, and use of contraceptives in the 1970s may indicate a lessening of this fear but this is an area where a number of attitudinal surveys, demographic, and social-psychological studies relative to the nature, rationale, and impact of such fears on black fertility behavior should be conducted.

2. As discussed earlier, blacks' actual fertility surpasses their desired and/or ideal family size. Research on the causes and the extent of this discrepancy are limited. More research in this area could prove valuable in providing the essential clues for helping couples to close the gap between their actual and desired family size, and thus avoid the adverse consequences of unwanted fertility in the black community.

3. Studies on the health effects of high/low fertility among blacks are in much demand. Social-psychological effects of alternative fertility control methods on the physical and mental health of blacks for various population subgoups need to be investigated.

4. Factors associated with adolescent pregnancy and fertility outside marriage need further research. Most needed are: (a) a more complete picture of the pattern of sexual activities among black teenage mothers, and its impact on family formation, family structure and stability; (b) information on black teenagers access to fertility control devices; (c) the social-psychological forces that shape these behavioral patterns; (d) the impacts of liberalized abortion

laws; (e) the role of poverty in black teenage fertility-related behavior; (f) parental attitudes toward premarital sex and pregnancy outside marriage; (g) the efficacy of parental rights to control fertility-related behavior of their minor children; and (h) the health consequences of all the above for the black community.

5. Research on the causes and consequences of black family stability are inconclusive. More studies employing fresh survey demographic data, in-depth social-psychological studies, and further examination of the relationship between fertility and family structure are suggested.

6. Death rates for blacks are higher than for whites below age 65, but after age 65 there is a crossover. A black man or woman aged 70 expects to live longer than a white man or woman of the same age. The components of this phenomenon are not fully known but further research in this area could prove valuable to gerontological studies.

7. Extensive research to find ways and means to reduce black infant mortality must be given special priority.

8. Data collection and quantitative analyses are important, but some human behavior cannot be explained in quantitative terms. It appears that better information on the qualitative aspects of some of the quantified variables is needed. Research designed to incorporate the qualitative aspects of the quantitative demographic studies should prove very useful. For instance, the number of blacks attending school has quantitatively increased, but what about the changes in the quality of the education? Quantitative studies that do not reflect qualitative changes are often misleading. Research in how to correct such methodological problems would be extremely useful.

9. We are in an age in which the collection of massive quantitative data has become routinized. As a result, there is a large quantity of information that is not yet fully analyzed and reflected upon. Further research designed to analyze and synthesize the existing data on black population should be encouraged and research on devising methods to avoid black undercount is overdue.

10. Philip M. Hauser (see item 574 in this volume) has said that the size, rate of growth, distribution, and composition of the black population both influence integration and provide some indication of the extent to which integration has been achieved. The precise way in which demographic factors influence racial integration is not fully studied. More research as to how the changes in black population affect racial integration must be given special priority.

References

Bean, Frank D., and Joseph P. Marcum. 1978. Differential Fertility and the Minority Group Status Hypothesis: An Assessment and Review. In **The Demography** of Racial and Ethnic Groups. Frank D. Bean and W. P. Frisbie, eds. New York: Academic Press, pp. 189-211.

Blair, A. O. 1967. A Comparison of Negro and White Fertility Attitudes. In Sociological Contributions to Family Planning Research, Donald J. Bogue, ed. Chicago: University of Chicago, Community and Family Study Center, pp. 1-35.

Bogue, Donald J. 1969. Principles of Demography. New York: John Wiley and Sons, Inc.

Coale, A., and N. W. Rives, Jr. 1973. A Statistical Reconstruction of the Black Population of the United States 1880-1970: Estimates of True Numbers by Age and Sex, Birth Rates, and Total Fertility. Population Index 39: 3-36.

Cutright, Phillips, and E. Shorter. 1979. The Effects of Health on the Completed Fertility of Nonwhite and White U.S. Women Born Between 1867 and 1935. Journal of Social History 13 (2): 191-217.

Farley, Reynolds. 1970. Fertility Among Urban Blacks. Milbank Memorial Fund Quarterly 48 (2, Pt. 2): 183-206.

Farley, Reynolds. 1971. Indications of Recent Demographic Change Among Blacks. Social Biology 18 (4): 341-47.

Farley, Reynolds, and Albert I. Hermalin. 1971. Family Stability: A Comparison of Trends Between Blacks and Whites. American Sociological Review 36 (1): 1-17.

Glick, Paul C. 1970. Marriage and Marital Stability Among Blacks. Milbank Memorial Fund Quarterly 48 (2, Pt. 2): 99-116.

Goldscheider, Calvin, and P. R. Uhlenberg. 1969. Minority Group Status and Fertility. American Journal of Sociology 74 (January): 361-72.

Hampton, Robert. 1979. Husband's Characteristics and Marital Disruption in Black Families. The Sociological Quarterly 20 (Spring): 255-66.

Henderson, Donald H. 1921. The Negro Migration of 1916-1918. Journal of Negro History 6 (October): 383-499.

Hill, Herbert. 1966. Demographic Change and Racial Ghettoes: The Crisis of American Cities. Journal of Urban Law 44 (Winter): 231-58.

Johnson, N. E. 1979. Minority Group Status and the Fertility of Black Americans, 1970: A New Look. American Journal of Sociology 84 (6): 1386-1400.

Jones, Marcus Earl. 1978. Black Migration in the United States with Some Emphasis on Selected Central Cities. Unpublished Ph.D. Dissertation. Southern Illinois University at Carbondale.

Landon, Fred. 1920. The Negro Migration to Canada After the Passing of the Fugitive Slave Act. Journal of Negro History 5: 22-36.

Lewis, L. Thomas. 1971. Some Migration Models: Their Applicability to Negro Migration. Unpublished Ph.D. Dissertation. Clark University.

Long, Larry, and Diane DeAre. 1981. The Suburbanization of Blacks. American Demographics 3 (8): 16-21, 44.

Moorhead, James William. 1971. Negro Suburban Migration: 1955-1960. Unpublished Ph.D. Dissertation. Brown University.

National Center for Health Statistics. 1982. Advance Report on Final Mortality Statistics, 1979. **Monthly Vital Statistics** 31, no. 6.

Pleck, Elizabeth H. 1974. Black Migration to Boston in the Late Nineteenth Century. Ph.D. Dissertation. Brandeis University.

Price Daniel O. 1969. **Changing Characteristics of the Negro Population: A Census Monograph**, Washington, D.C.: Government Printing Office.

Rao, S.L.N. 1973. On Long Term Mortality Trends in the United States, 1850-1968. **Demography** 10 (3): 405-19.

Scroggs, W. O. 1917. Interstate Migration of Negro Population. **Journal of Political Economy** 25 (December): 1034-44.

Stinner, W., and G. DeYong. 1969. Southern Negro Migration: Social and Economic Components of an Ecological Model. **Demography** 6 (4): 455-71.

U.S. Bureau of the Census. 1935. **Negroes in the United States, 1920-32**. Washington, D.C.: Government Printing Office.

U.S. Bureau of the Census. 1980. The Social and Economic Status of the Black Population in the United States: An Historical View, 1790-1978. **Current Population Reports**, Series P-23, no. 80.

U.S. Bureau of the Census. 1982a. Farm Population of the United States: 1981. **Current Population Reports**, Series P-27, no. 55.

U.S. Bureau of the Census. 1982b. Money Income and Poverty Status of Families and Persons in the United States: 1981. **Current Population Reports**, Series P-60, no. 134.

Wadley, Janet K., and Everett S. Lee. 1974. The Disappearance of the Black Farmer. **Phylon** 35 (3): 276-83.

Zelnik, M. and J. F. Kantner. 1970. United States: Exploratory Studies of Negro Family Formation—Factors Relating to Illegitimacy. **Studies in Family Planning** (60): 5-9.

Chapter 1
Black Fertility

001. Anderson, John E., and Jack Smith. 1975. Planned and Unplanned
Fertility in a Metropolitan Area: Black and White Differences.
Family Planning Perspectives 7 (6): 281-285.

Since 1960, the total fertility rate has declined for both blacks and
whites, with only slight changes in group difference. The pattern
has been very similar in the Atlanta area, in Georgia, and in the
United States as a whole: Black/white differences in fertility for
women aged 25 and older disappeared or became very small toward the
end of the period surveyed. Between 1960 and 1970, nonmarital
fertility became the most important factor in the nationwide
black/white difference in total fertility rate; while the importance
of marital fertility decreased. Results of the 1965 and 1970 NFS
suggest that much of the black/white convergence in marital fertility
was a result of the decrease in unwanted fertility among blacks.
Data from the 1971 Atlanta Family Planning Survey documented the
black/white fertility differences for married women and show that the
difference is due to higher levels of unplanned fertility among
blacks. Socioeconomic differences between whites and blacks, as
exemplified in their differential distribution according to education
appear to be an important underlying factor in the overall fertility
difference between the two groups; but such factors do not account
entirely for the higher levels of unplanned fertility reported by
black women. The similarity of fertility patterns in Atlanta to
those found in the national surveys tend to confirm the results of
the nationwide studies, and suggests that the factors underlying
racial fertility differences may be similar in different areas of the
country. The data reviewed here suggest that as both black and white
women continued to move toward more complete fertility control,

differences will continue to diminish and, eventually, may disappear altogether.★

002.   Bauman, Karl E. 1974. Birth Rates. In: The Media and Family Planning. J.R. Udry (ed.). Cambridge, Massachusetts: Ballinger. Pp. 147-153.

In order to determine whether the media campaign influenced the number of births, it is necessary to compare the numbers of births in campaign and non-campaign cities before, during, and after the campaign. Counts of live births for 1968-1971 are available for each of the 18 cities in the experimental design except 2. Portland and Utica are excluded from the present analysis since all of their 1968 and 1969 data have not been received, and the cities of Gadsden and Tuscaloosa, Alabama, have been added for analyses of vital events. 1972 data for some of the cities are available and will be available for all of them before the project's end. Included in this analysis are only those births which occurred during October, November, or December of 1968, 1969, 1971, and 1972. The trends for whites and blacks are presented separately and for total and illegitimate births. Comparisons between campaign and noncampaign cities revealed that fewer births could not be attributed to the media campaign. Although more vital data will be included in future analyses when the same question is asked again, this analysis suggests that there is no effect due to the campaign. ☆

003.   Bauman, Karl E., and J. Richard Udry. 1973. The Difference in Unwanted Births Between Blacks and Whites. Demography 10 (3): 315-328.

Blacks are more likely than whites to have unwanted births. A common explanation for that difference is that blacks use less effective contraceptive methods, use contraception less effectively, and use contraception less often than whites. Analysis of data from 17 cities in our family planning evaluation project suggested that, among women living in low-income neighborhoods, the black-white difference in unwanted births was not due to (1) blacks reaching desired completed parity at younger ages than whites, (2) differences in age or parity in our black and white samples, (3) black-white differences in current use of physician-administered contraception, or (4) blacks being more likely than whites to adopt physician-administered contraception after having an unwanted birth. Black-white differences which might have contributed to relatively more unwanted births among blacks were (1) blacks desired fewer children, (2) blacks were less likely than whites to use nonphysician-administered methods and more likely than whites to use no contraception, and (3) blacks had higher failure rates than whites subsequent to the adoption of physician-administered methods and when not using those methods. Comparisons are made with the 1965 and 1970 National Fertility Studies, and program implications of the findings discussed.*

004.   Bean, Frank D., and Charles H. Wood. 1974. Ethnic Variations in the

Relationship Between Income and Fertility.   Demography 11 (November): 629-640.

The effects of husband's potential and relative incomes on completed fertility, as well as their effects on certain parity progression probabilities, are examined within samples of Anglos, Blacks and Mexican Americans.   Relationships are estimated using data from the one-percent 1960 and 1970 U.S. Public Use Samples.   The results reveal different patterns of relationship by ethnicity between the measures of income and the measures of fertility.   The effects on completed fertility of the income measures are positive for Anglos and negative for Blacks, while in the case of Mexican Americans the effect of potential income is negative and that of relative income is positive.   Income effects on the parity progression probabilities are similar in pattern to those from the analyses using completed fertility, although somewhat different patterns tend to appear at different birth orders, especially among Anglos.*

005.   Bean, Frank D., and Joseph P. Marcum. 1978. Differential Fertility and the Minority Group Status Hypothesis: An Assessment and Review. In: The Demography of Racial and Ethnic Groups. Frank D. Bean and W. Parker Frisbie (eds.). New York: Academic Press. Pp. 189-211.

In this chapter Bean and Marcum present: (a) an overview of certain aspects of racial-ethnic group fertility differences in the U.S.; (b) review and evaluate the research efforts aimed at interpreting these differences; and, (c) suggest a particular research strategy for further investigation of the topic of minority group status hypothesis.   In this regard the authors argue that if minority group status affects reproductive behavior in the way suggested by Goldscheider and Uhlenberg (see annotation in this bibliography), then minority couples of higher socioeconomic status will exhibit lower fertility than majority couples of similar socioeconomic status.   Bean and Marcum have also hypothesized that a minority group status effect on fertility is more likely to emerge under conditons of less socioeconomic distance between majority and minority groups.★

006.   Beebe, G.W. 1942. Contraception and Fertility in the Southern Appalacians. Baltimore: Williams and Wilkins.

This monograph attempts to discover whether rural women in high fertility areas can be encouraged to practice birth control. A study focused on the population of the coal plateaus of the southern Appalachians.   The object of the study was to make birth control methods at once easy and pleasurable to use.   The monograph presents problems of this particular region, patterns of reproduction, the institution of the contraceptive service, the impact of the service upon fertility, and the prescription's acceptability.   Also included are organizational guidelines on contraceptive service in depressed rural areas and methodology of studies in clinical contraception. Observations have indicated that even half-hearted and unskilled

contraceptive practice produces a great decline in fertility.   At
initiation birth control services meet with rigid resistance.   More
diversified contraceptive methods requiring less sustained initiative
and interfering less with spontaneity but nevertheless providing
long-term protection are needed.☆

007. Blair, A.O. 1967. A comparison of Negro and White Fertility
Attitudes. In: Sociological Contributions to Family Planning
Research. Donald J. Bogue (ed.). Chicago: University of Chicago,
Community and Family Study Center. Pp. 1-35.

Data were collected from May 1959 to September 1961 on the attitude
of a sample of Negro and white women in Chicago on birth control and
childbearing in an effort to identify the reasons for the continuing
high fertility among urban Negroes in spite of increased availability
of birth control methods.   The data analyzed is part of a series of
studies sponsored by the Community and Family Study Center and the
National Opinion Research Center using material from the survey,
Problems of Living in the Metropolis. Most of the variables commonly
employed in studies of differential fertility were used.   The
nonwhite sample (96% Negro) was selected by the stratified cluster
method and contained a high proportion of respondents in slum areas,
ethnically concentrated neighborhoods and low income areas.   The
control group was formed of white persons living outside the slums
and was further classified as Catholic or non-Catholic.   Extensive
detail on sampling technique and data gathering along with numerous
tables detailing contraceptive attitudes and practices by color, age,
and religion are provided.   Specifically, attitudes toward the
general idea of family planning, practice of family limitation and
fertility, and toward desired and expected family size were
solicited.   In general, though nonwhite women and their husbands
approved of family planning and wanted slightly smaller families than
did white couples, they had higher rates of fertility and their
actual childbearing far surpassed their ideals. While some of the
difference in white-nonwhite fertility seems to be due to a greater
incidence of sterility or subfecundity among white women, the major
factor appears to be difference in use and use-effectiveness of contraceptives. Of women who reported themselves to be unsuccessful
family planners, 56.2% of the nonwhite wished they had had fewer
children while only 38.4% said they were not dissatisfied with their
family size.   The corresponding figures for white women are 8.7 and
64.7%, respectively.   The incidence of accidental pregnancy, defined
by attitude toward last pregnancy and number of children coming
earlier than planned, is about 41% among nonwhite and 20% among white
women.   Excessive fertility among Negroes thus appears to be
involuntary and undesired. Either a great discrepancy exists between
desired and actual behavior or there is a large white-nonwhite
difference in intensity of fertility attitudes or weak motivation but
rather because of lack of knowledge of modern contraception and
comparative availability of family planning services.☆

008. Bogue, D.J. 1975. A Long-Term Solution to the AFDC Problem: Prevention of Unwanted Pregnancy. Social Service Review 49 (4): 539-552.

Three hundred fifteen (315) AFDC women, drawn systematically from the files of the Cook County Illinois Department of Public Aid, were interviewed in 1972-1973 in order to discover the circumstances that preceded and accompanied the dissolution of their marriages. The results of these interviews were used to test the hypothesis that the most important single cause of dissolution among black conjugal unions is premarital and extramarital pregnancy, especially unwanted pregnancy. The high rate of marital dissolution among blacks had previously been explained by 3 hypotheses: the Negro culture, Negro family disorganization, and economic forces. The interviews provided a complete social history of the events preceding the acquiring of AFDC status. Each woman was assigned to 1 to 4 categories with respect to premarital pregnancy: 1) without premarital pregnancy; 2) premarital pregnancy-happy; 3) premarital pregnancy-unhappy; and 4) never married. 65% of all AFDC recipients became pregnant outside marriage. 45% of all 1st pregnancies of AFDC mothers were both extramarital and unwanted. The courtship and marriage of AFDC women, their aspirations and the reality of their situation was examined. The women had delayed middle-class aspirations about marriage but more than 2/3 had to leave high school because of pregnancy. 40% of AFDC mothers married the father of their 1st child in order to legitimize the child rather than for love. 90% of AFDC women failed to use contraception during their premarital or extramarital relations. The data strongly support the stated hypothesis. It is suggested that contraception information be made availale to unmarried women in the lower classes, by sex education courses in high school and during interactions with social workers and social welfare agencies. It is conceivable that the AFDC welfare rolls could be reduced.✩

009. Cain, Glen G., and Andriana Weininger. 1973. Economic Determinants of Fertility: Results from Cross-Sectional Aggregate Data. Demography 10 (May): 205-233.

Census data for areal units, SMSA's in 1960 and cities in 1940, are used to test hypotheses and estimate parameters concerning the influence of a variety of socioeconomic variables on fertility rates of ever married white and nonwhite women aged 25-29, 30-34, 35-44, and 45-49. An economic model of the demand for children is adopted as the theoretical framework. The principal findings are that the market earnings opportunities for wives have an important negative effect on the fertility rate and that male income, representing the income of husbands, has a small but positive effect on fertility. The implication of these results is that changes in economic variables, for example, improvements in the employment opportunities and wages for wives or the establishment of a children's allowance program, may be expected to affect fertility.*

010.   Curry, James P., and Gayle D. Scriven. 1978. The Relationship Between
       Apartment Living and Fertility for Blacks, Mexican-Americans, and
       Other Americans in Racine, Wisconsin. Demography 15 (4): 477-485.

       Recently published data from a sample of Bogota, Colombia public
       housing residents show that apartment dwellers, but not house
       dwellers, reduced their fertility in a tight housing market. We
       propose that the utility-cost theory of fertility accounts for this
       finding, and using this theory, we predict that (a) apartment
       residents will not decrease their fertility in an open housing market
       and (b) higher fertility will be associated with larger dwellings.
       Longitudinal data from a sample of Midwest urban blacks, Mexican-
       Americans, and other Americans support both predictions. The sub-
       stantive implications are discussed.*

011.   Cutler, W.B., C.R. Garcia, and A.M. Krieger. 1979. Infertility and
       Age at First Coitus: A Possible Relationship. Journal of Biosocial
       Science 11 (4): 425-432.

       Black women constituted twenty percent of the sample. Reported age at
       first coitus was shown to be associated with incidence and degree of
       infertility. Infertility patients reported later first coital ages
       than gynecological patients in a sample of 792 women seen in a major
       fertility service. Among the infertility patients, those who had
       never conceived presented a later first coital age than those who had
       previously conceived. Routine gynecological patients reported the
       youngest first coital age of the groups studied.*

012.   Cutright, Phillips, and E. Shorter. 1979. The Effects of Health on
       the Completed Fertility of Nonwhite and White U.S. Women Born Between
       1867 and 1935. Journal of Social History 13 (2): 191-217.

       This paper examines the effect of health on the completed fertility
       of nonwhites and whites. It concludes that the declining fertility
       of blacks before the Second World War and the increase after that war
       were primarily due to changes in the health of black women. The data
       presented suggest two reasons for the decline in the birth rate among
       blacks. One is increased lifetime sterility, or increased sterility
       after the birth of one or more children. The authors contend that
       most lifetime sterility probably was due to gonorrhea, but they offer
       little direct evidence for their argument. The second reason, for a
       decline in the fertility of very high parity mothers, is the harmful
       consequences of ceaseless childbearing. Mothers who had borne
       several children and who did not have gonorrhea at the time of a
       birth but contracted puerperal fever during a delivery, for whatever
       reason, would not bear more children because the postpartum infection
       would have blocked their tubes or damaged the endometrial lining of
       the tubes, thus making further conception unlikely.*

013.   Darney, P.D. 1975. Fertility Decline and Participation in Georgia's
       Family Planning Program: Temporal and Areal Association. Studies in

Family Planning 6 (6): 156-165.

Three (3) different analytic techniques are used to demonstrate a causal relationship between a Georgia statewide public family planning program and a subsequent decline in fertility. The Georgia family planning program developed rapid growth since 1967. By January 1973, 42% of the state's black women in the 15-44 age group had accepted contraception from a public family planning center; only 7.7% of white women in the same age groups had accepted. The proportions of young and of childless women increased over time. By 1969 oral contraceptives were the most popular method. The first analytic method, a temporal one, indicated an association between enrollment of black women 25 years or older in the family planning program and a subsequent decline in fertility. The second analysis showed that black fertility declined more than twice as much in counties with high rates of contraceptive acceptance than in counties with low rates of contraceptive acceptance. The third analysis, a multivariate regression technique to control for other factors that might influence fertility, controlled for the following factors: 1) female employment; 2) farm residence; 3) poverty; and 4) female education. The limitations of the model and the data are mentioned. This method indicated that socioeconomic factors became less important and contraceptive acceptance more important in declining fertility over time.☆

014.   Eckard, E. 1980. **Wanted and Unwanted Births Reported by Mothers 15-44 Years of Age: United States, 1976.** Advance Data 56 (January 24): 1-10.

Results of the 1976 National Survey of Family Growth in the U.S. show that an estimated 8.1 million or 12% of a total of 67.8 million live births that occurred to mothers 15-44 years of age were unwanted, representing a modest statistically nonsignificant decrease in the proportion of unwanted births since the 1973 Survey. Data were collected by means of personal interviews with a multistage probability sample of black and white women aged 15-44, who were currently married, previously married, or never married but with offspring presently living in the household, in the population of the conterminous U.S. Findings are reported in 2 tables: 1) number of mothers aged 15-44, number of live births, and percent distribution of births by whether wanted, unwanted, or undetermined, according to race, age, and parity; and 2) number of mothers aged 15-44, number of live births, and percentage distribution of births by whether wanted, unwanted, or undetermined, according to selected characteristics (hispanic origin; geographic region; women's education; husband's education; women's labor force status; religion; previous marriages, fetal losses; and desired family size). Results indicate that of an average 2.5 births per mother, 2 were wanted at the time of conception, .3 were unwanted at that time, and .2 births were undetermined. More than 4/5 of the births to white women were reported as wanted, compared with only 3/5 of the births to black

women. The proportion of unwanted births for black women, 25.8%, was
almost 3 times that for white women (9.5%). The wantedness of
another 13.8% of births to black women and 7% to white women was
undetermined because the women's feelings at the time of conception
were unknown. It is concluded that the summary data do not provide
the best basis for examining trends in wanted and unwanted fertility
in recent years because changes in these proportions between 1973 and
1976 might be obscured by the large overlap of births occurring in
1973 and earlier years reported in both surveys.★

015. Engerman, Stanley. 1978. Changes in Black Fertility, 1880-1940. In:
Family and Population in Nineteenth Century America. Tamara Hareven
and Maris A. Vinovskis (eds.). Princeton, N.J.: Princeton University
Press.

This preliminary foray into the patterns of black fertility and black
family structure has been more concerned with describing the broad
patterns of movement and with raising issues for further study than
with the detailed discussion of these movements. The intent was to
present the demographic experience of the black population as one of
many examples of the demographic transition, and to indicate the ways
it has been similar to other populations, rather than to regard this
as unique experience. It is possible that factors relating to
slavery did delay the onset of the transition and can explain the lag
of the U.S. black population behind the white in marked declines of
fertility. To study that we need know more about the determinants of
fertility in the slave period, a period for which systematic studies
are just starting. However, while the situation of American blacks
in the years between 1880 and 1940 was in many ways clearly different
from that of other groups, it seems that in the cross-sectional
differences, as well as in the movements over time, much of the black
fertility pattern resembles that of whites in the united States and
elsewhere, as well as that of free black populations in other parts
of the Americas.*

016. Engerman, Stanley, L. 1977. Black Fertility and Family Structure in
the U.S., 1880-1940. Journal of Family History 2 (2): 117-138.

Utilizing the unadjusted census data and employing Child-Woman-Ratio
as measure of fertility this paper examines the patterns of black
fertility and black family structure. This study is more concerned
with describing the broad patterns of movement and with raising
issues for further study than with a detailed discussion of the
transition in black fertility. The intent is to present the
demographic experience of the black population as another example
(one of many) of the demographic transition, and to indicate how it
has resembled the experience of other populations, rather than to
regard it as unique. This essay also discusses the nature of black
family life, since the author (quite accurately) contends that black
fertility is intimately linked to changes in family structure.
Engerman surmises that while it may be possible to analytically

separate the problem of explaining changes in black fertility from that of explaining changes in black family structure, there are obviously important relationships between the two.   Some of these links are discussed.★

017.   Family Planning Digest. 1972. 1970 National Fertility Study: Over 1960s Decade Unwanted Births Declined, Fertility Gap Between Poor and More Affluent Reduced. Family Planning Digest 1 (6): 9-12.

Several reports based on the 1970 National Studies are condensed. Since 1965 there has been a 36% decline in the rate of unwanted births among married couples, the groups which showed the largest declines being blacks (56%) and Catholics (45%).   Newly established family planning programs were thought to have some role in this change.   58% of married contraceptors were using either the pill, the IUD, or sterilization, the pill being used by 34%.   Voluntary sterilization became the most popular method for couples where the wife was 30 years of age or older.   This modernization of contraceptive practice has occurred quite uniformly among blacks and whites and across different socioeconomic groups.   The rate of IUD adoption is increasing and is likely to surpass use of "premodern" methods.   Despite these gains, it is still estimated that between 10 and 13 million American women need aid in their contraceptive practices to achieve their desired family size. ☆

018.   Family Planning Digest. 1973. Georgia Program: Black Fertility Drops When Service Offered. Family Planning Digest 2(6): 7.

In the period from 1960 to 1971, black fertility in Georgia dropped 28% and white fertility dropped 26.8%.   The major part of the decline in white fertility occurred in the years 1960-1965 with family planning services procured from private physicians.   In 1966 the statewide family planning program accelerated.   During the 1966-1971 period, the major part of the black fertility decline occurred.   The statewide program was patronized by only 6% of eligible white women and by 39% of eligible black women.★

019.   Farley, Reynolds. 1966. Recent Changes in Negro Fertility. Demography 3 (1): 188-203.

Crude birth rates for the Negro population of the United States indicate that fertility declined while Negroes remained in the South and then climbed in the last twenty-five years as Negroes became ur-banized.   Cohort rates show more precisely the effects of the depression upon childbearing as well as the magnitude and persistence of the post-Depression rise in fertility.   More Negro women now become mothers, average family size has increased, and the proportion of women bearing six, seven, or eight children has risen.   Negro fertility has risen despite the urbanization of Negroes and improvements in their socio-economic characteristics.   Negro fertility rates present the paradox of falling when demographic transition theory would predict the maintenance of high rates and then rising when a decline would be expected. Urbanization does not appear to have reduced Negro fertility. Traditionally, urban living has dampened childbearing in two ways--first, health conditions in cities were inferior to those of rural areas, and thus urbanization affected fecundity adversely; second, city residents are more likely to know about and adopt birth control than rural residents. Negroes migrated to cities at the very time when diseases were being controlled and when public health and welfare facilities were being expanded to serve all residents. This has contributed to higher Negro fertility rates. If fertility rates are to fall because of family planning, not only must birth control be available but there must be a desire to limit family size. Such a desire may be linked to opportunities for social mobility. Blacks have not been assimilated into urban society as previous immigrant groups were, and opportunities for mobility have been slow to adopt stable monogamous families and the intentional control of fertility.*

020.   Farley, Reynolds. 1970. Recent Changes in Negro Fertility. In: Growth of the Black Population: A Study of Demographic Trends. Chicago: Markham. Pp. 76-100.

In recent years the fertility rates of the black population have fluctuated most rapidly, and the future growth of the black population will be most influenced by fertility trends. In this chapter, Farley examines these trends and the changes in family size in great details. Some of his findings are: (1) completed family size among blacks declined over a long span. Women born between 1910 and 1914 averaged less than three children. This change resulted from a rise in childlessness and a decrease in large families; (2) during the 1940s, fertility began to climb, and during the 1950s, they increased very rapidly; (3) since the late 1950s fertility have decreased; and, (4) there is no way to know the completed family size of women who began child bearing in the late 1950s and the 1960s, for they have not yet completed their family size. As a whole, Farley discusses the high black fertility rates of the 19th century, the decline in fertility that occurred between the Civil War and the Depression, and the post-Depression rise in fertility.*

021.   Farley, Reynolds. 1970. Differentials in Negro Fertility. In: Growth of the Black Population: A Study of Demographic Trends. Chicago: Markham. Pp. 101-120.

In this chapter, Farley investigates black fertility differentials and describes fertility differences for women living in different places. He assesses the effects of urbanization on black fertility, and studies black fertility differentials by place of birth in an effort to measure the consequences of rural background on fertility. In the final section of this chapter, he examines black fertility differentials by socioeconomic factors such as education, income, and occupation of husband and discusses changes over time in these differentials. The major conclusion drawn is that the differentials in black fertility are very similar to those observed among white women in the United States. Black women in rural areas have higher fertility rates than black women in urban areas. Black women who are married to men with white collar jobs bear fewer children than those married to men with less prestigious jobs, and women who are well educated have fewer children than women who attended school for only a short time. In addition, women with urban background bear fewer offsprings than those of rural background.*

022.   Farley, Reynolds. 1970. **Fertility Among Urban Blacks**. Milbank Memorial Fund Quarterly 48 (Part 2): 183-206.

Black fertility rates in cities were at a low level 60 years ago, whereas the rates in rural areas were quite high. The socioeconomic characteristics of urban women and their more frequent marital disruptions help to explain why urban fertility rates were lower than were rural. Poor health conditions, however, were an additional and very important reason for the low fertility in cities. Prior to the mid-1930's, public health activities were modest in scope and little was done to control venereal disease. Descriptions of the life style of blacks in farm areas suggest that for some decades prior to 1940, rural blacks were becoming more impoverished as crops failed and farm prices fell. These lower standards of living and the spread of disease helped to reduce rural fertility rates although they always exceeded urban birth rates by a wide margin. The available evidence indicates that before World War II relatively few black women used birth control. In spite of this, growth rates were moderate and many women reached menopause with no children or with only a few children. This was particularly true of the Negro women who lived in cities. After World War II this changed and black women who did not use birth control undoubtedly found themselves bearing many children. The black women who were born in the early 1930's may complete their fertility with as many children as the women born during Reconstruction. The transition to controlled fertility and to lower fertility rates among blacks has been occurring for some time, but this transition has been accelerated in the past decade. The analysis of data from the Census of 1960 showed that educational attainment and coming from an urban background both had substantial independent consequences for fertility. This suggests that well-educated urban black women were among the first to effectively limit their family size. The Growth of American Families study, a survey that included a sample of 270 nonwhite couples in 1960, provided further support for this view. A very large proportion of the nonwhite women in the North and women with a college education had used contraception, but less than half of the women on farms or with no more than an elementary education had used birth control. Nonwhite women who had a high school education and who were not from a rural background had fertility rates and expectations similar to those of white women, but nonwhite women from a rural background or with a grade school education expected to have many more children than comparable white women.

Between 1959 and 1967, the general fertility rate for nonwhites and each of the age-specific fertility rates, declined by about 30 per cent. This is an indication of the fertility transition that is now occurring. It is likely that these fertility rates will continue to fall. Surveys such as the 1960 Growth of American Families study and the 1965 National Fertility study have discovered that nonwhite women desire to bear no more children than do white women. In fact, black women apparently desire smaller families than do white women. The control of fertility will be fostered by demographic and social changes occurring within the black population. First of all, educational attainment has increased. The cohorts of blacks born 1938 to 1942 are the first in which a majority will obtain a complete high school education and the school enrollment of teen-age blacks has continued to rise throughout the 1960's. Second, urbanization of the black population has continued and, because of the urbanization that followed World War II, a greater proportion of the women who begin their childbearing in the future will come from an urban background. Third, the development of new and apparently more effective contraceptives such as oral contraceptives and the intrauterine device is likely to lead to the more accurate control of childbearing. Although the oral contraceptives had been on the market for only five years, one-fifth of the black respondents contacted by the 1965 National Fertility study reported having used this method of birth control. It is reasonable to presume that these changes will lead to lower fertility rates and slower growth of the black population.*

023.   Farley, Reynolds. 1972. Fertility and Mortality Trends Among Blacks in the United States. In: Demographic and Social Aspects of Population Growth and the American Future, Research Reports, Volume 1. Charles F. Westoff and Robert Parke, Jr. (eds.). Pp. 111-138.

The vital rates of blacks in the United States are at a higher level than those of whites. The racial difference in crude rates is greater for fertility than for mortality and, as a result, the black population is growing more rapidly than the white. In 1969, the rate of natural increase approximated 1.7 percent annually among blacks; 0.7 percent among whites. Since the late 1950's, birth rates have decreased among both blacks and whites but the racial difference in fertility persists. Apparently many couples adopted more effective techniques of birth control during the 1960's but the incidence of unplanned or accidental pregnancies remains greater among blacks than whites. Although actual fertility rates are higher among blacks, desired family size is smaller among blacks than among whites. Racial differentials in mortality have traditionally favored whites. The racial gap in life expectation has narrowed a bit during the last 30 years. Nevertheless, impressive differences are evident. The current life expectation of nonwhites equals that of whites in 1940 while the current infant mortality rate of nonwhites is at the same level as that of whites in 1945. This paper summarizes racial trends and differentials with regard to fertility and mortality. Certain population projections are then presented.*

024.   Fried, E.S., and J.R. Udry. 1980. Normative Pressures on Fertility Planning. Population and Environment 3 (3): 199-209.

This paper is an exploration of normative responses, i.e. social or structural pressures, expected by potential parents, and of the effects of those pressures on their fertility planning. Interviews were obtained with 572 couples, black and white. Mean age of wife was 27, and of husband was 30. Blacks had a mean parity of 2.4, and whites of 1.7; whites were slightly better educated, and had moderately higher incomes than blacks. The survey showed that a substantial proportion of respondents had experienced direct social pressures with respect to childbearing, and, as expected, pressures were related to parity, pronatal pressure decreasing and antinatal pressure increasing with increasing parity. However, pressures were inconsistent, and there is no evidence of a normative consensus to which individuals may respond. Social pressure does not seem to have great influence on the final decisions of would-be parents.☆

025.   Gebhard, P.H., et al. 1958. Negro Woman. In: Pregnancy, Birth and Abortion, by P.H. Gebhard, W.B. Pomeroy, C.E. Martin, and C.V. Christenson. New York: Harper/Hoeber. Pp. 153-167.

The study sample of 572 Negro women is predominantly made up of young, urban women of above average education, generally living in the North. As such, the figures should be regarded with caution. However, findings agree in general with vital statistics and other studies. The sample showed attitudes toward sexuality distinctly different from the white sample. Coitus is regarded as a natural and desirable activity in and out of wedlock and pregnancy is accepted. This results in a high conception and live birthrate, a high spontaneous abortion rate (the result of poverty and disease), and minimal use of induced abortion. As socioeconomic status increases coitus before marriage starts at a later age, but is still 5 years before the white woman starts coitus. Birthrates decrease with education. Negro women have a higher proportion of late fetal deaths than white women and spontaneous abortion accounts for 28% of pregnancy outcomes for Negro women with grade school education. Among college-educated women 81% of pregnancies end in induced abortion, the same percentage as among white college graduates. Since she also has larger percentage of spontaneous abortions, the Negro college graduate has fewer children than her white counterpart.☆

026.   Gebhard, P.H., et al. 1958. The Prison Woman: Three Studies. In Pregnancy, Birth and Abortion, by P.H. Gebhard, W.B. Pomeroy, C.E. Martin, and C.V. Christenson. New York: Harper/Hoeber. Pp. 168-188.

This sample from 3 institutions covers 1250 women: 900 white, 309 Negro, and the rest from other races. This is about 1/4 the prison female population at the time for whites and 6% for Negroes. In

Prison A, a midwestern institution, 22% of the inmates had had premarital. In Prison C, a training school for Negro girls, the figures for premarital intercourse and pregnancy were similar to those for the Negro population as a whole: 59% for premarital intercourse for the prison population 2% for the same group. With both white and Negro population, imprisonment was not nearly as important as socioeconomic status. Outcomes of pregnancy are similar to others of similar socioeconomic background who have not been in prison. The fact that white women in prison show more premarital conceptions, more live births and spontaneous abortions, and fewer induced abortions than white women generally is probably due to the fact that most white women in prison are from lower socioeconomic backgrounds. The low marital conception rate and the high ratio of spontaneous abortion among Negro prison women seems largely the result of several factors, the most important being venereal disease. These factors are also found in nonprison women. The differences between prison and nonprison Negro women are smaller than among the 2 white groups because fewer nonprison Negro women are found in higher socioeconomic groups than nonprison white women.✩

027. George, Kochuparampil M. 1970. Family Structure and Fertility Among Lower Class Negroes: A Study in Social Demography. Unpublished Doctoral Dissertation. University of Kentucky. 145 pp.

The general thesis of this study is that family support tends to weaken the desire for effective family planning and thus contribute to higher fertility. Tests the hypothesis that family support in the extended family influences reproductive behavior of its members.★

028. Goldscheider, Calvin, and P.R. Uhlenberg. 1969. Minority Group Status and Fertility. American Journal of Sociology 74 (January): 361-372.

Most studies of minority group fertility assume that as assimilation proceeds the fertility of minority and majority populations will converge. Differences between minority and majority fertility are usually treated as temporary phenomena and often are interpreted in terms of the social, demographic, and economic characteristics of minority group members. Empirical evidence, however, does not fully support "characteristics" explanation of Negro, Jewish, Japanese-American, or Catholic fertility. An alternative hypothesis is presented with respect to the independent effect of minority group status on fertility. Some parameters of the interrelationship of minority group status and fertility are discussed.*

029. Grindstaff, C.F. 1976. Trends and Incidence of Childlessness by Race: Indicators of Black Progress Over Three Decades. Sociological Focus 9 (3): 265-284.

Patterns in childlessness rates for blacks and whites in the U.S. from 1950-1972 were examined using 1940, 1950, and 1960 census data and data from Current Population Reports for 1969 and 1972. Among ever married women, aged 15-49, the proportion of childless black women declined from 29.1%-13.6% from 1940-1972, while the proportion of childless white women declined from 22.9%-14.3% from 1940-1969 and then increased slightly to 15.6% in 1972. The decline in childlessness observed for both blacks and whites during this period was attributable, at least in part, to improved medical care. When age specific rates were examined 2 diverse patterns emerged. For females, aged 15-24, childlessness rates for blacks were lower than for whites throughout 1940-1972, and the differences between blacks and whites increased over time. However, for females, aged 30-39, childlessness rates were higher for blacks than for whites throughout 1940-1972, and the gap between white and black rates decreased over time. In general the data demonstrated a convergence in childlessness patterns for blacks and whites. Childlessness rates were viewed as an indication of social integration. Childlessness is not a norm in American society. The general decline in childless rates among blacks and especially among blacks over 30 years of age indicated that the wider society was serving as a reference group for blacks. Among blacks under 25 years convergence was less apparent and indicated that younger black women were less integrated into the larger society than older black women. On the basis of recent trends it was predicted that convergence between black and white childlessness patterns would continue; however, in view of the upturn in the childlessness rate observed for whites since 1969, it was expected that the childlessness rates for both blacks and whites would increase somewhat in the coming years.☆

030.   Groff, William. 1968. **An Analysis of White and Negro Fertility Differences.** Unpublished Ph.D. Dissertation. Brown University.

The focus of this analysis centers upon the possibility that racial fertility differences are related to segregation and its differential effect upon the Negro minority group. It is hypothesized that racial segregation contributes to a disruption of communication concerning family planning and the use of contraceptives. As a result, the recent improvements in the absolute level of living of a majority of the Negro population may have had a positive effect upon Negro fertility which has not been offset by the negative forces of family planning and the use of contraceptives. Negro fertility and racial fertility differences then would vary according to the level of the participation of the members of the Negro minority in the communication channels of the white majority. If this premise has merit, Negro fertility rates should be significantly higher than white fertility rates where segregation has its most restrictive effects and more similar or lower where it places the least restrictions on communication between whites and Negroes. Racial segregation appears to be more restrictive in the South, in the rural areas, and in the lower socio-economic strata. If this is valid, then Negro fertility rates should be significantly higher than white rates within these segments of the population. The increases in racial fertility differences between 1947 and 1957 should also reflect the greater increases in the fertility rates within these segments of the Negro population. The substantive analysis has shown that the observed patterns of racial fertility differences tended to conform fairly well to the expected patterns. When region, urban-rural residence, socio-economic status, income, and education were controlled, Negro fertility rates were higher than the corresponding white rates in the South, in the rural areas, and at the lower levels of control. Thus, the analysis lends tentative support for the hypothesis that racial fertility differences are associated with the differential effects of racial segregation. A similar pattern can be observed in the comparison of recent changes in racial fertility differences since 1940. Negro fertility rates increased significantly more than white fertility rates in those levels of control where racial segregation was assumed to be more restrictive. The resulting increases in racial fertility differences were in part offset by a decline in racial differences in some other levels of control where the increases in Negro fertility were similar or lower than the corresponding increases in white fertility. In general, these changes reflect a trend toward greater uniformity in the fertility of the white population which is not as evident in the Negro population. Racial fertility difference which tended to disappear when socio-economic status was controlled in 1940 now seem to be more inversely related to socio-economic status and reflect the differential effects of racial segregation. Any conclusions drawn from this analysis should be viewed as tentative and largely exploratory. Although the observed patterns tended to conform fairly well to the expected patterns, there were deviations, particularly at the lower levels of control, which cannot readily be explained within the context of the conceptual framework. The findings from this analysis point to the complexity of factors impinging upon racial fertility differentials and direct attention toward the possible significance of racial segregation in the evaluation of racial fertility differences and the prediction of future trends.*

031. Haney. C.A., et al. 1973. The Value Stretch Hypothesis: Family Size Preferences in a Black Population. Social Problems 21 (2): 206-220.

Data on the family size preferences and reproductive behavior of 990 black females are examined to determine the utility of Rodman's concept of a "lower-class value stretch" for understanding reproductive goals and behavior. An hypothesized inverse relationship between a measure of the range of acceptable number of children (ANC) and indicators of social class was clearly supported in the case of current social class (income level and education). An analysis of this relationship controlling for age, parity, and marital status suggests marital status to be a key control variable, with age exerting some influence. The findings of this study suggest that the concept of lower-class value stretch may have utility with respect to family size preferences among black females who have been ever married and who are older.*

032. Harig, T.J., A.H. Richardson, and J.B. Hardy. 1975. **Excessive Fertility Among a Black Inner-City Population.** Paper presented at the Second Annual Meetings of the World Population Society and International Population Conference, Washington, D.C., November 1975. 9 pp.

The objective in this research is to examine factors associated with the discrepancy between family size preference and actual family size. Several survey research studies indicate that the typical self-reported ideal family size is 2, 3, or 4 children, and literature documents that education is a major independent variable influencing fertility. The focus of this present research effort is "excessive fertility" or having more children than is desired. Interview data from the "Family Planning and Population Control: Attitudes, Knowledge and Behavior in the Inner City" study conducted by Richardson and Hardy between the fall of 1972 and the spring of 1973 are used. The present sample of 339 black mothers is a subsample of some 412 women who delivered children at the Johns Hopkins Hospital in Baltimore between January 1, 1964, and September 30, 1964. The mothers range in age from 20 to 43, and 49.5% were subfecund either by menopause, tubal ligation, hysterectomy, or other surgical contraceptive or therapeutic procedure. The sample group is of the lower socioeconomic level. The findings: 1) 25.5% of the study mothers express a subjective preference for more children than they have, and 26.2% indicate a preference for fewer children than they have; 2) education provides only a negligible contribution toward an explanation of either one's exposure to stressor events or excessive fertility; and 3) exposure to stressor events or excessive fertility was found to exert a positive influence on the degree of excessive fertility experienced, being particularly salient among the older rather than the younger subsample mothers. On the basis of the data it becomes clear that one's subjective family size goals alone provides only nebulous pragmatic information for family planning services and agencies. ☆

033. Heath, L.L., B.S. Roper, and C.D. King. 1974. **A Research Note on Children Viewed as Contributors to Marital Stability: The Relationship to Birth Control Use, Ideal and Expected Family Size.** Journal of Marriage and the Family 36 (2): 304-306.

The authors employ a tri-ethnic study of blacks, whites, and chicanos to determine the contributions of children to marital satisfaction and stability together with differences in fertility. These variables were found to be significantly related to ideal and expected family size; but not directly related to contraceptive use, although it did indicate a trend toward present use for those with low scores. The research's tentative findings suggest that a study using more refined measures may prove that attitudinal variables such as the one utilized in this study are important determinants of fertility.★

034. Hill, A.C., and F.S. Jaffe. 1965. **Negro Fertility and Family Size**

Preferences. In: The Negro American. Talcott Parsons and Kenneth
Clark (eds). New York: The Daedalus Library. Pp. 205-224.

This is an article that largely synthesizes the findings of previous
researches on black fertility. It is, however, based on the
theoretical framework suggested by Cornell University demographer,
Dr. J. Mayon Stycos. In his article entitled: Obstacles to Programs
of Population Control--Facts and Fancies (Marriage and Family Living,
Volume 25, February 1963), Stycos concluded that one of the major
obstacles to birth control programs in the developing nations is
rooted in the subjective explanations that the elite ruling class in
such countries offer for the high fertility of lower-class groups;
and, he identified a complex of related attitudes that he summed up
in the phrase that "procreation is the poor man's recreation." Stycos
also concluded that in achieving lower fertility levels in the
developing nations, the major hurdle that must be surmounted is the
attitude of their elite ruling class. In the present article, Hill
and Jaffe examine Stycos' model of upper-class stereotypes blocking
the development of sound fertility control policies, and assess its
relevance and applicability to the socioeconomically disadvantaged
groups in the developed societies in general and to the black
fertility behavior in the United States in particular. This article
also reviews studies that attribute high black fertility to the
effects of social-class (socioeconomic variables) on reproductive
behavior.★

035.   Hirsch, M.B., J.R. Seltzer, and M. Zelnik. 1981. Desired Family Size
of Young American Women, 1971 and 1976. In: Predicting Fertility:
Demographic Studies of Birth Expectations. G.E. Hendershot and P.J.
Placek (eds.). Lexington, Massachusetts: D.C. Heath.

Trends and patterns in family size preferences among American black
and white females, aged 15-19, were examined using data obtained in
the 1971 and 1976 National Surveys of Young Women. Sample size was
4359 in the 1971 survey and 2183 in the 1976 survey. Desired family
size decreased significantly between 1971 and 1976, from 2.68 to 2.52
for the total group. The trend toward smaller family size preference
was observed among both the black and white female adolescents. Between 1971 and 1976, the proportion of blacks wanting 2 or fewer
children increased from 61.9% to 64.4% and the proportion of whites
wanting 2 or fewer increased from 50.3% to 55.6%. An examination of
the reasons behind the teenagers' family size preferences showed that
these preferences were influenced by economic conditions and exhibited more rationality than expected. The relationship between desired
family size and a number of socioeconomic variables was examined
using bivariate and multivariate analysis. Investigated variables
included race, age, religion, religiousity, family stability, number
of siblings, marital status, number of live births, educational
attainment of the parents, and the educational aspirations of the
respondents. Bivariate analysis revealed that white adolescent
females who had no sexual experience, who were never married, and who

grew up in stable family environments were more likely to have larger
family size preferences than those who did not have these traits. For
blacks there was no significant relationship between these variables.
For whites, but not for blacks, there was a positive relationship
between desired family size and the respondent's number of siblings.
For both groups, those with 0 parity or with a parity of more than 1
were more likely to desire a larger family than those with a parity
of 1. Unexpectedly, there was a positive association between
educational aspiration and family size preference for blacks in 1971
and for whites in 1976. Multivariate analysis indicated that the
variables with the largest predictive value for family size
preferences for both 1971 and 1976 were: 1) race; 2) religious
affiliation; 3) religiousity; 4) number of siblings; and 5) the
number of previous live births. In 1976 the predictive value of
educational aspiration was also relatively high. Findings were presented in tabular form. ☆

036.   Hofferth, S.L., and K.A. Moore. 1979. Early Child Bearing and Later
Economic Well-Being. American Sociological Review 44 (5): 784-815.

In a study of 1268 women, aged 20-24 in 1968, who were surveyed in
1968 and reinterviewed in 1973 and 1975 as part of the National
Longitudinal Surveys of the Labor Market Experience of Young Women,
the economic situation of the women at age 27 was compared for those
who had given birth to a child during their teen years with those who
did not bear a child until after age 18. The effects on economic
status of early childbearing were primarily negative and operated
indirectly through intervening variables such as, decreased educational levels and higher fertility rates. For each year a birth was
postponed, annual earnings at age 27 were increased by $197. Surpris-
ingly, women who had a child at age 15 or 16 experienced fewer negative economic effects at age 27 than those who had a child at age 17
or 18; perhaps the younger girls continued to live with their
parental family and remained in school while the slightly older girls
left the parental family and dropped out of school. The negative
economic effects at age 27 for black women who bore a child at an
early age were less pronounced than for white women. Policy makers
should be aware of these long-term negative economic effects on early
childbirth and efforts should be made 1) to increase child care programs which enable young mothers to continue their schooling; 2) to
provide family planning services to young mothers who are at greater
risk of subsequently having large families; 3) to encourage young
mothers to remain living with their parental family; and 4) to
provide additional training and job counseling for young mothers.
Tables depict 1) mean and standard deviations for 50 sociodemographic
variables for women who were less than 19 at first birth and for
women who were 19 or older at first birth; 2) estimated structural
equations for the total sample, for whites only, for blacks only, for
those 19 years or older at first birth, and for those less than 19
years of age at first birth; and 3) effect on economic well-being at
age 27 of delaying birth by one year by age at first birth and by

race.☆

037. Hout, Michael. 1979. Age Structure, Unwanted Fertility, and the Association Between Racial Composition and Family Planning Programs: A Comment on Wright. Social Forces 57 (4): 1387-1392.

This analysis has shown that Wright's (for abstract see Gerald C. Wright, Jr. in the section on family planning in this bibliography) charge of racism in the provision of family planning services is unfounded. Although he considers the political climate of an area important, the cornerstone of his charge is the observed correlation between racial composition and the availability of family planning services. Without that correlation, no charge of racism can be made. This analysis has shown that the correlation he reports is spurious. Net of controls for need for family planning services in the construction of the measure of family planning availability and controls for socioeconomic conditions in the multiple regression, the effect of racial composition on the availability of family planning services is not significantly different from zero.*

038. Johnson, N.E. 1979. Minority Group Status and the Fertility of Black American, 1970: A New Look. American Journal of Sociology 84 (6): 1386-1400.

Two opposing explanations, the "characteristic hypothesis" and the "minority status hypothesis" as to why black fertility rates have declined more rapidly than the rates for whites in recent years, were tested using data from the 1970 National Fertility Study; the findings support a weak form of the "characteristic hypothesis." The strong form of this hypothesis states that race itself has no effect on fertility and that differences in black and white fertility arise from varying social, demographic, and economic conditions; therefore, as social change equalizes these conditions, fertility differences will disappear. The weak form states that racial differences will disappear, but that distinctive family size will disappear first among the highly educated blacks. The "minority status hypothesis" holds that race itself has an independent influence on fertility and that fertility among educated blacks will continue to be lower than among whites because blacks must invest more effort than whites in the struggle for success and child rearing efforts are sacrificed in this struggle. In the present study, social, demographic, and economic factors accounted for a significant proportion of the variance in fertility; the remaining significant proportion of variance was jointly explained by race and education. In order to assess the various hypotheses, the variance attributed jointly to education and race was decomposed and the variance was accounted for by differences in education and not race; thus the minority status hypothesis was not supported. This study overcomes methodological limitations inherent in previous studies and permits a reinterpretation of previous findings. Analysis of the relationship obtaining between race, education, and fertility since 1970 should be undertaken as well as studies of other American minority groups, such as the Jews, Chinese, and Japanese, who had low fertility in the past, but who have high status, in order to determine if family size for these groups continues to differ from family size for the majority. A graph depicting the 4 hypothesized relationships of education and race on fertility is included as well as tables displaying: 1) contrast vector coefficients and mean comparisons for decomposition of joint race and education effect on fertility; 2) means and standard deviations for race by education groups; and 3) analysis of variance in fertility jointly attributed to education and race.*

039.   Karashkevych, Boris. 1964. **The Postwar Fertility of the American Negro.** Unpublished Ph.D. Dissertation. New York University.

Measures rise in black fertility in postwar years and compares trends in fertility differentials among blacks and whites. Finds higher fertility rates among black, especially lower socioeconomic groups, in spite of rapid black urbanization. Black baby boom was not a result of earlier marriage nor was it a result of greater stability of the family.*

040.   Kiser, C.V. 1958. **Fertility Trends and Differentials Among Nonwhites in the United States.** Milbank Memorial Fund Quarterly 46 (April): 190-195.

Documented analysis of data, mainly from the census of 1910, 1940, and 1950, regarding children ever born by color, age, urban-rural residence, and socioeconomic factors; the major focus of the paper is on trends in fertility, trends in proportions married, fertility rates and percent changes, 1940-1950, trends and differentials in fertility ratios, proportions with large families, differentials in fertility, fertility ratios by education of wife and major occupation group of husband, and concomitants of increase in nonwhite fertility.*

041.   Kiser, Clyde V., and Myrna E. Frank. 1967. **Factors Associated with Low Fertility of Nonwhite Women of College Attainment.** Milbank Memorial Fund Quarterly 45: 427-449.

Here the authors are concerned with the interrelationship of color, fertility and socioeconomic status in the United States. Frequently, this relationship is studied by comparing the socioeconomic differentials in fertility among the whites with that among the nonwhites. This study, however, is concerned mainly with differentials in fertility by color at different socioeconomic levels and particularly upon factors associated with low fertility of nonwhite women reporting one or more years of college attendance. According to this study, among married women 25 years of age and over the fertility of nonwhites tends to surpass that of whites in the United States except at upper socioeconomic levels. For the women under age 25 the fertility of nonwhites tends to surpass that of whites at the upper as well as other socioeconomic classes. This study is based on the 1960 census data.*

042.   Kritz, Mary M., and Douglas Gurak. 1976. Ethnicity and Fertility in the United States: An Analysis of 1970 Public Use Sample Data. Review of Public Data Use 4 (May): 12-23.

Data from 1970 public use sample files are used to analyze the fertility patterns of currently married women in three age cohorts--20 to 29, 30-39, and 40-49. These women belong to twenty-five different ethnic groups and are of various socio-economic levels.*

043.   Kronus, S. 1967. Fertility Control in the Rural South: A Pretest. In: Sociological Contributions to Family Planning Research. Donald J. Bogue (ed.). Chicago: University of Chicago, Community and Family Study Center. Pp. 129-160.

The study attempts to evaluate the effectiveness of a family planning communication program on a rural, agrarian, low-income population and to identify the sociological factors that correlate with differential acceptance or rejection of family planning. The study was done on a population of 50 Black females between the ages of 15-45 who had ever had a child selected by the random area probability method in Bullock county, the county in Alabama with the poorest and most illiterate inhabitants. In 1960, Bullock county had a crude birthrate of 31.0/1000 as compared with the national crude birthrate in nonmetropolitan areas of 23.3/1000. The sample was interviewed 3 times, initially in September 1963 at which time aerosol foam, condoms, and 3 booklets on family planning were distributed, and then twice for follow-up, in December, January 1963-1964 and in February, March 1965. The study is concerned with changes that took place between the 1st and 2nd interviews. The sample was divided into 3 age groups, 16-20 (N=15), 30-39 (N=19), and 40-45 (N=16). The majority of the husbands were found to be in the same age groups as their wives. 82% of the sample was married 4% had never married, and 14% were separated for various reasons. The never marrieds were all in the young group. The modal marriage age was 18 or 19 and over 40% of all age groups married at 20 or above. Happiness was the dominant characteristic of the marriages. 66% of the sample said they liked Bullock county very much, and only 6% expressed a positive dislike for it. However, about 40% in each age group said they had considered leaving, mostly for better economic opportunities in Northern or Midwestern cities. With the exception of the young group who in general had not completed their family size, the number of living children was much larger than the expressed ideal number. Over 50% favored small families, and of those remaining a large percentage was ambivalent as regards family size. The sample expressed a favorable attitude toward planning in general. The majority in each group had used some method of contraception but the methods used were not the most effective and had been used inefficiently. 19 of the 50 women had to be eliminated in the final analysis because of the inability to accept family planning for various reasons. <15 of the 31 women left changed to or adopted a reliable method of contraception as a result of the communication and all 15 reduced the number of times they took a chance. Adoption or improvement was significantly and positively related to younger age of female and high parity; higher educational level of female, female employment, and higher family income; female as head of household and female in an unhappy or averaged marriage; attitude that children provide security; early discovery of birth control and total number of methods used; and use of the written material by females. It is concluded that the motivation to use contraception is present and that the major emphasis of fertility control programs should be on dissemination of materials and instructions in their use.*

044.   Lantz, H., and L. Hendrix. 1977. The Free Black Family at the Time of the U.S. Census: Some Implications. International Journal of Sociology of the Family 7 (1):37-44.

Using data from the Federal census of 1790, the authors compare black family size with that of the white family size. Factors contributing to the smaller size of black families, such as higher infant mortality and higher rates of unreported illegitimacy, are discussed. The authors also present the hypothesis that certain voluntary constraints on black fertility existed in the 18th century such as Puritan attitudes toward sex and marriage in the north and stable family patterns in the south.*

045.   Lantz. Herman, and L. Hendrix. 1978. Black Fertility and Black Family in the Nineteenth Century: Re-examination of the Past. Journal of Family History 3 (3): 251-261.

This study examines some features of black fertility in the 19th century to see if differential fertility patterns were present; variations attributable to regional and socioeconomic differences are discussed.*

046.   Lee, Everett S., and Anne S. Lee. 1952. The Differential Fertility of the American Negro. American Sociological Review 17 (4): 437-447.

Utilizing the data from the 1940 census relative to women aged 15-49, this paper examines fertility differentials for the black population. The authors find that the pattern of black fertility is remarkably similar to that of native whites. With both races fertility declines as the marks of socioeconomic status become more favorable. Like whites, black fertility is lower outside the south, and the fertility of rural nonfarm residents is greater than that of urban residents but less than that of rural farm residents. Employment of women and ownership of home is found to be associated with lower fertility. Similarly, a fairly regular decline in fertility is observed as the monthly rental value of home and the years of schooling completed by women increased. The second major findings of this paper is that the fertility patterns of the black most closely approached those of the

native whites in those areas where the blacks have been permitted to
share most freely in the general culture, that is, in the North and
the West and in urban South.*

047. Lee, Anne, and Everett Lee. 1959. **The Future Fertility of the
American Negro.** Social Forces 37 (3): 228-231.

According to the authors a number of factors have been noted which
would tend to keep black fertility at its present high level or
perhaps even to increase it. These factors include the continued
improvement in general health and the lowering of the incidence of
venereal disease, the decrease in maternal and fetal deaths, the
possibly increasing stability of black family, and the probably
continuing economic development. These, however, are factors the
major effects of which have already been felt. On the other hand, we
can expect a reduction of unwanted births, whether illegitimate or of
high birth order, because of increasing knowledge of birth control.
The parents of today's black babies were born 15-45 years ago, the
great majority of them in the South where educational levels are
extremely low. A few years from now the cohorts of potential parents
will be more sophisticated in these matters and will have absorbed
much more of the white attitudes toward family size. Even today the
higher black fertility can be explained in terms of differences in
education and socioeconomic levels. Whenever blacks and whites are
equated in these matters, no matter how roughly, black fertility
seldom appears much higher than white and it is often lower. In
particular the decrease in fertility of blacks with increasing
education is especially sharp, and this is an area in which the
improvement of blacks can hardly be doubted. As blacks become more
middle class in orientation and enter white-collar and supervisory
jobs, they may try to counteract some of their disadvantages by
redefining or limiting child bearing. An indication that this may be
the case is found in the extremely low fertility of black college
graduates.*

048. Lewis, T.B. 1969. **Fertility Trends and the Community: A Consumer's
Point of View.** Journal of Medical Education 44 (11, Part 2): 93-97.

Black community's view of Family Planning trends is described. Family
Planning and the general community are related. The family planning
movement can make its greatest impact in the countries where
population control and family planning are most needed through the
use of Community Development Methods. Community development ideas and
principles are outlined. Community development means not merely
servicing a woman with birth control information and devices but also
training that woman to service her neighbors. This may involve a
community extension of medical schools and creation of entirely new
professional and paraprofessional roles. The article further solicits
the idea and principles of community development in family planning
as follows: 1) Plans for redesigning family planning programs to
provide for maximum feasible participation of the consumer; 2) What

do we mean by freedom of choice?; 3) How do we develop communities to control family planning program?.☆

049. Littlewood, T.B. 1977. **Prelude to Change Black Birth Rates...and the Powerhouse.** In: The Politics of Population Control. T.B. Littlewood (ed.). Notre Dame, Indiana: University of Notre Dame Press. Pp. 12-24.

The history of the increasing black birth rates and the efforts by the Catholic Church to suppress contraceptive information are discussed. Competition between the Yankees of New England and the immigrants sets a framework for American political behavior. In the early 1900s the Protestants and the Catholics were in agreement that the dissemination of contraceptive information should be made a criminal act. The Comstock laws were passed in 1873. Margaret Sanger devoted herself from 1912 until World War 2 to the cause of birth control for the poor. By 1920 her attention shifted to the large families in the lower classes and she considered "the chief issue of birth control" to be a goal of "more children from the fit, less from the unfit". Social Control is usually associated with race. The black fertility rate rose after World War 2 to 160/1000 in the 1950s, and illegitimate births are more frequent among blacks. In 1970, 1/3 of the black population lived in 15 cities, and these are centers of commerce built by immigrants, many of them Catholic. The Catholic Church has been opposed to the use of tax-supported facilities for birth control services. In the 1960s politicians and laymen were conscious of a "new consensus" in favor of birth control help available to the poor at government expense.☆

050. Littlewood, Thomas B. 1977. **Birth Rates in the Bayous...the Sage of Joe Beasley.** In: The Politics of Population Control. Thomas B. Littlewood (ed.). Notre Dame, Indiana: University of Notre Dame Press. Pp. 88-106.

Dr. Joseph D. Beasley was instrumental in bringing subsidized family planning services to Louisiana in the mid-1960s, a time when it was still a criminal offense to disseminate information about contraceptives. Aiming at eventual comprehensive health services, he started with family planning. The state's political and medical establishments responded favorably because they were concerned with rising black birthrates and increasing welfare costs. He worked to gain the support of the Catholic Church and the state welfare-health bureaucracy before he started his family planning clinics. By enlisting local leaders' support, he avoided the politics of confrontation. With the 1st OEO family planning grants for the area, Dr. Beasley soon set up 144 birth control clinics over the state which were receiving support from 31 different granting sources. His high visibility and extreme popularity caused opposition to develop. Blacks raised the black genocide issue. Public health department officials and private doctors objected to his incursions into comprehensive health care. Politicians were worried by his network of statewide clinics. Catholic support dissolved over the abortion issue. His extraordinary, semiillegal methods of raising family planning funds led to federal criminal prosecution.☆

051. Lunde, A.S. 1965. White-Nonwhite Fertility Differentials in the United States. Health, Education, and Welfare Indicators (September 1965): 23-38.

Data utilized in this study relate primarily to the annual vital statistics of the United States. This paper examines the higher non-white fertility; white-non-white trends in birth, 1909-1963; factors affecting the trend of non-white fertility--differentials by educational level, husband's occupation, and income; white-nonwhite differences by characteristics at birth (age of mother, birth order, birth weight, plural births, illegitimate births, and attendant at birth). The last part of the article discusses the implications of white-nonwhite fertility differentials.★

052. Lunde, A.S. 1971. Recent Trends in White-Nonwhite Fertility in the United States. In: International Union for Scientific Study of Population (IUSSP). International Population Conference, London, 1969. Volume 3. Liege, Belgium, IUSSP. Pp. 2062-2073.

Upward trends in white and nonwhite annual birthrates in the U.S. were parallel between 1920-1947, but declined and diverged in 1947, with white rates declining through 1950 and steadily after 1957 and nonwhite rates rising to a peak in 1956 then declining. The downward trend since 1957 has been similar for whites and nonwhites, but the proportional decrease has been greater for whites than for nonwhites reflecting the higher fertility of nonwhite women. Between 1957-1967 nonwhite rates dropped 29.2%, from 35.3 to 25.0/1000, and white rates 30.0%, from 24 to 16.8/1000. The birthrate in 1967 was the lowest ever officially recorded in the U.S. at 17.8/1000 as compared with 25.3/100 in 1957. Birthrates have declined for all women of child-bearing ages (15-44 years) in recent years, with the greatest overall declines in age groups 35-39 and 40-44 years, which is consistent with conditions of completed fertility and reduction of family size though this is more true of whites than nonwhites. Trends in rates of natural increase have followed those in birthrates; nonwhite rates continued to climb between 1947-1956 while white rates dropped and leveled off. Both rates fell between 1956-1967, at a rate of 7/1000 or 50% for whites and 10/1000 or 40% for nonwhites. General fertility rates by color followed somewhat the same pattern peaking in 1957 and declining thereafter. The overall rate fell from 122.9/1000 in 1957 (117.7/1000 for whites and 163.0/1000 for nonwhites) to 87.6/1000 in 1967 (83.1/1000 for whites and 119.8/1000 for nonwhites). There will certainly be an increase in the number of births in the U.S. In the 1970s as the bulk of babies born in the 1950s comes of age, and while in the last 10 years the point differences in numbers between white and nonwhite have tended to decrease it is too soon to project any convergence.★

053.   Masnick, G.S., and J.A. McFalls. 1978. Those Perplexing U.S.
        Fertility Swings: A New Perspective on a 20th Century Puzzle.
        Population Reference Bureau Report, November 1978. Pp. 1-12.

        By viewing 3 classical fertility determinants as dynamic variables
        having a temporal dimension, and having both independent and inter-
        active effects , an attempt is made to decipher the process by which
        some individuals gain control of their childbearing while others do
        not. With a starting point of recognition that childbearing can take
        place over a broad period in a woman's life, a proposed theory recon-
        siders the role of 3 major variables that have influenced fertility
        across all populations throughout human history: 1) fecundity, or the
        biological capacity to reproduce; 2) mate exposure, including the
        frequency of premarital intercourse, marital stability, and coital
        frequency within marriage; and 3) use-effectiveness of birth control,
        including abortion and contraception. It is viewed that childbearing
        or childlessness evolves out of each woman's ongoing experience,
        particularly during adolescence, as shaped by societal norms and
        circumstances prevailing at the time. This shaping process determines
        the crucial variable in accounting for varying fertility patterns:
        how effectively birth control is learned. Findings from a 1975
        Philadelphia survey of 3 generations of black women strongly suggests
        that the new perspective clarifies perplexing swings in U.S. fertil-
        ity. In all 3 cohort studies, the number of children ever-born was
        inversely related to age at regular intercourse, age at 1st union,
        and time spent out of unions. All of the evidence suggests that the
        explanation of the American fertility swing for black women is under-
        standable in terms that are entirely generalizable to the entire U.S.
        population.☆

054.   McFalls, J.A., Jr. 1973. The Impact of VD on the Fertility of Black
        Population, 1880-1950. Social Biology 20 (1):2-19.

        In his book entitled: Growth of the Black Population (Markham,
        Chicago, 1970), Reynolds Farley advanced the general "poor-health
        lower fertility" hypothesis. VD is the most cited and probably the
        most important fertility-inhabiting factor in this hypothesis. In
        this paper, McFalls criticizes the principal arguments which support
        the hypothesis that VD was the dominant factor explaining the 1880-
        1950 black fertility trend. McFalls maintains that it is unlikely
        that VD was the dominant architect of the decline in black fertility
        from 1880 to 1936. According to McFalls, even if the unrealistic
        assumptions of a zero to 25% syphilis prevalence increase and a zero
        to 50% gonorrhea prevalence increase are accurate, such increases
        could account for only about 20% of the observed natality change.
        Under lower and more realistic assumptions, this estimate would
        become substantially lower. McFalls believes, however, that the black
        fertility trend was probably fashioned essentially by the same
        traditional factors that determined its white counterpart, although
        health factors undoubtedly played a more significant role in the
        former.★

055.   McFalls, J.A., Jr., and G.S. Masnick. 1981. Birth Control and the
        Fertility of the U.S. Black Population, 1880-1980. Journal of Family
        History 6 (1): 89-106.

        Black fertility in the U.S. declined sharply in the latter part of
        the 19th century and continued declining up to 1940. Common expert
        opinion has held that this decline in fertility was not attributable
        to an increse in birth control practice. Instead, experts hypothe-
        sized that the fertility decline was due almost entirely to delete-
        rious changes in health factors among blacks. The health hypothesis
        is faulty because those black groups with socioeconomic advantages
        most conducive to good health were the very groups with the lowest
        fertility rates. A number of recent fertility studies seem to show
        fairly widespread use of birth control among blacks during the 60
        years up to 1940. This widespread use did not increase precipitously
        in the 1930s but grew gradually over the previous 1/2 century. Knowl-
        edge and acceptance levels of birth control were also high during
        those years among blacks. Similarly, the experts' beliefs that birth
        control, even if practiced among blacks, did not have much effect on
        black fertility because ineffective methods were used, birth control
        was not practiced "effectively," and blacks started birth control
        practice too late in their reproductive lives have been shown by
        studies to have no empirical bases.☆

056.   McKay, R.B. 1975. One-Child Families and Atypical Sex Ratios in an
        Elite Black Community: Class Contrasts in Black Family Size. Paper
        presented at the American Association for the Advancement of Science
        Annual Meetings, New York, January 25, 1975. 10 pp.

        In 1960 an elite black social club in Baltimore, Maryland provided a
        population of 162 families, typically comprised of 2 college-educated
        parents, both working, with 1 child (63%). In the 1-child families
        there were almost twice as many girls as boys, with a sex ratio at
        birth of 61.9. This atypical ratio is explained as the interaction of
        a biological trend (evidence that the secondary sex ratio decreases
        as the age of the father increases) with a cultural pattern (the
        delay of childbearing until the 2-income family is ensconced securely
        enough in the elite class to afford the temporary loss of 1 income).☆

057.   McKenney, Nampeo, D. 1964. Socioeconomic Fertility Differentials of
        the Negro Population in the District of Columbia: 1960 and 1950.
        Unpublished M.A. Thesis. American University.

        This thesis is concerned with an investigation of the relationship
        between fertility and socioeconomic variables--education, occupation,
        and income in 1950 and 1960. The major hypotheses of the study seeks
        to establish the relative importance of each of the variables, when
        considered separately and combined, to fertility. The hypotheses
        tested are: (1) there exists an inverse relation between fertility
        and each of the socioeconomic variables; and, (2) the relation
        between fertility and each of the variables--education, occupation,

and income--when considered separately or jointly diminished between 1950 and 1960. The results indicate that the relative importance of the three socioeconomic variables, when combined, diminished from 1950 to 1960. However, this was not found to be true when variables were related to fertility separately (individually). Also, the data fail to lend support for the hypothesis of inverse relationship between fertility and socioeconomic variables in its entirety. The inverse relationship between fertility and education and occupation variables are supported. The relative importance of education and income to fertility declined over the decade, while the importance of occupation increased.*

058. Menken, James A. 1972. Teenage Childbearing: Its Medical Aspects and Implications for the United States Population. In: Demographic and Social Aspects of Population Growth. Commission on Population Growth and the American Future, Research Reports, Volume 1. Charles F. Westoff and Robert Parke, Jr. (eds.). Pp. 331-354.

A sizable proportion of infants born in the United States in recent years have teenage mothers. These infants have higher mortality rates than infants born to mothers in their twenties, both in the period just after birth when most deaths are attributable to biologic causes and in the latter part of the first year, when environmental causes of death predominate. In addition, a review of the medical literature concerning maternal age shows that infants of young mothers have higher risks of premature birth and of suffering from severly handicapping conditions including epilepsy and mental retardation. The available data suggest that infants of mothers aged 17 or less are an especially high risk group. These findings have two possible interpretations: (1) the increased risks to the infant are caused by biological immaturity of the mother and would decrease if child-bearing were postponed beyond the teens and (2) that risks result from social and economic factors leading to the selection of girls who become teenage mothers. In the latter case, unless postponement of childbearing is accompanied by changes in these social influences, infants born at a later time to these girls may be subject to the same higher mortality and disease risks. In either case, to increase the welfare of both parents and infants, increased attention to the problems of teenage mothers and their infants and access for teenagers to efficient means of fertility control are strongly recommended.*

059. Moore, K.A. and S.B. Caldwell. 1976. The Determinants of Out-of-Wedlock Fertility: Data Analysis. In: Out-of-Wedlock Pregnancy and Childbearing, by S.B. Caldwell. Washington, D.C.: Urban Institute. Working Paper 992-02. Pp. 88-157.

Out-of-wedlock (o-w) fertility is presented. The micro set is based on individual survey interviews conducted in 1971 with a sample of 4611 females aged 15-19. The macro data consist of state-level observations on o-w fertility rates and other contextual variables

for 1974. Micro analysis determined that women are more likely to be
sexually active as teenagers if they are older, their father is less
educated, they live on the West Coast (U.S.), and they are from more
recent age cohorts. Teenage females are less likely to be sexually
active if they are religious, white, come from intact families, and
live on a farm. Catholicism, mother's education, welfare benefits,
and family planning availability do not seem to be important
influences. The probability of pregnancy among sexually active
teenagers appears to be highest among blacks, black Catholics, those
15 or older, females from nonintact families, and those with poorly
educated mothers. Teenagers who are religious, less recent age
cohorts, and older teens from states with high unmet needs for family
planning services are at slightly more risk of pregnancy. The
probability of abortion among premaritally pregnant teenagers is
highest among whites and those with college-educated fathers. The
likelihood of carrying the pregnancy to term without marriage is
greatest among blacks, those raised by a father without a college
education, those living in states with conservative abortion laws,
those desiring pregnancy, and those becoming pregnant prior to 1970.
Macro analysis indicates that family planning availability, measured
as the proportion of those in need served and the age of consent for
contraception predicts low o-w rates for blacks, while availability
of abortion lowers such rates for whites. No association was found
between welfare programs and o-w childbearing. White and black
probabilities indicate 70% unplanned pregnancies. It is projected
that the use of perfect, consistent contraception among adolescents
would reduce the expected o-w pregnancies by age 20 from 229 to 52
for whites and from 2538 to 795 for blacks.☆

060. Mosher, W.D. 1981. Reproductive Impairments Among Currently Married
      Couples: United States, 1976. Advance Data (55): 1-11.

      Preliminary estimates, based on Cycle 2 of the National Survey of
      Family Growth conducted in 1975 by the National Center for Health
      Statistics, are provided of fecundity impairments, or involuntary
      conditoins that make it difficult or impossible to have additional
      children, among currently married couples in the U.S. Fecundity
      classifications included: 1) contraceptively sterile; 2)
      noncontraceptively sterile; 3) long interval (3 years without
      contraception or pregnancy); and 4) subfecund (difficulty in carrying
      a pregnancy to term). Findings are presented in 4 tables: 1) number
      of all currently married women 15-44 years of age and percent
      distribution by fecundity status according to selected
      characteristics (age; parity; years since wife's 1st marriage;
      hispanic origin); 2) number of currently married women 15-44 years of
      age and percent distribution by fecundity status according to
      selected characteristics; 3) number of currently married black women
      15-44 years of age and percent distribution by fecundity status
      according to selected characteristics; and 4) number and percent of
      currently married women 15-44 years of age with fecundity impairments
      who intend to or would like to or have a future baby, by fecundity

status and parity. Findings indicate that in 1976 about 6.9 million couples, or 25% of all married couples with the wife of childbearing age, had fecundity impairments with most couples having 1 child or more and not wanting additional children. A significant minority of couples with impaired fecundity--about 2.7 million--wanted to have a baby or another baby, with about 848,000 of these couples childless and 688,000 with only 1 child. In all, couples with impaired fecundity who wanted to have a baby made up about 10% of the married couples with the wife of childbearing age.✩

061.   Okun, Bernard. 1958. Secular Trends in the Birth Ratio of Negroes, By Selected States, and for the United States, 1870-1950. In: Trends in Birth Rates in the United States Since 1870. Baltimore: Johns Hopkins Press. Pp. 102-156.

In the 101-page long essay preceding the present essay Okun confines his investigation to the analysis of birth ratio (a measure of fertility) of the white population. In the present essay, he makes a parallel analysis for the black population. This 54-page long essay is one of the few important studies of black fertility since 1870. The "summary and conclusion" section to this essay is six pages long, the reproduction of which here is beyond the scope of this bibliograhy. However, some of the Okun's fundings are: (1) levels and trends of black birth ratios are in many respects similar to those for whites. The crude birth ratio (ratio of children age 0-4 to women age 15-44), declined over time and is found to be greater in the South than in the North; (2) urbanization made an important contribution to the decline in the refined birth ratio (ratio of children 5-9 to women aged 20-24) between Period I (1870-1910) and Period II (1910-1950), and that it definitely accounted for from 25% to 50% of the decline between 1910 and 1930; (3) in some of the states, the redistribution of blacks from smaller to larger communities did contribute significantly to the decline in urban fertility between 1910 and 1930. The corresponding effect of urban intensification for whites was found to be much smaller. Black-white fertility differentials and factors accounting for the differentials are also fully discussed.★

062.   Pearl, R. 1934. Contraception and Fertility in 4945 Married Women: A Second Report on a Study of Family Limitation. Human Biology 6 (2): 355-401.

This is the 2nd report in an ongoing study on the prevalence of contraceptive efforts among a sample of 4945 recently delivered married women. Women were classified by race, income, religion, and education. Women were further classified by contraceptive genus; that is, the manner in which contraception is practiced. There were 4 genera: no contraception, regular and steady contraception, contraception with intervals for planned pregnacies, and erractic contraceptive practices. 45.3% of the whites and 25.7% of the blacks practiced some form of contraception. Contraceptives were positively associated with economic status among whites and, to a lesser degree, among blacks. Careless contraceptive practices seemed to cut across class lines. An examination of "contraceptive species"--the particular devices and methods used, indicates the following preferences, in descending order, for regular contraceptive users: condom, medicated douche, coitus interruptus, water douche, vaginal suppositories with jellies, rhythm, pessary with medicated jelly, other methods, pessary, pessary with douche, and intrauterine device. Whites and blacks differed in their choice of methods. Whites, and good contraceptors generally, favored the condom, while blacks favored the douche. The percentage of women using the condom rose with economic status. There were startling differences in pregnancy rates for contraceptors and noncontraceptors. While the mean pregnancy rate for all classes of women who did not practice contraception was similar, the rate was reduced by 57% among good contraceptors and by nearly 70% by efficient contraceptors of the upper classes. Poor contraceptors experienced about 35% fewer pregnancies than noncontraceptors. White contraceptors of all genera shared similar pregnancy rates in each economic class, and statistics for blacks reflect this pattern, indicating a natural fertility that is similar to whites. It is suggested that removal of legal restrictions on contraceptive information and devices might increase contraception among the poor and lead to a greater fertility balance among all classes.☆

063.   Pearl, R. 1936. Fertility and Contraception in Urban Whites and Negroes. Science 83 (May): 503-506.

This is a study based on a sample of 25,316 white and 5,633 black women overtly fertile in 1931 or 1932, who were residents in or near 26 large cities in 14 states and the District of Columbia. The major purpose of the study is to discuss contraceptive practice and fertility as observed in this sample of white and black women. Some of the findings and conclusions of this study are (1) 42.7% of the whites and 16.4% of the black women practiced contraception. (2) In the absence of contraceptive efforts the pregnancy rates of whites and black women were identical. (3) Among the white women contraception, as practiced, was found to be significantly effective in reducing pregnancy rates below those of corresponding classes of noncontraceptors. (4) Among the black women contraception as practiced, was found to be without statistically significant effect in lowering pregnancy rates below those of comparable classes of non-contraceptors. However, it was found that in two age groups (15-19 and 20-24 age groups) there was some lowering of pregnancy rates, but only about 10 to 18 percent. (5) The data presented confirm and extend the experience of birth control clinics to the effect that blacks generally do not practice contraception effectively, even after they have been instructed.★

064.   Pearl, R. 1939. The Effect Upon Natural Fertility of Contraceptive Efforts. In: The Natural History of Population, by R. Pearl. New York: Oxford University Press. Pp. 198-248.

Actual contraceptive efforts among women differing in economic status, education, and religious affiliation are analyzed. Data were collected for 22,657 urban women during the depression. There is a significant difference in contraceptive use between women with only 1 child and women with more than 1. Mean total period from marriage to 1st conception in the white primiparae contraceptors was 2 times as long as in corresponding noncontraceptors. Negro primiparae postponed pregnancy only .22 year compared with Negro noncontraceptors, implying less efficient means. Efficiency in contraception also increased with economic status. Average increase per woman in "married years free of pregnancy" among white contraceptor multiparae over noncontraceptor were: very poor, .40 year or 8% of noncontraceptor mean; poor group, .88 year or 20%; moderate circumstances, .96 or 23%; well-to-do and rich, 2.13 years or 57%. Corresponding figures for the Negro multiparae are: very poor, .412 year or 8%; poor, .46 or 11%; and moderate, 1.60 or 42%. (None of the Negro respondents were in the well-to-do class). The number of induced abortions per 100 pregnancies and the percentage of total reproductive wastage due to induced abortion are 3-4 or more times greater among contraceptors than noncontraceptors in this material. The rate for whites is roughly twice that for Negros. Whites had a lower live birth rate with increasing education while exactly the reverse was true for Negroes. Among Negroes the college-educated had the highest birth rates. A possible explanation is that the low fertility of the illiterate and low education Negro groups reflects real and serious under nutrition or malnutrition. There was no religious differential among Negros as almost all were protestant. Among whites there is little religious difference in birthrates among noncontraceptors and effectiveness of contraception was essentially the same for both Catholic and protestant contraceptors. Jewish women had the highest proportion of contraceptors and admitted induced abortions. Protestants and no religion had the next largest number of contraceptors while the no religion group had more admitted abortions. Catholics were least likely to practice either contraception or abortion. ✩

065. Pick, J.B. 1977. Correlates of Fertility and Mortality in Low-Migration Standard Metropolitan Statistical Areas. Social Biology 24 (1): 69-83.

Significant determinants of fertility and mortality were looked for among 17 demographic and socioeconomic variables characterizing the populations of 29 low-migration standard metropolitan statistical areas (SMSAs). Regression analysis showed density to be correlated negatively with life expectancy of white females and positively with the gross reproduction rate (GRR) of nonwhites. The GRR of whites was inversely related to the level of medical care, but the GRR of nonwhites was most closely linked to the percent of nonwhites in an area, with higher percentages lowering the GRR. Greater white income increased nonwhite infant female mortality, possibly because of competition for medical services. ★

066. Pohlman, Vernon C., and Robert H. Walsh. 1975. Black Minority Racial Status and Fertility in the United States, 1970. Sociological Focus 8 (2): 97-108.

Reversal in the trend toward convergence of black and white fertility rates in the United States between 1940 and 1970 has given rise to the theory of independent effect of minority racial status. The 1970 Public Use Sample is used in this study to extract data on a 1/1000 sample of all black and white women (excluding Spanish Americans) ages 15 to 59 in order to analyze relationships between fertility and other census variables. The results tend to support the theory of independent effect of minority racial status on fertility. The relationship is more pronounced for women under 35 than for women 40 and over. Distinctive patterns emerge by race and age cohorts.*

067. Population Reference Bureau. 1974. Family Size and the Black American. Population Bulletin 30 (4): 1-26.

Birth control among blacks began to be an issue in the 1930's and 1940's in America. A particularly prevalent attitude in the 1940's was that birth control was a vehicle by which Afro-Americans, as a minority group, could decimate themselves. In the 1950's "race genocide" became the fashionable phrase. In the 1960's and 1970's, eminent blacks usually considered moderates and antiseparatists have mostly supported birth control. The NAACP in general believes in family planning as a social value. Many black women are even claiming the right to exercise freedom of choice in the matter of their own fertility. But acceptance by some blacks of family planning has only increased the skepticism of others. Nationalist and radical organization like the Black Panther Party reject birth control. Needless to say, punitive birth control legislation has not been enacted. And the politics of numbers of blacks is playing an important role in prohibiting others from forcing birth control measures on them. Today blacks are still producing more children than whites, but their numbers are declining and they are beginning to use contraceptive methods. The fear of genocide has not disappeared, however, and the black population is expected to increase at least 15% by the turn of the century.☆

068. Presser, H.B. 1971. The Timing of the First Birth, Female Roles and Black Fertility. Milbank Memorial Fund Quarterly 49 (3, Part 1): 329-361.

The author postulates the hypothesis that timing of first birth is a critical factor in generating subsequent fertility; i.e. the earlier the timing of the first birth, the higher the completed fertility. In 1960, white mothers aged 40-44 years had an average of 2.9 births per mother; nonwhite mothers averged 3.9. Data from National Fertility Study of 1965 show blacks had more unwanted (never-wanted) first births than whites, 12% and 4%, and more timing failures among first births than whites: 50% and 36%, respectively. Black women have earlier first births than white women, and spacing of subsequent births is shorter. Impact of mother role on participation in other roles is greatest at time of first birth, having a restricting effect on woman's social and economic status. If role options are limited to low-status choices, motivation to practice contraception/abortion may be minimized. Black women have first birth about 2 years earlier than white. Motivation to effectively control fertility may emanate basically from preference to participate in nonfamilial activities; when such participation is a necessity, motivation may be minimal. The author concludes that delaying birth of first child would reduce completed fertility and enhance social and economic status if rewarding alternatives to early motherhood exist.★

069.   Ram, B. 1976. Regional-Subcultural Explanation of Black Fertility in the United States. Population Studies 30 (3): 553-559.

The independent effect of Southern origin of black fertility was reexamined by studying the relationship between region of birth and fertility in a multivariate framework using data from the 1970 census. Marital status, number of times married, age at 1st marriage, educational attainment, and rural/urban residence were assumed to be the variables through which the region of birth would influence fertility. In order to examine the influence of regional origin, net of the above mentioned variables, the dummy regression variable technique known as multiple-classification analysis was applied to a sample of 2316 ever-married black women aged 15-44 who had had at least 1 live birth. For comparative purposes a 1/5000 sample of corresponding white mothers was also drawn (4339 cases). Examination of census data showed that with few exceptions, fertility for Southern-born blacks between the ages of 20-44 was higher than for those born in any other region. The multivariate analysis, however, indicated that Southern origin was not effective in increasing black fertility; in fact, when controlled for the effects of other variables, there was an increase in fertility in every region but the South. Other things being equal, being born in the South increased black fertility, but much less so than being born in the North Central Region. It did not seem logical, therefore, to conclude that being born in the South was a unique factor influencing fertility. Southern blacks probably showed higher fertility because of their lower socioeconomic status and rural background while those born in the North and West showed lower fertility because of their relatively higher socioeconomic status and urban backgrounds.☆

070.   Riemer, Robert J. 1971. Child-Spacing and Economic Behavior in a Black Community. Unpublished Ph.D. Disserttion. University of Notre Dame.

This research focuses on childspacing as the independent variable in a study of economic behavior in a black community. Four aspects of economic behavior are considered: family income, occupation of head of the family, employment of the family head, and family debt. The interval between marriage and last child in male-headed families and the interval between first and last child in female-headed families are utilized as measure of rate of family growth. The results indicate that the rate of family growth has a consistent relationship with the socio-economic position of black couples. For the maleheaded families in the study the slower the rate of family growth, the better is the financial position of the families, the fewer the unemployed, the more rewarding are the wages of the husband, and the greater is the possibility of the family owning its own home. Families in which the mother bore her first child before marriage are particularly in a disadvantaged position. This relationship is not the function of family size, duration of marriage, personal satisfaction with family size, nor age of wife at time of marrige and first birth is found to be important in determining the interval between marriage and last child. No association is found to link childspacing with economic behavior in female-headed families or with number of mothers in the work force. On the contrary, former marital status of husbandless mothers and education emerge as strong factors relating to socio-economic position of female-headed families. Likewise, number of children and marital status are more closely related to number of mothers in the work force than is the rate of family growth. Some limitations are found in the study. Due to the typological approach in the analysis the data is categorized according to rate of family growth. This approach is followed because of the comparatively small sample size. Another limitation is that the statistical tests show only the existence of the relationships while the strength of these relationships is inferred from the consistent and persistent tendency of the associations to go in the same direction. The findings of this research have theoretical interest because they indicate that the relationship between rate of family growth and economic behavior apparently cuts across racial lines. The practical value of the findings arise from the fact that the circumstances surrounding the relationship become clearer.*

071.   Rindfuss, Ronald R. 1976. Fertility Rates for Racial and Social Subpopulations Within the United States: 1945-1969. ix, 155 pp. University of Wisconsin, Center for Demography and Ecology. Working Paper Series.

Examines fertility rates for various subgroups based on race--black and white--education, residence (rural and urban), and ethnicity (e.g., Mexican American, American Indian, Japanese American, and Chinese American). The rates are based on the data from the 1960 and 1970 censuses.★

072.   Rindfuss, Ronald R. 1978. Changing Patterns of Fertility in the South: A Social-Demographic Examination. Social Forces 57 (2): 621-635.
This paper examines the trend in the fertility differences between the South and the remainder of the United States--a differential which has existed since colonial times. The paper begins with a

consideration of the reasons why there might be a regional fertility differential. The rest of the paper examines the trend in this differential. It is found that the long-standing higher fertility of the South, relative to the rest of the country, has ceased. But this does not mean that the differential has disappeared. The South currently has lower levels of fertility than the non-South, and this is because southerners prefer fewer children than nonsoutherners.*

073.   Rindfuss, R.R., and J.A. Sweet. 1977. **Postwar Fertility Trends and Differentials in the United States.** New York: Academic Press. x, 225 pp.

The authors examine fertility trends and levels within social and economic subgroups in the United States. The focus of the study is on period rather than cohort fertility. The major part of the study deals with the 1945-69 period. However, the last chapter extends the findings through the first half of the 1970s. This study is based on data from the 1-in-100 public use samples of the 1960 and 1970 censuses.★

074.   Ritchey, P. Neal. 1973. **The Fertility of Negroes Without Southern Experience: A Re-examination of the 1960 GAF Study Findings with 1967 SEO Data.** Population Studies 27 (1): 127-134.

The 1960 Growth of American Families Study (GAF) found that black couples with no southern rural experience had the same number of births as similar whites. Data from the SEO (Survey of Economic Opportunities) demonstrated that the residence background classification utilized in the GAF study defeated, in part, the attempt to remove the effects of rural experience on fertility. The category of "no southern rural experience" employed in the GAF study contained a relatively homogeneous group of blacks--almost all were urban of urban background. However, this classification of whites contained a sizeable proportion of whites who were rural residents (non-southern rural whites) or of rural background (non-southern rural-to-urban migrants). Non-southern rural whites were found to have the highest fertility among whites. Comparing blacks and whites with no southern rural experience resulted in a comparison of one population which rural experience had been minimized with another population containing a substantial proportion of couples with rural experience. Indigenous urban blacks had 25% higher fertility than indigenous urban whites, a finding contrary to that implied by the GAF study. Both the sample size and the residence background categories used in the GAF study contributed to the overestimation of the effects of southern rural background on the racial differential in fertility. The fertility of black migrants out of the rural South was sharply curtailed in contrast to those remaining in the rural South. Although urban blacks of southern rural background had nominally higher fertility than indigenous urban blacks, the difference was neither statistically nor substantively significant. Both the fertility on in-migrants and of indigenous urban blacks contributed to population pressures in urban areas. Proportionately, their contributions were about equal. However, indigenous urban blacks out numbered black migrants two to one, and in absolute numbers, their share of births was disproportionate in the same ratio. The data suggest that a high youth dependency burden, and the extent to which it limits social and economic mobility, is characteristic of all urban blacks and not simply an attribute of in-migrants from the rural South. The greatest excess of black over white fertility occurred in the rural South where it appeared and white fertility continued to decline precipitously. In all likelihood, this increasing gap marks a greater social and economic differential between blacks and whites in this area which will continue to widen. As the influence of southern rural patterns of mating and childbearing diminishes, the white-black fertility differential will decline, as was suggested by the authors of the GAF study. However, it is evident that other factors, in addition to those associated with rural backgrond, must be sufficiently altered before the white-black differential in fertility ceases to exist.*

075. Ritchey, P. Neal. 1975. The Effect of Minority Group Status on Fertility: A Re-examination of Concepts. Populatiton Studies 29 (2): 249-257.

Some studies have shown a tendency to generalize white-black fertility differentials in a majority-minority context. In this paper, Ritchey examines the assertion that the minority group status is, indeed, relevant to the study of black fertility. He reviews the limited literature on the topic and brings together the set of ideas currently available. This study is based on the 1970 Census Public Use Sample. Ritchey departs from previous analyses by positing that conceptual and empirical consideration of the structural milieu is necessary for correctly interpreting and assessing the effects of the individual's attributes on his behavior. That is, the attribute of being black--and thus, of minority group status--gains its significance as an independent influence on behavior to the extent that the social milieu maintains social distance and discriminates on the basis of this attribute. Ritchey's findings support this approach and strongly suggest a minority group status effect. But they also suggest, in contradiction to Goldscheider and Uhlenberg (see abstract in this bibliography), that with the assimilation of minority groups, the fertility of majority and minority converge.★

076. Roberts, R.E., and E.S. Lee. 1974. Minority Group Status and Fertility Revisited. American Journal of Sociology 80 (September): 503-523.

This paper reexamines the effect of minority group status on fertility to discover the efficacy of two positions outlined by Goldscheider and Uhlenberg (1969) and Sly (1970). The problems raised focus on the definition "ethnic group," the failure to control for the effects of age at marriage and employment status of women in fertility analyses, and the failure to examine current as well as cumulative fertility. Results tend to support Goldscheider and Uhlenberg's position that ethnicity has effects on fertility independent of other dimensions and point toward their recommendation that social psychological factors be examined to determine how fertility is influenced by ethnicity.*

077.   Ross, J. 1966. United States: The Chicago Fertility Control Studies. Studies in Family Planning 1 (15): 1-8.

In January 1962 the Community and Family Study Center of the University of Chicago started a family planning program which stressed mass communication and mass motivation. This type of program can achieve major results with little expenditure of funds, manpower, and time. The program concentrated in a low-income Negro neighborhood. The program was preceded in the neighborhood by an attitude study of contraception and related topics. It was found that high fertility resulted from careless and inconsistent use of contraceptives, not from an unfavorable attitude toward them. 60% of the women responding to the program chose pills, of whom 80% continued to use them at least 6-8 months. Mass media methods provided information in the neighborhood about birth control specifics and the location of family planning services. The program employed mobile vans and emphasized nondoctor methods. It urged word-of-mouth information exchange. The birthrate in the area has dropped substantially in the last 5 years as a result of the program.★

078.   Ryder, N.B., and C.F. Westoff. 1969. Fertility Planning Status: United States, 1965. Demography 6 (4): 435-444.

Data concerning the planning circumstances of the interval preceding each pregnancy, collected from a national sample of 4810 married women, are used to establish the fertility planning status of each respondent as one of five classes: (1) never-pregnant; (2) number failure; (3) at least one timing failure; (4) at least one timing success; (5) neither success nor failure. For the ever-pregnant women who intended no more children, 32 percent of the exposed were number failures and 52 percent of the rest were timing failures. For the ever-pregnant women who intended more children, 67 percent of the exposed were timing failures. Women not exposed to the risk of timing failure because they claimed to want all of their pregnancies as soon as possible had similar characteristics to women reporting failures; accordingly the reliability of their reports is suspect. The probabilities of failure are well-patterned by race, religion and education: higher for Blacks than for Whites; within the latter, higher for Catholics than for Non-Catholics; and inversely related to education, except among White Catholics. Although uniformly high, the proportions classified as failures are probably under-estimates of the true values for completed families, because of misreporting and continuing exposure to risk, subsequent to interview.*

079.   Ryder, N.B. and Charles F. Westoff. 1971. Racial, Religious, and
Socioeconomic Differences in Fertility. In: Reproduction in the
United States, 1965. Princeton, N.J.: Princeton University Press. Pp.
53-95.

Black women expect to have more children than white women because
they already have more, but the number they say they want is, on the
average, about the same as for whites. This indicates the racial
difference in the control of fertility. The less education a woman
receives, the more the number of children expected exceeds the number
desired--a generalization that holds for both whites and blacks. The
number of children desired varies inversely with education only among
blacks, and this association diminishes when parity is held constant.
The racial differential in total number of children expected are
found to vary directly with the age of the woman. Another findings of
this study is the sharp inverse relationship between indices of
socioeconomic status and the number of children expected by blacks.
Working women were found to have lower fertility. Fertility differentials by religion is also discussed. The chapter also includes
an analysis of socioeconomic and residential differences in fertility
and trends in these differentials.*

080.   Sly, David F. 1970. Minority Group Status and Fertility: An Extension
of Goldscheider and Uhlenberg. American Journal of Sociology 76 (3):
443-459.
It has been common to approach the study of differences in Negro-
white fertility from an assimilationist perspective. A recent paper
criticized this approach, suggesting as an alternative a social
psychological argument which approaches the differential in terms of
the insecurities associated with minority-group status. This explanation suggests that (1) minority-group status exercises an independent effect on fertility, and (2) minority-group status and certain
structural factors interact to effect fertility. This paper attempts
to test these two aspects of the "minority-group status hypothesis."
The use of simple descriptive statistics early in the analysis tends
to support the minority-group status hypothesis; however, the use of
more rigorous inductive statistical techniques suggests that the
hypothesis does not stand when applied to Negro-white fertility
differences. It is suggested that the hypothesis be reformulated to
take account of the extent of structural assimilation.*

081.   Stearns, R. Prescott. 1974. Factors Related to Fertility Values of
Low-Income Black Males: A Case Study. Unpublished Ph.D. Dissertation.
Case Western Reserve University. 138 pp.

This was a case study of demographic characteristics and selected
themes relating to fertility values of a group of ninety-two young,
low income urban black males, ages, 14-27, who were recruited from
clients and potential clients of a program of services to young
families located within an inner-city ghetto. Their fertility values
were found to be considerably below the achieved fertility of thier

parents and similar to fertility values of other groups reported in the literature. The four fertility value measures utilized were "general ideal," "status restricted ideal," "self ideal" and "life-time fertility ambition." The latter was introduced in this study as a measure which would be independent of the concept of the lifetime marriage. This case study demonstrated that studies of males by the interview method can yield useful data. The group was generally interested in the subject and responsive to the interview. The level of knowledge and acceptance of family planning was generally high and especially among the older and more experienced males. However, there was a general rejection of abortion and sterilization. There was greater favor for male responsibility for decisions in family planning matters among those who had caused pregnancy. Communication between sexual partners was higher for those who were older and more experienced. Difference in the meaning of children in fulfilling the masculine role existed with subgroups and in some cases these experiences related to expressed fertility values. The group generally had low concern for the threat of genocide in family planning programs. In the older high school graduates this concern was inversely related to fertility values. Concern for overpopulation was similarly low and was related to lower fertility values. The findings suggest the feasibility of surveying young, black ghetto males regarding their participation in family planning matters. Family planning programs designed to include males could find males to be interested and responsive participants. Lower knowledge and acceptance of family planning among the younger and less experienced presents a challenge for education and motivation of youths to prevent their risking unwanted pregnancies. It was concluded that further studies of family planning issues would be feasible.*

082.   Stokes, C. Shannon, et al. 1977. Race, Education, and Fertility: A Comparison of Black-White Reproductive Behavior. Phylon 38 (2): 160-169.

There are two general explanations of racial differentials in fertility: (1) Traditional, which emphasizes that differences in racial fertility are attributable to differentials in social and cultural environment; and, (2) the most recent approach which largely attributes racial differences in reproductive behavior to an index of the effects of social class on fertility. In line with these two theoretical frameworks, the authors examine the relationship between age, race, and fertility in a metropolitan area. They also assess the extent to which racial differentials in ideal, actual, and expected family size are affected by educational differences. This study is based on the data from the 1971 Metropolitan Atlanta Family Planning Survey, conducted by the Family Planning Evaluation Activity Unit of the Center for Disease Control. A total of 1,026 women 15-44 years of age whose interview questionnaires were complete constitute the sample. But the analysis is restricted to 715 ever-married females only. The major findings of this study are found to be congruent with

the minority group status explanation of black-white fertility
differences.★

083.   Tolnay, Stewart E. 1980. Black Fertility in Decline: Urban
Differentials in 1900. Social Biology 27 (4): 249-260.

This paper describes variation in urban black fertility near the turn
of the century. Differentials in both average numbers of children
ever born and percent childless are considered. The data source is a
1 in 750 sample of households from the 1900 census manuscripts.
Higher status Blacks are found to have lower fertility and a greater
incidence of childlessness than are lower status Blacks. In addition,
women experiencing marital disruption have considerably lower
fertility than women in stable unions. The results support previous
inferences of deliberate fertility control by Black women before 1900
and demonstrate the importance of marital instability as a source of
fertility variation in the nineteenth century.*

084.   Tolnay, Stewart E. 1981. The Fertility of Black Americans in 1900.
Unpublished Ph.D. Dissertation. University of Washington.

This dissertation provides an in-depth analysis of Black fertility in
the late nineteenth century. Data from a 1 in 750 sample of households from the 1900 census manuscripts are used to describe trends
and differentials in completed and current fertility of Black
Americans. The results indicate clear variation in fertility by
literacy and residence--urban versus rural. In recognition of the
importance of place of residence, separate analyses are conducted for
women living in cities and those located in the countryside. The
investigation into rural reproduction presents several hypotheses
positing relationships between childbearing and such factors as: land
availability, child labor, urban proximity, farm size, farm
mechanization, and county industrialization. The failure of these
variables to adequately predict rural fertility led to the
speculation that rural Black residents may have been a "natural
fertilty" population. In contrast, the analysis of urbanites reveals
significant variation in fertility by female labor force participation, social status of husband's occupation, and marital stability.
The results for urban women strongly suggest that Blacks in cities
were exercising some control over their childbearing. Finally,
separate urban and rural trends in total fertility and age-specific
marital fertility rates are estimated for the last several years of
the nineteenth century. The results imply that urban residents began
the transition to lower fertility levels much earlier than their
rural counterparts; and that urban fertility fell faster than rural
fertility in the last fourteen years of the nineteenth century--
despite their much lower fertility at the outset of the period. The
notion that rural Blacks were a natural fertility population, and
that urbanites were controlling their childbearing, also receives
support from the analysis of trends and variations in age-specific
marital fertility rates.*

085. Tolnay, Stewart E. 1981. **Trends in Total and Marital Fertility for
      Black Americans, 1886-1899.** Demography 18 (4): 443-463.

      Total fertility rates and age-specific marital fertility rates are
      estimated for the urban and rural black populations during the last
      fourteen years of the nineteenth century. The data source is a
      1-in-750 sample of households from the 1900 census manuscripts. The
      results show sharp differences in the levels of urban and rural
      reproduction, as well as differences in the timing of the well-known
      black fertility transition. Calculation of Coale-Trussell m-values
      suggests that, up to 1899, rural blacks were essentially a "natural
      fertility" population while urban residents apparently had a history
      of family limitations. These findings support the inference that at
      least some segments of the black population were practicing birth
      control before the turn of the twentieth century.*

086. Trussell, J., and J. Menken. 1978. **Early Childbearing and Subsequent
      Fertility.** Family Planning Perspectives 10 (4): 209-218.

      Data from the National Survey of Family Growth which was conducted by
      the U.S. National Center for Health Statistics in 1973-1974 were
      searched for the relationship between early childbearing and sub-
      sequent fertility. The data show that early age at 1st birth,
      especially if the mother is a teenager, correlates with more rapid
      and higher levels of subsequent fertility. Women who start their
      childbearing in their teen years tend to have more unwanted and
      out-of-wedlock births. This is true within racial, educational, and
      religious subgroups. Marital status at 1st birth had little effect on
      subsequent fertility. Previously observed fertility differences
      between blacks and whites are largely attributable to differences in
      age at 1st birth. Blacks, in fact, seem to have slowed the pace of
      their current childbearing, perhaps due to the growth of federally
      subsidized family planning programs in recent years. There are still
      differences in subsequent fertility between Catholics and non-
      Catholics when age at 1st birth is controlled. Subsequent child-
      bearing seems to have no relation to whether the 1st birth was
      considered wanted or unwanted. Education proves to be an important
      predictor of contraceptive use and success. The reasons for this are
      complex.✰

087. Udry, J.R., and K.E. Bauman. 1973. **Unwanted Fertility and the Use of
      Contraception.** Health Services Report 88 (8): 730-732.

      Two (2) different data sources were used to determine the answers to
      the questions: 1) Are the poor less likely to use physician-
      administered contraception (PAC) than the nonpoor? 2) Are the poor
      more likely to use drugstore methods than the nonpoor? 3) Do the poor
      have higher rates of unwanted births than the nonpoor? and 4) Can the
      higher rates of unwanted births to the poor be attributed to their
      lower use of PAC? It was determined that there are no important
      differences in the use of PAC among whites by income but that among

blacks, PAC is more common among high income women than among low. The poor are not more likely to use drugstore method than the nonpoor. The poor of each race have higher rates of unwanted births. It is unlikely that the differences in rates of unwanted fertility as large as those observed could be caused by the trivial differences in method use. Increases of the use of PAC among the poor would not substantially reduce the gap in unwanted fertility between the poor and nonpoor. ☆

088.   U.S. Bureau of the Census. 1976. Fertility of American Women: June 1975. Current Population Reports: Population Characteristics, Series P-20, No. 301. Washington, D.C.: Government Printing Office.

The data presented in this final report focus on changes that have occurred in fertility expectations for currently married women 14-39 years of age from the 1st Census Bureau study of birth expectations in 1967 to the present study based on the June 1975 survey. Other areas dealt with in this report include differentials in birth expectations by current marital status, education, and the sex distribution of children already born, and variations in completed fertility of older women in different socioeconomic strata. According to the data, American wives between the ages of 18-39 were expecting fewer births during their lifetime in 1975 (2.5 births/woman) than in 1967 (3.1 births/woman), yet the childless family does not appear to be the anticipated way of married life. For both races and women of Spanish origin in 1975, about 3-5% of reporting wives 18-39 years old expect to be childless. However, the statistics indicate an increase from 1967 to 1975 in the percentage of wives of all races who expect to have a 1-child family. Approximately, 11% of wives 18-39 years old in 1975 anticipate a 1-child family as compared with 6% in 1967. A decline in the mean number of expected lifetime births occurred between 1967-1975 for all educational and age strata. Among both white and black women aged 18-29 years old, widowed, divorced, and separated women anticipate fewer additional births/1000 women than either currently married or single women. 40 detailed tables are provided. ★

089.   U.S. Bureau of the Census. 1977. Fertility of American Women: June 1976. Current Population Reports: Population Characteristics, Series P-20, No. 308. Washington, D.C.: Government Printing Office.

The June 1976 Current Population Survey conducted by the U.S. Census Bureau collected data on the childbearing experience and fertility expectations of American women. All data findings are presented in detailed tabular form. Sources for all data and calculations are identified. An overview of fertility trends, consisting of the total fertility rate and the average number of lifetime births expected by all currently married 18-24 year old women for the 1960-1976 period is presented. The birth expectations and fertility of young single (never-married) women are included in the Population Survey for the 1st time. Birth expectations of married women in 1971 are compared with actual fertility during the period. Such short-term fertility projections are shown not to be precise analytical tools. Birth expectations were quite high in the early 1960s. Childbearing has declined in recent years to the point that the total fertility rate has dropped below 2.0 since 1972. Some portion of expected fertility seems to be deferred at this point. Large fertility differentials by race are observable in the data. Educational attainment is shown to be inversely related to fertility.☆

090.   U.S. Bureau of the Census. 1978. Fertility. In: **Characteristics of American Children and Youth: 1976.** Current Population Reports: Special Studies, Series P-23, No. 66. Pp. 29-32. Washington, D.C.: Government Printing Office.

In the U.S. wives age 18-24 surveyed in 1976 anticipated only 2.1 lifetime births, continuing a downward trend from 2.9 in 1967 and 2.4 in 1971. Single women of the same age group expected 1.9 lifetime births, and a subgroup of black wives expected 2.3 births. In 1976, 75% of young married women expected to have a maximum of 2 children as compared to 45% in 1967. This trend is reflected in the rise in proportion of married women age 20-24 who are childless from 24% in 1960 to 42% in 1976. Data on births to single women indicate that 5% of white single women had borne at least 1 child as opposed to 44% of black single women.   Since the number of illegitimate births/1000 live births has risen steadily since 1950 for women aged 15-24 of all races, the recent decline in birth rate is due entirely to a decline in the number of legitimate births.☆

091.   Weller, Robert H. 1979. **The Differential Attainment of Family Size Goals by Race.** Population Studies 33 (1): 157-164.

In this paper Weller examines the extent to which number and timing of birth failures occur to blacks and whites and the effect that removing these would have on the cumulative fertility history of various birth cohorts. His analysis is restricted to currently married women who have been married once only. The author's major conclusions are: (1) blacks have higher fertility than whites primarily because they have more unwanted births; and, (2) removing number and timing failures from the past reproductive histories of American women would have reduced their fertility significantly. These reductions would be greater for blacks than for whites and would be greater if some wanted pregnancies continued to terminate in fetal loss. The author points at several limitations of his study. Because it is restricted to the universe of currently married, once-married who have not had multiple births, and because it refers to past behavior only, generalization of future behavior or to other universe of women should be made with great caution. Another limitation is that cumulative, rather than completed fertility has been used as the dependent variable.*

092.   Westoff, L.A., and C.F. Westoff. 1971. Black Fertility and

Contraception: From African Tribes to American Plantations. In: From
Now to Zero: Fertility, Contraception, and Abortion in America. L.A.
Westoff and C.F. Westoff (eds.). Boston: Little, Brown, and Company.
Pp. 234-277.

Black fertility and contraception are discussed. Historical
background data are presented. Ghetto life is described and the
difference between the family life of the poor black and the poor
white is pointed out. It is socially easier for blacks to have
children and raise them without a man around. In the area of
reproduction, maternal and infant mortality rates for blacks are much
higher than for whites. Surveys have shown that black couples under
the age of 30 have intercourse less frequently than whites and after
that age, whites and blacks appear to have the same frequency. 87% of
blacks under age 30 in the cities have used contraception compared
with 83% of whites. There are still a great number of unwanted births
among blacks; according to the women themselves, 1 out of every 3
births is not wanted. There is a strong relationship between the
extent of unwanted fertility and poverty. The rates of reproduction
for blacks in the U.S. have recently been running about 50% above
replacement compared with about 15% for the white population. A small
group of militant blacks accuse those who are concerned about population numbers of genocide. It is known that as blacks improve their
economic situation, their fertility declines.☆

093. Zelnik, Melvin. 1966. Fertility of the American Negro in 1830 and
      1850. Population Studies 20 (1): 77-83.

      Zelnik provides an estimate of the female black birth rate as of
      1850, derived on the assumption that the black population as of that
      date was 'destabilized' to some degree--i.e., that black fertility
      had been declining for some (short) period of time prior to 1850. The
      birth rate can be estimated, using stable population techniques, from
      some measure of the age distribution, as in the present analysis from
      the cumulative proportions under successive ages in the 1850 census
      age distributiton and one other parameter. This procedure provides a
      series of estimates of birth rate, and from a consideration of the
      pattern of these estimates of birth rate, a final estimate can be
      made. However, if a population has been experiencing declining fer-
      tility, as appears to be the case for the black population prior to
      1850, then the use of this procedure will provide biased estimates of
      the birth rate. The last section of this paper contains the develop-
      ment of a set of relationships which make it possible to obtain an
      unbiased estimate of the birth rate using stable population tech-
      nique.★

094. Zelnik, Melvin. 1969. Socioeconomic and Seasonal Variations in
      Births. Milbank Memorial Fund Quarterly 47: 159-165.

      This paper examines the relationship between seasonal variation in
      births and socioeconomic status. It is based on births to Baltimore

City residents for the period between 1961-1965. The determination of socioeconomic status is done by matching census tract of residence of mothers with census tract data on median rental or value of dwelling property. The analysis is done for black and white populations and in both instances for the highest and lowest socioeconomic fifths only. On the basis of the Kolmogorov-Smirnov statistical one-sample test, the monthly distribution of births for the highest socioeconomic category is not rectilinear. Although upper socioeconomic status categories can modify the effects of climate to a greater extent than can lower socioeconomic status categories, practice better nutritional habits, and utilize birth control devices more frequently and more efficiently, these activities need not necessarily lead to a uniform monthly distribution of births.☆

095.   Zelnik, M., and J.F. Kantner. 1972. Some Preliminary Observations on Pre-Adult Fertility and Family Formation. Studies in Family Planning 3 (4): 59-65.

In 1970 a survey, designed as a pretest for a national study of American female teen-ager, was conducted among 372 never-married white and black women between the ages 15-19. 13% of the white females and 39% of the blacks had ever had intercourse, less than 25% of whites had experienced intercourse before age 16 while the percentage was 46% for blacks. Sexually-active white had intercourse more frequently than their black counterparts. Blacks, however, had a higher pregnancy rate than whites largely because contraceptives are 1st used by blacks about 1 year after 1st intercourse. White women, on the other hand, begin using contraception soon after 1st intercourse and use contraception more regularly. Whites would prefer to have the 1st baby at a slightly later age than black women--23.5 as opposed to 22.3. Both races expressed an ideal family size of more than 3 children, with whites preferring slightly more on the average☆

- - - - - -O✳O✳O✳O✳O✳O- - - - - -

Chapter 2
Black Nuptiality, Family, and Fertility Outside Marriage

096. Anonymous. 1978. U.S. **Women Marrying Later, Having Babies Later, Spacing Them Further Apart Than in Earlier Years.** Family Planning Perspectives 10 (5): 302.

   According to a 1975 Current Population Survey, during the early 1970s U.S. women married later, waited longer to have their 1st child, and allowed more time between subsequent births than did women in previous decades. 33% of the white women aged 21-25 at the time of the survey had married as teenagers, and 69% had married by the age of 23, compared with 41 and 79%, respectively, of those aged 36-40. By age 23, 53% of the younger black women had married. 5% of the white women aged 21-25 had had a child by the time they were 17, and 16% had given birth before age 20, compared with 6 and 22%, respectively of white aged 36-40 at the time of the survey, representing a 27% decline in teenage childbearing between the 2 cohorts. 40% of the younger white women had borne a child by age 23, contrasted to 64% of those aged 36-40, representing a 38% decline. 68% of women marrying in 1955-1959 had their 1st child within 2 years, compared with 48% of those marrying in 1970-1974. The median interval between 1st and 2nd births was found to be 32 months, 7 months longer than that in 1960-1964. Women with more education were found to have fewer children. The report attributes the slow down in childbearing tempo to increasing acceptance and usage of effective contraception and a desire for smaller families. ☆

097. Aug, Robert G., and Thomas Bright. 1970. **Study of Wed and Unwed Motherhood in Adolescents and Young Adults.** Journal of the American Academy of Child Psychiatry 9 (October): 577-594.

Study involves the urban black and rural white population of Lexington-Bluegrass area. Notes case study of how girls viewed themselves and their babies, past experience and their relationships with family and husband. Demographic characteristics revealed.★

098. Bianchi, Suzanne Marie. 1978. Household Composition and Racial Inequality: 1960-76. Unpublished Ph.D. Dissertation. University of Michigan. 254 pp.

Since the mid-1960's, there has been increased attention given to race and sex based discrimination in the labor market. Most sociological and economic analysis of racial inequality have focused upon the educational, occupational and earnings attainments of individuals. When larger units, such as families or households have been studied, analysis has been superficial. Little attention has been paid to the economic consequences of racial differentials in household size and structure. In this dissertation, we use the 1960 and 1970 one-in-one thousand Public Use Samples of the Census of Population and the March 1976 Annual Demographic File of the Current Population Survey to assess the trend in racial inequality in household well-being. Two indicators of well-being, a ratio of total household income to member needs and a per capital income measure, are used. Racial comparisons and time trends in household well-being are decomposed into that due to differences in household size or needs and that due to income differentials. Household income sources are investigated. Differentials in the larbor force activity and earnings of household members are assessed and employment and earnings functions of household heads are analyzed in detail. Analysis is accomplished for all black and white households and for households of different type. We find that size differentials are important to the assessment of the trend in racial inequality. Ignoring these differentials results in an understatement of racial inequality in well-being. In addition, the decline in household size has been an important factor in well-being improvements over time for both blacks and whites. Improvements over time are underestimated by income comparsions which do not adjust for household size and composition changes. Perhaps the most startling finding to emerge from this investigation of racial inequality concerns not race inequality directly but rather sex inequality. While well-being improvements have occurred for all types of households since 1960, improvements have been least substantial in female headed households, the most economically disadvantaged type of household. This has resulted in a widening of inequality among households. Children living in female headed households were relatively more economically disadvantaged, compared to children living in husband-wife households, in 1976 than they were in 1960. This takes on increased importance because a growing proportion of white and black children, but particularly black children, reside in these type households. Because of the increasing importance of women's economic roles in households and because of widening racial differentials in living arrangements, sex inequality has become an

ever larger component of the inequality in well-being enjoyed by
black and white individuals.*

099. Burnham, Drusilla. 1977. Black-White Differentials in Illegitimacy:
An Examination of the Effects of Socio-Economic Differences, Marital
Stability and Educational Attainment. Unpublished Ph.D. Dissertation.
Florida State University. 153 pp.

This study examines the significance of certain social, structural,
and demographic factors associated with the differing incidence rates
of illegitimacy in the United States between black and white subgroups, and in particular, the effects of socioeconomic differences,
marital stability and educational attainment upon illegitimacy within
the black subgroup. The research is divided into two parts. Part I
examines the effect of socioeconomic differences resulting from the
effects of minority group status on the total, white, and black illegitimacy rates for twenty-five selected states. The measure of
minority group differentials in an "Index of Structural Deprivation"
consisting of several variables that reflect the structural inequality between blacks and whites within the selected states. Part II
analyzes differing illegitimacy rates and ratios within the black
subgroup for levels of structural deprivation, marital stability and
individual educational attainment. The measure of minority group
status is the same as that used in part I, the "Index of Structural
Deprivation." The measure of marital formation is an "Index of
Marital Patterns" constructed from several variables characterizing
the family structure in the selected states. Individual educational
attainment is measured by the educational attainment for each unwed
black mother in the selected states. Part I uses aggregate state
data, both vital statistics data for 1970, and census data for 1970.
Part II uses individual vital statistics data for selected states
obtained from the public use tape of the detailed natality file for
1970 as well as aggregated state data from the 1970 census. Several
control variables are used in both parts I and II such as the relative size of the minority group, the relative size of the population
at risk, urbanization geographic region and age of mother. Generally,
structural deprivation resulting from minority group status within a
given area does not seem to affect illegitimacy rates of groups in
that area if the relative size of the minority group is controlled.
The examination of individual data, however, found a slightly greater
incidence of illegitimacy among blacks living in areas with moderate
levels of deprivation even when all control variables had been introduced. Among blacks living in areas with neither particularly stable
nor unstable marital patterns, the incidence of illegitimacy is
higher than among blacks living in either areas of low or high
marital stability. Finally, the data demonstrate that illegitimacy
decreases sharply among women with a high school education or more
regardless of the influence of age or minority group status. The
immediate importance of the findings of this study is that, because
differentials in black-white illegitimacy rates do not appear to
depend significantly upon differentials in the life style opportun-

ities between blacks and whites, the nonmarital fertility of blacks may be expected to continue exceeding that of whites notwithstanding efforts to equalize these opportunities. Accordingly, projections regarding population growth and composition in the United States must explicitly take into account the disparate illegitimacy rates for blacks and whites.*

100. Butts, J.D. 1979. Adolescent Sexuality and the Impact of Teenage Pregnancy from a Black Perspective. Washington, D.C., George Washington University, Institute for Educational Leadership, Family Impact Seminar. 24 pp.

The author notes that teenage pregnancy is gaining attention but states that federally funded programs are inappropriate, geared toward teaching teenagers parenting skills rather than prevention by contraceptive education. It is proposed that characteristics of black adolescent sexuality are an outgrowth of culturally valued sensuousness, or prevalence of the sense of touch as a means of communication between family and friends and perceiving the world. This, in turn, is seen as being linked to the historical African merging of religious fervor and sensuality, and leading to a "sex-positive view" to lead to greater likelihood of "natural" sexual expression and avoidance of contraceptives, and therefore to pregnancy, than in the case of white adolescents, who have been found more likely to participate in nonreproductive sexual practices. Racism and sexism are seen as contributing to the problem. 10 black health care professionals interviewed by phone found federally funded programs discriminatory and insensitive, often discouraging the husband from living with his family and failing to adequately aid women and poor people. They recommended policies geared to keeping families intact and incorporating self help.☆

101. Carter, Hugh, and Paul C. Glick. 1966. Trends and Current Patterns of Marital Status Among Nonwhite Persons. Demography 3: 276-288.

Conclusion: The evidence from vital records and census data points in the same general direction. Where comparable data of acceptable quality are available though nonwhite persons as a group tend to have increasingly more marriage instability than white persons, there are noteworthy exceptions to this generalization for some of the detailed nonwhite racial groups. Further research and better vital and census records are needed to provide additional clarification of the marital status trends among the several races.*

102. Cohen, Patricia, et al. 1980. The Effect of Teenaged Motherhood and Maternal Age on Offspring Intelligence. Social Biology 27 (2): 138-154.

Causal models of the effect of maternal age on offspring intelligence were generated using three large data sets. The direct and indirect

effects of two components of maternal age, teenage motherhood and
linear maternal age, were investigated separately for white and black
children. The intervening variables investigated as routes of indirect effect were family structure, parental education, parental employment, family income, and family size. The findings indicate that
there are no direct effects of teenage maternity on offspring intelligence, and that the observed negative relationship is primarily
attributable to parental education. In contrast, the overall effect
of maternal age, while very small and positive, is primarily direct,
that is, not mediated by any of the social or economic conditions
included in the model. The consistency of these findings and the
impact on children's intelligence of the other variables included in
the model are demonstrated and discussed.*

103.   Cutright, P. 1974. Teenage Illegitimacy: An Exchange. Family Planning
        Perspectives 6 (3): 132-133.

        The writer comments on "Teenage family Formation in Postwar America,"
        an analysis of recent California trends by June Sklar and Beth
        Berkov. Their emphasis on teen-age illegitimacy rates obscures other
        data in their report. The general fertility rate in California de-
        clined from 84.6 to 63.6 in the years from 1970 to 1973. The drop in
        black fertility was even sharper. There was a drop in all illegiti-
        macy rates (black and white teen-agers and total married women).
        Black illegitimacy rates are still higher than white, but the total
        fertility of the 2 races differs little. Sklar and Berkov ignore the
        role family planning programs could play among lower class blacks and
        whites in California.☆

104.   Davis, Lenwood G. 1978. The Black Family in the United States: A
        Selected Bibliography of Annotated Books, Articles, and Dissertations
        on Black Families in America. Westport, Connecticut and London:
        Greenwood Press.

        Many entries in this comprehensive bibliography by Davis (with the
        assistance of Janet Sims) delineate demographic characteristics of
        black families.★

105.   Deasy, Lelia C., and O.W. Quinn. 1962. The Urban Negro and Adoption
        of Children. Child Welfare 41 (November): 400-407.

        Discusses why black families do not adopt children. There are many
        black children born under adverse circumstances who need a home but
        adoption agencies find it hard to locate parents. Authors seem to
        feel that the new value system of blacks which see children as a
        handicap is the reason couples are not having or adopting children.★

106.   DuBois, W.E.B. 1932. Black Folk and Birth Control. Birth Control
        Review 16 (6): 166-167.

        In this short essay, DuBois reviews the socioeconomic conditions of the black people and indicates that the more "intelligent" blacks secretly practiced birth control even during the slavery era, when as slaves every incentive was provided to raise a large family. DuBois calls on blacks to "clearly recognize concept of proper birth control, so that the young people can marry, have companionship and natural health, and yet not have children until they are able to take care of them." DuBois points out that some blacks have been "quite led away by the fallacy of numbers. They want the race to survive. They are cheered by a census return of increasing numbers and a high rate of increase. They must learn that among human races and groups, as among vegetables, quality and not mere quantity really counts."★

107. Edwards, G. Franklin. 1953. Marital Status and General Family Characteristics of the Nonwhite Population of the United States. Journal of Negro Education 22 (3): 280-296.

The author compares the marital status and general family characteristics of the nonwhite population of the United States, during the 1940-1950 period. Edwards concludes that lack of comparable data for the two population groups (Non-whites and Whites) makes it difficult to portray an accurate demographic picture of marital status and family characteristics. Edwards, like Frazier, finds nonwhite families to be more disorganized than white families as measured by the statistics on separations, widowhood, and divorce. During 1940-50 decade [as is true even today] a larger percentage of nonwhite than white families were headed by females.★

108. Farley, Reynolds, and Albert I. Hermalin. 1971. Family Stability: A Comparison of Trends Between Blacks and Whites. American Sociological Review 36 (1): 1-17.

From the 1890 to the present, writers have commented upon the instability of Negro family life. Most have observed that discrimination in the job and housing markets have made it difficult for black men to support their wives and children. As a result, desertions occur commonly. Family stability has been of interest because of the belief that children who grow up apart from their parents will be adversely affected. Indeed, some investigations imply that being raised in a home which did not have both parents is linked to lower rates of achievement in school, higher rates of delinquency and lower occupational status. While commentators have discussed family stability, there has been little consensus as to how this concept should be measured. Moreover, there are only a few demographic indicators available for operationalizing this concept, particularly if one desires to study long-term trends or to compare blacks and whites. The major portion of this paper examines Negro and white trends on a number of indicators related to a specific definition of family stability. This study concludes that (1) the majority of both blacks and whites are in the statuses indicative of family stability. Contrary to the images which are sometimes portrayed, most black families are husband-wife families, and the majority of black children live with both parents. (2) In every comparison, the proportion of people in the status indicative of family stablility is greater among whites than among blacks. (3) In recent years there have been changes in family status, although most of them have been small. Some changes suggest a trend toward greater stability while others indicate a trend in the opposite direction.*

109.   Farley, Reynolds. 1971. **Family Types and Family Headship: A Compari-son of Trends Among Blacks and Whites.** The Journal of Human Resources 6 (3): 275-296.

The decrease in the proportion of husband-wife black families in recent decades has led to discussions of the breakdown of the Negro family. This hypothesis is examined, along with the hypothesis that the economic status of black men accounts for the instability of black families. The findings indicate that a growing proportion of adult Negroes are heading families. Differential rates of increase, especially the sharp rise in headship rates among black women, ex-plain the changing distribution of families by type. Rather than con-firming a trend toward a breakdown of the black family, these data report the changing living arrangements of adults. Available informa-tion indicates that socioeconomic status is positively related to the likelihood that a man will head a husband-wife family.*

110.   Frazier, E. Franklin. 1932. **An Analysis of Statistics on Negro Ille-gitimacy in the United States.** Social Forces 11 (December): 249-257.

In surveying the statistics on black illegitimacy, the author shows that there has been a slight upward trend in illegitimate births for the whole registration area during the period from 1917 to 1928. Des-pite this general trend, the rates have gone down in recent years. In some states the rate has been relatively stationary. Marked differ-ence in rates for northern and southern states with northern states having a lower rate. Estimates that at the present time (1932) about 15 percent (as opposed to 25 percent two decades ago) of black births is illegitimate.★

111.   Frazier, E. Franklin. 1939. **The Negro Family in the United States.** Chicago: University of Chicago Press.

Throughout this classic work by Frazier, there are many references to black nuptiality. More specifically, chapter 18 entitled **Divorce: Script From Law** (pp. 376-392) provides statistics on marriage and divorce in the black community.★

112.   Gispert, M., and R. Falk. 1976. **Sexual Experimentation and Pregnancy in Young Black Adolescents.** American Journal of Obstetrics and Gyne-cology 126 (4) 459-466.

Interviews were conducted with 214 black adolescents in North

Carolina matched for age and socioeconomic status, and with their parents. The adolescents were divided into 3 groups: 1) the abortion group, those who had become pregnant and chose abortion (N=80); 2) the term group, those who chose to have their babies (N=64); and 3) the control group, those who had not been pregnant (N=70). The interviews focused on academic functioning and educational goals, sexual history, use of contraceptives, the impact of the pregnancy, and adolescent and parental attitude toward abortion. The Rodgers Combined MMPI-CPI was also administered. The girls in all 3 groups were in general physically healthy, attractive, and related well to the interviewer. The psychological testing did not yield any causal inferences about factors which might identify a population at high risk of pregnancy. Age at conception was an important factor in deciding pregnancy outcome; girls over 16 were considered to be more able to make their own decisions in that regard, while the younger the girl the more justified she and her parents felt in seeking abortion, and thus more pressure was applied to younger girls to terminate. Mean age of the abortion group was 14.6 and of the term group was 16.4. Nonpregnant girls reported the fewest problems in school, had better grades, and expressed a greater desire to go to college than did the pregnant girls. There was very little difference between age at 1st intercourse; about 1/3 of each pregnant group began at 13 or younger, 1/3 at 14, and 1/3 at 15. Term girls more frequently reported having intercourse more than 15 times; the incidence of 6-15 times was almost equal for both pregnant groups. As might be expected, there was a high rate of consistent contraceptive use among the sexually active controls, while the highest rate of never-use was that of the term group. <46% of the abortion group and 25% of the term group described the relationship with the putative father as casual and 48% and 75%, respectively, as serious. The majority of both pregnant groups denied the wish to become pregnant. The abortion group expressed more open discomfort and opposition to pregnancy continuation whereas the term group was more inclined to acceptance, mainly because they and their parents were opposed in principle to abortion. Also, term girls reported a greater number of friends who had had babies. In all 3 groups a remarkable inability to discuss sexual matters with parents was reported. The report is part of an ongoing longitudinal study.☆

113. Glick, Paul C. 1970. **Marriage and Marital Stability Among Blacks.** Milbank Memorial Fund Quarterly 48 (2, Part 2): 99-116.

This paper has demonstrated that blacks made more headway than whites during the 1940's in advancing the proportion married among those approaching middle age. The direction of change continued for whites during the 1950's, but reversed for blacks, with the net effect of more gain over the 20 years from 1940 to 1960 for whites than blacks. During the early 1960's, all indicators showed increasing marriage and marital stability for both blacks and whites of mature adult age, but more change in this direction for whites. In this period, the proportion with marriage intact went up at least partly because of

increasing joint survival of husbands and wives. Increases in divorce
were offset to some extent by declines in separation. A growing
tendency to delay first marriage increased the proportion of young
single adults; increasing marriage at older ages reduced the ranks of
bachelors and spinsters. Blacks on farms in 1968 had a consistently
lesser tendency than whites toward marriage and marital stability at
young, intermediate and older adult ages. Young adult blacks in nonfarm areas were delaying marriage more than were their white counterparts, whereas blacks of more mature adult ages in nonfarm areas
tended to show far less evidence of marriage intactness than corresponding whites. For both blacks and whites of native parentage,
variations in separation by size of place greatly exceeded those by
region of residence. However, the situation was mixed with regard to
variations in divorce. The marital situation seems to have been deteriorating somewhat since around the mid-1960's among blacks in
their late twenties and early thirties. Most of these persons are
parents of young children. At the same time, the proportion of young
children who were living with separated, divorced or unwed parents
went up by one-half among both blacks and whites between 1960 and
1968. One of the factors behind this change is more immediately
demographic than social--the decline in the birth rate since 1957;
fewer young children now than a decade ago are in the very young ages
when most children live with both parents. Yet, many parents of today's children had married for the first time in the late 1950's when
the average age at marriage was the youngest on record. Now this same
cohort of parents has a record proportion divorced. During the last
decade, however, the average age at marriage has been rising, and the
proportion of youth who dropped out of school before completing high
school has been falling. Therefore, to the extent that early marriage
and dropping out of school weaken the chances for stable marriage,
the developments in these respects during the 1960's should be reducing the prospects for continued escalation of divorce in the
decade ahead.*

114.   Glick, Paul C. 1981. A Demographic Picture of Black Families. In:
Black Families. Harriet Pipes McAdoo (ed.). Beverly Hills and London:
Sage Publications. Pp. 106-126.

Glick examines changes in the diversity of black family life in the
U.S. during 1970, with an emphasis in comparisons between the family
patterns of the black population and the population of all other
races combined. The analysis is organized around these major topics:
(1) family composition; (2) marriage and divorce; and, (3) employment
and income. The major conclusion of this chapter is that "many of the
racial differences in family characteristics persist but are demon-
strably smaller within socioeconomic levels than they are for all
levels combined. If racial differences in socioeconomic stratification should diminish during coming years, one might reasonably expect
that more of the residual differences in family characteristics will
become matters of choice to fulfill aspirations rather necessary to
cope with their unique problems of adjustment."*

115. Godfrey, Daniel Douglas. 1975. The Utilization of Selected Services
      by Household Types, White and Black, in Region Q, North Carolina.
      Unpublished Ph.D. Dissertation. Cornell University.

      The major purpose of this study was to determine the variations in
      the utilization of selected services by white and black households in
      a multi-county planning district (Region Q) in the Coastal Plains
      area of North Carolina. Data for analysis were drawn from a survey of
      1,086 households in the five-county region, one of 17 multi-county
      planning districts in the state. The survey was conducted in 1973 by
      the Economic Research Service of the U.S. Department of Agriculture
      and North Carolina State University as part of a study of the effects
      of mechanization in the production of flue-cured tobacco. Excluded
      from the random systematic block sample were all households which
      fell below certain minimum criteria for earnings in 1972 (e.g., a
      gross income of less than $250 from farm or self-employment). The
      general hypothesis was that the utilization of selected services is
      influenced by household type. Eight types of household were construc-
      ted based on sex and marital status of head and presence and age of
      children, four types for complete households (that is, with both
      husband and wife present) and four for households with incomplete
      families. All analyses were made holding color of household (white
      and black) constant. The services included selected indicators of
      housing, transportation, welfare and public assistance payments as
      well as the distance to certain medical and commercial services.
      Contingency and simple least squares multiple regression analyses
      were utilized to test the variations by household type and other
      independent variables. The major hypothesis was supported by the
      data. Type of household had the most influence on selected housing
      services and the least influence on the value of food stamps received
      and distance to selected medical and commercial services. However,
      then three other independent variables--namely, age, sex of head and
      number of children under 12--were introduced into the regression
      analysis, the predictability of household type was negligible. The
      correlations between household type and age of head for both white
      and black households were significantly positive. Therefore, the
      variable included in the household typology tended to tap the same
      values in the dependent variable, utilization of selected services.
      Of the 1,086 households selected for this study, 60 percent were
      white and 40 percent black. Black households generally traveled a
      shorter distance than white households to obtain medical and com-
      mercial services and entertainment. More black households reported
      receiving net household incomes below $4000 than did white house-
      holds--46 and 13%, respectively. Likewise, more black households
      reported receiving food stamps and welfare payments than whites. The
      1970 Census of Population revealed that the region's population was
      more rural than urban, 66 and 34 percent, respectively. Pitt County,
      which contains the region's largest city, Greenville, also had the
      largest total population and accounted for 60 percent of the urban
      and 31 percent of the rural residents in 1970. Greenville gained 27

percent in population from 1960 to 1970, which was the greatest single gain for the region. Overall, the region experienced a slight (0.8%) decline in population. Approximately 20 percent of the white and 16 percent of the black households had changed their place of residence during the five years prior to the survey. More white than black households indicated plans to relocate during the next five years. The internal and external mobility of black and white households is expected to affect the service mix from the provider perspective and cause variations in the utilization profile of the household types. Therefore, if the plans of the survey respondents can be considered reliable indicators, the projected service mix for the area will require some adjustments.*

116. Gustavos, Susan, and K.G. Mommsen. 1973. **Black-White Differentials in Family Size Preferences Among Youth.** Pacific Sociological Review 16 (1): 107-119.

Historically, birth rate in the black population has been higher than in the white population. But, since 1963, there has been some drop in birth rate in the black population. In this study, Gustavos and Mommsen examine black-white differentials in family size preferences among youth. Their major findings are that the black youth "do desire to limit their family size and, more often than whites, think that their parents had too many children. Further, they are concerned with economic reasons for limiting family size, as are whites. Since 1957, both white and black fertility rates have declined, but there has been a slightly large drop for blacks. If the present data on the family size preferences of black youth are at all representative, white and black fertility rates may continue to converge."★

117. Hampton, Robert L. 1979. **Husband's Characteristics and Marital Disruption in Black Families.** The Sociological Quarterly 20 (Spring): 255-266.

Throughout the 1960s and the 1970s a great deal of scholarly and popular literature has addressed the status of blacks in American society, some of it concerned with the stability of black family life. This paper, concerned with the relationship between husband's characteristics and marital disruption, focuses on 575 intact black families and identified several factors associated with disruption. Although husband's age is the strongest bivariate predictor of marital disruption, husband's income is the most important predictor; and husband's employment problems and religiosity are also strong predictors. A causal model of marital disruption shows that education, employment and age at marriage influecne marital disruption through their influence on income. Only age, income and religiosity had a significant direct effect.*

118. Haney, C. Allen, et al. 1972. **Legitimacy, Illegitimacy, and Live Birth Ratios in a Black Population.** Journal of Health and Social Behavior 13 (3): 303-310.

This investigation focuses on the influence of illegitimacy on pregnancy wastage among black women. Unlike other studies of pregnancy wastage that have utilized period rates, the data consist of longitudinal pregnancy histories for a sample of 990 women. It was hypothesized, on the basis of past research and theory, that illegitimate conceptions would be less likely than legitimate conceptions to result in live births. The hypothesis was not supported, however. Illegitimate conceptions have a slightly better chance of resulting in live births, even when control variables, such as economic status, education, and age, are introduced. Three possible explanations for the results are suggested: (1) Most illegitimate conceptions occur at a younger age when the risk of stillbirths, miscarriages, and other complications is minimal. (2) A younger woman experiencing an illegitimate pregnancy is likely to be residing in the parental home where she would be urged to get proper care. (3) Illegitimacy may not carry a great deal of social stigma for the black women. Therefore, the unwed black woman may not have a greatly different image of herself than does the married woman. The community probably does not make much distinction either. Therefore, emotional and financial support may be removed from the unwed mother, as it often assumed.*

119.   Hansen, H., G. Stroh, and K. Whitaker. 1978. **School Achievment: Risk Factor in Teenage Pregnancies?.** American Journal of Public Health 68 (8): 753-758.

New York State Health Department statistics pertaining to live births, spontaneous fetal deaths, and induced abortions were used to analyze trends in teenage pregnancy among upstate New York white and nonwhite females, aged 12-17, from 1971-1974. An unexpected finding was that students, in some age and race categories, with either below average or above average school achievement, measured by the highest grade completed at delivery or abortion were at greater risk or pregnancy than students with average school achievement. White girls, who were 12-13 years old and who were either below average or above average in school achievement, had an excess number of pregnancies; those who were 14-15 years old and above average in school achievement, had an excess number of pregnancies, and those who were 16-17 years old and below average in school achievement, had an excess number of pregnancies. Nonwhite girls, who were 12-13 years old and above average in school achievement, had an excess number of pregnancies, and those who were 14-17 years old and below average in school achievement, had an excess of number of pregnancies. Other findings were 1) the number of live births remained relatively constant for both nonwhites and whites from 1971-1974; 2) the number of induced abortions increased from 1971-1974, especially among nonwhite teenagers; 3) the number of pregnancies increased for all age and racial groups from 1971-1974 except for 12 year old white females; and 4) among whites, aged 12-15, and among nonwhites, aged 12-13, the number of induced abortions surpassed the number of live births. Tables provide 1) the distribution of teenage pregnancies by school

grade and 2) the number of live births, induced abortions, spontaneous fetal deaths, and the pregnancy rate/1000 years of risk by age
and school grade for whites and nonwhites, aged 12-17, from 1971-
1974. Bar graphs depict the number of abortions and live births by
age and grade for white and nonwhite teenagers, 1971-1974.☆

120. Harrison, Algea. 1981. **Attitudes Toward Procreation Among Black
Adults.** In: **Black Families.** Harriet Pipe McAdoo (ed.). Beverly Hills
and London: Sage Publication. Pp. 199-208.

In this chapter, Harrison examines the attitudes toward procreation
among black adults, by reviewing the literature on family planning,
specifically fertility rates and birth control practices. Also
discusses parental roles and behaviors toward procreation. The
chapter delineates important demographic differences. One major
conclusion of this chapter is that there has been a decline in
fertility rates among blacks for the past two decades; but the author
also discovers important differences. She finds significant
differences in motivation for birth control by sex.★

121. Hoeppner, M. 1977. **Early Adolescent Childbearing: Some Social
Implications.** Santa Monica, California: The Rand Corporation. 24 pp.

During the period 1960-1974, the teenage birthrate declined, but
the number of women aged 10-19 increased from 15 million to over
20 million, and the annual total of births to teenagers remained
relatively stable, only dropping from 609,000 to 608,000. In
consequence, births to very young women has scarcely been diminished.
This paper examines the effects of adolescent childbearing upon the
mother, the child, and the society. It points out that fertility
rates, both legitimate and illegitimate, are consistently higher for
blacks than for whites, although between 1970 and 1974 black birth
rates for the very young fell while the birth rates for whites rose.
The illegitimate birth rate has risen significantly among teenagers
and constituted 53% of the total illegitimate births in 1974. The
author reviews the health chances for young mothers, educational and
financial disadvantages, emotional effects, and suicide rates, as
well as the life chances for the illegitimate child. In addition, the
author assesses the ability of unwed adolescent mothers to socialize
their children and other reasons that help to explain why young
teenagers become pregnant. These reasons include misconceptions about
reproductive biology, failure to use contraception and desire to
become pregnant. There is also an increasing tendency to keep
children rather than to offer them for adoption. The author concludes
by identifying some of the implications for policy-making, especially
concerning sex education.☆

122. Johnson, Leanor Boulin, and R.E. Staples. 1979. **Family Planning and
the Young Minority Male: A Pilot Project.** The Family Coordinator 28
(October): 535-543.

This paper is a report of the first coordinated program of its kind aimed at young Black, Spanish speaking, Asian and American Indian males in relation to family life education, family planning and parental concerns. The project sought to develop an approach to the promotion of sexual responsibility and the reduction of repetition of unwanted, out-of-wedlock pregnancy through goal-directed support and assistance to unwed fathers and potential unwed fathers, 14 to 24 years of age.*

123.   Kantner, J.F., and M. Zelnick. 1969. United States: Exploratory Studies of Negro Family. Studies in Family Planning 1 (47): 10-13.

A study was made of 166 Negro females to discover contraceptive attitudes, knowledge, and use. The black genocide issue, used against contraception by Black Nationalist leaders, was not a concern. Semantic confusion arose in discussion of family planning and the various methods of contraception. There was widespread misunderstanding of when the safe period occurs in the ovulatory cycle. Abortion was generally condemned, as was (to a lesser extent) putting the unwanted child up for adoption. The varied age groups, regions, or socioeconomic groups differed little with respect to contraception and related subjects, the one difference being a greater use of pills by younger women.☆

124.   Kephart, William, and Thomas P. Monahan. 1952. Desertion and Divorce in Philadelphia. American Sociological Review 17 (December): 719-727.

Using data (from court records) based on a random 20 percent sample of marriage licenses issued in Philadelphia in 1950, this paper examines the status of marriage, divorce, desertion, and nonsupport in Philadelphia. The findings are that blacks were underrepresented in divorce actions in Philadelphia, and over-represented in desertions and non-support cases. Proportion of divorce among white families was higher than among nonwhites. There was a backlog of nonwhite families characterized by separation or desertion for which no formal divorce proceedings have been initiated.★

125.   Kiser, Clyde V. 1935. Fertility of Harlem Negroes. Milbank Memorial Fund Quarterly 13 (3): 273-285.

Previous studies of birth rates by social class conducted by the staff of the Milbank Fund have been limited to the study of white women. In the present study similar data relative to blacks have been collected and analyzed. The analysis is based on a house-to-house survey among 2,256 Harlem black families in 1933. Variables studied are nativity, date and duration of marriage, age of the husband and wife, usual or last occupation of the husband, and a complete birth-date roster of all children born. The analysis concentrates on the study of birth rates by occupational groups. Two major findings of this study are: (1) the black families included in this study are too "much alike with respect to nativity and occupational level to afford an adequate analysis of class differences in fertility; and, (2) the birth rates among Harlem blacks are generally "very low".★

126. Lammermeier, Paul J. 1973. The Urban Black Family of the Nineteenth Century: A Study of Black Family Structure in the Ohio Valley, 1850-880. Journal of Marriage and the Family 35 (3): 440-456.

This study of the black family structure in seven Ohio Valley cities is an effort to fill the void in historical literature on the origins of the present-day urban black family, especially the phenomenon of the lower-class "black matriarchy." Based on the manuscript census, all male- and female-headed families are compared with such demographic data as the age, sex, and family structures; size and number of children; and socioeconomic data of real estate ownership and occupations. The basic conclusions are twofold: (1) the urban black family structure during the nineteenth century was basically a two-parent, male-headed family that showed little evidence of retaining structural characteristics of the slave family, and (2) despite the increasing trend towards residential segregation, the only sign of a lessening of the two-parent family is a rise in the proportion of female-headed extended families.*

127. Liebow, Elliot. 1970. Attitudes Toward Marriage and Family Among Black Males in Tally's Corner. In: Demographic Aspects of the Black Community. Milbank Memorial Fund Quarterly 48 (2, Part 2): 151-165.

The article opens with making a distinction between marriage and common law. How the man on the streetcorner sees them. Concludes that as compared with consensual unions, marriage is clearly the superior relationship. With marriage comes higher status and greater respectability than consensual union. Not only the rights and duties of marriage are better defined and supported with greater public force but it is only through marriage that a man and a woman can lay legitimate claim to being wife and husband. The article also discusses reasons for the failure of marriages and the theory of manly flaws; and, concludes that not all men hold to the theory of flaws in accounting for the failure of their marriage. The paper is a modified version of the chapter entitled: Husband and Wife, in the author's book, Tally's Corner: A Study of Negro Streetcorner Men. 1967. Boston: Little, Brown, and Company.★

128. Linn, M.W., J.S. Carmichael, P. Klitenick, and N. Webb. 1978. Fertility Related Attitudes of Minority Mothers with Large and Small Families. Journal of Applied Social Psychology 8 (1): 1-14.

The relationship between certain attitudes and levels of fertility in five cultural groups--Blacks, Cubans, American Indians, migrant Chicanos, and white Protestants--was explored. Mothers, aged 35-45, with one or two children (small family, N = 253) or five children (large family, N = 196) were comparted. Subjects responded to semantic differentials measuring attitudes toward pregnancy, family, abortion, sex, birth control, and parent. Large family mothers were generally more negative toward birth control, sex, and family. Cultures differed significantly on all six attitudes, with those toward abortion and pregnancy being the best discriminators. Significant interactions between culture and size were found on attitudes toward birth control and pregnancy. In general, large families wanted fewer children than they had and their negative attitudes toward birth control might be associated with their ineffective experiences; however, the trend was reversed toward birth control. Since small family mothers among migrant Chicanos were difficult to find and their estimates of ideal family size was large, it is likely that their negative attitudes toward birth control reflected an aversion to its use.*

129.   Littlewood, T.B. 1977. Teen Sex: Double Standards of Feasibility. In: The Politics of Population Control, by T.B. Littlewood. Notre Dame, Indiana: University of Notre Dame Press. Pp. 133-143.

The double moral standards of society concerning interests in curtailing illegitimacy in black neighborhoods but consideration of sex as family responsibility in middle-class homes are discussed. In Raleigh, North Carolina, an OEO-sponsored program answered questions that black teenagers had about sex and prescribed contraceptives for girls before they became pregnant. Compulsory eugenic sterilization and state-financed birth control services were widespread in North Carolina for years, and condoms and vaginal foams were dispensed free to black youths. In most societies the sexual behavior of the young is thought best handled by the family. The rate of illegitimate births in the U.S. tripled between 1940-1968, and the rate is much higher for blacks. Abortions or adoptions are more easily arranged among middle-class whites. "Family-centered approaches" are seen by the public as an unrealistic option for the black welfare class. The middle-class mind-set is that easy access to contraceptives will encourage sexual promiscuity. The proper role of the public schools in sex education is an even larger controversy. "The same parents who fought sex education classes in their childrens' schools approved contraceptive stations in the ghetto."★

130.   Monahan, Thomas P. 1970. Interracial Marriage: Data for Philadelphia and Pennsylvania. Demography 7 (3): 287-299.

Our knowledge of interracial marriage in the United States is fragmentary, inadequate and fraught with contradictions. A major methodological finding of this study, discovered by a comparison of statistical records for Philadelphia (1960-1962 and 1965-1966) with marriage license applications, is that there has been a 32 percent error in reporting mixed race cases. The full significance of this as regards existing data can only be conjectured at present. In Pennsylvania, it would seem, areas of high concentration of nonwhites show the lowest intermarriage rates. In the state, excluding

Philadelphia, the figure is 52 percent. To some extent nonresidents seem to be attracted to Philadelphia for their intermarriages, but, on the other hand, a considerable number of the 84 percent who are residents declared to have the same address. As measured by the interval from application to performance of the ceremony, they do not marry in haste, nor do they show a strong urge to use their license elsewhere in the state. There is no remarkable age disparity for these couples. They do marry somewhat later--about 2 years later for those who are entering upon their first (primary) marriage; and a large proportion of the couples show a prior divorce experience. These data for Philadelphia and Pennsylvania disclose a tendency, noticed also in other studies, for the rate of such marriages to increase, so that now about 2 percent of Philadelphia and nearly 5 percent of Pennsylvania nonwhites are marrying interracially.*

131. National Center for Health Statistics. 1975. **Summary Report: Final Natality Statistics, 1973.** Monthly Vital Statistics Report 23 (11, Supplement 1): 1-15.

Live births in the United States in 1973 declined 3.7% from the year before. No further decline is noted in provisional data through November 1974. For women 15-44 the fertility rate of 69.2 births per 1000 in 1973 was the lowest ever recorded in the United States. Vital statistics were tabulated to give the following information about births in the United States in the year 1973: 1) age of mother and father; 2) geographic distribution; 3) sex ratio at birth; 4) race differentials; 5) month of birth; 6) birth weights; 7) medical condition of delivery; 8) multiple births; 9) illegitimate births; 10) interval since last birth; 11) education of mother and father; and 12) prenatal health care. Birth after the second are falling off substantially.*

132. O'Connell, M. 1980. **Comparative Estimates of Teenage Illegitimacy in the United States, 1940-44 to 1970-74.** Demography 17 (1): 13-23.

A comparison of data on teenage illegitimacy was made between the June 1978 Current Population Survey (CPS) and similar data published by the National Center for Health Statistics in order to evaluate the extent of suspected underreporting of illegitimate 1st births in the vital records system since the 1940s. The CPS data derive from a large national sample survey of retrospective marriage and fertility data and do not suffer the incompleteness of national coverage that Vital Statistics data do because of a consistent nonreporting of legitimacy status on birth certificates in many states. In the data, differentiations are made among premarital, legitimated, and postmarital births. There is indication of a 15% underreporting of white illegitimate 1st births by Vital Statistics during the 1940s and early 1950s. The fact that the 2 data sources were closer for nonwhite than for white figures on out-of-wedlock births may indicate the less serious social stigma attached to illegitimacy in the nonwhite than in the white society. However, overall comparison indicates a general consensus between the 2 sets of data on the incidence of illegitimacy among both white and nonwhite teenagers for the 1940-4 and 1970-4 periods. It is interesting to note that figures increased from a range of 77-92 illegitimate 1st births/1000 1st births in 1940-54 to approximately 135/1000 1st births in 1955-74. Potential sources of data error in both data collection systems are mentioned.☆

133.   Pope, Hallowell. 1967. **Unwed Mothers and Their Sex Partners.** Journal of Marriage and the Family 29 (3): 555-567.

Data from 387 white and 552 Negro women who were not married when they had the first child were used to characterize the prepregnancy relationship between unwed mothers and the fathers of their children. The universe sampled was those women in selected North Carolina counties recorded on 1960-1961 birth certificates as mothers of illegitimate children. Field interviews were conducted in 1962, with 32 percent of the white and 65 percent of the Negro women sampled providing completed schedules. Only a minority of these women had a liaison unknown to and in isolation from social ties of family and friends. Before becoming pregnant, most of the women had "gone with" their sex partner exclusively for at least six months, were committed to them (indicated by regular dating or planning marriage), and were in love with them. The comparison of the sex partners' social statuses (age, education, and social class) indicates that these couples were similar to courting couples generally. Most of the women had sex partners who were never-married; however, 13 percent of the white women had partners who were married and living with their wives. The data supported the conclusion that, in general, these "courtships" cannot be characterized as deviant, exploitative, or lacking in exposure to the normal social controls. Reasons were discussed for Negroes' less often planning to get married at the time of their pregnancies even though, in comparison to whites, they were more frequently in a long-term courting relationship.*

134.   Price, Daniel O. 1969. **Marital Patterns and Household Composition.** In: **Changing Characteristics of the Negro Population: A 1960 Census Monograph,** by Daniel O. Price. Washington, D.C.: U.S. Bureau of the Census: Government Printing Office. Pp. 219-240.

For both whites and nonwhites, the 1890-1950 trend in marital status showed an increase in proportion married and a decrease in proportion single, with the greatest change coming in the 1940-1950 decade. During the 1950-1960 decade, this trend continued for whites but was apparently reversed for nonwhites, and between 1960 and 1965 the trend seemed reversed for both whites and nonwhites. Examination of the data by age in cohorts, however, indicates that the percent single in the population was apparently a function of changing age distribution rather than any change in the trend toward increasing proportions getting married. It is possible that improved enumeration of single males may have been responsible for part of the increase in percent single. The proportion of nonwhites that was either married with spouse absent or divorced was much higher than the corresponding proportion of whites and showed evidence of continuing to increase. The proportion of nonwhites with these "broken marriages" was no higher in the South than in the rest of the country. A consequence of the high proportion of nonwhites with "broken marriages" was the high proportion of nonwhite households with female heads. In 1965 about 30 percent of nonwhite households had female heads while the corresponding percentage for whites was about 16 percent. Households with female heads were primarily an urban phenomenon among both whites and nonwhites. Between 1950 and 1960 the average size of nonwhite families increased by a larger amount than did the average size of white families. Among nonwhites, families with female heads showed nearly as large a percentage increase in average size as did husband-wife families while white families with female heads decreased in average size. The nonwhite household was more likely than the white household to be made up of three generations, and the 3-generation nonwhite households were more likely to have a parent of the husband or wife present. Approximately twice as large a proportion of nonwhite families as white families had individuals other than members of the immediate family living in the household.*

135. Ram, Bali. 1975. **Instability of Unions and Black Fertility in the United States.** Unpublished Ph.D. Dissertation. The Ohio State University.   218 pp.

The influence of instability of union defined as marital dissolution, remarriage, and matricentricity on black fertility was studied. A comparison with whites was also made. Drawing upon the theories of instability and fertility among American blacks, a conceptual framework employing social-causation and social-selection models was developed. Data were selected from the public-use sample tapes of the United States Census of 1970. The sample included 2316 black and 4339 white ever-married women aged 15-44 years. Each woman in the sample had given birth to at least one child. Analyses relied upon the multiple-classification and multivariate nominal-scale techniques. Besides independent and dependent variabels, nine control variables (age, age at first marriage, years of schooling, completed status of schooling, region of birth, region of residence, rural-urban residence, poverty status, and chief-income recipient status) were used. The following conclusion were reached: (1) the instability, however defined, reduced black fertility more than whites. Other things being equal, the largest reduction in black fertility was among divorced women, followed by widowed and separated. Remarriage generally reduced both black and white fertility, apparently more in the case of blacks. The daughter of a househead had substantially lower fertility among blacks as well as whites, but this was so of the househead only in the case of blacks; (2) age at first marriage and educational attainment were the most salient variables acting to suppress the inverse relation between instability and fertility; (3) the region of birth had little or no cultural meaning in explaining either instability or fertility; (4) blacks were more sensitive than whites to the socio-economic variable; (5) black-white differentials in family formation and disruption were clearly noticeable even after controlling the effects of background variables; (6) the higher the socio-economic status, the lesser the influence of instability on the reduction of fertility; and (7) contextual variables such as the birth cohort and the region of residence did not modify the relation between instability and fertility. It was concluded that the distorted (primarily suppressed) and modest inverse association between instability and black fertility is an artifact of social and cultural background. This observation, is more marked, however, for less mobile blacks than others. The general conclusion reached was that cultural context and social class rather than the opportunity structure offer the most powerful set of explanations for family formation among blacks.*

136. Reed, Ruth. 1926. **Negro Illegitimacy in New York City.** New York: Columbia University Press.

The author contends that the triats of family life existing among blacks at the present (i.e., 1926) time show some variations from the family life characteristics of the remainder of the community: marriages take place earlier, a large number of women widowed, and fewer married women at the child bearing ages. There are also higher illegitimacy rates among blacks than among any other population class. However, Reed concludes that there is no conclusive evidence that black women are meeting their problems of family life in any way which may be regarded as characteristically racial.★

137. Shah, F., M. Zelnik, and J. F. Kantner. 1975. **Unprotected Intercourse Among Unwed Teenagers.** Family Planning Perspectives 7 (1): 39-44.

A total of 976 teen-aged women were asked about contraceptive practices in a nationwide survey. 70% of respondents who did not use contraception felt they could not become pregnant; among white women the most common reason given was the "wrong time of month" while for black women the reason was a belief in subfecundity, "too young to get pregnant," or a general belief one would not get pregnant. 30% cited nonavailability of contraceptives, both black and white. Those who used medical methods were far more likely to cite nonavailability than those who used nonmedical methods. 25% said it interfered with pleasure, spontaneity, or convenience of sex. 1/8 cited moral or medical reasons. 1/6 said they wanted to become pregnant or did not mind becoming pregnant. These women generally had low educational status, were raised by a woman with low educational status, and generally were planning to be married within 6 months. Consistent use of contraception is positively related to the mother's educational background and the teenager's educational aspirations. Since most of the teenagers who cited "unavailability" were from higher socioeconomic backgrounds, more attention should be given to health delivery systems for this group. Also, regular contraception is not easy to establish when sex is episodic and when planning is in conflict with the high value placed on spontaneity by this age group.☆

138.   Sherline, D.M., and R. A. Davidson. 1978. **Adolescent Pregnancy: The Jackson, Mississippi.** American Journal of Obstetrics and Gynecology 132 (3): 245-255.

From September 1971 to July 1976, the Jackson Separate School District and the University of Mississippi ran and administered an adolescent pregnancy center in Jackson, Mississippi. 763 students were enrolled in the center, which provided for their educational, medical, and social needs. 99% of the students were black and from poor and single-parent homes. The mean age was 16; ages ranged from 12 to 19 years. School retention rate was 78%, but an attempt to reduce dependence upon welfare assistance failed. When hematocrit, hypertension, low birth weight, medical complications, and difficult deliveries were compared in center, noncenter, faculty, and drop-in patients, no notable differences were detected. Medical complications were primarily venereal diseases. A survey to test the awareness of the community about the project revealed a remarkable lack of information and interest.☆

139.   Spanier, Graham B., and Paul C. Glick. 1980. **Mate Selection Differentials Between White and Blacks in the United States.** Social Forces 58 (3): 707-725.

The greater excess of women among blacks than among whites during the years in which mate selection and first marriage typically occur is documented. The extent to which this imbalance has implications for differential patterns of mate selection and marital history is explored through the use of data from the U.S. Bureau of the Census Current Population Survey for June 1975. The data are weighted to reflect estimates of the resident civilian, noninstitutional population of the United States age 14 and over. Findings establish that demographic necessity requires black females to have a more restricted field of marriage eligibles than white females. It is demonstrated that black women enlarge their fields of eligibles by marrying males who tend to be older, who have lower educational attainment, and who have previously been married. The findings suggest that the "marriage squeeze" young marriageable black women experience may have important consequences for courtship during adolescence, entrance into marriage, and marital dissolution.*

140.   Stickle, G., et al. 1975. **Pregnancy in Adolescents: Scope of the Problem.** Contemporary Ob/Gyn 5 (6): 85-91.

Adolescent pregnancy contributed significantly to the annual increase in live births in the U.S. from 1950 to 1960. The number of births to mothers under 16 rose by 37%, by 44% for those aged 16 and 17, and by

39% for women aged 18 and 19 during the decade. More moderate gains were recorded for women in their 20s and 30s. Since 1961, annual totals have declined continuously, but the number of mothers aged 16 and 17 increased by 25% between 1960-1973, while the number under 16 increased by 80%. There are indications, however, that the upward trend is becoming more gradual. Virtually all mothers under 16 are primiparas. In 1973, 22% of births to 18- and 19-year-olds were 2nd births and 4% 3rd or subsequent. For mothers aged 16 and 17 the corresponding proportions were 11% and 1%. Data from 1968 indicated that low birthweight ratios for both whites and nonwhites were highest for girls under 15 and lowest for women in their late 20s. However, among girls under 15, 21% of nonwhite newborns weighed 2500 gm or less as compared with 13% of white newborns. It has been found that infant mortality rates vary by maternal age in much the same manner as low birthweight ratios; the rate for the youngest maternal age group is more than twice as high as for women aged 20-34. Also, maternal complications (e.g., precipitate or prolonged labor, toxemia, hypertension, postpartum infection) are encountered frequently among very young women, and there is a pronounced tendency toward maternal mortality at either end of the age scale. There is also some evidence of lower IQs in children of parents at either extreme of reproductive age. In short, the pregnant adolescent is subject to all the medical and social risks that confront the more mature woman, but is even more vulnerable due to physiologic immaturity, economic dependency, poor nutritional status, lack of education, inadequate medical care, and in some cases, racial discrimination. A recent study done in New York City indicated that if mothers at highest risk had been identified early, a realistic possibility, and had received adequate medical attention, the City's infant mortality rate could have been reduced by 33% during the study period. Applying those findings to the country suggests high quality medical care could have saved 22,000 babies in 1972 and moved the U.S. infant survival rate from 15th to 6th place internationally.☆

141. Sweet, James A., and L. L. Bumpass. 1974. Differentials in Marital Instability of the Black Population, 1970. Phylon 35 (3): 323-331.

In this paper the authors document differential marital instability among blacks on the basis of data uniquely appropriate for the study of marital disruptions. They first examine differentials in separation and divorce among blacks, comparing these differentials to those among whites; then, they briefly consider the extent to which aggregate black-white differences in marital instability result from composition differences on the variables studied. The paper concludes with a methodological analysis of alternative definitions of instability, with particular focus on the measurement of black-white differences.*

142. Teele, James E., and W. M. Schmidt. 1970. Illegitimacy and Race: National and Local Trends. Milbank Memorial Fund Quarterly 48 (2, Part 2): 127-145.

This paper has presented some data on trends in illegitimacy rates and ratios by color and race for the United States and for selected local areas. For the United States as a whole the published data show that the extent of illegitimate births has been and still was, in 1965, far greater for blacks than for whites. Nevertheless, a leveling-off process has been taking place in the 1960's for blacks while rates and ratios for whites appear to be increasing. In Boston, illegitimacy rates could not be estimated because of the lack of population estimates by sex, age, color and marital status. However, illegitimacy ratios were computed by color, the result was that the illegitimacy ratio for whites was higher than the national figure for whites; that for nonwhites was lower than the national illegitimacy ratio for nonwhites. The question of validity of ratios and rates alike was considered, using the findings from several local-area studies in the United States and Scotland. Essentially, it was found that the apparently more useful statistic--illegitimacy rate--was inappropriate because it assumes that all illegitimate births are to unmarried women. Specifically, it was noted that a number of researchers have stated or found a substantial number of illegitimate births among married women, both concealed and not apparently concealed. It was also noted that, because of administrative decisions and concealment practices, the number of illegitimate births is likely to be overestimated among blacks, a fact that inflates both the illegitimacy ratio and rate for blacks. Present methods for obtaining illegitimacy ratios and rates leave much to be desired because of the lack of uniformity among reporting states, the lack of data from nonreporting states, the inclusion of children of consensual marriages as illegitimate, the exclusion of many illegitimate births to married women that are concealed, the exclusion of married women having illegitimate babies from the denominator on which rates are based and the failure to take proper count of unconcealed illegitimate births to married women. If illegitimacy is worth being studied at all, it should be studied thoroughly. If it is to be studied, students in the area will have to deal with some of the neglected issues and questions raised in this paper. By doing so they may even alleviate the present negative publicity being focused on the unmarried and the black. Moreover, it is emphasized that the care of children should be of first concern, and not whether a child is legitimate or illegitimate. Indeed, in view of the temptation that many people apparently have to punish unwed mothers and illegitimate children, the time has come for society to think seriously about eliminating both labeling children as illegitimate and brutalizing their mothers.*

143.   Thompson, K.S. 1980. A Comparison of Black and White Adolescents' Beliefs About Having Children. Journal of Marriage and the Family 42 (1): 133-139.

This research compares the beliefs, perceptions, and decisions of 150 black adolescents with those of 150 white adolescents as they are related to having children. Responses to a 35 item inventory were factor analyzed and subjected to multi-and univariate analysis of variance. From the numerous findings, it was concluded that both black males and females expressed stronger beliefs than comparable white respondents about the promotion of greater marital success, personal security, and approval from others through having children. Black respondents also expressed stronger beliefs that couples should have as many children as they wish. Females of both groups perceived themselves as exposed to stronger social pressures to have children than did males. Both black and white males placed more value on having children, a finding for males that has now been replicated in several studies.**

144.   Udry, J. R. 1979. **Age at Menarche, at First Intercourse, and at First Pregnancy.** Journal of Biosocial Science 11 (4): 433-441.

Data from an urban sample of American women of reproductive ages demonstrate that age at menarche is correlated with age at first intercourse, that age at first intercourse is correlated with age at first pregnancy, and that menarche is therefore correlated with age at first pregnancy. This applied to both blacks and whites when examined for the early years of the reproductive cycle. Girls with early menarche, compared to those with late menarche, are more than twice as likely to have given birth or had a pregnancy terminated by age 18. It is therefore useful to think of the timing of menarche as an indicator of the probability of early intercourse and early childbearing.*

145.   Uhlenberg, Peter. 1972. **Marital Instability Among Mexican Americans: Following the Patterns of Blacks?.** Social Problems 20 (2): 49-56.

While existing literature repeatedly states that rates of marital instability are low among Mexican Americans, data from the 1960 Census suggest otherwise. Furthermore, a comparison of subgroups defined by generation and place of residence indicates a trend toward rapidly increasing rates of marital instability for this population. Third-generation Mexican Americans living in California, the most rapidly growing segment of the minority, have a level of marital instability closely resembling that of blacks. As among blacks, the inability of many Mexican American males to adequately provide for their families at the level they deem necessary, due to low wages and widespread unemployment, appears to be an important source of marital strain. While increasing marital instability may be viewed as an adaptation to their currently deprived circumstances, it is also possible that this may hinder the group's future economic advancement.*

146.   U. S. Bureau of the Census. 1975. **Marital Status and Living Arrangements: March 1975.** Current Population Reports, Population Characteristics, Series P-20, No. 287. Washington, D.C.: Government Printing Office.

Detailed statistics on the marital status and living arrangements of the noninstitutional population of the U.S. are presented. Included in the report is information on the marital status of the population 14-years-old and over by age, race, and sex, family relationship, presence of parents for persons under 18-years-old, and household headship by marital status for regions. The text focuses particularly on information on recent increases in age at 1st marriage, in the percent remaining single among young adults, in the proportion of the young single population maintaining their own households, in marital disruption through divorce and separation; in the number of female family heads, and in the frequency of children living in families where only 1 parent is present. The data presented were derived from the March 1975 Current Population Survey conducted by the Bureau of the Census and are subject to sampling variability. The proportion of single people among persons 20-24 years old increased from 28% in 1960 to 60% in 1975 for men. As the proportion of young adults who remain single has increased, the tendency for these individuals to maintain their own households has also increased. Between 1970-1975, the number of single persons 25-34 years old increased by about 50% while the number of these persons who were heads of their own households approximately doubled. There have also been marked increases in the incidence of marital disruption by divorce or separation due to marital discord. In 1975, 10% of all ever-married persons 25-54 years old were reported as either divorced (and not remarried) or separated. Additionally, the number and proportion of women who head families and of children who live in homes where only 1 parent is present has also increased. 8 detailed tables are presented.☆

147.   U. S. Center for Disease Control. 1978. **Unintended Teenage Childbearing: United States, 1974.** Morbidity and Mortality Weekly Report 27 (16): 131-132.

According to a study by the Center for Disease Control (Family Planning Division), there were an estimated 273,000 unintended births in the U.S. in 1974 to women aged 15-19. This figure does not include the estimated 237,000 abortions in the same age group or the 322,000 intended births. The fertility rates of teenagers ranged from 32/1000 (15-19) in Massachusetts and 101.6/1000 in Mississippi. The estimated intended fertility rate for black teenagers was 44% higher than for whites, 43.2/1000 versus 29.9/1000. The national estimated unintended fertility rate for black teenagers was 75, compared to 18.7 for whites. White teenagers in the South have higher fertility rates than their counterparts in the North. In 1974 12,000 births occurred to women 14 and younger. If all their births were unintended, the total unintended births for that year would be 285,000.☆

148.   Ventura, Stephanie J. 1980. **Trends and Differentials in Births to Unmarried Women: United States, 1970-76.** U.S. Department of Health and Human Services, National Center for Health Statistics. DHHS

Publication No. (PHS) 80-1914. Washington, D.C. : GPO. 74pp.

This is an analysis of trends and differentials in childbearing by unmarried women. Discusses variations relative to maternal age, live-births order, race, educational attainment, and place of residence. Also examines the relationship of childbearing by unmarried women with health factors such as birth weight and prenatal care. Relative to black mothers, the author concludes that there is a larger incidence of illegitimacy for black population than for the white. This is true regardless of the measure used. A number of factors are examined, but a substantial racial difference persists, with the measure for the black population being several times larger than that for the white population.*

149.   Vincent, Clark E., C. A. Haney, and C. M. Cochrane. 1969. Familial and Generational Patterns of Illegitimacy. Journal of Marriage and the Family 31 (4):659-667.

Data on ages at which significant sexual-reproductive events occurred for one generation, and on trends in illegitimate births for three generations are reported from a study of 793 poverty-level (PL) and 239 lower-middle income (LMI) black females ages 15 to 39. The general hypothesis that illegitimacy "runs in families" is supported by data on three generations for both income groups. A strong trend toward increased illegitimacy in each succeeding generation is compounded by a marked increase in illegitimacy among the 15 to 24 year-old females in the current generation (respondents) of both income groups. When increases in illegitimacy by five-year age groupings are compared for the two income groups, it is obvious that if the rapid increase in illegitimacy among the younger LMI females continues it will soon cancel out the present difference in illegitimacy between the two income groups. One interpretation of the findings is that economic improvement will not serve as a deterrent to illegitimacy, unless it is achieved at a far faster pace and to a much higher income level than is generally believed.*

150.   Werton, Pamela C. 1975. Sociodramatic Play Among Three and Four Year Old Black Children. Unpublished ED.D. Dissertation. Ball State University. 104 pp.

The purpose of this study was to determine the frequency of occurrences of sociodramatic play behavior during the dramatic play of black male and female children three and four years of age using the six elements of sociodramatic play identified by Smilansky (1968). This study attempted to determine whether there was relationship between sociodramatic play and age among black children and whether the same relationship between age and sociodramatic play was the same for black males as for black females. Sociodramatic play is a combination of all of the elements of dramatic play which include: imitative role play, make believe in regard to objects, make believe in regard to actions and situations, persistence, interaction, and verbal communication. In order to be termed sociodramatic play all of the six elements must be present. Most children engage in some form of dramatic play, but interaction and verbal communication are the two elements that make the dramatic play sociodramatic. Forty-eight black children who were three and four years of age were selected on a convenience basis from three day care centers located in midwestern Indiana. All of the children lived in cities having an excess population of 70,000 people. The children were observed individually as a member of a group of four, in a structured play setting. Two observers made narrative records of the play behavior of the same child systematically every thirty seconds for five minutes, in order to have a total of 20 observations, 10 from each observer, per child, per day for each of six consecutive days. The child's actions were recorded on the specimen portion of the instrument and, after analysis, were later transferred to the checklist portion of the instrument. The C.W.S. (Chirstman, Werton, Schurr) Observation Instrument was an adaptation and refinement of the instruments used by Smilansky and the Ohio State University Research Group (1970). The two observers who participated in the study were trained in the use of the C.W.S. Observation Instrument. The application of the Pearson Product Moment Correlation technique produced an interrator reliability on scoring of the play behavior of .94 for six days observation. A univariate analysis of variance has been applied to the collected data. Sex and age of the child constituted the independent variables. Each of the six elements of sociodramatic play have been treated as a dependent variable. Testing the hypotheses on the variables of sex and age produced no significant differences at the .05 level of significance, although several of the dependent variables approached the level of significance. Eleven of twenty-four three-year-old black children did not engage in all six of the elements of sociodramatic play. Five of twenty-four four-year-old black children did not engage in all six of the elements of sociodramatic play. The remaining thirty-two of the forty-eight black children in this study did engage in all six of the elements of sociodramatic play. Consistent differences appeared in both the age of the black child in regard to the six elements of sociodramatic play and sex of the child, but these differences did not prove to be statistically significant.*

151.   Wilkinson, Doris Y. 1978. Toward a Positive Frame of Reference for Analysis of Black Families: A Selected Bibliography. Journal of Marriage and the Family 40 (November): 707-708

        Several enteries in this selected bibliography by Wilkinson discuss demographic characteristics of black families.*

152.   Zelnik, M., and J. F. Kantner. 1973. United States: Exploratory Studies of Negro Family Formation: Factors Relating to Illegitimacy. In: Readings in Family Planning: A Challenge to the Health Professions. D.V. McCallister, V. Thiessen, and M. McDermott(comp.). St. Louis, Missouri: Mosby. pp.196-204.

An effort will be made to identify the factors that might be related to illegitimacy, giving special attention to the explanation of high levels of illegitimacy among Negroes. Various students of the problem of illegitimacy in the U.S. have analyzed the illegitimacy sequence and have shown that the approximately 1:7 ratio between white and nonwhite illegitimate fertility rates is, to a large degree, a compound of differences in out-of-wedlock conceptions and differential tendencies to conceal these through marriage. It would appear from a study by Pratt that as of 1960 the white-nonwhite illegitimacy differential was partially a function of differences in the frequency of both premarital conception and the decision to marry prior to delivery. Relatively earlier and relatively more frequent intercourse among Negro women than among white women is expected, because the social environment of the Negro women is more conducive to sexual activity and the penalties for illegitimacy are less stringent. Although the connection between premarital intercourse and illegitimacy could be weakened by the effective use of contraception, contraception appears to have a psychic "cost" which many young women are unwilling to bear until they have had 1 or 2 illegitimate children. The configuration of attitudes and behavior with respect to sex, birth control, and marriage is undoubtedly contributory to high levels of illegitimacy, It does appear that given comparable socioeconomic background and holding educational attainment constant, the black female as compared with her white counterpart is more likely to engage in premarital intercourse; less likely to use contraception; more likely to conceive; less likely to attempt to alter that condition; more likely to have and raise her illegitimate child; less likely to be censored for doing so; and better able to feel that her child has as good a chance in life as any legitimate child of her race.☆

153. Zelnik, M. and J.F. Kantner. 1970. United States: Exploratory Studies of Negro Family Formation--Factors Relating to Illegitimacy. Studies in Family Planning (60): 5-9.

Given comparable socioeconomic background and holding educational attainment constant, the black female as compared with her white counterpart is more likely to engage in premarital intercourse; less likely to use contraception; more likely to conceive; less likely to attempt to alter or change that condition (through abortion, falsification of legitimacy, or marriage); more likely to bear and raise her illegitimate child; less likely to experience any condemnation for doing so; more likely to experience parental acceptance and assistance together with a more independent status; and better able to feel that her child has as good a chance in life as any legitimate child of her race born into similar economic circumstance. These considerations, which need to be submitted to further research, provide essential clues to the phenomenon of illegitimacy as it exists among blacks in the United States.★

154.   Zelnik, M., and J.F. Kantner. 1972. Some Prelimianry Observations on
        Pre-adult Fertility and Family Formation. Studies in Family Planning
        3 (4): 59-65.

        In 1970 a survey, designed as a pretest for a national study of
        American female teen-agers, was conducted among 372 never-married
        white and black women between the ages 15-19. 13% of the white
        females and 39% of the blacks had ever had intercourse, with the
        percentage increasing with age. Of those who had intercourse, less
        than 25% of whites had experienced intercourse before age 16 while
        the percentage was 46% for blacks. Sexually-active whites had
        intercourse more frequently than their black counterparts. Blacks,
        however, had a higher pregnancy rate than whites largely because
        contraceptives are 1st used by blacks about 1 year after 1st inter-
        course. White women, on the other hand, begin using contraception
        soon after 1st intercourse and use contraception more regularly.
        Whites would prefer to have the 1st baby at a slightly later age than
        black women--23.5 as oppossed to 22.3. Both races expressed an ideal
        family size of more than 3 children, with whites preferring slightly
        more on the average.☆

155.   Zelnik, M., and J.F. Kantner. 1978. First Pregnancies to Women Aged
        15-19: 1976 and 1971. Family Planning Perspectives 10 (1): 11-20.

        The results of the abortion question did not correspond to national
        figures for black respondents, so it is hard to determine changes in
        use of abortion by blacks. Contraceptive use also increased. The
        larger number of miscarriages reported by whites in 1976, 14.9 vs.
        7.6%, may represent self-induced abortions. In 1971 more than 2/5 of
        1st pregnancies among whites ended in live births, while in 1976 only
        1/4 ended thus. These infants were more likely to be wanted and to
        remain with the mother or a relative. Despite increasing contracep-
        tive usage, only a minority of either race used contraception at the
        time pregnancy occurred. About 50% thought they had a good chance of
        becoming pregnant. Part of the explanation is a low degree of confi-
        dence in "drugstore" methods of contraception, and the fact that
        other methods are not readily available. In general, fewer women of
        either race are relying on marriage as a solution to out-of-wedlock
        pregnancy. However, the proportion of babies delivered out of wedlock
        has not changed since 1971. The increase in teenage abortions is due
        to increase in teenage sexuality and resulting pregnancy.☆

- - - - - -O✣O✣O✣O✣O✣O- - - - - -

Chapter 3
Black Fertility Regulation

A. FAMILY PLANNING AND BIRTH CONTROL

156. Anderson, J.E. 1977. **Planning of Births: Differences Between Blacks and Whites in the United States.** Phylon 38 (3): 282-296.

During the period 1960-1974, the fertility rate in the U.S. declined for both blacks and whites; however, the black fertility rate remained considerably higher than the rate for whites despite a decline in the % of unplanned marital births for both groups. The major factor which accounted for the difference in fertility between the 2 groups was the greater increase in the % of unplanned out of wedlock births among blacks in recent years. Higher fertility rates for blacks were also attributed to the fact that black women tended to give birth to their 1st child at a younger age than white women. These were some of the conclusions reached in a statistical analysis of U.S. vital statistics and of data derived from a number fertility surveys. In 1968 the total fertility rate for blacks was 4.5/1000 women and for whites it was 2.5. In 1974 the rate for blacks was 2.3 and for whites it was 1.8. The % of women, aged 15-19 who gave birth was higher for blacks than for whites throughout the period from 1920-1974. For whites, it was estimated that 94.5% of the births in 1969 and 94.0% of the births in 1972 were legitimate while 5.5% of the births in 1969 and 6.0% in 1972 were illegitimate. For blacks, it was estimated that 65.1% of the births in 1969 and 56.1% in 1972 were legitimate while 34.9% in 1969 and 43.9% in 1972 were illegitimate. Tables comparing birth data for blacks and whites in the U.S. include: 1) cummulative 1st births/1000 women, aged 15-19 and 20-24 according to birth cohorts for 1919-1974; 2) the % of illegitimate births for 1940-1974; 3) selected fertility measures, 1960-1974; 4) mean number of births per married couple by birth planning status for 1961-1965 and 1966-1970; 5) the % of births to married women by birth planning status for 1968, 1969, and 1972; and 6) estimated % of births by marital and birth planning status for 1969 and 1972.☆

157. Anonymous. 1954. Is Birth Control A Menace to Negroes?. Jet (August 19): 52-55.

In this article differing views of three prominant individuals are compared: (1) Dr. Julian Lewis, a pathologist and former University of Chicago Professor who advocated high black birth rate; (2) Dr. E Franklin Frazier, a Howard University Sociologist, who flatly de-bunked the advocates of high birth rate; and, (3) Margaret Sanger, who believed that if blacks practiced birth control, a large pro-portion of 17,000 stillbirths to black mothers annually could be pre-vented. The article ends without drawing any definitive conclusion one way or the other relative to the question raised as its title.★

158. Anonymous. 1973. First Black Woman Heads Center For Family Planning. Jet 43 (17): 20.

Reports that Marjorie A. Costa, a veteran public health teacher and worker has been named as the first black female to head the National Center for Family Planning Services at the Department of Health, Education and Welfare's Health Service and Mental Health Admini-stration. The aim of the department is to make family planning ser-vices available to people who cannot afford such services and makes project grants to state and local health departments.★

159. Anonymous. 1976. Black Organizations Strongly Support Family Plan-ning, but Oppose any Form of Coercion Incentives. Family Planning Perspective 8 (1): 27.

At the 1975 annual meeting of the American Public Health Association 75 predominantly black national, regional, and local leaders were interviewed regarding their background, attitudes, and organizations, and were asked to rate 40 possible family planning policies on a 6-point scale. There was the most approval for policies which would make family planning widely and freely available. 88% approved the suggestion that maternal health care programs have family planning as a core element. Policies which suggested restriction of individual freedom or coercion were the least popular. All said there would be opposition to a proposal that women be allowed to have only 2 children, or that only certain women be allowed to bear children, or that licenses be required for having children. Policies placing special pressure on poor people to limit births were disapproved.☆

160. Arnold, C.B. 1973. A Condom Distribution Program for Adolescent Males. In: Readings in Family Planning: A Challenge to the Health

Professions. D.V. McCalister, V. Thiessen, and M. McDermott (eds.).
St. Louis, Missouri: Mosby. Pp. 138-145.

A program aimed at providing adolescent males with condoms was
initiated in a city in Wake County, North Carolina, in May 1969.
Inner city adolescent males are believed to be hard to reach,
reluctant to use condoms for hedonistic reasons, and militantly
opposed to birth control. It was found that they were willing to use
condoms and assume a major share of responsibility for preventing
unwanted births. The program was characterized from the beginning as
being primarily interested in the psychosexual development of young
people and only secondarily concerned about the provision of contraception in its presentation to the influential members of the black
community who gave their support and approval. Home visits and sex
information sessions held in local recreation centers provided en-
hanced communication with the adolescents. Despite vigorous efforts
for 4 months, only 12 adolescent girls visited the public family
planning clinic; arrangements with private physicians proved equally
unsuccessful. At this point, condoms were made available at no cost
in the project office and at an antipoverty youth program. In 6
months, 1200 condoms were distributed. New sites were developed for
condom distribution, 2 grocery stores and a barber shop; these were
expanded to 9 sites in the target area. In 2 surveys done 1 year
apart, 60% of respondents indicated they had used a condom within the
past weeks, and between 69-81% had used a condom the last time they
had sexual intercourse. Only 15% indicated that their sexual partners
used contraception. Many problems in organizational staffing and
functioning were experienced in the program. The demographic effort
of the project showed a 19% decline in the target area for the
fertility rate of black women aged 10-19 years as compared with
elsewhere in the county. This difference was statistically significant using a 1-tailed chi-square test. This decline may be attributed
to the condom distribution program as no new social forces in the
area could have accounted for the change.☆

161. Bauman, Karl E., and J.R. Udry. 1972. Powerlessness and Regularity of
      Contraception in an Urban Negro Male Sample: A Research Note. Journal
      of Marriage and the Family 34 (1): 112-114.

      In an urban Negro sample of 350 married, recent fathers interviewed
      in 1966, powerlessness is found to be relatively strong predictor of
      the regularity of contraceptive practices, even when eight other
      related variables are controlled. We think this variable is worth
      including in future research on fertility.*

162. Beasley, J.D., et al. 1966. Attitudes and Knowledge Relevant to
      Family Planning Among New Orleans Negro Women. American Journal of
      Public Health 56 (11): 1847-1857.

      Information obtained from this representative sample of ever-married
      and/or ever-pregnant Negro women age 15 to 45 in metropolitan New

Orleans indicates substantial ignorance about reproductive physiology, the ovulatory cycle, and effective means of contraception.
Forty-nine per cent did not have a rudimentary knowledge of reproductive physiology and 86 per cent did not know the time women who have
had sterilization operations, 57 per cent used no method of family
planning during their most recent year of cohabitation. Minimally,
then, about one-half of these women lack sufficient knowledge or
means to control their fertility. These data indicate that about
three-fourths of these women do not ever want to become pregnant
again, two-thirds of them want more information about how to keep
from getting pregnant, and nine-tenths think they should have the
right to plan the size of their families. Furthermore, nine-tenths of
the sample think family planning clinics should be available for the
indigent, and nine-tenths of them want their sons and daughters to be
informed of birth control technics. This suggests that motivation to
use effective family planning technics may be present. But such motivation is apparently frustrated by the lack of information and the
unavailability of services needed to control fertility. Beasley has
obtained data which suggest strongly that ignorance of family planning technics and the inaccessibility of family planning services
contribute to family instability among Negro mothers. In his study of
50 Negro mothers, Beasley found that 38 per cent had no mate. There
was a direct positive relationship between age of mother and the
absence of paternal family head. It is plausible that the economic
pressure of undesired increases in family size without increasing
income, and the related emotional trauma, build up beyond endurance
and the paternal head leaves the home to seek a less troubled
environment. The result is a breakdown in the stability of the family
structure. While the present data are drawn from a single metropolitan area, we believe that the instability of family structure, particularly the absence of a paternal family head, is one of the major
problems, if not the major problem facing Negroes across America. Our
New Orleans data indicate that one-third of the ever-married and/or
ever-pregnant Negro women age 15 to 45 do not have husbands living
with them. Futhermore, we have shown that many of these women are
unable to plan their fertility because information on the possibility
and means of planning family size is not available to them. This
suggests a hypothesis that we are now examining: that random fertility resulting from the lack of knowledge on how to control fertility
serves as a major factor contributing to family disruption.*

163. Beasley, J.D., and R. F. Frankowski. 1970. Utilization of a Family
      Planning Program by the Poor Population of a Metropolitan Area.
      Milbank Memorial Fund Quarterly 48 (2, Part 2): 241-268.

The Orleans Parish Family Planning Demonstration Program sought to
develop (during the period July 1, 1967 to June 1970) a system for
the delivery of family planning information and services for all
indigent families of the metropolitan area and to evaluate the
system. Studies showed a marked lack of information concerning reproductive physiology and contraceptive technology, an absence of

organized planning services designed to meet the needs of patients, and the lack of an adequate health delivery system in which family planning could be incorporated. An appropriate system was designed for the delivery of health care. From the family planning program's start to July 1, 1967 through June 30, 1969, 17,459 families have become active participants. 85% of the patients who enrolled during this period are continuing. Over 95% of the families are black. By estimate at least 80% acceptance of services has been achieved in the 20-24 year old group of New Orleans black women. Black patients have kept their appointments 6 times as frequently as white patients. Traditionally problems in family planning have been due not to the patients but to the lack of an effective system. The article closes with a discussion among the authors and several other researchers concerning the program, family planning, and the state of Jamaican family planning (as one participant was a Jamaican doctor). Beasley estimates at least 65 to 75 dollars per patient per year will be necessary to provide adequate family planning in the U.S.☆

164.   Beasley, J.D. and R.F. Frankowski. 1970. United States: Utilization of a Family Planning Program in a Metropolitan Area. Studies in Family Planning 1 (59): 7-16.

The achievements of the Orleans Parish Family Planning Program during its first 2 years are described. In 1966, the program was established after studies were conducted which demonstrated the need for such a program for the indigent. The program's clinic system is composed of a central clinic and 3 satellite clinics. In the first 2 years, 24,230 initial contacts were made through the program which resulted in 17,459 first admissions to the clinic program. As a result of their first admission experience, 16,762 women adopted some method of family planning. The major source of patients is the postpartum referral system. A woman entering the program would most likely be black (94%), 24 or younger (56%), at parity 3 or less (65%), and educated at less than high school level. The type of contraceptive most frequently chosen was the pill (65%). 44% of the black financially eligible population were admitted to the program while .8% of the financially eligible white population were. It is estimated that 3 out of 4 women admitted to the program will be active contraceptors 18 months later. It is noted that a system is needed to provide information about family planning and the means to deliver health care to the indigent.☆

165.   Beasley, J.D. et al. 1971. Louisiana Family Planning. American Journal of Public Health 61 (9): 1812-1825.

In 1967 the Orleans Parish Family Planning Clinic was established with the aim of providing services to the indigent population of New Orleans. It was composed of a central clinic and 3 satellite clinics providing prenatal care, postpartum care, prescription and supervision of contraception, screening for chronic disease, and social and medical counseling. From June 1967-June 1969, 16,762 women accepted some method of family planning. 94% were black; 56% under 25 years of age; 65% at parity 3 or less; and 69% had less than a high school education 61% entered as a result of postpartum referral. It was estimated that 75% of the women would be active contraceptors 18 months after initiation of contraceptive use. This project was pre- dicated on: 1) demographic and social studies of the patients; 2) studies on availability and usage of existing health services; 3) evaluation of facilities that could be used for family planning; 4) operation research on design and administration of the program; 5) establishment of a private, nonprofit corporation; 6) development of a health care delivery system where family planning could be incor- porated; and 7) development of a system for evaluation of services.★

166.   Beebe, G.W. 1942. **Contraception and Fertility in the Southern Appala- chians.** Baltimore, Maryland: Williams and Wilkins. 277 pp.

This monograph attempts to discover whether rural women in high fer- tility areas can be encouraged to practice birth control. A study focused on the population of the coal plateus of the southern Appala- chians. The object of the study was to make birth control methods at once easy and pleasurable to use. The monograph presents problems of this particular region, patterns of reproduction, the instituion of the contraceptive service, the impact of the service upon fertility, and the prescription's acceptability. Also included are organization- al guidelines on contraceptive service in depressed rural areas and methodology of studies in clinical contraception. Observations have indicated that even half-hearted and unskilled contraceptive practice produces a great decline in fertility. At initiation birth control services meet with rigid resistance. More diversified contraceptive methods requiring less sustained initiative and interfering less with spontaneity but nevertheless providing long-term protection are needed.☆

167.   Blake, R.R., et al. 1969. **Beliefs and Attitudes About Contraception Among the Poor.** Chapel Hill, N.C.: Carolina Population Center, Mono- graph No. 5. 38 pp.

A study was conducted among black and white female residents of 2 public housing projects in a North Carolina city to determine a methodology of distinguishing between attitudes and beliefs of contraceptors and noncontraceptors. The methodology of testing, the demographic charcteristics of the respondents, and questions included on the questionnaire are included. Husbands seem to play a crucial role in the decision to contracept. Family planning campaigns should be directed toward couples and husbands. The practice of contracep- tion was associated with a more positive belief in the effectiveness of contraception. Educational campaigns should focus on effective methods of birth control and the necessity for correct and consistent use of the chosen method. Educational programs should stress the fact that positive aspects of family life are not disturbed by contracep- tion. Nonwhites seemed to value large families less than whites in

the survey. Campaigns directed toward nonwhites should seek to in-
culcate middle-class values and, then, to emphasize the fact that the
practice of family planning will help to achieve these values. 'Unwanted' fertility among the poor seems to account for only 25% of the
excess fertility in the U.S. The rest of the excess fertility must be
handled by more general acceptance of the small family norm and
increased contraceptive practice among all classes in the society.☆

168. Bogue. Donald J. 1970. **Family Planning in the Negro Ghettos of**
Chicago. Milbank Memorial Fund Quarterly 48 (2, Part 2): 283-299.

This is a study based on interview of 1,010 women age 18 to 44 from
all Chicago's census tracts in which the median family income has
been less than $5,500 per year in 1960. Bogue's finding is that the
low income black population in Chicago's ghettos possess ideals of
reproduction that are very favorable to birth control. Their attitudes toward the use of contraception were found to be overwhelmingly
favorable, although a small but vehement resistance group existed-
-true of men as well as women. The level of contraceptive knowledge
among the population has been found to be very high; almost every
respondent had known at least one reliable method of fertility
control.★

169. Bousfield, M.O. 1932. **Negro Public Health Work Needs Birth Control.**
Birth Control Review 16 (6): 170-171.

Bousfield asserts that among blacks large families of undernourished
children, with economically depressed and hopeless parents constitute
a major problem. Birth control is at least one method of partially
alleviating this problem. He concludes his article by pointing out
that if birth control is to progress among black people, it is
important that black physicians, women practioners, black nurses, and
black social workers be thoroughly educated about birth control. As
Bousfield sees it, this is one of the "vital considerations to which
the proponents of the movement have not given sufficient consideration."★

170. Campbell, Arthur A. 1965. **Fertility and Family Planning Among Non-**
white Married Couples in the United States. Eugenics Quarterly 12
(3): 124-131.

The birth rate of the nonwhite population of the United States is
higher than that of the whites. In this paper Campbell makes white-
nonwhite comparisons on the past, expected, and desired number of
births, use/nonuse and methods of contraception as well as white-
nonwhite comparisons on fecundity. One major conclusion of this paper
is that the influence of Southern rural patterns of mating and
child-bearing account for the white-nonwhite differentials in birth
rate. That is, nonwhite couples with no Southern farm background
have/expect the same number of children as whites. Other findings of
this paper are: (1) that the nonwhites desire fewer number of

children than they actually have. (2) No significant white-nonwhite differential in fecundity impairments are found. (3) A lower pro- portion of nonwhites than whites use contraception, and a smaller proportion **expect** to use contraception by the end of childbearing period. And, (4) nonwhites are found to be less successful in con- trolling fertility than their white counterparts.★

171.   Champion, P. 1967. A Pilot Study of the Success or Failure of Low Income Negro Families in the Use of Birth Control. In: Sociological Contributions to Famly Planning Research. Donald J. Bogue (ed.). Chicago: University of Chicago, Community and Family Study Center. Pp. 112-128.

The study was designed to test the significance of values held by low-income Negro families with respect to regular and persistent use of an effective birth control method received on the initial visit to a Planned Parenthood Clinic in Chicago. A random sample of 78 women who had visited mobile clinics between July 1961-January 1962 and who favored birth control, knew effective contraception was possible, and had decided to try it was used. 43% had finished high school and 12% had never reached high school. Preliminary testing revealed 86% of the sample had very poor knowledge of the physiology of reproduction. Notwithstanding, all had attempted some means of contraception before visiting the clinic; in fact, many unwanted pregnancies may have resulted from misunderstanding of the effectiveness of the methods they tried along with nonpersistence in their use. Each of the women was provided with a reliable method of her choice at the clinic. the pill being the most popular (32 acceptors). Follow-up interviews were conducted 3-9 months after the initial visit. The follow-up revealed that of 72 women (3 were lost and 3 had unknowingly been pregnant at the time of the visit), 64 had persisted in the use of the chosen method for an average of 6 months, 3 were using what Planned Parenthood would consider an unreliable method, and 5 were using no method at all. 1 definite and 3 possible pregnancies were reported, but in no case had the women used acceptable methods. The success of the remaining acceptors must, in large measure, be attributed to the effectiveness of the pill. When asked about the future, only 2 said they would not continue using some method of birth control. In order to account for the success or failure of the sample, they were divided into 3 groups; successful, partly successful, and failures, and were then cross-classified by variables representing hypotheses to be tested, i.e., 1) communication between spouses on family matters, 2) aspirations for children, 3) apathy and resignation (about the figure), 4) dissatisfaction with the neighborhood, and 5) female attitude toward sexual intercourse. Each of the tests failed to be significant; i.e., if the values represented in the 5 hypotheses do affect family planning, the effect is rather small. It is suggested that while low income and educational attainment and poor knowledge of reproduction may be barriers to family planning, individuals can and will be successful if given easy and sympathetic access to the best family planning methods at prices they can afford.☆

172.   Chasteen, E.R. 1971. Barriers to Birth Control. In: The Case for
       Compulsory Birth Control, by E.R. Chasteen. Englewood Cliffs, N.J.:
       Prentice Hall, Inc. Pp. 125-147.

       A number of barriers exist in America today which act to lessen the
       dissemination of contraceptive information and the practice of con-
       traception. Barriers relating to the nation's diversity involve
       opposition of Negroes fearful of genocide, lack of understanding of
       population pressures by people living in low-density areas, unavail-
       ability of birth-control services to certian poor women, and opposi-
       tion by organized religious groups. Psychological barriers include
       desire for a male child, fear of loneliness or rejection on the part
       of wives, and refusal of husband to allow his wife to use contracep-
       tives out of fear she will then engage in extramarital intercourse.
       Social and legal barriers include tax deductions allowed for child-
       ren, opposition by American business, and past and present legal poli-
       cies (e.g., 1873 Comstock Laws). Contraceptive technology is remark-
       ably crude when compared to other medical technologies. The greatest
       barrier is probably the ignorance of the educated.☆

173.   Cochrane, Carl M., C.E. Vincent, C.A. Haney, and R. Michielutte.
       1968. Motivational Determinants of Family Planning Clinic Attendance.
       Journal of Psychology 84 (May): 33-43.

       Southern, black, poverty-level, female subjects were classified as
       Actives, Dropouts, or Never-Beens in regard to attendance at a
       family-planning clinic. The subjects took a story-telling test
       designed for lower social class subjects and rated a variety of
       persons and activities along semantic differential dimensions. Women
       who had dropped out were significantly lower than the other groups in
       their needs for achievement and for controlling life events. Actives
       perceived more difficulty in controlling events. Several significant
       differences were also found in the semantic differential ratings. The
       results can be interpreted to yield a consistent set of hypotheses
       about motivations related to birth control decisions.*

174.   Cutright, P., and F.S. Jaffe. 1977. Impact of Family Planning Pro-
       grams on Fertility: the U.S. Experience. New York: Preager. 150 pp.

       The hypothesis that U.S. family planning programs reduce unwanted
       fertility among subgroups from which clinic patients are drawn was
       confirmed. The study divided white and black females within counties
       into age, marital, and socioeconomic (SES) subgroups. The coincidence
       of a decennial census in 1970 and availability of national county-by-
       county studies of organized family planning programs in 1969 provided
       the data used for this systematic national evaluation of the demogra-
       phic impact of U.S. programs. 51 tables and 2 figures show that the
       overall program effects, independent of other factors, on the fertil-
       ity of lower SES women in the U.S. were both statistically and sub-
       stantively significant, suggesting that the programs have the poten-
       tial to sharply reduce historical class differentials in fertility.

The level of program enrollment had a negative impact on fertility of women in all lower SES subgroups and was statistically significant (p < .05) in 28/36 comparisons and only slightly less significant (p < .1) in 2 others. In contrast, program enrollment was unrelated to fertility in 19/24 tests involving subgroups of upper SES women. Hence, it is recommended, a policy to expand the enrollment of lower SES persons in family planning clinics would be the most cost effective means of reducing the class differences in fertility by assisting in avoidance of unwanted and mistimed pregnancies, which in recent years have accounted for the remaining class differentials in the U.S.☆

175.   Daily, E.F., and N. Nicholas. 1975. Tubal Ligations on General Service Patients Seen by Peer-Level Family Planning Counselors in Thirty New York City Voluntary and Municipal Hospitals. American Journal of Obstetrics and Gynecology 123 (6): 656-659.

From July 1969 to September 1974 185,927 obstetric-gynecologic and 87,989 abortion patients were seen by peer-level counselors selected, trained, and employed full time or part time by the New York City Dept. of Health's Maternity, Infant Care-Family Planning Projects. The counselors are instructed never to recommend a sterilization procedure unless a patient states she and her husband do not wish more children, at which time the pros and cons of sterilization by vasectomy or tubal ligation are discussed. An almost negligible number of couples covered by this report would consider vasectomy. Obstetric-gynecologic patients having a tubal ligation increased from 5.7% in 1969 to a high of 7.3% in 1972, then declined to 5.4% during the 1st 9 months of 1974. Abortion patients requesting tubal ligation remained at 2% during 1970-1972, then decreased to 1.0% during 1974. 2 detailed samples conducted in 1971 and 1974 showed obstetric-gynecologic patients requesting sterilization rose from .8% (1971) or 1.0% (1974) with 1 pregnancy to 70.8% (1971) or 66.9% (1974) for 4 or more pregnancies. Similar increases were found for abortion patients. Puerto Rican or Spanish background obstetric patients request almost 3 times as many ligations as black women and almost 6 times as many as white women. Similarly, Peurto Rican or other Spanish background abortion patients request and receive tubal ligations at a rate double that of both black and white women.☆

176.   Darity, W.A., and C.B. Turner. 1972. Family Planning, Race Consciousness, and the Fear of Race Genocide. American Journal of Public Health 62 (1): 1454-1459.

The black genocide notion has been an issue since 1933 and 1938 with the philosophies of Frazier and Dubois, which have evolved in the contemporary idea that the black man's security in the U.S. lies in strength in numbers. A project was done in a medium-sized New England city in which black neighborhoods were divided into 2 groups by the aid of census data and street lists: low-income neighborhoods (a 60% sample of households) and middle-to-upper income (40%). From the

total group of households 160 (2.5%) were a random sample and provided a stratified view of the black community. 10 interviewers were
employed to interview the head of the household or a female member of
the reproductive age and determine the relationship between family-
planning practices and the belief in race genocide and race consciousness. 66% of the sample were females of median age 27; the
median age for males was 30. Of a sample of 117 subjects, 3 had no
preference (either Negro or colored) in color designation, while 82
desired to be called either black or Afro-American. 21 (60%) of the
no-preference group wanted 0-2 children, while 14 (40%) wanted 3 or
more. 40 (49%) of the black or Afro-American group desired 0-2
children, 42 (51%) wanted 3 or more. A tendency to desire more
children is shown by the race-conscious group. In a sample of 142, 8
(26%) of the no-preference group agreed with the idea of birth control, 74% disagreed   In a sample of 138, 15 (47%) of the no-preference group agreed that birth control clinics in black neighborhoods should be controlled and operated by blacks, 17 (53%) disagreed. In the race conscious group, 80 (75%) agreed, 26 (27%) disagreed. The black people feel estranged from the larger society in
more ways than birth control ideology with an underlying notion that
family planning is a way of eliminating blacks.☆

177.   Darity, W.A., and C.B. Turner. 1973. **Attitudes Toward Family Planning: A comparison Between Northern and Southern Black Americans: A
Preliminary Report.** Advances in Planned Parenthood 8: 13-20.

An attitude study was conducted of 1890 blacks residing in
Philadelphia, Pennsylvania, and Charlotte, North Carolina. The purpose was to compare Northern and Southern black attitudes on the
following family planning aspects: 1) sex education programs,
including birth control information, in junior and senior high
schools; 2) use of and attitudes towards family planning services; 3)
attitudes toward different methods of birth control; 4) belief that
family planning programs are aimed at genocide; and 5) ideal family
size. A large part of all the respondents favored sex education programs in public schools. This conflicts with other attitudes discovered in the study, i.e., the limited actual use of birth control
methods and the belief in genocidal aims of family planning programs.
Part of this conflict may be due to the fact that people will give
verbal acceptance to birth control in general but not accept it as a
personal habit. The Southern blacks seemed to have a more positive
attitude toward family planning programs in general. Northern black
males were less accepting of sterilization as a method of birth
control. Negative attitudes toward family planning programs were
evident. Large numbers of the respondents felt that these programs
are aimed at elimination of low-income groups. A lesser number felt
they were aimed at eliminating blacks. The fact that Northern blacks
felt more negative toward the programs indicates their general
heightened state of alienation.★

178.   Darity, W.A., C.B. Turner, and H.J. Thiebaux. 1972. **An Exploratory**

Study on Barriers to Family Planning: Race Consciousness and Fears of Black Genocide as a Basis. Advances in Planned Parenthood 7: 20-32.

Many black leaders have expressed strong feeling that family planning programs are forms of black genocide. This paper aims at exploring some of the historical and general aspects of the problem, reviews some contemporary thoughts, and reports on part of a research project comparing the 30-and-under age group with the over 30 age group of a random sample of black males and black females. The study is conducted among a random sample of 159 black households to determine the extent of this feeling. It was found that although 68% of the total sample agreed that birth control projects are aimed at low-income people, 72% disagreed with the statement: "Encouraging blacks to use birth control is comparable to trying to eliminate this group from society"; 44% of the females under 30 and 36% over 30 had received birth control information from a clinic or a doctor. On the other hand, 84% of the total would not be sterilized even if they had all the children they wanted. Sixty-two percent agreed that blacks should operate birth control clinics in black neighborhoods. Only 28% felt blacks should not limit their family size. However, among males 30 and under 47% opposed family limitation.★

179. Darney, P.D. 1975. Fertility Decline and Participation in Georgia's Family Planning Program: Temporal and Areal Associations. Studies in Family Planning 6 (6): 156-165.

Fertility change in Georgia from 1960 to 1972 is examined in relation to development of the statewide family planning program. A temporal association between enrollment of black women aged 25 and over and decreasing fertility levels among this group of women is demonstrated. A comparison of fertility change in counties with high contraceptive acceptance rates among black women and counties with low rates shows that fertility declined twice as much in high as in low acceptance counties. Because socioeconomic factors might also account for fertility change, regression analysis was used to demonstrate that from 1965 to 1971 selected socioeconomic variables became progressively less strongly correlated with declining black fertility levels but remained constant in their correlation with white fertility levels.*

180. Darney, P.D. 1975. A Statewide Family Planning Program's Effect on Fertility. In: The Demographic Evaluation of Domestic Family Planning Programs: Proceedings of a Research Workshop. J.R. Udry and E.E. Huyck (ed.). Cambridge, Mass.: Balinger. Pp. 85-89.

The 1st step in evaluating a family planning program is to look for temporal relationships between program activity and decline in fertility levels. In assessing the program in the State of Georgia it was found that white fertility declined 21.5% during the 5 years preceding the program while black fertility decline 12.7% during this period; during the 5 years after the program white fertility declined 5% while black fertility 15%, or 3 times white fertility. Program records showed nearly 39% of Georgia's black women but only 6% of the white women aged 15-44 had accepted contraception through the program. Comparisons of counties with high and low acceptance rates showed that the counties with the highest acceptance rates had 43% decrease in black fertility while the counties with the lowest had a 21% decrease (p less than .005). Multiple linear regression analysis of black and white fertility rates showed family planning program variables did not account significantly for intercounty variations in white total fertility but 7.8% of the intercounty black variation was explained by oral contraceptive acceptance rates and 3.4% by IUD acceptance rates.☆

181. Delcampo, R.L., et al. 1976. Premarital Sexual Permissiveness and Contraceptive Knowledge: A Biracial Comparison of College Students. Journal of Sex Research 12 (3): 180-192.

392 college students, both black and white, were surveyed to investigate the relationship between knowledge of contraceptive devices and techniques and attitudes toward premarital sex. It was found that more permissive students also had greater knowledge of contraceptive techniques (p less than .01). Both blacks and whites held similar permissive attitudes towards sex but the mean correct knowledge of contraceptive techniques was 58% for whites and 26% for blacks. For whites there was a linear relation between knowledge and permissiveness while for blacks the permissiveness and the knowledge varied independently of each other. The highest permissiveness scores were found for white males, then black males, then white females, then black females. This contradicts an earlier study which found black females more permissive than whites. White females were the most knowledgeable about birth control followed by white males, black females, and black males. Subjects with family incomes about $10,000 were significantly more knowledgeable than others; income was not related to permissiveness.☆

182. Dhaliwal, Manmohan S. 1970. Preferences in the Size of Family Among Senior Girls in Black Segregated High Schools in the South, Central, and Western Parts of Mississippi. Unpulbished Ph.D. Dissertation. Utah State University.

This study seeks to discover the attitudes of the young black senior high school girls of South, Central, and Western parts of Mississippi regarding their preferences for the ideal and desired family sizes. This study attempted to determine the ideal family size, to identify the socio-economic factors that influence family size preferences, to determine the norms of expected and desired family size and to provide guidelines and delineate important information to plan further research in this area. In order to achieve these objectives the hypotheses were formulated and tested. The following relationships were found: (1) The girls whose parents have either the lowest or the highest levels of education have indicated the larger family size as compared to those whose parents have slightly less than a high school education. (2) The group of respondents belonging to the Catholic faith have indicated the largest desired and the ideal family size. (3) The females with a longer rural background have indicated larger desired and ideal family size. (4) Those respondents who have belief in birth-control have indicated a smaller desired and ideal family size as compared to those who do not believe in birth control. (5) There is a slight tendency to prefer larger ideal and desired family size among respondents who desire to marry at relatively young ages compared to those who desire to marry after 25 years of age. (6) A strong positive relationship between the grade point average and the desired and ideal family size exists; the higher the grade point average, the larger the preferred size of the family. (7) The findings of this study regarding the spacing interval between the successive births indicated that those females who prefer a shorter period of spacing indicate a larger desired and ideal family size.*

183. DuBois, W.E.B. 1932. Black Folk and Birth Control. Birth Control Review 16 (6): 166-167.

In this short essay, DuBois reviews the socioeconomic conditions of the black people and indicates that the more "intelligent" blacks secretly practiced birth control even during the slavery era, when as slaves every incentive was provided to raise a large family. DuBois calls on blacks to "clearly recognize concept of proper birth control, so that the young people can marry, have companionship and natural health, and yet not have children until they are able to take care of them." DuBois points out that some blacks have been "quite led away by the fallacy of numbers. They want the black race to survive. They are cheered by a census return of increasing numbers and a high rate of increase. They must learn that among human races and groups, as among vegetables, quality and not mere quantity really counts." ★

184. Elifson, K.W., and J. Irwin. 1977. Black Minister's Attitudes Toward Population Size and Birth Control. Sociological Analysis 38 (3): 252-257.

The attempt was made to explain the various influences upon a black minister's stance toward the issue of population control. Attitudes toward ideal black population size and genocidal efforts by whites were assessed in conjunction with a larger study of 154 black ministers in Nashville, Tennessee. A variety of demographic and experiential indicators which hypothetically should serve as predictors of the stance taken by the ministers were considered. A consistent and sharp linkage was identified between the extent to which a person is disenchanted with the general relationship between blacks and whites and the manner in which he perceives a crucial population issue. This was demonstrated in terms of attitudes and in 2 behav-

ioral measures. The more rhetorically active men were at the quantitative end of the continuum. If the black minister is in fact
effective in influencing the members of his congregation, a shift
toward the quantitative approach on the part of churchgoing laymen
might be anticipated. Those who were rhetorically inactive and qualitatively oriented should have little if any influence.**

185. Erhardt, C.L., et al. 1971. **Seasonal Patterns of Conception in New
York City.** American Journal of Public Health 61 (Nov.): 2246-2258.

To establish a basis for investigation of variations, by month of
conception, among factors associated with pregnancy, a study was
conducted to determine seasonal pattern of conception in New York
City for an 8-year period. Data was pulled from 1,387,851 certificates of live births and fetal deaths (of all durations of gestation)
routinely reported to the Dept. of Health. Date of conception was
estimated from the initial date of the last menstrual period (LMP) in
a range from January 1960 to December 1967. Seasonal index (ratio of
observed to expected) for all conceptions, all years combined, shows
a low of .954 for March and a high of 1.077 for December. Of the 30
ethnic-service-gravidity groups, 25 showed a maximum index for conceptions in November or December. 27 of the 30 showed a low index
between May and July. Other variables examined were legitimacy,
plural birth rates, and sex ratios. The basic pattern or consistency
was maintained from 1 group to another. In sum, conception is most
likely to occur in November or December regardless of pregnancy
order, hospital service, or ethnic group (white, black and Puerto
Rican). No significant differences appear in distributions, by month,
of births to residents of high socioeconomic areas as compared to
births among residents of low socioeconomic areas.☆

186. Ewer, P., and J.O. Gibbs. 1975. **Relationship with Putative Father and
Use of Contraception in a Population of Black Ghetto Adolescent
Mothers.** Public Health Reports 90 (5): 417-423.

Pregnant black girls under 17 who were attending high schools in
Atlanta were interviewed as to their contraceptive use and relationship with putative fathers of their babies. The study results indicate fewer close relationships with the father over time. At 9 months
postpartum, 58% of girls who described their relationships with the
father as regular before conception had less close relationships. All
the girls were provided with contraception at the 6th week post delivery examination. Having a continuing relationship with the putative
father was positively associated with contraceptive continuation.
Those who initially chose IUDs or pills were more likely to continue.
More than 1/3 of the girls discontinued use of contraception by 9
months postpartum. 24% of all girls reported unprotected coitus at
that time. If the relationship with the father was never close or
became less close, unprotected coitus was more likely. If that relationship was terminated, contraception was often not recommenced when
a new sexual relationship was established. Married adolescents had

more unprotected coitus and higher contraceptive discontinuation rates than unmarried girls. Divorced and separated girls had the highest rates of unprotected coitus and lowest continuation rates for contraception. Education is needed about the ill effects on maternal health of too frequent maternity.☆

187.   Fisch, Maria Alba. 1973. Internal Versus External Ego Orientation and Family Planning Effectiveness Among Poor Black Women. Unpublished Ph.D. Dissertation. Columbia University.

Rainwater (1960) observed that the fatalistic world view of the poor contributes to their ineffective family planning behavior. The current study was designed to investigate several hypotheses derived from his observation and Frankenstein's (1966) concept of overall internal/external ego development. It was hypothesized that, among the poor, effective planners, when compared with ineffective planners, would show greater belief in internal control of reinforcements, field independence, and psychological differentiation. Also, a positive correlation was predicted among those variables. Thirty-four Black women on welfare were interviewed and classified as Effective or Ineffective Planners. They were given a modified Rotter I-E Scale to test their belief in internal/external control of reinforcements and the Portable Rod and Frame Test to measure field independence. They were also asked to make human figure drawings, which were rated according to the Peck-Goldstein Body Sophistication Scale to measure psychological differentiation. No significant differences were found between Effective and Ineffective Planners on the measures used. There were also no significant correlations among the measures. Since a high degree of intrasubject variability was observed on the Portable Rod and Frame Test, asymmetrical scorers with high variability were eliminated. The PRFT scores of the remaining $\underline{S}$s were revised to reduce variability further, and were compared. After these procedures, Effective Planners were found to be less field dependent than Ineffective Planners. It was also found that, when compared with other populations, the Black lower income women studied, as a group, showed a strong belief in external control of reinforcements and a high degree of field dependence. Overall, the hypotheses formulated for the current investigation were not supported. While the data did indicate that the poor Black women studied tended to have a fatalistic, external orientation, as Rainwater observed, this orientation, as measured, is not necessarily a simple and uniform orientation of the individual ego. Finally, field independence may be related to family planning behavior, but its role for these $\underline{S}$s seemed, at best, to be limited. Background data gathered during the interviews were explored to evaluate possible areas for future research. The most striking significant findings were that Effective Planners more often than Ineffective Planners were younger, came from somewhat smaller families, had had a special ordinal position in their families of origin, had husbands who took a specific stand on desired number of children, expressed interest in a man as a partner with regard to long-term life goals, gave more discrete reasons for family planning, and mentioned the mother's needs as an important reason. These data were interpreted to suggest that the Effective Planners have responded to society's recent encouragement to plan smaller families because, in contrast to Ineffective Planners, that "norm" was congruent with the behavior of their own familial groups, as represented by their mothers and husbands. It was further speculated that Effective Planners had a special modelling relationship with their mothers and were, therefore, able to establish a greater sense of themselves as having needs worthy of consideration. This sense-of-self, then, received support from their marital partners and permited the Effective Planners to implement their family planning choices successfully. It was concluded that future research in family planning among the poor should explore issues of self worth, attitudes towards need gratification, and view of the opposite sex in both men and women. The influence of the family of origin as well as the marital relationship should be studied.*

188. Fisher, Constance. 1932. **The Negro Social Worker Evaluates Birth Control.** Birth Control Review 16 (6): 174-175.

Fisher assesses the changes in the black attitudes on family size from a time when every child born to a family was regarded as an economic asset, to the present time (1932) when family case workers frequently hear that each new baby born is inevitably more burden than the last one. Fisher also discusses the role birth control has played, and indicates that there is increasing demand for birth control information in the black community because "they feel that if they go on resenting themselves and their mates for physical, economic, and emotitonal reasons, greater problems are certain to arise, and the existing tensions in their family life are bound to be stretched to their logical ends--the breaking point."★

189. Fischman, S., et al. 1974. **The Impact of Family Planning Classes on Contraceptive Knowledge, Acceptance, and Use.** Health Education Monographs 2 (3): 246-259.

In order to evaluate the impact of classes in family planning on the acceptance and use of contraception, a study was conducted in Harlem Hospital, New York in 1970. 100 postpartum women completed questionnaires before attending a class on family planning, and 100 completed the questionnaires attending the class. The median age of the women was 21 years and median number of children 2.1. There was a significant increase in knowledge about methods of contraception after the class. Acceptance of contraception was not influenced by whether the women had attended the class or not. Those in the after class group did not differ in their acceptance of contraception when high scores on quizes were compared to low scorers. However those women who understood the mechanism of action for oral contraceptives had significantly higher continuation rates. ✰

190. Ford, K. 1978. **Contraceptive Utilization in the United States: 1973**

and 1976. Advance Data (36): 1-12.

A comparison of results of the 1973 and 1976 National Surveys of Family Growth, conducted by the National Center for Health Statistics, indicates increased use of highly effective contraceptive methods by married couples but a decreased reliance on nonsurgical techniques. The 1976 study involved personal interviews with 27,185 women aged 15-44 who were currently or previously married, or were never married but had offspring living in the household. The data on currrently married women show a decrease of 5 percentage points in use of fertility control methods other than sterilization and an increase of 6 percentage points in the proportion of surgical sterilization, with the largest increase (10 points) taking place in the 30-44 age group. This statistic is due almost entirely to the increase among white couples. The percent sterile among black couples increased less than 2 percentage points between the 2 studies, and decreased by 1 point among Hispanics. The percent of sterilizations performed on male partners remained at 38% for white couples, but was very small for black couples in both years. The percent of white women at risk of an unplanned pregnancy and using a contraceptive method remained stable at 87%, while this proportion rose from 72 to 77% among black women. Although use of oral contraceptives has not increased among married women using methods other than sterilization (47% in 1973 and 46% in 1976), the pill remains the most popular nonsurgical contraceptive technique.☆

191.   Ford, K. 1978. **Contraceptive Use in the United States, 1973-1976.** Family Planning Perspectives 10 (5): 264-269.

The data presented were collected in the 1973 and 1976 National Survey of Family Growth. The survey showed that the pill and, increasingly, sterilization are the main methods used by U.S. married couples to prevent pregnancy. Although the majority of couples exposed to unplanned pregnancy use contraception, socioeconomic differentials persist in the proportion of women protected. In both years, low-income black women were less likely to use a contraceptive method than were higher income women and white women. In 1973, black wives were as likely as white wives to use the most effective methods (the pill, IUD, and surgical sterilization), but by 1976 this was no longer true because more blacks turned to traditional and folk methods. Between 1973-1976 there was a dramatic rise in the prevalence of surgical sterilization among white couples, but not among blacks. A slight decline occurred among women of both races in the use of oral contraceptives, although the pill remains the dominant method (aside from sterilization) among all couples who practice contraception.☆

192.   Ford, K. 1978. **Contraceptive Practice Among U.S. Couples.** Forum 1 (2): 5-7.

Major findings of a 1976 National Survey of Family Growth indicate new trends in contraceptive usage since 1973. The survey, which focused on black and white married women between the ages 15-44, was conducted in two cycles, 1973-1974 and 1976. Participants were interviewed to determine their contraceptive practice, plans for future pregnancies, birth spacing, utilization of family planning services, and socioeconomic characteristics. Comparison of the data collected in both segments of the survey demonstrated several trends. Surgical sterilization increased as a method of contraception for whites, but not for blacks. Although sterilization for noncontraceptive reasons increased by 6.5% in 1976, sterilization for contraceptive reasons increased dramatically by more than 16% in 1976. Although oral contraceptives continue to be the most popular technique.★

193.   Frazier, E. Franklin. 1933. The Negro and Birth Control. Birth Control Review 17 (3): 68-70.

E. Franklin Frazier, a prominent black sociologist at Howard University, presents a strong argument countering those who advocate high (or even higher than its present high level) birth rate for blacks on the grounds that high birth rate is necessary to ensure the survival of the black race in America. Frazier's argument is very much in tune with Margaret Sanger's views also cited in this volume. Frazier concludes his article by stating that: "Planned parenthood is not a panacea for the ills of the Negro. But together with other equally important health and social measures, it can help Negro to survive and to attain his desired goal. For to live decently and efficiently, whether his relative numbers are greater or smaller, will depend upon knowledge and the intelligent ordering of his life rather than upon ignorance and uncontrolled impulse." According to Frazier, the key to survival is how many babies can properly live, not how many are born.★

194.   Ferebee, D. Boulding. 1942. Planned Parenthood as a Public Health Measure for the Negro Race. Human Fertility 7 (1): 7-10.

This is an eloquent argument by Dr. Ferebee that family planning is desirable for all women irrespective of race. Ferebee argues that there are two major reasons for this: (1) it reduces maternal death rate by enabling mothers with severe constitutional diseases to avoid pregnancy; and, (2) as a result of improving maternal health, it helps to reduce infant mortality, which is very high among blacks, through pregnancy spacing, and enabling parents to better cope with economic matters which have bearing on parental adjustment to family size. Ferebee concludes the article by stating that "those of us who believe that the benefits of family planning as a vital key to the elimination of human waste, must reach the entire population, also believe that a double effort must be made to extend this program as a public health measure to Negroes whose need is proportionately greater." ★

195.   Garvin, Charles H. 1932. The Negro Doctor's Task. Birth Control Review 16 (9): 269-270.

The June 1932 issue of Birth Control Review had focused attention on the important question of birth control in the black community. This stimulated activities among the black physicians. In this article Dr. Charles H. Garvin, a prominent black surgeon of Cleveland, Ohio, examines the need for birth control as a means for improving the socioeconomic and racial conditions of the blacks in the United States.★

196.   Gettys, J.O., et al. 1974. A Review of Family Health's Latest Evaluation of the Demographic Impact of the Louisiana Family Planning Program. Journal of the Louisiana State Medical Society 126 (3): 81-88.

A critique of the Family Health Foundation (FHF) report of the demographic impact of family planning programs in Louisiana is presented. The starting dates of analysis in the FHF report precedes a wide-scale establishment of family planning clinics. Comparison of figures between Louisiana and Mississippi were made from estimates of the Mississippi data. The assumption that the Louisiana family planning program has had significant impact on "vital forces" in the state is questioned.★

197.   Goldsmith, S., et al. 1972. A Study of Teenage Contraceptors: Their Sexual Knowledge, Attitudes and Use of Contraceptives. Advances in Planned Parenthood 7: 33-46.

To elucidate possible differences in knowledge, attitudes, and behavior among sexually active girls 17 years or younger in a contraception group, abortion group, and maternity group, a study was carried out between November 1969 and July 1970 by means of an anonymous, self-administered questionnaire. The contraception groups consisted of 210 consecutive new patients, never pregnant, attending the Teen Clinics of San Francisco or Oakland Planned Parenthood (PP). The abortion group consisted of 100 consecutive new patients seeking counseling at PP for a problem pregnancy. The maternity group consisted of 67 girls at 2 Bay Area maternity homes. The girls were predominantly Caucasian. Blacks made up 10% and 11% of the contraception and maternity groups, but 30% of the abortion group. Somewhat higher scores on the sexual and birth control knowledge questions were obtained by the contraception group, but the differences lacked significance. Among the pregnant girls the higher scorers of the maternity group were thought to have reflected the educational programs and social interaction at the maternity homes. Of the 3 groups, the contraceptors were obviously least anxious about masturbation, although in all groups masturbation was viewed with more censure than intercourse. Sexual knowledge was found to be directly related to age. An acceptant attitude towards one's own sexuality seemed a more important correlate with contraceptive use than other factors. Girls in the 3 groups began intercourse at an average age of 14 to 15. A large majority of all groups found intercourse enjoyable, but the contraceptors were more likely to select "extremely" while the pregnant girls chose "somewhat". A majority of girls had used some method of birth control. The most common methods cited were withdrawal, the condom, and rhythm. The contraception group had higher educational goals and more plans to postpone marriage than the pregnant groups. The authors stress the need for teenage centers for contraception, sexual counseling, and abortion referral in their closing remarks. ☆

198. Graves, W.L., and B.R. Bradshaw. 1974. Some Social and Attitudinal Factors Associated with Contraceptive Choice Among Low Income Black Teen-agers After an Illegitimate Birth. Advances in Planned Parenthood 9 (2): 28-33.

In a study of 289 black, unmarried girls under 19 years of age who had been pregnant one year previously, it was found that active use of contraception at one year was strongly associated with the initial choice of method. Two hundred and fifty-seven (89%) selected some method of contraception after delivery. Of the 150 patients who originally selected oral contraception, 45 were pregnant, 62 had discontinued use and 19 were lost to follow-up one year later making a total of 126 (84%). By contrast, of the 87 who originally selected an IUD 8 were pregnant, 17 had discontinued use and 7 were lost to follow-up making a total of 32 (37%). Since oral contraception is the preferred, but least successful method, it is important to gain a better understanding of why patients select a particular type of contraception. Data are presented which show that patients who experienced strong family disapproval of the earlier illegitimate pregnancy were more likely to choose the IUD than patients who did not experience such disapproval. Furthermore, among patients who experienced family disapproval, those who scored high on a scale of passivity were more likely to choose the IUD. These findings suggest that family pressures may play a role in initial choice of contraception in this population.*

199. Graves, W.L., and B.R. Bradshaw. 1975. Early Reconception and Contraceptive Use Among Black Teenage Girls After an Illegitimate Birth. American Journal of Public Health 65 (7): 738-740.

Contraceptive continuation and early reconception rates among a group of low income, black, teenage primiparous women were examined. It was found that: (1) Subjects who subsequently married following their first pregnancy were significantly more likely to conceive again within 1 year, but, when the association was examined by method of contraception chosen, the difference persisted only for those who selected oral contraceptives. (2) There was no association between method of contraception chosen and subsequent marriage within 2 years postpartum, although patients who did not marry but reported at the time of delivery that they had plans to marry were more likely to choose oral contraceptives. (3) Selection of IUD was associated with a set of social situational factors which suggest that family pressures may be an important factor in the choice of this method of contraception. And, (4) active use of contraception at 1 year does not appear to be related to social situational factors in this population. Psychological attributes seem to be more critical. It was shown that passivity was related to continued use of the IUD and discontinued use of oral contraceptives.★

200. Gray, N.T. 1964. Family Planning and Agricultural Migrant Workers: A Case Study. In: International Planned Parenthood Federation (IPPF). Proceedings of the Seventh Conference of IPPF, Singapore, February 10-16, 1963: Changing Patterns in Fertility. Pp. 263-269.

PPFA-WPEC cooperated in a research project to develop methods and techniques for teaching preventive health care to a selected group of agricultural migrant workers from 1956 to 1961. 1 of the 1st needs expressed, particularly by the women migrant workers, was help in limiting their families. As family planning services were not incorporated in the Children's Bureau project, the assignment given by the International Planned Parenthood Federation was to assist the health department in establishing its family planning program along with a team of 2 public health nurses, a health educator, a nutritionist, an environmental sanitarian, a medical social worker, and a "liaison worker." Family planning services were integrated into the ongoing maternal and child health services of the local health department. For 3 to 4 weeks each year the project area was visited, lived in, and observed. The majority of the migrant workers lived in the Glades' area in 5 farm labor camps housing a total of 1559 families. In order to provide information about reproduction and medically approved contraceptive methods, the following combination of techniques were used: 1) determination of the attitude and knowledge of the crew leaders about family planning as this person has been identified to have a leadership role among the migrant workers; 2) use of a "liaison worker" who was formerly a migrant worker and who is someone with whom the migrant worker can easily identify and confide their problems; and 3) mothers classes which offered family planning education as an integral part of the discussion of general health problems. The public health nurses were trained to instruct the women in easy to use family planning methods, and the health educator assisted in the preparation of a simple leaflet geared to the worker's educational level. In addition to establishing rapport with the migrant workers, cooperative programs have been developed with other health services and organizations. Mobile units have been used to take the simple and easy to use contraceptives directly to the worker. Public health nurses distribute contraceptives to the mothers in their homes. Efforts are being made to provide additional family planning services along the travel routes of migrant workers.☆

201. Hansen, Christian M., Jr. 1972. The Pediatrician and Family Planning in a Very Poor Community: An Appraisal of Experiences in the Tufts Delta Health Center, Bolivar County, Mississippi. Clinical Pediatrics 11 (6): 319-323.

This paper describes a family planning program which was developed by a pediatrician for 154 low-income rural black mothers by the Office

of Economic Opportunity's Tufts Delta Health Center in Mississippi.
It emphasizes the importance for child health of family planning services as a part of total family health care for better acceptance,
rather than merely a categorical program. The age of these black
mothers were between 14 and 42 years with an average age of 26 years.
Their average number of years of schooling was found to be 8. Almost
50% of them were married. They had an average of 5.5 pregnancies.
About 48% had had five or more pregnancies, including 30 with 9 or
more pregnancies. And, 39% of them had never used any form of contraceptives in the past. The major conclusion of this research   is
that there was no resistance to family planning services in the community (rural community of Mound Bayou, with a total population of
3,000 all of whom are blacks), and black mothers stand to gain by
integrating family planning practices in their family health care
program.★

202.   Heath, L.L., B.S. Roper, and C.D. King. 1974. A Research Note on
Children Viewed as Contributors to Marital Stability: The Relation-
ship to Birth Control Use, Ideal and Expected Family Size. Journal of
Marriage and the Family 36 (2): 304-306.

A tri-ethnic study of Blacks, Whites and Chicanos was employed to
determine the contributions of children to marital satisfaction and
stability together with differences in fertility. These variables
were found to be significantly related to ideal and expected family
size. This value was not directly related to contraceptive use but
did indicate a trend toward present use for those with low scores.
The findings of this research suggest that a study using more refined
measures and a larger sample may prove that attitudinal variables
such as the ones utilized here are important determinants of fertility.*

203.   Hendershot, G.E. 1980. Trends in Breast Feeding. Advance Data 59
(March): 1-3.

An analysis of data, which was collected as part of the Cycle 2 study
of the National Survey of Family Growth, undertaken by the National
Center for Health Statistics in 1976, and which was obtained from a
sample of American mothers who gave birth in 1973-1975, indicated
that the proportion of mothers who breast-fed their infants increased
from 25% in 1973 to 35% in 1975. The proportion of mothers who
breast-fed their infants during the 1973-1975 period and the proportional increase in breast-feeding from 1973 was greater for white
women than for black women and greater for women with higher
educational levels than for women with lower educational levels. In
1973, 27.1% of the white mothers and 12.3% of the black mothers
breast-fed their infants. The respective proportions in 1975 were 37%
and 16.8%. In 1973, 42.2% of the mothers with more than 12 years of
schooling and 19.2% of those with 12 or fewer years of schooling
breast-fed their babies. The respective proportions in 1975 were 5.9
and 28.2%. The duration of breast-feeding in 1973-1975 was relatively

short and did not differ significantly from the duration of breast-feeding observed in 1970-1973 Cycle 1 study. An estimated 4% of all the infants born from 1973-1975 were breast-fed for 3 or more months. U.S. data shown in tabular form included 1) the estimated number of infants who were born during 1973-1975, and who resided with their mothers for at least 2 months, by birth order, sex, race, mother's education level, and birth year and 2) the % of infants breast-fed by birth order, sex, race, and mother's educational level for the years 1973-1975.☆

204.   Herson, J., C.L. Crocker, and E. Butts. 1975. **Comprehensive Family Planning Services to an Urban Black Community.** Journal of the National Medical Association 67 (1): 61-65.

This is a description of the Howard University Center for Family Planning Services which operates in 4 locations in Washington, D.C. Patient services began October 1, 1970. Family planning is viewed as not only fertility control but also infertility correction and the promotion of responsible parenthood through information, education, and counseling. Patients are 91% black, 4.7% white, 3% Puerto Rican or Latin American, and 1.4% other ethnic groups. About 55% are living at or below the federal poverty level and about 70% are living below 150% of the poverty level. Overall median parity is 1 and overall median age is 22.65 years. Approximately 62% were single, 11% separated, divorced, or widowed; 27% were married. There has been a steady increase in the percentage of single parents, rising from 48% in 1971 to 70% in 1973. This may be due to increased awareness of the program among single people and the trend toward delayed marriage in the population served. Oral contraceptives are the most popular method, 76.34% of patients. IUDs were chosen by 19.55% while foam was considered an interim method and the diaphragm was used by 2.32%. About 82% of oral users are still using them after 1 year compared with 62% of diaphragm and IUD users.★

205.   Hicks, Florence J. 1970. **Variables Associated with Participation of a Group of Nonwhite Mothers in a Selected Health Department Birth Control Program.** Unpublished Ph.D. Dissertation. University of Maryland.

The overall objective of the study was to determine variables that are associated with participation of a group of nonwhite women in a selected Health Department Birth Control Program. The secondary purposes were threefold: (1) to develop a predictive model for selecting hospitalized pregnant women who will voluntarily participate in a birth control program. (2) to test the effectiveness of a selected educational technique in encouraging a specific segment of women to avail themselves of a birth control service, (3) to describe selected attitudinal and demographic characteristics of a group of eligible women who elected not to participate in a Health Department Birth Control Program. Two basic populations were used for this undertaking. For the predictive model, 5,192 nonwhite females who delivered at the city hospital in 1965 comprised the population. The population from which the sample was drawn for the experiment and the survey consisted of 2,748 AFDC recipients as of September 1967, who were 49 years of age or younger and non-participants in the Health Department Birth Control Clinic. A 20 percent random sample was selected for the prediction model and a 10 percent random sample was utilized for the experiment and survey; these procedures yielded 1,038 subjects for the prediction model of the research phase and 275 cases for the experiment and survey. As a result of the attrition of subjects for various reasons, the final samples numbered 1,000 and 106 respectively. Twenty-four variables were studied either collectively or independently to determine if they could predict participation in the Health Department Birth Control Clinic. The discriminant analysis technique was utilized to ascertain the discriminating power of the following five quantitative variables: (1) age, (2) number of children, (3) years of residence, (4) days in hospital, and (5) weight of infant. The effects of these variables collectively were studied for the total study unit consisting of 1,000 subjects, a subgroup of 527 women who experienced an illegitimate birth in 1965, and the 339 women who delivered in 1965 without the benefit of prenatal care. For each of the three analyses, the five variables were able to distinguish more efficiently than chance between participants and nonparticipants of the Birth Control Clinic; the results were statistically significant beyond the .05 level, the criterion arbitrarily selected for the research. A subset of variables consisting of years of residence and days in hospital was analysized with respect to its effectiveness in discriminating between participants and nonparticipants of the total study unit. The result was statistically significant; however, but no more efficient than the five original variables. Nineteen qualitative, or nominal, variables were subjected to the chi-square test of independence to determine their ability to distinguish between the two groups. Each variable was considered independently of the others. The nineteen variables selected for the analyses were: (1) pregnancy complications, (2) prenatal clinic attendance, (3) pregnancy history, (4) prior hospital admission, (5) past history of illness, (8) medical school service (Catholic--non-Catholic physicians), (9) method of delivery, (10) delivery month, (11) legitimacy status of 1965 birth, (12) occupation of respondent, (13) occupation of respondent's mother, (14) occupation of respondent's father, (15) past history of illness (duration), (16) marital status, (17) birthplace of respondent, (18) birthplace of respondent's mother, and (19) birthplace of respondent's father. Of the nineteen pregnancy complications, prenatal clinic attendance, and pregnancy history were found to predict participants and nonparticipants beyond the .05 level of significance. The experiment involved five health aides visiting the homes of 51 experimental group subjects, teaching them information regarding reproductive anatomy and physiology, imparting information relative to the various methods of birth control and their effectiveness, informing them of the public and private birth control facilities in the city, and referring them to a birth control clinic. While in the home, the health aides interviewed the experimental group subjects using a prepared questionnaire. The 55 control group subjects were visited for the purpose of obtaining information relative to the demographic and attitudinal variables contained within the questionnaire; the control group subjects were not encouraged to attend a birth control clinic. Seven experimental subjects and no control group subjects attended a birth control clinic during the study period; this result was found to be statistically significant beyond the .05 level when the chi-square test was applied. The survey provided much new information regarding a selected group of nonwhite AFDC recipients who did not participate in the Health Department Birth Control Program prior to the interview.*

206. Hill, J.G. 1972. **Birth Control Usage Among Abortion Patients.** Journal of the Kansas Medical Society, June 1972. Pp. 293-301.

The 1642 single Caucasian and 167 black patients therapeutically aborted at the Kansas University Medical Center from March 23, 1970 to October 1, 1971, were interviewed on the day of surgery in an effort to offer advice about contraception. Ages of patients varied from 13 to 40 years. Data concerning contraceptive use at the time of conception were obtained. The use of contraceptives by these single patients, at the time of conception, was shown to be less than that of those in a parallel report who had at some time in their lives been married. Those in conditions different from ever-married had not differed among themselves as to use of contraceptives. However, there was a significant difference between the two groups (probability less than .01). There was also a difference between single blacks and single Caucasians. The blacks used contraceptives more often and were more effective in their usage (probability less than .001). In Caucasian patients the proportion of those using contraceptive devices increased with age (probability less than .001). The number of abortions obtained by single women at different ages was not proportional to the number of females at those ages in the U.S. population (probability less than .001). Cultural factors in our society are responsible for most of these findings. More education in sexual matters, especially for young people is needed.★

207. Holmes, S.J. 1932. **The Negro Birth Rate.** Birth Control Review 16 (6): 172-173.

Starting in 1880 the black birth rate has been declining. This is attributed to increasing birth control practice in the black community. Holmes points out that "in fact, the downward course of birth rate among the Negroes is approximately parallel to that of the whites. For the most part, the difference is simply a case of lag." According to Holmes, as blacks become more enlightened and prosperous, birth control is more often used to limit the size of the families. Holmes concludes his essay by asserting that birth rate problems among blacks are much the same as those among whites, and the forces that cause the decline of birth rate operate alike in both blacks and whites.★

208. Jaffe, F.S. 1964. Family Planning and Poverty. Journal of Marriage
      and the Family 26 (4): 467-470.

      Using data from the 1960 Growth of American Families study, Jaffe
      examines family size preferences, fertility levels, and contraceptive
      practices among Americans of different socioeconomic groups--whites
      and nonwhites. One of the findings of this study is that there is a
      clear trend toward uniformity of fertility values and practices among
      these groups. But, many low income families still remain outside the
      area of effectively controlling their fertility. Jaffe explains the
      significant gap between lower-class fertility control aspirations and
      performance in terms of unequal access of poor families to effective
      birth control instructions and guidance. He draws the readers' atten-
      tion to aspects of the institutional and social mechanisms that
      govern birth control services. One of the significant observations
      made by Jaffe is that nonwhites wanted (desired) a significantly
      smaller average number of children than whites. Nonwhites wanted a
      minimum of 2.7 and a maximum of 3.0, while whites wanted 3.1 and 3.5.
      Forty-six percent of nonwhites, as compared to only 29 percent of
      whites, wanted no more than two children.*

209. Jaffe, F.S., and P. Cutright. 1977. Short-Term Benefits and Costs of
      U.S. Family Planning Programs, 1970-1975. Family Planning Perspec-
      tives 9 (2): 77-80.

      A short-term cost benefit analysis of family planning programs showed
      an estimated 1,097,596 total births averted by women of low and mar-
      ginal income in the years 1970-1975. These data are broken down
      year-by-year and for each age and race subgroup. Of these 1.1 million
      averted births, 767,000 were among white women and 330,000 were among
      blacks. Nearly 2/3 of these averted births were the result of ser-
      vices to patients in the last half of the 1970-1975. 2/3 of the
      averted births also occurred among white and black women aged 20-29,
      who comprised the bulk of the clinic patients during the 1970-1975
      period. Nearly 3/10 of these averted births were among teenagers. The
      following types of medical costs were calculated in the cost benefit
      ratios for averted births: medical care associated with pregnancy and
      birth; public assistance during the 1st year for children of poor
      women; and selected social services such as food stamps and public
      housing. Also reflected in computations were losses of income when
      women gave up employment for pregnancy and early child rearing. The
      cost to government/birth has increased from an estimated 488 dollars
      in 1970 to 1021 dollars in 1975. Estimated average national cost of
      cash assistance, social services, food stamps, and public
      housing/public assistance recipient ranges from 792 dollars in 1970
      to 1353 dollars in 1975. Based on certain assumptions, the estimated
      saving in governmental expenditures (16-19% of family planning
      patients received public asistance) per birth averted among all
      family planning patients ranged from 151 dollars in 1970 to 216
      dollars in 1975. Overall, these averted births resulted in short-term
      savings to the government for health and social welfare services of

1.1 billion dollars--a cost benefit of 1.80:1 government dollar.☆

210.   Johnson, L.B., and R.E. Staples. 1979. Family Planning and the Young
Minority Male: A Pilot Project. Family Coordinator 28 (4): 535-543.

In Los Angeles the first coordinated program, the Young Inner-City
Males Project, sought to reach Black, Spanish speaking, Asian, and
American Indian males in relation to family life education, family
planning, and parental responsibilities. The project developed an
approach to the promotion of sexual responsibility and the reduction
of repetition of unwanted, out-of-wedlock pregnancy through goal-
directed support and assistance to unwed fathers and potential unwed
fathers, aged 14-24. The Young Males Pilot Project was implemented in
1974 by Naomi Gray Associates (NGA), funded by an HEW contract. Each
ethnic community has a peer outreach counselor who works within the
community, and with the participating delegated agency. Within 12
months approximately 1000 sexually active young men were reached
through face-to-face contact with 40-50% participating in the ongoing
program. 118 were surveyed as to knowledge, attitude, and practice of
birth control, venereal disease, and other sexually related topics.
Of those who confined their sexual partners to 1 woman, 76% were
12-14 year olds; 26% were aged 15-17, and 30% were 18-20. Education
about venereal disease was most relevant to the older teenager who
had more than 1 partner. 79% of those aged 15-17 and 40% of those
aged 18-20 had little or no knowledge of birth control.☆

211.   Kahlil, Brother. 1971. Eugenics, Birth Control and Black Man. Black
News 27 (14 January): 20-21.

Eugenics, a word of Greek derivation, means **selective breeding.**
Kahlil surmises that in recent times this word has taken a more "sin-
ister meaning; it has become a synonym for racial genocide". The entire article is an attempt by Kahlil to convince the readers as to
how eugenics and birth control are genocide in disguise against black
people.★

212.   Kammeyer, K.C., et al. 1974. Family Planning Services and the
Distribution of Black Americans. Social Problems 21 (5): 674-690.

Data from a 1968 Planned Parenthood/Office of Economic Opportunity
study on the availability of family planning services in all 3072
countries in the U.S. was used to correlate availability of services
to poverty, fertility, urbanism, and racial composition. The percentage of the county population that was black and the availability of
services was more highly correlated than the percentage of families
below the poverty line or the percentage of women in need of subsidized family planning. In no region was poverty highly correlated
with availability of services. High fertility was correlated highly
with availability of services only in the North Central region.
Urbanism was positively correlated to availability of services. The
study demonstrates that counties that have made family planning

services available are more likely to have a higher percentage of
blacks than counties that have not. It also indicates that race may
be a crucial latent determinant of policies and programs in which it
is usually assumed that such considerations are absent.☆

213.   Kammeyer, Kenneth C.W., N.R. Yetman, and M.J. McClendon. 1975.
        Family Planning Services and the Distribution of Black Americans. In:
        Population Studies: Selected Essays and Research. Kenneth C. W.
        Kammeyer (ed.). Chicago: Rand McNally. Pp. 475-499.

There are several perspectives from which the findings of this
research may be viewed. First, it must be emphasized that the unit of
analysis in this study is the county. The act is one of making family
planning services available to the population of that county. This
research has demonstrated that counties that have made family
planning services available are more likely to have a high percentage
of blacks in the population than the counties that have not. We do
not know which people in these counties took what precise action, and
we certainly do not know from these data what motivated them to do
what they did. We only know that in most regions of the country, in
poor counties and rich counties, in rural and urban counties, the
same pattern appears: family planning is more likely to be available
if there are black Americans in the population. It may be that public
officials have been more responsive to pressures by black poor, who
in the past decade have been more strident and insistent in their
demands for equal justice. Thus higher "visibility" of black poor may
have been a function not of higher fertility or of the salience of
race, per se, as by the fact that blacks had made their demands for
equal justice and for programs of governmental assistance more keenly
felt in the minds of officials responsible for making decisions. Thus
the patterns we discerned could be attributed to a responsiveness on
the part of those in power to the needs of poor black Americans. A
problem with this "responsive" interpretation is that, given the
relative dearth of black political power in most local communities in
the United States, the "success" of obtaining family planning services would appear to be an anomaly. Even if there were black pressures for the establishment of such programs (and how frequently this
occurred is problematic), in order for such programs to be implemented some person or persons in power in each county had to make those
decisions. That would raise the question why there was acquiescence
of agreement on the part of local officials on this particular program "to do something for" blacks? Since the family planning movement continues to grow, it would appear that most places in the
country will have some family planning services within a few years.
The Planned Parenthood/Office of Economic Opportunity follow-up study
of 1969 (eighteen months after the original survey) revealed that
there had been a 20 percent increase in the number of counties providing services, even in that short period of time (Planned Parent-
hood/Office of Economic Opportunity, 1972). This could be interpreted
to mean that our findings have only transitory historical significance. However, we feel that this research is important not only for

the substantive issue investigated, but also for what it reveals about public policy formation. This study indicates that race may be a crucial latent determinant of policies and programs in which it is generally assumed that such considerations are absent.**

214. Kantner, J.F. and M. Zelnik. 1969. United States: Exploratory Studies of Negro Family Formation--Common Conceptions About Birth Control. Studies in Family Planning (47): 10-13.

This paper is based on 24 group discussions with black women in Philadelphia, Raleigh, and Wilson County (North Carolina), and New Orleans to test a new approach to the study of fertility of blacks. A total of 166 black females in the 15-49 age group (reproductive age) had participated in the discussions. All discussions were videotaped and analyzed. The discussions had dealt mainly with issues broadly related to contraception knowledge, attitude, and practice (KAP), and with the language used by the blacks to discuss these topics, with the hope of greater understanding of the factors influencing family formation. One of the most significant findings of these discussions has been that black women discuss fertility and birth control without any racial overtones. That is, the genocide issue was found to be completely lacking in salience and when introduced was "greeted as slightly preposterous". The discussions had also revealed that the language adopted by the professionals for discussing fertility and family planning can be a source of misunderstanding for the laywoman. The semantic footing was found to be of particular significance in relation to abortion. Regarding birth control knowledge, the wide-spread understanding of the ovulatory cycles was found to be striking.*

215. Lees, Hannah. 1966. The Negro Response to Birth Control. The Reporter 34 (10): 46-47.

This is a discussion of the question: can blacks as a minority group in the United States afford birth control, raised at a panel on birth control in a prosperous Germantown, Pennsylvania, church with a largely black congregation. The author has been one of the partici-pants in the panel. The main point of this essay is that although these educated and responsible black participants were aware of the charge from other blacks that birth control is a concealed form of genocide, their response was that blacks should and can afford birth control. The author cites several examples of the cases where enlightened blacks have either advocated the necessity for birth control or even (in the case of some medical doctors) have voluntarily established clinics to help black women in need of birth control. The major trust of this article is perhaps best expressed in the statement that despite the negative attitudes expressed by some other blacks, "...it is remarkable how far and how fast many Negro leaders, whatever their inner anxieties, are moving toward awareness that birth control is a weapon in their fight for equality. The number of Negroes on the national and local boards of planned parenthood is fast multiplying." ★

216. Lester, Julius. 1969. Birth Control and Blacks. In: Revolutionary
      Notes, by Julius Lester. New York: Richard W. Baron. Pp. 140-43.

      Lester surmises that the statements made by some black militants
      relative to birth control is in line with the Pope's recent encycli-
      cal. The differences between the two, however, is that Pope's opposi-
      tion is based on moral grounds, but black militants see it as a geno-
      cidal weapon against the black community. In this, Lester asserts,
      militants are highly misguided. Lester presents an argument opposing
      the view held by the black militants. According to Lester, the mere
      number does not necessarily mean power, if this is what the militants
      want in order to achieve their revolutionary goal. Lester's view is
      best described in his statement that: "There is power in numbers, but
      that power is greatly diminished if a lot of those numbers have to
      sit at home and change diapers..." ★

217. Lewis, Julian. 1945. Can the Negro Afford Birth Control. Negro Digest
      3 (May): 19-22.

      Lewis, a top-ranking pathologist and former Professor at the Univer-
      sity of Chicago, presents an argument that for the preservation of
      their race, blacks cannot afford birth control. He dismisses the
      argument that birth control and/or family planning are necessary for
      improving the quality of blacks' life. He maintains that the quality
      of the black race must be accomplished without "involving the risk of
      tampering with its greatest factor of safety--its high birth rate." ★

218. Lindsey, Kay. 1970. Birth Control and the Black Woman. Essence 1
      (October): 56-57, 70-71.

      Kay Lindsey, a black woman free-lance writer and painter and a
      graduate of Howard University, discusses the conflict surrounding
      birth control among black people. By citing the example of closing
      down of a family planning center in Pittsburg by calling it a center
      for "black genocide" only to be reopened by the very women in the
      community which it served, she illustrates the conflict and demon-
      strates the fact that some blacks are rejecting the idea that birth
      control is genocide. Lindsey asserts that the problem of birth
      control is a personal matter that must be left to the woman involved
      to decide on, depending on her socioeconomic ability. Lindsey
      expresses the view that the question of birth control must not become
      a political issue or an instrument for political propaganda. ★

219. Maultsby, D.M. 1971. Conjugal Role Structure, Joint Action, and
      Contraception Adoption. Unpublished Ph.D. Dissertation. Tulane
      University. 184 pp.

      The focus of this research is on the practice of contraception among lower class Negroes to specify family and interpersonal variables which are associated with the initial attempts to begin family planning. Research findings indicate that task sharing is more descriptive of .patient couples than non-patient couples and that such sharing is positively associated with socioeconomic variables. Joint-ness in conjugal role sharing also appears to be positively associated with the frequency and range of communication between spouses. One of the theoretical reasons for the relevance of the task sharing variable is supported by both the evidence of its association with communication and the empirical findings demonstrating the effects of communication between spouses. One of the theoretical reasons for the relevance of the task sharing variable is supported by both the evidence of its association with communication and the empirical finding demonstrating the effects of communication on interpersonal variables and the significance of the latter for clinic participation. ☆

220. Mayhew, Bruce H., Jr. 1968. Behavioral Observability and Compliance with Religious Proscriptions on Birth Control. Social Forces 7 (1): 60-71.

Differences in behavioral observability, as determined by the pre-valence of religious endogamy, account for differences in compliance with the religious proscription against the use of artificial means of birth control. Data are presented on fertility differences among Negro women members of Roman Catholic and Pentecostal-Holiness churches. Differences in behavioral observability for these women are determined by differences in the church membership status of their husbands. High behavioral observability systematicaly predicts high fertility. These findings suggest that a stronger emphasis on the ex-planatory power of situational or external constraints would be pro-fitable in the study of religious organizations.*

221. McFalls, J.A., Jr., and G.S. Masnick. 1981. Birth Control and the Fertility of the U.S. Black Population, 1880-1980. Journal of Family History 6 (1): 89-106.

Black fertility in the U.S. declined sharply in the latter part of the 19th century and continued declining up to 1940. Common expert opinion has held that this decline in fertility was not attributable to an increase in birth control practice. Instead, experts hypothe-sized that the fertility decline was due almost entirely to deleteri-ous changes in health factors among blacks. The health hypothesis is faulty because those black groups with socioeconomic advantages most conducive to good health were the very groups with the lowest fertil-ity rates. A number of recent fertility studies seem to show fairly widespread use of birth control among blacks during the 60 years up to 1940. This widespread use did not increase precipitiously in the 1930s but grew gradually over the previous 1/2 century. Knowledge and acceptance levels of birth control were also high during those years among blacks. Similarly, the experts' beliefs that birth control, even if practiced among blacks, did not have much effect on black fertility because "infective" methods were used, birth control was not practiced "effectively," and blacks started birth control practice too late in their reproductive lives have been shown by studies to have no empirical bases.★

222.   Misra, B.D. 1966. A Comparison of Husbands' and Wives' Attitudes Toward Family Planning. Journal of Family Welfare 12 (4): 9-23.

A study of family planning attitudes was conducted among a random sample of 118 low income black couples in Chicago. Attention was focused on attitudes toward family size, spacing of births, motives for wanting a small or large family, and birth control. It was hypothesized that the communication, concurrence,and empathy aspects of the couples' relationships would affect their attitudes and practice regarding birth control. It was found that couples who communicated more were more likely to communicate this knowledge to their husbands. Male approval, however, was instrumental in causing the communication. The high fertility among these couples did not derive from high fertility aspirations. Fertility motives of both men and women were found often to be ambivalent, which may account for the fact that achieved fertility was often higher than desired fertility. There was a lack of concurrence between husbands and wives as to the absolute number of children desired in a majority of couples. Men preferred shorter spacing intervals than their wives. More than 3/4 of the respondents were favorable to birth control practices. Parity was the essential element in controlling empathy, communication, and concurrence between the partners; i.e., as family size increased, communication regarding birth control increased.☆

223.   Misra, B.D. 1967. Correlates of Males' Attitudes Towards Family Planning. In: Sociological Contributions to Family Planning Research. Donald J. Bogue (ed.). Chicago: University of Chicago, Community and Family Study Center. Pp. 161-271.

The effort is made in this study to determine what role men play in maintaining high fertility and how they behave when participating in programs to reduce fertility. The following correlates are examined: 1) the male's use of contraceptives; 2) effectiveness of this use; 3) his ability and willingness to communicate to his spouse and to others about birth control; and 4) his perception of the population explosion problem as it relates to his aspirations for himself, his children, and his society. The objective is to provide information that may prove helpful in formulating a better program aimed to reduce the rate of population growth. A representative sample of 118 black males and their wives living in a low income area of Chicago were interviewed concerning their family planning attitudes and behavior. It was learned that both males and females in the sample preferred a family of 3 children, and there was no evidence to support the assumption that the higher fertility among blacks is a result of a desire for large families. The excess of black fertility appears to be both involuntary and undesired. Most of the males seem aware that too many children would block their economic goals. Males want their children to be better educated than they and to have jobs with more prestige than theirs. A majority of males in the sample approve of birth control. Only 12% of the sample of males had not used contraception at any time in the past. Approval of family planning increases significantly for males with higher education and with larger families, and maximum approval is reached between the ages of 30 and 39. An inaccurate understanding of the reliability of the different contraceptive methods and resorting to chance were found to be the reasons for high fertility among blacks. The males were not indifferrent to family planning. It is suggested that a communication program is necessary to provide males with complete and correct information about family planning.☆

224.   Morehead, J.E. 1975. Intrauterine Device Retention: A Study of Selected Social-Psychological Aspects. American Journal of Public Health 65 (7): 720-730.

A study was conducted of 270 black, low income women who received an IUD at a New Orleans, Louisiana, clinic to determine whether there are social-psychological factors which differentiate continuers of the IUD from terminators. 314 patients were in the sample. 4 major "dimensions" were used as independent variables: 1) sociodemographic variables, 2) sexuality image, contraceptive attitudes, 3) side effects and somatization, 4) conjugal reaction. It was found that a greater number of terminators are younger, more mobile and have experienced more changes in marital partners. Continuers are at a greater health risk in pregnancy as rated by the clinic at time of admission, but do not verbalize this as a concern. Terminators tend to have more positive attitudes toward pregnancy, to dislike the internal string check, and to report a heavier menses flow. There were few signficant differences in IUD side effects between the 2 groups.☆

225.   Morris, N.M., and B.S. Sison. 1974. Correlates of Female Powerlessness: Parity, Methods of Birth Control, Pregnancy. Journal of Marriage and the Family 36 (4): 708-712.

To determine if powerlessness is an intervening variable influencing family size, contraceptive practice and/or method selection, a 5-item scale was administerd to 2 samples of ever-married women ages 15-44: Guamanians surveyed in island wide public health clinics, and U.S. white and black women interviewed at home in low-income census tracts of 17 cities. Female powerlessness directly correlated with parity in all but U.S. black women when controlled for age, education, husband's occupation, and family income. Difference in powerlessness failed to appear between contraceptive users and nonusers, or among users of different methods and no method. Pregnancy failed to increase powerlessness, and there was no evidence that female powerlessness results in high fertility through nonuse of contraception. Data support the hypothesis that high parity generates female powerlessness in some populations.★

226.   Pearl, R. 1934. Contraception and Fertility in 4945 Married Women: A
        Second Report on a Study of Family Limitation. Human Biology 6 (2):
        355-401.

        This is the 2nd report in an ongoing study on the prevalence of
        contraceptive efforts among a sample of 4945 recently delivered
        married women; nearly 85% were white. Women were classified by race,
        income, religion, and education. Women were further classified by
        contraceptive genus; that is, the manner in which contraception is
        practiced. There were 4 genera: no contraception, regular and steady
        contraception, contraception with intervals for planned pregnancies,
        and erratic contraceptive practices. 45.3% of the whites and 25.7% of
        the blacks practiced some form of contraception. Contraceptives were
        positively associated with economic status among whites and, to a
        lesser degree, among blacks. Careless contraceptive practices seemed
        to cut across class lines. An examination of "contraceptive species"
        - the particular devices and methods used, indicates the following
        preferences, in descending order, for regular contraceptive users:
        condom, medicated douche, coitus interruptus, water douche, vaginal
        suppositories with jellies, rhythm, pessary with medicated jelly,
        other methods, pessary, pessary with douche, and intrauterine device.
        Whites and blacks differed in their choice of methods. Whites, and
        good contraceptors generally, favored the condom, while blacks
        favored the douche. The percentage of women using the condom rose
        with economic status. There were startling differences in pregnancy
        rates for contraceptors and noncontraceptors. While the mean preg-
        nancy rate for all classes of women who did not practice contracep-
        tion was similar, the rate was reduced by 57% among good contracep-
        tors and by nearly 70% by efficient contraceptors of the upper
        classes. Poor contraceptors experienced about 35% fewer pregnancies
        than noncontraceptors. White contraceptors of all genera shared
        similar pregnancy rates in each economic class, and statistics for
        blacks reflect this pattern, indicating a natural fertility that is
        similar to whites. It is suggested that removal of legal restrictions
        on contraceptive information and devices might increase contraception
        among the poor and lead to a greater fertility balance among all
        classes.☆

227.   Pearl, R. 1939. The effects Upon Natural Fertility of Contraceptive
        Efforts. In: The Natural History of Population, by R. Pearl. New
        York: Oxford University Press. Pp. 198-248.

        Actual contraceptive efforts among women differing in economic
        status, education, and religious affiliation are analyzed. Data were
        collected for 22,657 urban women during the depression. There is a
        significant difference in contraceptive use between women with only 1
        child and women with more than 1. Mean total period from marriage to
        1st conception in the white primiparae contraceptors was 2 times as
        long as in corresponding noncontraceptors. Negro primiparae postponed

pregnancy only .22 year compared with Negro noncontraceptors, implying less efficient means. Efficiency in contraception also increased with economic status. Average increase per women in "marrried
years free of pregnancy" among white contraceptor multiparae over
noncontraceptor were: very poor, .40 year or 8% of noncontraceptor
mean; poor group, .88 year or 20%; moderate circumstance, .96 or 23%;
well-to-do and rich, 2.13 years or 57%. Corresponding figures for the
Negro multiparae are: very poor, .41 year or 8% poor, .46 or 11%; and
moderate, 1.60 or 42%. (None of the Negro respondents were in the
well-to-do class.) The number of induced abortion per 100 pregnancies
and the percentage of total reproductive wastage due to induced
abortion are 3-4 or more times greater among contraceptors than
noncontraceptors in this material. The rate for whites is roughly
twice that for Negros. Whites had a lower live birth rate with
increasing education while exactly the reverse was true for Negros.
Among Negros the college-educated had the highest birthrates. A
possible explanation is that the low fertility of the illiterrate and
low education Negro groups reflects real and serious under nutrition
or malnutrition. There was no religious differential among Negros as
almost all were Protestant. Among whites there is little religious
difference in birthrates among noncontraceptors and effectiveness of
contraception was essentially the same for both Catholic and
protestant contraceptors. Jewish women had the highest proportion of
contraceptors and admitted induced abortions. Protestants and no
religion had the next largest number of contraceptors while the no
religion group had more admitted abortions. Catholics were least
likely to practice either contraception or abortion.☆

228.   Pilpel, Harriet F. 1966. Birth Control and a New Birth of Freedom.
Ohio State Law Journal 27 (4): 679-690.

The author analyzes Griswold v. Connecticut and other recent developments in the birth control movement and explains their significance
for constitutional theory. The Griswold case raised the principle of
voluntary family planning to the status of a constitutional right. It
also recognized the standing of those in the helping professions to
assert the rights of their patients and clients. The Court's recognition of a right of privacy and restoration of meaning to the ninth
and tenth amendments may be a protection against the increasing
threat of a "big brother" society. Recent administrative and judicial
decisions emasculating the Comstock laws demonstrate the importance
of constitutional checks and balances. The ultimate question posed by
the Griswold case is whether it will be recognized that the government has an affirmative obligation to make the exercise of constitutional rights possible.*

229.   Polgar, S., and F. Rothstein. 1970. Research Report: Family Planning
and Conjugal Roles in New York City Poverty Areas. Social Science and
Medicine 4: 135-139.

The compatibility between methods of birth control and conjugal role

relationships was investigated in New York City in a research project
initiated in 1965 by the Planned Parenthood Federation of America. 12
neighborhoods in New York, of approximately 70,000 persons each, were
selected based on the following criteria, and divided into control
and experimental groups: 1) designation as a poverty area and/or the
lowest average incomes in the borough; 2) willingness of a neighborhood agency to house a mobile birth control service; and 3) the absence of family planning clinics in the vicinity. The only ethnic
groups large enough for detailed analysis were Negroes and Puerto
Ricans. The conjugal role measure combined 2 distinct components:
joint vs. separated roles and among the latter, husband-dominant vs.
wife-dominant relationships. Among both Negroes and Puerto Ricans,
women reporting a joint relationship had fewer children, with age
controlled, than those with separated/female-dominant conjugal roles.
Natality was higher among Puerto Rican women reporting male-dominant
than female-dominant separated relationships. Looking at completed
family size desires, controlled by children born, in both ethnic
groups those with joint roles wanted larger families. Women with
higher natality desired fewer additional children on the average, and
those with lower natility were more likely to want additional
children, with the exception of separated-role Puerto Rican women
reporting male dominance who both had more children and wanted more.
Joint vs. separated roles made little difference in the likelihood
that some method of contraception will be used. Among Negroes, those
in separated roles were more likely than those in joint roles to be
using the coitus-independent methods in 1965 and to have switched to
them more often. Both Negro groups were switching from male-partici-
pating to female methods, but the separated-role wives were quicker
to adopt the new coitus-independent methods than the joint-role
wives. Among Puerto Ricans, all 3 conjugal role groups had switched
from coitus-connected female methods, but the women reporting joint
relationships were more likely to be using pill or IUD than those
with separated roles. The results indicate that in both ethnic groups
when the woman has more of the responsibility, she is more ready to
adopt the pill and IUD.☆

230. Pomeroy, R., and A. Torres. 1972. Family Planning Practices of Low
Income Women in Two Communities. American Journal of Public Health
62: 1123-1129.

1351 white, black and Spanish-American women between the ages of 18
and 44 from the low income districts of Grand Rapids, Michigan and
Albuquerque, New Mexico, were interviewed regarding their use of
contraception. The areas sampled in the 2 communities were poverty
designated areas with family planning clinics within their bounda-
ries. The data are summarized in subsamples based on ethnicity and
income levels with those designated by the Social Security Administration as "poor" or "near poor" compared with the remaining low
marginal income group. Findings indicate that except for white women
in albuquerque, about 1/3 of the sample had never used contraception.
The majority of each subsample were either now using or had used

contraception in the past. Black and Spanish-American women were less
likely to be or to have been users of contraception than their white
counterparts and were more likely to be at risk of an unwanted pregnancy. The poor generally used contraception as much or more than the
women of low marginal incomes. Of all women using contraception at
the time of the interview, over 1/2 were using oral contraception.
Despite family planning clinics in the area, 2/3 of the poor white
subsamples and 2/3 of the users of contraception received their 1st
prescription from a private doctor. For all ethnic subsamples the low
marginal income respondents use public medical sources less than the
poor. The greater use of public family planning services by the poor
appears to explain their slightly more effective contraceptive use as
compared to the low marginal income group. However, it is the relative lack of use of the private doctor that puts minorities at a comparative contraceptive disadvantage with the whites. The role of subsidized family planning services is different both in perception and
actuality for whites and minorities. The poor whites appear to have
both greater preference for and apparent access to private medical
care than do correspondingly poor nonwhites. ★

231.   Presser, H.B., and L.L. Bumpass. 1972. The Acceptability of Contraceptive Sterilization Among U.S. Couples: 1970. Family Planning
Perspectives 4 (4): 18-26.

An analysis of data from the National Fertility Studies of 1965 and
1970 tabulates sex, percent sterilized, percent considering sterilization, and percent either sterilized or considering it. Independent
variables are race, age, parity, timing of failures, number of
failures, method used, religion, and wife's education. Vasectomy,
which is accelerating in numbers, is used chiefly by low-parity
whites who are highly educated and have used effective contraception,
with few failures. Tubal sterilization is more common in blacks,
especially Protestants and the less educated. Sterilization was
prevalent among older couples but seriously considered among more
younger people. Sterilized whites averaged 2.7 children, blacks 5.1,
including twice as many unwanted children. Use and acceptability is
directly related to parity for female sterilization and for blacks,
but not for vasectomy on whites. Despite misinformation about vasectomy, contraceptive sterilization for both sexes is widely accepted
amongst U.S. couples.☆

232.   Rochat, R.W., et al. 1971. The Effect of Family Planning in Georgia
on Fertility in Selected Rural Counties. Excerpta Medica International Congress Series 224: 6-14.

To assess the possible effect of family planning fertility was
examined by 3 variables (race, age, parity) in 2 groups of matched
counties in rural Georgia, one with family planning programs (test
group); one without (control). Women in need of public contraceptive
service were defined as fecund (age 18-44), household income less
than $3000, and desired to avoid pregnancy. Characteristics of con-

traceptive users in the study area were: 90% Negro, 83% between 15-34 years, 65.9% married, 94.1% had children, 55% used the IUD, and 36.7%, oral contraceptives. Negro fertility declined in both groups at the same rate between 1960-1966 but in 1966-1968, the rate declined more (3 times greater) in the study group. Negro fertility declined more in all age groups of the study area than that of the control (50% decline for the women 25-39). The decline in fertility was greater for active contraceptors going to family planning clinics. More frequent and precise measurements of population characteristics will be needed to show the impact of family planning services. ☆

233.   Rochat, R.W., et al. 1972. Program Evaluation. In: Seminar in Family Planning. A.W. Isenman, E.G. Knox, and L.B. Tyrer (eds.). Chicago: American College of Obstetricians and Gynecologists. Pp. 90-92.

The necessity for evaluating family planning programs is briefly discussed, and data are presented from matched study and control counties in Georgia used to determine the relationship between fertility change and family planning programs. Characteristics of the contracepting group are summarized as 1) 90% Black; 2) 15-34 years of age (83%); 3) 66% married; 4) 94% proven fertile; 5) 55% using IUD; and 6) 37% using oral contraceptive agents (OCAs). Black fertility rates in 1960-1966 and 1966-1968 declined as follows: 1) Georgia overall; 3.4% and 6.3%, 2) control women, 2.3% and 8.3%; and 3) study counties, 3.2% and 15.2%. Estimated fertility changes did not correlate exactly with the age distribution of contraceptives. It was concluded that clear impact of family planning programs on fertility awaits more precise measurements and analysis of populations involved. ★

234.   Ryan. G.M., and P.J. Sweeney. 1980. Attitudes of Adolescents Toward Prergnancy and Contraception. American Journal of Obstetrics and Gynecology 137 (3): 358-366.

In-depth interviews with 87 percent teenagers in the University of Tennessee Center for the Health Sciences prenatal clinics found that 94% were knowledgeable about contraception and 66% made conscious choices not to use it. Of 87 pregnancies, 26 (30%) were intended. 6 pregnancies occurred among contraceptive users. Only 32 (37%) pregnancies were unwanted. Most of the sample (92%) were black, single, aged 15-17. Attitudes toward abortion were primarily negative; only 21 considered abortion as an alternative. 9 patients wanted an abortion but for various reasons carried to term. A high degree of pleasure or acceptance was found in attitudes. 24% reported problems, mostly with school. 76% of the study patients had friends with babies. Most patients maintained some type of relationship to the father of the child. 75 of the 80 women who had not finished high school expressed the desire to do so. 13 patients were working; 26 were seeking employment. Less than half the patients were seeking employment. Less than half the patients were receiving welfare, but the same group planned to use it to support their children. 11% planned to marry a responsible husband. 20% felt they could earn the money to support their children. Parents were viewed as important social assets. Only 23 patients planned to assume personal responsibility for the upbringing of their children.☆

235. Ryder, N.B., and C.F. Westoff. 1966. Use of Oral Contraception in the United States, 1965. Science 153 (3741): 1199-1205.

In only 5 years oral contraception has become a major means of regulating fertility. The American birthrate has fallen by more than 20% in the last 8 years. 26% of married women under age 45 have used oral contraception. Use among younger women is much greater. Of women under 30, more than 40% have already used the pill. With rising age, as women complete their families, use of pills should rise as a prevention of fertility. The majority of women who have been to college have used pills. Use by Negroes is somewhat less than by whites, which is partially explained by concomitant racial differences in educational levels. It is too soon to know whether pills will limit a couple's eventual number of children or whether they will merely be used to delay the start of families. Both lower eventual parity and delayed fertility contribute to a decline in the number of births annually.★

236. Rydman, Edward J., Jr. 1965. Factors Related to Family Planning Among Lower Class Negroes. Unpublished Ph.D. Dissertation. Ohio State University.

Observations suggest that social and cultural factors may have an influence upon family planning practices. Reveals that there are very few factors which have a strong influence on family planning but many which may have a small influence. Subjects behave in many inconsistent ways and additional areas of cultural and social milieu need further investigation before any valid conclusion on contraceptive practices can be drawn.★

237. Ryser, P.E., and W.H. Spillane. 1974. The Effect of Education and Significant Others Upon the Contraceptive Behavior of Married Men. Journal of Biosocial Science 6 (3): 305-314.

Summary: A survey of married men living with their wives revealed that they had, on the average, been married for 14 years and had 2.8 children. The men in this survey were found to be positively oriented towards family planning. Seventy-nine percent were using a contraceptive at the time of survey. The analysis revealed that race and education explained differences in contraceptive practices. Black males reported using more effective methods, namely pill, than white males. The examination of the effect of education revealed that as education increased, the racial differences persisted except for those men with education beyond high school.*

238.   Sanger, Margaret. 1946. Love or Babies: Must Negro Mothers Choose?
       Negro Digest 4 (1): 3-8.

       Margaret Sanger, pioneer of birth control movement who set up the
       first birth control clinic in the United States in 1916, makes a
       strong appeal to the black population for birth control. Her appeal
       is best explained in her own words as follows: "Last year 40,000
       Negro mothers and babies died in childbirth in this country. They
       died, for the most part, as a result of inadequate medical attention,
       poor living conditions, improper diet and many other ills, which
       taken together made for mothers who were poor maternity risks from
       the start....Negro parents need birth control to help alleviate some
       of the needless suffering and heartbreak, to get firmly established on
       the road to health and better living....The Negro race has reached a
       place in its history when every possible effort should be made to
       have every Negro child count as a valuable contribution to the future
       of America. Negro parents, like all parents, must create the next
       generation from strength, not from weakness; from health, not from
       despair." ★

239.   Sastry, K.R. 1973. Female Work Participation and Work-Motivated Con-
       traception.   Unpublished Ph.D. Dissertation. University of North
       Carolina.

       This study seeks to answer 2 questions: 1) What part of the work-
       related variance in fertility can be attributed to fecundity and what
       part to contraception? and 2) Does the relative strength of these 2
       variables (fecundity and contraception) change by race and class? As
       it is not possible to answer the question of causal relationship from
       cross-sectional data, the author has tried to determine the propor-
       tion of work-related variance in fertility due to the contraception
       once the infuence of fecundity is removed. The data is drawn from 2
       surveys. One set of data was collected as part of a base line survey
       from 17 American cities during 1969-1970. For this survey, more than
       3000 low-income married women between the ages of 15 and 44, about
       equally divided between blacks and whites, were interviewed. The 2nd
       set of data is drawn from the 1965 National Fertility Survey. Here, a
       sample of 5617 women under the age of 55 and living with their
       husbands were questioned. The ratio of whites to blacks was about 4
       to 1. Work variables are considered well-measured by the 1st survey;
       fecundity and contraceptive measures by the 2nd. A sub-sample from
       each survey was selected for analysis. The only general conclusion
       from an analysis of the data is that fecundity explains a greater
       proportion of work-related variance in fertility than contraception
       across race and class. No consistent support was found for the hypo-
       thesis that work-related variation in fertility due to contraception
       was higher for whites than blacks or for white collar employes of
       either race as opposed to blue collar workers. The implications of
       these findings in regard to attempts to control fertility by
       encouraging female participation in the labor force are explored. ☆

240. Sewell, Lemuel T. 1933. The Negro Wants Birth Control. Birth Control
      Review 17 (3): 131.

      As the opening sentence of his article, Dr. Sewell refers to the
      frequently asked question: Do the masses of black Americans accept
      and practice birth control? As an answer to this question, Sewell who
      operated two prenatal clinics and an obstetrical service in a black
      hospital asserts that at least 75 percent of the women visiting him
      are anxious for birth control information and that most of them will
      carefully follow the instructions given. Dr. Sewell asserts that
      women tend to ignore what the sociologist, the scientists, or the
      politicians say about birth control. They want birth control for two
      simple reasons: economic and health. The author concludes his article
      by stating that: "The Negroes are interested in birth control; they
      welcome it, and they will practice it." ★

241. Siegel, E., et al. 1969. **Measurement of Need and Utilization Rates
      for a Public Family Planning Program.** American Journal of Public
      Health 59 (8): 1322-1330.

      To determine the number of women in need of family planning services
      in the Charlotte, North Carolina area, and the proportion of these
      women currently served by the present family planning clinic, 1693
      randomly selected households in low-income districts were surveyed.
      Interviews were obtained from women between 15 and 44 years of age in
      94.3% of the eligible households, resulting in 800 usable interviews
      on a broad variety of items including socioeconomic background,
      sexual history, and family planning practices. 63% of the sample were
      determined to be financially eligible for the county's family plan-
      ning program because of their poor or near-poor status. The
      proportion of these poor was twice as great among nonwhites as
      whites. 18.7% of these eligible women were infertile or had been
      sterilized. Significantly more white fell into this category than
      nonwhites (p less than .05). 32.5% of the eligible women were
      determined to be temporarily not in need of family planning services
      because they were sexually inactive, using nonclinic contraception,
      or were in some states of pregnancy. Thus 48.8% of the eligible women
      were found to be currently in need, and 34.2% were going unserved by
      the clinic. Significantly more nonwhite women were in need than
      whites (p less than .01). Of the 292 women not financially eligible
      for the county's program, 12.7% were found to be infertile or
      sterilized and 42.5% temporarily not in need. Significantly more
      whites fell into the latter category than nonwhites (p less than
      .001) due to their more frequent use of nonclinic contraception.
      Significantly more nonwhites were sexually active and not using
      contraception in this group than whites (p less than .001). The poor
      and financially eligible respondents were significantly more sterile
      (p less than .05), less using nonclinic contraception (p less than
      .05) and more sexually active without contraception (p less than .05)
      than the financially ineligible. It is concluded that the greatest
      need for family planning in this area is among the nonwhite poor.✩

242. Singer, A., et al. 1969. **Contraceptives** and **Cervical Carcinoma.** British Medical Journal 4: 108.

The authors express reservations similar to those expressed by others relating to the recently published rates of carcinoma-in-situ in women using the diaphragm as compared with those using contraceptive oral steroids. Data from the Planned Parenthood Clinics in New York City compared 3 ethnic groups: white, Negro, and Puerto Rican. All were shown to have variations in incidence rates for invasive cervical carcinoma, possibly due to such etiological factors as early sexual activity, multiparity, and low socioeconomic status. Those using oral contrceptives were 78% of the possibly high risk groups and therefore might be expected to have more cervical carcinoma. The simultaneous random matching procedure employed may have reduced the differences somewhat. Larger groups on an international scale and over extended periods of time are needed for study. It is suggested that the proposed coital mutagen may have gained entry during adolescence or before the use of either a mechanical barrier or oral contraception. ☆

243. Sinquefield, J.C. 1974. **The Effects of Personal Efficacy on Resistance to Family Planning.** In: A Social-Psychological Study of Resistance in Family Planning in Rural Alabama. J.C. Sinquefield (ed.). Chicago: University of Chicago, Community and Family Study Center. Pp. 20-32.

In this portion of a study of low-income, rural Negro Adopters and non-adopters of family planning, the hypothesis "The lower a woman's degree of internal control, the higher the probability that she will resist family planning" is tested. 58% of resisters and 42% of adopters felt God-fate determined the number of children you have. Questions further probing attitudes showed 57% of resisters and 43% of adopters thought both fate and human decision played a part while 30% of resisters and 70% of adopters thought human decision could play a major part. Both resisters and adopters felt human decision was the major factor in the person one marries, having friends, the government, and whether children grow up to be considerate of others. 95% of both groups felt God-fate determined when and where one dies but 95% of resisters and 82% of adopters felt fate determines sickness. 45% of resisters and 40% of adopters felt fate determined success. To test institutional fatalism, a series of questions were asked relating to economic betterment and ability to improve ones life by working harder. 27.5% of resisters and 38.5% of adopters felt it unlikely that their husbands (or boyfriends) would ever have a better job than they have right now. 12% of resisters and 5% of adopters felt their neighbors had stopped trying to better their lives; 15% of resisters and 7.5% of adopters said they themselves had stopped trying. More than 1/2 of both groups felt that in the community if you are Negro there is nothing you can do to get ahead. 30.8% of resisters and 55% of adopters felt it was an individual's fault if he stayed poor all his life. To measure the effect of experience in controlling ones own activities, voting was chosen. This is extremely difficult for a Negro women in the South as black were disinfranchised effectively until the 1960s. This hypothesis was supported at the .005 level. Women who had taken the trouble to register, pass the literacy test, and vote were much more likely to adopt birth control. Findings suggest that a woman's degree of personal efficacy affects resistance and personal efficacy can be measured both from social-psychological and behavioral perspectives.☆

244. Sinquefield, J.C. 1974. Source of Resistance to Innovation. In: A Social-Psychological Study of Resistance to Family Planning in Rural Alabama. Chicago: University of Chicago, Community Study Center. Pp. 1-19.

This study of rural, low socioeconomic status women in Alabama attempts to compare late adopters with resisters and to develop and test hypotheses that would explain the behavior of the resisters group. Innovation studies was adopted of family planning. From a previous study of adoption of familly planning by hard-core resisters, 2 groups were paired. The 1st group were women who had adopted family planning after home visits by a nurse. These were the "late adopters" of the community. The 2nd group were women who did not adopt, the "resisters." All were Negro with 3 or more living children, under age 35, and sexually active. They were paired by age, education, and number of children. 40 pairs were finally obtained and interviewed in detail. Previous studies had emphasized social-demographic factors and attitudes toward traditionalism. These had found little difference between late adopters and resisters. This study focuses on socio-psychological variables and their interaction with sociodemographic factors. Particular variables chosen for study are: feelings of efficacy, as measured by feelings of fatalism and attempts to control the external world; family communication and stability; basic attitude toward family planning; her view of the social acceptability of family planning; her desire for more children; and her perception of the consequences of family planning. The final hypothesis also includes the women's aspirations for her children, the feelings toward health and pregnancy, the degree to which she sees family planning as a way to raise the economic condition of the family, and the side effects she attributes to the use of family planning.☆

245. Sinquefield, J.C. 1974. Family Factors in Resistance of Family Planning. In: A Social-Psychological Study of Resistance to Family Planning in Rural Alabama. Chicago: University of Chicago, Community and Family Study Center. Pp. 33-46.

This study of rural, low socioeconomic status Negro women in Alabama found no difference in adoption of contraception by marital state. About 59% of both resisters and adopters were in legal marital relationships while 25% were in stable, long-term common-law relationships. Only 16% were having regular sexual relations with their

current boyfriends. A most interesting finding was that approximately
60% of adopters and 80% of resisters never talked with their spouses
about family planning. However, 75% of adopters and 52.5% of resisters talked with neighbors. It appears easier to talk with female
neighbors about such a delicate subject. Neither the pill nor the IUD
require the spouse's cooperation for use. Marital happiness seemed
correlated with family planning. 75% of the resisters but only 25% of
the adopters said they often wished for a different spouse (p = .015)
while 10% of resisters and none of the adopters found sexual relations unpleasant or neutral. Adopters were found to have more legitimate and fewer illegitimate children than resisters (p = .05). Attitude questions also showed that the more a woman approved of the concept of family planning in general, the more likely she was to adopt
it for herself. None of the adopters but 8% of the resisters disapproved for religious or health reasons. Nearly 1/2 the resisters but
only 2% of the adopters were neutral. About 97% of the adopters
approved of the financial or maternal health aspects of family planning while less than 1/2 of the resisters did. This leads to the
conclusion that for a sizable proportion of the resisters nonadoption
is a positive decision, not just apathy or lack of motivation.☆

246. Smith, Mary. 1968. Birth Control and the Negro Woman. Ebony 23
      (March): 29-37.

      With the birth of each child, the Negro mother must today face the
      growing issue of birth control. Census figures show the black birth
      rate to be double that of whites in some areas. Yet, many individuals
      are reluctant to use contraceptives and suspect discrimination in
      public family planning clinics.*

247. Stycos, J.M. 1977. Some Minority Opinions on Birth Control. In:
      Population Policy and Ethics: The American Experience. New York:
      Irvington Publishers. Pp. 169-196.

      The views of militant blacks, feminists, and radical leftists
      regarding governmental population programs are examined. New Leftists
      oppose programmatic provision of birth control by the government on
      ideological and political grounds. Birth control is a high priority
      issue for the Women's Liberation Movement. However, many feminists
      distrust the family planning movement because of a basic mistrust of
      males, a rejection of tokenism, and an antifamily bias. Some, but by
      no means all, blacks view population programs, especially such
      programs as punitive sterilization as intended genocide. Blacks are,
      in fact, divided and ambivalent on the population/family planning
      issue. The need (and desire, on the part of many black women) for
      improved birth control services conflicts with goals of group power
      and suspicions of the white majority. For all 3 of these minority
      groups, governmental birth control programs raise the specter of the
      dominant social groups--whites, males, and the Establishment. None of
      these groups wants the issue of birth control to divert them from
      issues they consider more basic. Birth control services followed by

birth control information programs are viewed as least controversial.*

248.   Thorpe, C. 1973. Social Status and the Pill at a Black Woman's College. College Student Journal 6 (2): 66-73.

A survey was conducted in 1969 among undergraduate students, (ages 16-26) at Bennett College for women in North Carolina to determine the relationship between socio-economic status and the use of the pill. 143 responses were useable. 17% of the women used the pill and 83% did not. There was no significant effect of parental home influence on pill use. Students whose family incomes were above $7000 were more likely to use the pill than the other students. There was no significant difference between users and nonusers in attitudes towards sex. 72% of the nonusers approved of but did not use the pill, and only 18% used another method of contraception.*

249.   Tobin, P., W. Clifford, R. Mustain, and A. Davis. 1975. Value of Children and Fertility Behavior in a Tri-racial, Rural County. Journal of Comparative Family Studies 6 (Spring): 46-55.

In this study the authors assess the relationship between the values toward children and actual fertility and family size preferences. In this connection they test two hypotheses: (1) the more an individual disregards the costs and problems of rearing a large family and emphasizes the emotional benefits attributed to large families, the more likely he (she) will both desire and have large number of children; and (2) that men and women assess the worth of children differently. In addition, the study examines the effect of subcultural influences on the value of children. The analysis is based on a sample of 526 currently married women aged 18 to 49, and their husbands, residing in Robenson County, North Carolina, during the summer 1972. The populatiton of this county is basically tri-racial consisting of 43 percent white, 26 percent black, and 31 percent Indian residents. The researchers employ an area probability sampling technique to ensure proportional representation in the sample of all three races in the County. In connection with fertility behavior, family planning among the three racial groups is also discussed.*

250.   Valien, P., and A. Fitzgerald. 1949. Attitudes of the Negro Mother Toward Birth Control. American Journal of Sociology 55: 279-283.

Of 136 black mothers in Nashville, Tennessee, approximately one-half had unfavorable attitudes toward birth-control practices. Religious or moral reasons and a belief that birth-control practices are insufficient or injurious to health were the chief reasons given. Age, number of children, urban or rural birthplace, and amount of education appear to be associated with differential attitudes toward birth control.*

251.   Valien, Preston, and Ruth E. Vaughan. 1951. Birth Control Attitudes and Practices of Negro Mothers. Sociology and Social Research 35 (6):

415-421.

This is a small study on birth control attitudes and practices of urban blacks. It concentrates on variables such as rural or urban birthplace, level of education, employment of the mother outside the home, source of information regarding contraception, and length of residence in the city of interview. The data is based on a random interview of 100 black mothers under age 40 living in one of the five census tracts of Nashville inhabited predominantly by blacks. The major findings of this study are: (1) three fifth of the mothers had favorable attitudes toward birth control; (2) one fifth of the mothers reported practicing birth control; (3) fifty percent of those who opposed birth control gave religious reasons; (4) the percentage of urban-born mothers practicing birth control was found to be more than twice the percentage of rural-born mothers; (5) education beyond high school was found to have significant effect on attitudes and practice of birth control; (6) working mothers exhibited more favorable attitudes than non-working mothers; (7) almost all those who had reported practicing birth control had received their information from physicians; and, (8) seventeen out of the eighteen mothers who were practicing birth control had lived in Nashville 10 years or longer.*

252. Varky, George, and C.R. Dean. 1970. Planned Parenthood Patients: Black and White. Family Planning Perspectives 2 (1): 34-37.

A study made of two samples of Planned Parenthood Affiliates showed that the proportion of non-white new patients served by Planned Parenthood nationwide from 1966 to 1968 was about the same as that of non-whites among all medically indigent women in need of family planning in the communities which these Affiliates served. Non-whites appeared to be slightly over-represented in those Affiliates located in the North Central census region, and somewhat under-represented in the large city Affiliates of the Western Region. While there was some indication that nonwhites tended to be over-represented among the patients of Affiliates in smaller cities and towns, this finding should be viewed with some caution in light of the imprecision of the data base for these communities. Nationally the proportion of non-whites among Planned Parenthood patients, poor and non-poor, declined between 1966 and 1968.*

253. Weisbord, R.G. 1973. Birth Control and the Black American: A Matter of Genocide? Demography 10 (4): 571-590.

During the 1960's and continuing into the 1970's the charge that birth control and abortion are integral elements of a white genocidal conspiracy directed against Afro-Americans has been heard with increasing frequency and stridency in black communities. The genocide theory finds greatest acceptance among spokesmen for black nationalist and black revolutionary groups, but suspicion of family planning programs is not limited to them. An analysis of black leadership opinion on birth control is provided in this paper. The black debate

over the desirability of population limitation is traced back
approximately fifty years. It began with a dispute between those
blacks who believed that in sheer numbers there was strength and
those blacks, such as W.E.B. DuBois, who argued that among human
races, as among vegetables, quality and not quantity counted. An
appreciation of the sexual exploitation of the chattel slave in the
ante-bellum period, which did not end with emancipation, is also
essential to an understanding of the roots and rationale of the
genocide notion which are the foci of this paper.*

254.   Weisbord, R.G. 1975. Blacks on the Distaff Side. In: Genocide? Birth
Control and the Black American. Westport, Ct.: Greenwood Press. Pp
110-123.

Women's liberation is basically a white, middle-class movement. There
has been some question among black women as to the relationship
between the women's liberation movement and the black movement. There
is no necessary conflict between feminism and racial justice. Black
women have more burdens to bear than white women. Black female
leaders have recognized that family planning and legal abortion can
ease these burdens. The poor, especially minorities, were the main
victims of restrictive abortion legislation. Legalized abortion has
reduced the economic burdens of black families, the illegitimacy rate
among blacks, and health hazards associated with illegal abortion.*

255.   Weisbord, R.G. 1975. Reservations Among the Most Reasonable.
In: Genocide? Birth Control and the Black American, by R.G. Weisbord.
Westport, Connecticut: Greenwood Press. Pp. 124-136.

Many respectable black organizations, especially the biracial,
middle-class, prointegrationist ones, support the practice of family
planning among black people. They point out that excessive numbers of
children are particularly disadvantageous to poor people, of which
group blacks make up a large proportion. Respected black leaders have
spoken out for the low-cost provision of family planning services to
the black community. Other equally reasonable black leaders and
organizations fear that family planning would become compulsory and
amount to black genocide.☆

256.   Westoff, C.F., and N.B. Ryder. 1970. Contraceptive Practice Among
Urban Blacks in the United States, 1965. Milbank Memorial Fund
Quarterly 48 (2, Part 2): 215-233.

Based on extensive data from the first National Fertility Study, a
report of the practice of contraception and success of fertility
planning among urban blacks in the U.S. in 1965 is presented. For
comparative purposes, data are included for blacks and whites in 4
residential categories: large cities, suburbs, smaller cities and
rural areas. Indices of contraceptive practice included whether contraception was ever used, the proportion of couples at risk of conception who were currently not using contraception, types of current

exposure of risk of conception, contraceptive method most recently used, and extent of use of newer methods. Infuences of education, region and income were considered. Blacks and whites in large cities had used contraception to these extent; but in totality, the proportion of black couples using no contraceptive was greater for all age groups and communities. Urban blacks had a lower incidence of subfecundity and were less likely to be fecund contraceptive nonusers than other blacks. The pill was the most popular method used for almost every race-residence category. Amount of knowledge of the ovulatory cycle was found dependent on level of education; 1/4 of urban blacks compared to 1/2 of urban whites were correctly informed. Blacks were found less successful than whites in preventing excess fertility. ☆

257.   Williams, Barbara A. 1973. **Family Planning and the Black Perspective.** Essence 4 (September): 18.

In this brief article Williams presents the view that with the rise of black consciousness comes the cry for better education and the shout of "power to the people". But how can black people have more power if they are unable to adequatly feed, clothe, and shelter their children? Or, how can they ask for better education for their young, if there are so many in the family that individual parental attention is impossible? Williams concludes that birth control, like preventive medicine, will help black people to control their destiny. ★

258.   Wolfe, S.R., and E.L. Ferguson. 1973. **The Physician's Influence on the Nonacceptance of Birth Control.** In: Readings in Family Planning: A Challenge to the Health Professions. D. V. McCalister, V. Thiessen, and M. McDermott (eds.). St. Louis, Missouri: Mosby. Pp. 226-230.

Observations on unconscious factors influencing the interaction between physician and patient were made in the Prenatal Clinic of a large metropolitan hospital, with frequent "spot" interviews of the same patients. A series of 12 intensive interviews were tape-recorded and analyzed. Records and follow-ups of over 300 clinical psychiatric interviews with clinic patients were studied. The patients were mainly poor black women from the Baltimore inner city area. The analysis of the observed and recorded data revealed 6 repetitive patterns: 1) overenthusiastic and authoritative behavior makes patients suspicious; 2) patients feel that the physicians are not interested in them personally when broad social problems are stressed; 3) physicians wait for patients to raise questions on birth control but patients do not out of embarrassment or fear; 4) although condoms may be the optimal method of contraceptive for some patients, phsyicians concentrate on sophisticated methods; 5) patients who were treated for gonorrhea in adolescence beleived themselves sterile because of comments by physician at that time; and 6) genital injury at an early age, especially if bleeding occurred, left patients thinking they were sterile. Physicians need to anticipate the fears, superstitions and preconceptions of this population which may keep the patient from utilizing a contraceptive method.☆

259. Wright, N.H. 1970. Vital Statistic and Census Tract Data Used to
      Evaluate Family Planning. Public Health Reports 85 (5): 383-389.

      In an estimated total eligible population of 50,000 disadvantaged
      women, most nonwhite, living in Fulton and Dekalb Counties, Georgia,
      12,000 to 15,000 were new contraceptive patients in a postpartum
      clinic at Grady Memorial Hospital in the Emory University Family
      Planning Program from September 1962 to the end of 1966. Attempts to
      determine whether the Program influenced the birth rate, especially
      among nonwhites (90% of the new clients), were made using vital
      statistics and census tract data. For Fulton County, which included
      80-95% of the eligible population, crude birth rates for white and
      nonwhite declined yearly at an average 2.8% and 3.9%, repectively,
      for 1960-1967. The greatest yearly declines were in 1965-1967. Oral
      contraceptives and the IUD were introduced in the Program in mid-1963
      and late 1964, respectively. The decline of the white birth rate is
      due in part to the aging of the white population of Fulton County
      resulting mainly from the exodus of its younger members to suburban
      counties. Since among nonwhites both emigration from Atlanta to the
      north and immigration to the Atlanta area from rural southern areas
      occurred, it is unlikely that the age composition of the nonwhite
      population changed significantly. The IUD seems to have been a
      particularly important means of nonwhite contraception. Some problems
      were found in using intercensal population data for relatively small
      areas.☆

260. Wright, Gerald C., Jr. 1977. Racism and the Availability of Family
      Planning Services in the United States. Social Forces 56 (4): 1087-
      1098.

      Previous research (Kammeyer et al.) has found that the availability
      of family planning services in U.S. counties is positively related to
      precent black in the population, but has not established the correct
      interpretation for this linkage. Two competing explanations of this
      relationship are developed and tested in the present study. A racism
      interpretation is found to best explain county provided family plan-
      ning services, and little support is found for an altruistic inter-
      pretation. Services provided by Planned Parenthood and O.E.O. are
      mainly due to urbanism and are not consistent with either the racial
      or the altruistic interpretation.*

261. Zelnick, M., and J.F. Kantner. 1972. Sexuality, Contraception and
      Pregnancy Among Young Unwed Females in the United States. In:
      Demographic and Social Aspects of Population Growth and the American
      Future, Research Reports, Volume 1. Charles F. Westoff and Robert
      Parke, Jr. (eds.). Washington, D.C.: Government Printing Office. Pp.
      359-374.

      Some of the salient features of the sexual knowledge and behavior of unwed young women between the ages 15 to 19 are described. Results of the study indicate that sexuality increases with age in this group. On the average, blacks have intercourse sooner than whites, and proportionately more of them have intercourse. Most of the sexually active girls did not have intercourse in the month preceding the survey and most had had intercourse with only 1 partner. Whites are somewhat better informed about the menstrual cycle than blacks and become better informed as they become older or more sexually experienced. The principal reason given for not using contraception is the belief that pregnancy could not occur. Although the teenagers are reasonably poorly informed regarding the basic facts of life, there is widespread contraception which increases with age. With respect to method last used, blacks favor the condom, Pills, and douche; whereas whites opt for withdrawal, condom and the Pill. Blacks are much more likely to become pregnant than whites. This evidently has something to do with the effectiveness of use and a degree, perhaps, with the somewhat lesser reluctance of blacks to become pregnant. Among the currently pregnant and unmarried, few of either race contemplate either abortion or marriage. Overall, there is evidence of fairly widespread sexuality, pervasive misinformation about the risk of pregnancy, a high degree of unprotected coitus, and a good bit of pregnancy, most of which appears to have been unwanted at least at conception but without recourse to abortion.☆

B. ABORTION

262. Abernathy, James R., B.G. Greenberg, and D.G. Horvitz. 1970. **Estimates of Induced Abortion in Urban North Carolina.** Demography 7 (1): 19-29.

In 1965, Warner developed an interviewing procedure designed to eliminate evasive answer bias when questions of a sensitive nature are asked. He called the procedure "randomized response." The authors have been studying the technique for several years and, in this paper, are reporting some of the estimates of induced abortion in urban North Carolina using randomized response. Estimates of the proportion of women having an abortion during the past year among women 18-44 years of age were 0.0139 for the white population in the sample and 0.0681 for the nonwhite population. Estimates were higher for the never married than the ever married. For the study population indices were developed relating induced abortion to total conceptions for whites and nonwhites. The illegal abortion rate per 100 conceptions was estimated to be 14.9 for whites and 32.9 for nonwhites. Estimates of the proportion of women having an abortion during their lifetime among women 18 years old or over are also shown. Among ever married women, the proportion having an abortion during their lifetime declined as education increased. Estimates were high for women whith 5 or more pregnancies. Most of the respondents stated that they were satisfied that the randomized response approach would not reveal their personal situation. Furthermore, they did not think their

friends would truthfully respond to a **direct** question regarding
abortion. Results from this study clearly indicate that the
randomized response procedure is a worthwhile tool in the hands of
the survey designer.**

263. Acevedo, Z. 1979. Abortion in Early America. Women and Health 4 (2):
      159-167.

Abortion was frequently practiced in North America during the period
from 1600 to 1900. Many tribal societies knew how to induce abortions. They used a variety of methods including the use of black root
and cedar root as abortifacient agents. During the colonial period,
the legality of abortion varied from colony to colony and reflected
the attitude of the European country which controlled the specific
colony. In the British colonies abortions were legal if they were
performed prior to quickening. In the French colonies abortions were
frequently performed despite the fact that they were considered to be
illegal. From 1776 until the mid-1800s abortion was viewed as
socially unacceptable; however, abortions were not illegal in most
states. During the 1860s a number of states passed anti-abortion
laws. Most of these laws were ambiguous and difficult to enforce.
After 1860 stronger anti-abortion laws were passed and these laws
were more vigorously enforced. As a result, many women began to
utilize illegal underground abortion services. Although abortion was
legalized in 1970, many women are still forced to obtain illegal
abortion or to perform self-abortions due to the economic constraints
imposed by the Hyde Amendment and the unavailability of services in
many areas. Throughout the colonial period and during the early years
of the republic, the abortion situation for slave women was different
than for other women. Slaves were subject to the rules of their
owners, and the owners refused to allow their slaves to terminate
pregnancies. The owners wanted their slaves to produce as many
children as possible since these children belonged to the slave
owners. This situation persisted until the end of the slavery era.✩

264. Anonymous. 1972. Use of Abortion by Poor is High. Ob. Gyn. News 7
      (7): 39.

Maryland liberalized the indications for therapeutic abortion in
1968. Since then, the number of abortions performed in the state has
increased yearly. More early abortions were performed in fiscal year
1971. Almost 1/2 of the abortions during the year were for women
under 22 and 1/2 were for unmarried women. Service (nonprivate)
patients accounted for 31% of all hospital abortions. Blacks accounted for 37% of the abortions and 23% of the live births in the
state for the year. Figures indicate an abortion to live birth ratio
of 145/1000 during the year.★

265. Anonymous. 1973. Black Churchmen Oppose Abortion as Genocide. Jet 44
      (July): 44.

Reports on a resolution adopted recently by the Progressive National Baptist Convention deploring abortion as a form of genocide. The convention consisted of some 3,000 black delegates.★

266.   Ashe, Christy. 1970. **Abortion...or Genocide?**. Liberator 10 (8): 4-9.

This essay is not based on any research. It is a journalistic review of anti-abortion issues. More specifically, the author attempts to look at the negative aspects of various statements made by different authorities in the field of abortion.★

267.   Bailey, R.T. 1974. **Arkansas Therapeutic Abortions.** Journal of the Arkansas Medical Society 71 (3): 134-137.

Arkansas Department of Health statistics for legal abortions per-formed in State hospitals during 1973 are summarized. A total of 1138 legal abortions were performed, 89.9% of which were obtained by white women. Unmarried women constituted about 67% of the total, and abor-tions sought by married women increased from 31% to 32.5% during 1971-1973 though the national figure for married women decreased. About 88% of the abortions were performed by Week 12 of gestation and only 2 abortions were performed as late as Weeks 22 and 23. Maternal mental health was the indicated reason for abortion in about 75% of the cases.✩

268.   Binkin, N., J. Gold, and W. Cates, Jr. 1981. **Illegal Abortion Deaths in the United States: Why Are They Still Occurring.** A paper presented at the 109th Annual Meetings of the American Public Health Associ-ation, Los Angeles, California, November 2, 1981. 6 pp.

Overall, the number of abortion deaths in the U.S. has markedly declined during the period 1972-79. The rate of illegal abortion deaths declined from 0.46 (per million women 15-44 years old) during the period 1972-74 to 0.07 in 1975-79. The ratios of illegal abortion deaths per million live births per year were 6.6 for 1972-74 and 1.0 for 1975-79. During 1972-74, the age groups with the highest inci-dence of illegal abortion deaths were the 20-24 (34.9%) and 25-29 (28.6%) age groups; this trend was reversed in 1975-79, when the 15-19, 30-34, and 35+ age groups registered the highest incidence of illegal abortion deaths (23.5% rate for each group compared to 11.8% for the 20-24 age group and 17.6% for the 25-29 age group). During both periods blacks had the highest incidence of death, 68.3% in 1972-74 and 64.7% in 1975-79; Whites had 19.0% deaths in 1972-74 and 17.6% in 1975-79. The demographic characteristics of women who died of illegal abortion in 1975-79 are as follows: 47.1% were married, 35.3% were single; 64.7% had 2 or more previous pregnancies; 41.2% had 2 or more living children; 58.8% did not have previous induced abortions (23.5% had 1, and 17.6% had 2 or more previous induced abortions) 76.5% had abortions in their state (23.5% were from out-of-state); 76.5% were urban residents (23.5% were non-urban), and majority came from the South (52.9%) and Northeast (23.5%) regions of the U.S. During the same period, 35.3% of women who died of illegal deaths were in the 9-12 weeks gestational age; an equal proportion were in the 13+ weeks gestational age. The method of abortion was self-induced in 52.9% and by a non-physician in 41.2%. Septicemia was the major cause of death in 58.8%, followed by air embolus in 17.6% and pulmonary embolus, respiratory arrest, potassium phosphate poisoning, and pennyroyal toxicity in the rest. The primary reasons for seeking illegal abortions were financial, geographic, ignorance, secrecy, ethnic, previous experience, and countercultural.☆

269. Blake, J. 1973. Elective Abortion and Our Reluctant Citizenry: Research on Public Opinion in the United States. In: The Abortion Experience: Psychological and Medical Impact. H.J. Osofsky and J.D. Osofsky (eds.). Hagerstown, Maryland: Harper and Row. Pp. 447-465.

Elective abortion still faces resistance in the American public. American attitudes toward abortion were studied in Gallop polls from 1962-1972. Approval for abortion increased until 1970 but has held constant since then. In 1972, approximately 2/3 of those responding disapproved of abortion. Abortion done for the mother's health had almost unanimous approval. Men disapproved of abortion less than women, non-Catholics less than Catholics. The dividing line was not along religious but along social class lines. College educated people approve abortion much more than do less educated people. Age did not correlate with views on abortion. Neither did race. These findings corroborate 2 National Fertility Studies, done in 1965 and 1970. The findings show much less support for abortion than Planned Parenthood studies have found. Biases in the questions of the Planned Parenthood surveys may account for the difference. It is possible that elective abortion might be supported if it were not linked to demands for radical sociocultural changes.☆

270. Bracken, M.B., and T.R. Holford. 1979. Induced Abortion and Congenital Malformations in Offspring of Subsequent Pregnancies. American Journal of Epidemiology 109 (4): 425-432.

In connecticut, a case-control (n=1427 and 3001, respectively) study was conducted to determine the risk for congenital malformations due to the effects of previous induced abortion. Increased risk of congenital malformations could result from the abortion technique it-self or from procedure complications. Complications due to abortion, although rare, include retention of products of conception, excessive curettage of the basal layers of the endometrium, the development of uterine synechise and Asherman's syndrome, cervical incompetence, abruptio placentae, and placenta previa. Using a standard question-naire, information was obtained concerning demographic characteris-tics, contraceptive practice, smoking, and exposure to risk factors. Black mothers aged 25-29 who delivered a congenitally malformed in-fant were more likely to have previously aborted, overall odds ratio=2.6, 95% confidence limits=1.2, 5.8, and p < .05. This racial difference is possibly due to more frequent histories of illegal and

septic abortions or to other characteristics of these women. The results of the study found no relationship between delivery of a congenitally malformed infant and overall previous experience of induced
abortion (o=.9, 95% CL=.7, 1.1). This indicates that legal abortions
performed under safe clinical conditions impose no increased risk for
subsequent delivery of a malformed infant.☆

271. Cates, Willard, Jr. 1977. **Legal Abortion: Are American Black Women
Healthier Because of It?** Phylon 38 (3); 267-281.

Despite relatively greater disapproval of abortion by black women,
they use legal abortion at approximately twice the rate of their
white counterparts. Moreover, the disproportionate use of legal
abortion by black women has been increasing since the 1973 Supreme
Court decisions made legal abortion available at the local level.
Because legal abortions are safer than either of the other alternatives facing black women with unwanted pregnancies, namely illegal
abortions or term births, they have a positive effect on their
health, as demonstrated through reduced levels of morbidity and
mortality from pregnancy and childbirth. Moreover, legal abortion has
probably contributed to the reduction of unwanted births to married
black women, reducing such births to the same level as that of white
women. For these reasons, it is apparent that black women have shared
in the health benefits accompanying increased availability of legal
abortion within the United States, probably to an even greater extent
than white women.*

272. Charles, Alan, and Susan Alexander. 1971. **Abortion for Poor and
Nonwhite Women: A Denial of Equal Protection?** The Hastings Law
Journal 23 (November): 147-169.

The abortion cases which will be heard by the Supreme Court during
its 1971 Term will consider three issues: whether the old-style laws
limiting abortion to preservation of the woman's life alone are
unconstitutionally vague; whether any categorical restriction on
abortion violate a woman's right to personal, marital, sexual and
family privacy without a compelling state interest; and whether the
strong empirical evidence of discrimination against poor and nonwhite
women in obtaining abortions under such laws is a denial of equal
protection. In the privacy argument, the Court will be asked to
determine that abortion is an expression of these fundamental and
consitutionally protected interests, best articularted in the famous
birth control case Griswold vs. Connecticut. If the Court is willing
to do so, then it must also determine an issue which was not present
in Griswold--whether the state interest in protecting a previable
fetus outweights a woman's rights. The equal protection argument does
not require the Court to go so far. It holds that there is
infringement of a fundamental interest to receive proper and lawful
medical care which is otherwise available to women able to pay and
that the state had no compelling interest which can justify the
denial of such care to poor and nonwhite women. One conclusion to be

drawn is that the equal protection argument is in direct conflict with the due process argument, since the former is not based on asserting a fundamental right to abortion, per se, nor is it based on contending the state has no interest in protecting the fetus. Its strategic usefulness in the cases, however, is as an important backstop to the due process argument. If the Court is unwilling, as it may be to say that there is a due process right to abortion, and/or is unwilling to say that the state has no compelling interest in protecting the previable fetus, that unwillingness would not dispose of the problem of unequal treatment. If successful, the equal protection argument would leave states with the choice of forbidding abortions to all, an unlikely and itself constitutionally questionable alternative, or changing their laws to assure equality of treatment to poor and nonwhite women. Hopefully the later will be the end result.*

273.   Craven, Erma C. 1972. **Abortion, Poverty and Black Genocide: Gifts to the Poor?**. In: Abortion and Social Justice. Thomas W. Higlers, and Dennis J. Horan (eds.) New York: Sheed and Ward. Pp. 231-243.

Poverty and Black genocide are realities in the United States. The introduction of abortion has poignantly brought this into clear perspective. IT MUST NOT BE ALLOWED TO GO FURTHER! If we are truly a nation who speak of civil human rights, then we must prove that we carry no prejudices. The abortion issue, with its gnawing ability to make one honest, may very well be the ultimate test. If we can openly admit our prejudice, then perhaps we can begin to move forward. If we cannot, then we will move one step further down into the valley of death, The blood-and-guts problem is our lack of compassion and our lack of concern. More and more, women are being seen as wombs to be deactivated rather than human beings with lives to be fulfilled. Only when this impoverishment is eliminated can we fully expect to enter the new frontier.*

274.   Ezzard, N.V., W. Cates, Jr., and C. Tietze. 1981. **Race Specific Patterns of Abortion Utilization, United States, 1972-1978.** A paper presented at the 109th Annual Meetings of the American Public Health Association, Los Angeles, California, November 3, 1981.

Estimates of abortion ratios by age at conception and race, and by parity and race, for the U.S. from 1972-78 are presented, and the impact of the increasing availability of legal abortion on race-specific abortion patterns is inferred from the trends. The data was from 3 sources: the distribution of abortions from the Center for Disease Control's (CDC) annual abortion surveillance activities and CDC's multicenter study of abortion morbidity; the number of abortions from the Alan Guttmacher Institute's annual survey of abortion providers; and live births from the National Center for Health Statistics. The abortion ratio was defined as the number of abortions/1000 known pregnancies. Abortion ratios were calculated by the age at conception. To relate births and abortions to the same age at conceptions, births were "deaged" by 9 months and abortions by 3 months. Annual race specific abortions ratios were then calculated for all women, for 6 different age subgroups, and for 5 different birth order subgroups. For each year, the legal abortion ratio for black and other women was higher than the ratios for white women. Between 1972 and 1978 both racial groups had increases in their abortion ratios, but the percentage increase in the ratio for black and other women was 1.5 times that for white women. In 1972 the abortion ratio for black and other teenagers was lower than the ratio for white teenagers but had become higher by 1974, and increased faster through 1976. The greatest race specific differences in the abortion ratios occurred for women between the ages of 25 and 34 and for women with 1 and 2 previous live births. Declines in abortion ratios after 1976 for high parity women of both races may be because of the increased use of tubal sterilization during the 1970's. In sum, following national availability of legal abortion, abortion ratios increased for women of all ages, races, and birth orders. Minority women were more affected by improved access to legal abortion. The data suggest that young nulliparous minority women now use abortion to nearly the same extent as their white counterparts.☆

275. Furstenburg, Frank, Jr. 1972. **Attitudes Toward Abortion Among Young Blacks.** Studies in Family Planning 3 (4): 66-69.

Interviews in 1970 with 300 young black women in Baltimore, Maryland, mostly from low-income families, indicated a low level of acceptance of abortion as a method of family planning. There was an increasing acceptance of abortion as a woman approached or exceeded the family size she desired. 2 different groups were involved: 1/2 the women were young mothers and 1/2 were classmates of the mothers. All had been part of a study begun 4 years earlier, and at that time they shared many background characteristics although a slightly higher percentage of mothers came from broken families and fewer had parents who had completed high school. By 1970, the following differences were noted: all the mothers had at least 1 child, 1/2 had 2, but only 1/3 of the classmates had ever been pregnant; a little more than 1/2 the mothers had been or were married which was the case with only 1/5 of the classmates, but more mothers had broken marriages; fewer mothers had completed high school (42% vs 67%); far fewer attended school (16% vs 46%); and 2/5 of the mothers and 3/5 of the classmates expressed mixed feelings although they generally disapproved of abortion as a means of family limitation. More than 4/5 of those opposed to abortion felt so for moral reasons; the others opposed abortion because of health factors, cost, and illegality. As the mothers reached their desired family size, almost 1/3 said they might have an abortion. The majority of the women strongly favored birth control, which suggests that well-designed contraceptive programs are indispensable in helping these women avoid unwanted pregnancies.☆

276. Gebhard, Paul H., et al. 1976. **The Negro Woman.** In: Pregnancy, Birth

Control and Abortion, by Paul H. Gebhard, et al. Westport, Connecticut: Greenwood Press. Pp. 153-167.

The differences between Negro and white women stem primarily from differences in cultural and socio-economic background. Some of these differences may be the heritage of the peculiar sexual and reproductive behavior associated with slavery. The grade school and high school educated Negro women, for the most part, belong to the lower socio-economic level where social sanctions against pre-marital coitus, pregnancy, and live birth are high in comparison with the white women. Owing to a relative scarcity of induced abortion and to adverse health factors, pre-marital spontaneous abortion is also prevalent among the Negroes. One also finds that the Negro wives have relatively high rates of conception, live birth, and spontaneous abortion. The single college educated Negro woman presents a different reproductive pattern. A recent product of vertical social mobility, she retains vestiges of the lower socio-economic sexual pattern, which accounts for her exceeding the college educated white woman in premarital coital experience and pregnancy. However, she aborts spontaneously and deliberately the same percentage of her pre-marital conceptions as does the white woman, and presumably for the same reasons. The married college educated Negro, often striving for status on a rather adverse social and economic environment, tends as a result to be less fertile than the white wife. Equaling the white wife in percentage of pregnancies ended by induced abortion, the Negro wife has a larger proportion of spontaneous abortions; hence the percentage of her pregnancies resulting in live birth is lower than that for the white woman.*

277.   Glass, Leonard, et al. 1974. Effects of Legalized Abortion on Neonatal Mortality and Obstetrical Morbidity at Harlem Hospital Center. American Journal of Public Health 64: 717-718.

Studies have shown that as a result of the 1970 New York abortion law, leaving the termination of pregnancy at the discretion of patient and her physician prior to the 24th week of gestation, there has been a significant decline in the maternal and neonatal mortality rates, as well as a decline on the number of illegitimate births in New York State. This study examines these effects relative to the patients--mostly blacks--using the Harlem Hospital Center. More specifically, it deals with an examination of the effects of the new abortion law on perinatal, neonatal, and maternal mortality rates as well as maternal morbidity at the Harlem Hospital Center, with a predominantly poor black patients. The Hospital's neonatal and obstetrical data for 1966 through 1971 were analyzed. The major findings of this study were:(1) the in-hospital neonatal mortality rate declined from an average of 33.9/1,000 live births during the 1966-69 period to 18.9/1,000 live births in 1971; (2) the frequency of admissions for incomplete abortions in relation to the annual number of deliveries was found to be significantly lower in 1971 than during the 1966-69 period; (3) from July 1970 through 1971 only two maternal death had occurred--one of these had occurred on a woman with sickle cell anemia who died as a result of complications of her primary illness; (4) the neonatal mortality rates at Harlem Hospital Center which prior to 1970 far exceeded those of both the white and nonwhite population of the United States declined following the legalization of abortion.★

278.   Gold, Edwin M., et al. 1965. Therapeutic Abortions in New York City: A 20-Year Review. American Journal of Public Health 55 (7): 964-972.

This paper deals with trends in therapeutic abortions in New York City during the 1943-1962 period. The data for this study are derived from the routine reporting of fetal deaths to the Department of Health of the City of New York. According to this study although the number of therapeutic abortions has shown a downward trend, the influence of professional and social factors exhibit considerable differentials by race/ethnicity--whites, nonwhites, and Puerto Rican groups. Another finding of this paper is the high rate of abortion deaths among nonwhite and Puerto Rican women. The authors call upon health departments to examine these problems in their jurisdictions and to take the necessary corrective actions. More specifically, they suggest that from the public health point of view, the development of an effective family planning program presents the most practical approach, not only to the population expansion problem, but also to bring about a significant reduction in the puerparal loss (abortion deaths) associated with criminal abortions. Additionally, they suggest that the health department has the obligation to carry on an intensive and continuous program of public health education, especially among the lower socioeconomic groups such as nonwhites and Puerto Ricans.★

279.   Hale, C. B., and S. C. O'Neil. 1979. Southern Black and White Women Who Seek Abortion: A Comparative Analysis. Paper Presented at the 107th Annual Meetings of the American Public Health Association, New York, November 4-9, 1979.

Results of a survey utilizing self-report questionnaires of Alabama women under 21 seeking abortions at a private clinic in Montgomery show that inadequate sexual knowledge and contraceptive behavior are characteristic of younger adolescents, regardless of race. Attitudes toward self and parents were measured by Likert items, as were psychological factors often associated with inadequate contraceptive practice. 236 women completed usable questionnaires; 58.9% were white, 41.1% were black, and the mean age for black and white was 17.9. Results indicate that white women under 19 express negative or ambivalent attitudes toward 1 or both parents more often than do those 19-20. White women under 17 are more likely to express negative or ambivalent feelings toward themselves than either older white adolescents or black women under 17. Analysis of contraceptive and sexual knowledge, attitudes, and practice showed that among those

19-20, whites report significantly more partners than do blacks, and whites at each age are more likely to report frequent intercourse than are blacks. Both black and white women under 17 are less likely to use contraception than are older adolescents.*

280. Hill, J.G. 1972. Birth Control Usage Among Abortion Patients. Journal of the Kansas Medical Society, June 1972. Pp. 293-301.

The 1642 single Caucasian and 167 single Negro patients therapeutically aborted at the Kansas University Medical Center from March 23, 1970, to October 1, 1971, were interviewed on the day of surgery in an effort to offer advice about contraception. Ages of patients varied from 13 to 40 years. Data concerning contraceptive use at the time of conception were obtained. The use of contraceptives by these single patients, at the time of conception, was shown to be less than that of those in a parallel report who had at some time in their lives been married. Those in conditions different from ever-married had not differed among themselves as to use of contraceptives. However, there was a significant difference between the 2 groups (p less than .01). There was also a difference between single Negroes and single Caucasians. The Negroes used contraceptives more often and were more effective in their usage (p less than .001). In Caucasian patients the proportion of those using contraceptive devices increased with age(p less than .001). The number of abortions obtained by single women at different ages was not proportional to the number of females at those ages on the U.S. population (p less than .001). Cultural factors in our society are responsible for most of these findings. More education in sexual matters, especially for young people is needed. *

281. Hill, E. L., and J. W. Eliot. 1972. Black Physicians' Experience With Abortion Requests and Opinion About Abortion Law Change in Michigan. Journal of the National Medical Association 64 (1): 52-58.

66 black physicians were surveyed in the Detroit Medical Society in 1969 on their experiences with abortion in their practices and their attitudes toward abortion laws. The response rate was 34% of the 196 surveys mailed, and it is not clear how representative the sample is in terms of age, background, and type of medical practice. 96% of the respondents favored a liberalization of the Michigan abortion law and 49% favored elimination of abortion from the criminal code entirely. All of the psychiatrists surveyed favored such a move, but only 25% of the obstetricians approved of this change. Approval of the repeal of the abortion law increased with age and the number of patients seeking abortion the physician had had. 59% of the responding physicians had recieved a request for abortion in the 6 months preceding the survey, with a few physicians receiving the large number of requests. The majority of the women seeking these abortions were young (89% under the age of 34), unmarried (61%), and nonindigent (63%). The 37% of the women who were indigent indicate that the idea that poor women do not seek abortion is clearly

inaccurate. 82% of the responding physicians agreed that a more liberal abortion law would benefit black women. A wide range of recommendations were made by the respondents if such a law were passed, includinng careful standards of abortion procedure, liberal means of financing, expanded facilities, and careful attention to the psychological needs of the patients.☆

282. Howell, E. M. 1975. A Study of Reported Therapeutic Abortions in North Carolina. American Journal of Public Health 65 (5): 480-483.

Legislation in 1967 allowed abortions in North Carolina for reasons of mental or physical danger to the mother or child or in cases of rape. In 1971 the Statute was changed to require 2 rather than 3 physicians in agreement, to reduce residency requirements from 4 months to 30 days, and mandatory reporting of all abortions. A study of reported abortions since 1967 is undertaken for time trends, differences, distribution, and complications of patients in 1971 voluntary versus mandatory reporting, and abortion ratio for mandatory reporting period. 4378 abortions were reported for 1971. 70.6% of the women were white; 29.4% nonwhite. The most frequent indication was for psychiatric reasons (90%) and the most frequent procedure was suction curettage. Mean age was 23.6 years; mean gestation was 11.9 weeks. In comparison to national data for 1971, North Carolina had similar age distribution, later performance of abortion in terms of gestational age, and similar distribution of operational procedures.☆

283. Hughes, Blanche R. 1973. **Abortion: Perception and Contemporary Genocide Myth: A Comparative Study Among Low-Income Pregnant Black and Puerto Rican Women.** Unpublished Ph.D. Dissertation. New York University.

In this research, Hughes compares perceptions of abortion, held by low-income black and Puerto Rican women, after the 1970 implementation of the New York State's liberalized abortion law, with the contemporary genocide myth. The sample used consists of 200 applicants to the abortion and prenatal clinics of a selected hospital's out-patient department. Subjects are evenly divided into ethnic-clinic subgroupings: black abortion seekers, Puerto Rican abortion seekers, black prenatals, and Puerto Rican prenatals. The majority of the respondents in the sample are between ages 16 and 25 years. More than 50 percent (50.5%) of the sample are single and 37.5% are married with the remaining separated, widowed, or divorced. About half (49%) of the Puerto Ricans and only 26% of the blacks are married. The study concludes that both ethnic groups are different in how they perceive of abortion for medical-social and religious reasons, but there is no probable difference between their perception of abortion in genocidal terms. Neither ethnic or clinic group, according to this study, perceives abortion as significantly associated with genocide. The male ethnics, appear to pose the greatest threat to the females's interruption of pregnancy. This is because progeny appears to represent a thrust for survival and power for minority males. In discussing the implications of this study, the author asserts that if progeny as a thrust for survival and power has any validity, it is important that human development experts and educators embark upon programs designed to allay minority males genocide fears. The author also suggests that research designed to ferret out causal factors related to the genocidal fears must be undertaken in order to find appropriate means to resolve these fears, for if such fears remain unresolved, it can result in irrational acts of violence.*

284.   Johnson, Robert E. 1973. Legal Abortion: Is it Genocide or Blessing in Disguise? Jet 43 (26, March 22): 12-19.

In this essay Johnson examines a discussion of abortion by a teacher and his class of teenage girls, discusses legalization of abortion in Illinois and other states in the union, and reviews the issue of legal abortion from a disguised genocidal point of view. He points out that while black women, who regard legalized abortion as a "blessing in disguise", took their burdens to the Friendship Medical Center in Chicago and left them there, the black men, who saw legal abortion as white racist genocide, demonstrated in front of the medical facility trying to persuade the black women not to terminate their unwanted pregnancies. The author talks about the director of the above mentioned medical facility as a "lunch hour" abortionist. Himself an anti-abortionist, the author attempts to convince his readers to believe in his views.*

285.   Kramer, M.J. 1975. Legal Abortion Among New York City Residents: An Analysis According to Socioeconomic and Demographic Characteristics. Family Planning Perspectives 7(3): 128-137.

The social, economic, and demographic characteristics associated with abortion procedures are discussed. The sample population consisted of 1.7 million women 15-44 years of age in New York City between September 1970 and August 1971. It was found that women were obtaining legal abortions at a rate equivalent to 1.21 procedures over the reproductive span and that the abortion rate for blacks and Puerto Ricans doubled that for whites. Moreover, legal abortion was utilized most among women from low income areas and among areas where education is low and where only a small percentage of school-age children attend parochial schools. But it was only because blacks were concentrated at the low-income, low-education, low-labor-force-participation end of the spectrum that the neighborhood pattern of abortion rates showed the mentioned trends. The overriding importance of race as a factor in utilization of legal abortion emerges as one of the principal findings of Kramer's study. Prior to liberalization of New York's abortion law, the total fertilitty rate of blacks was 2.85, as compared to 2.15 for whites. In the course of just 1 month, Kramer finds that the rate of blacks fell to 2.11, the replacement level, while white fertility declined much more modestly to 1.84. From this evidence it is concluded that by enabling blacks to avert what must have been a significant number of unwanted births, and thereby to reproduce at a rate more compatible with the well-being of the family unit, abortion legalization may rank as one of the great social equalizers of its time.★

286. Lamman, J.T., S.G. Kohl, and J.H. Bedell. 1973. **Reduced Delivery Rates of Immature and Premature Infants Following Liberalization of New York State Abortion Law.** Pediatric Research 7 (4): 289.

Liberalization of the New York State abortion law was followed closely by a significant decrease in the rate of immature and premature deliveries at Kings County Hospital Downstate Medical Center, serving a predominantly black population. A similar finding among 6 white hospitals was absent. After the first 6 months following passage of the law, numbers of children placed for adoption also declined. ☆

287. Leavy, Zad, and Jerome M. Kummer. 1966. **Abortion and the Population Crisis: Therapeutic Abortion and the Law: Some New Approaches.** Ohio State Law Journal 27 (4): 647-678.

Induced abortion is one of the most popular, if not the most widely used, single means of personal population control in the United States and throughout the world today. In the United States, however, criminal sanctions against performing abortions have resulted in many pregnancies being terminated under septic conditions by unskilled persons. The authors contend that our abortion laws are badly in need of reform in order to bring them into conformity with accepted medical practice, and to permit termination of pregnancy for medical and humanitarian reason by qualified physicians. Notwithstanding the religious opposition to efforts of the medical profession and the public toward social progress, the law of therapeutic abortion is on the threshold of change, either by legislative enactment or court decisions.*

288. McCormick, P. 1973. **Attitudes Toward Abortion Among Women Undergoing Legally Induced Abortions.** Paper Presented at the Annual Meetings of the Population Association of America, New Orelans, Louisiana, April 1973. (Transnational Family Research Institute Working Paper No. 5). 25 pp.

200 women who had applied for legal abortions were interviewed to determine the extent to which they perceived abortion as an alternative rather than as a supplement to contraception. The influences of race, contraceptive use, religion, social class, and marital and procreational history upon abortion attitudes were also examined. All the women were undergoing abortion for psychiatric reasons. Most were from the middle and lower middle classes, and they were about equally divided between blacks and whites. 95% were undergoing abortion for

the first time, and 81% had used contraception at some point but most had not used it prior to their present pregnancy. 4 major conclusions were derived from the research. 1) Most women who undergo legally induced abortions accept the use of abortion as a supplementary means of regulating fertility, but only a minority consider it acceptable as an alternative means of contraception. 2) There is a substantial racial differential in attitudes toward abortion, with black women being less favorably inclined to use abortion either as a supplement or alternative to contraception. This difference persisted throughout controls for contraceptive use, religion, education of respondent and her mother, economic and marital status, future child desired, and number of siblings. Only when education of respondent's father and parity were introduced did the black women respond more favorably than whites. 3) Aborting women who have used contraceptives in the past are more favorably inclined toward abortion than women who have never used them. 4) The most important underlying theoretical variable responsible for the intercorrelations seems to be the "racial-religious-family matrix" factor. These variables seem to suggest that the greater opposition to abortion among black women may be attributable to their experiences growing up in a large, religiously oriented family which fostered their attitudes toward religion, family, and procreation. Among the suggested avenues for further research is the exploration of these psychosocial influences.☆

289. McCormick, E.P. 1975. Attitudes Toward Abortion: Experiences of Selected Black and White Women. Lexington, Massachusetts: D.C. Heath. 159 pp.

An attempt is amde to ascertain attitudes toward the use of abortion as an alternative or supplement to contraceptives use. 200 women about to undergo an induced abortion in the summer of 1971 in the Washngton, D.C and Baltomire, Maryland, area were interviewed. 82 people were from an abortion clinic, 18 from a private physician, and 100 from the clinic of a municipally controlled hospital. 51% were white; 49% black. The influences of race, contraceptive use, religion, social class, and marital and procreational history upon attitudes toward abortion are examined. Race was used as a control variable. Data were analyzed by cross-tabulation, correlation matrices, and factor analysis. 4 major conclusions were derived from the study: 1) most women who undergo legally induced abortions accept it as a supplementary means of regulating fertility; only a few regard it as an acceptable alternative to contraception; 2) a substantial differential exists in racial attitudes toward abortiton, with black women being less receptive to it for any reason; 3) aborting women who have used contraceptives sometime in the past are more likely to be favorable toward abortion than those who have never used contraceptives; and 4) the most important underlying theoretical variable seemingly responsible for the above is the "racial-religious-family maxtrix" factor. This attributes greater opposition to abortion among blacks to their experience of growing up in a large, religiously oriented family environment that fostered the development of their own religiousness and attitudes toward family and procreation.☆

290. Miller, J. 1973. The Social Determinants of Women's Attitudes Toward Abortion: 1970 Analysis. University of Wisconsin (Mimeo). 28 pp.

The determinants of women's attitudes toward abortion were examined. 3 populations were considered: blacks, white non-Catholics, and white Catholics. It was determined through the analysis 1) that the specific stage and circumstances of women's life experiences do not influence their attitudes on justifications for abortion, and 2) that there is variation in the predictive accuracy of the remaining independent variables among the 3 populations. The effects of educational attainment, total family income, political ideology, and total intended family size interact with race and religion. The white Catholic position on abortion is dominated by religious obligation, but the religiosity also indirectly influences ideas on the ideal family size norms and intended number of children. Although the emotional aspect of these norms is also evident in the white non-Catholic females, they do tend toward a more rational social evaluation. The important determinants for white non-Catholics are the percieved sex role, including social opportunities and responsibilities, and socioeconomic status. Black attitudes toward abortion are only very slightly influenced by religion but are influenced greatly by background characteristics. The analysis suggests that as the social environment changes and new social and psychological needs develop, there will be changes in the social norms prescribing acceptable conditions for abortion.☆

291. Oppel, W., and S. Wolf. 1973. Liberalized Abortion and Birth Rate Changes in Baltimore. American Journal of Public Health 63 (5): 405-408.

To investigate the effect of liberalized abortion laws, all recorded abortions and births in Baltimore City from July 1, 1970 to December 31, 1970, were compared with births from July 1, 1968 to December 31, 1968. Both black and white in-wedlock observed births were lower than expected 1970 births, but the out-of-wedlock births were higher. Both black and white in-wedlock abortion rates showed similar patterns. Out-of-wedlock abortions, which had been rising steadily for the past few decades continued to rise. The differences observed could not be attributed only to a liberalized abortion policy. There is no record of the number of illegal abortions performed in 1968, and the study did not measure changes in birth rate which might have been attributable to differences in family planning practices caused by adverse publicity about the pill. Although abortions have increased since liberalization of the law, there may still be limited access to abortion.★

292. Pakter, J., and F. Nelson. 1971. Abortion in New York City: The First Nine Months. Family Planning Perspectives 3 (3): 5-12.

An analysis of New York City's experience in providing approximately 47,000 abortions in the first 9 months (July 1, 1970-March 31, 1971) after the state's liberalized abortion law went into effect shows that safe prompt terminations of pregnancy can be performed upon women of all socioeconomic groups. The morbidity rate was 5.7% for abortions under 12 weeks and 28% for those over 12 weeks. Hospital admissions for septic abortions and illegitimate births decreased to the lowest point since such data have been recorded. The data indicate that women have sought and obtained abortions earlier in pregnancy and abortion mortality rates have markedly decreased. Legal abortions should help reduce the incidence of infant mortality by reducing the number of high-risk pregnancies, encouraging birth spacing, and averting unwanted births.☆

293. Redford, Myron H., and Edgar K. Marcuse. 1973. **Legal Abortions in Washington State: An Analysis of the First Year Experience.** Seattle, Washington: Battelle Human Affairs Research Center, Population Study Center.

This is largely an analysis of the 1971 abortions performed in Washington State. According to this report women of different ages, social, ethnic/racial and religious affiliations obtained legal abortion in Washington State in 1971. The age of the abortion patients ranged between 13 and 51 years, but the majority were under 24 years of age; the majority had never married. According to the statistics for the first six months of 1971, blacks and orientals had significantly more abortions per 1,000 live birth than Caucasians (268 abortions per 1,000 births for blacks; 244 abortions for orientals, and, 167 abortions per 1,000 live births for Caucasians and Spanish Americans combined). This is despite the fact that National Fertility Surveys show that blacks use contraception less frequently than Caucasians. As a result the investigator did not expect the higher abortion rate for blacks in Washington State, especially because the black areas of Seattle voted against Referendum 20 (a measure to reform Washington's abortion law, passed on November 3, 1970, with a 56.5% majority vote, the first time in the continuing controversy over abortion that the people were able to decide directly the abortion issue). The irony is that blacks voted against abortion law, but once the law passed, they appeared to be the major beneficiaries. One of the major findings of this report is that women of varying parity, marital status, religious and ethnic/racial backgrounds obtained abortions. Use of contraception was very limited. Therefore, factors other than contraceptive failure were believed to be responsible for demand for abortions. ★

294. Roghmann, Klaus J. 1975. **The Impact of the New York State Abortion Law on Black and White Fertility in Upstate New York.** International Journal of Epidemiology 4 (1): 45-49.

The availability of abortions on demand, as provided by the new New York State abortion law, had a profound effect on fertility in a

large community with previously very restricted access to illegal
abortions. Improved family planning and the availability of abortions
as a backup measure combined with a preference for a smaller family
size led to a one-third reduction of live births in the short period
since the new law became effective. Planning for paediatric and
obstetric care had to be adjusted accordingly. The frequently hypothesized or reported secondary effects on illegitimacy or infant
mortality could not be observed. The trend towards increasing illegitimacy was slowed down, but not reversed. Infant mortality continued
its short-term erratic pattern; the trend towards a high proportion
of teenage pregnancies cancelled the effect that pregnancies at high
risk for infant death are also at higher risk for abortion.*

295. Rosen, R.H., J.W. Ager, and L.J. Martindale. 1979. Contraception,
Abortion and Self Concept. Journal of Population 2 (2): 118-139.

This paper deals with the relationship between preconception and
postconception decision making among women who have unwanted
conceptions, and with 2 dimensions of self concept as a factor in
decision making patterns: perceived competence and female role
orientation. This study was done throughout Michigan in 1974-75. The
sample was 1746 women with unwanted conception, selected by means of
a two stage, stratified sampling design. A standardized questionnaire
included items on demographics, background of pregnancy, relationship
with partner, pregnancy resolution and birth control use, as well as
a feminism scale and a scale to measure perceived competence. Several
multiple regressions analyses were carried out. A hypothesis that
prior use of contraception would be positively related to choice of
abortion was strongly supported. A hypothesis that choice of abortion
would be negatively associated with traditional attitudes toward the
female role also was supported, but a hypothesis that choice of
abortion would be positively associated with perceived competence was
not borne out. Other important predictors of pregnancy resolution
decisions among various subgroups of differing age, race, and marital
status were mother's influence and partner's influence.*

296. Rosenwaike, Ira, and Robert J. Melton. 1974. Abortion and Fertility
in Maryland, 1960-1971. Demography 11 (3): 377-395.

In the brief period between 1967 and 1971 about one-third of the
state legislatures passed abortion reform bills, and in states such
as Maryland the number of legal abortions soared. Maryland with its
good demographic representativeness, appears to offer an ideal "test
situation" for assessing the impact of fertility of the new
liberalization. Data on live births and reported induced abortions to
residents of the state have been compiled and analyzed in an effort
to interpret the recent changes in birth rates. Variables examined
include maternal age, birth order, race, and legitimacy. Since 1968,
Maryland, along with higher than national average abortions ratios,
has experienced a rate of decline in fertility greater than that for
the nation....Nonwhites, with relatively high abortion usage, did not

have a greater change in fertility than whites. In addition, most of the age and parity groups with high abortion ratios show fertility declines greater than those for groups not using abortion as extensively. Nevertheless, because a number of different factors simultaneously influence fertility, it is hazardous to make accurate cause-and-effect statements on the relationship of any single one of these to the observed change.*

297.   Sarvis, Betty, and Hyman Rodman. 1974. Social and Cultural Aspects of Abortion: Class and Race. In: The Abortion Controversy, by Betty Sarvis and Hyman Rodman. New York and London: Columbia University Press. Pp. 153-172.

A study on the effects of socioeconomic status (income, education and employment), race (Whites, African Race (Puerto Ricans and Blacks)) and smoking on weight-definend (< or = 2500 grams) and gestational prematurity (< or = 37 weeks) using data on 45,000 live single births from the Collaborative Perinatal Project of the National Institute of Neurological and Communicative Disorders and Strokes (NINCDS) showed a higher prevalence of prematurity among neonates of African ancestry as compared with White neonates, at each income and occupational level, parity-corrected or not, smoking or not. The incidence of prematurity decreased as the level of mother's education increased, suggesting that higher educated women have greater nutritional knowledge, greater interest in health care, and better prepregnancy status than mothers with lesser education. However, the effects of socioeconomic correlates are debatable, since issues can be raised regarding income groupings and educational groupings, or levels at special risk. Although infants of African ancestry tended to be smaller at birth and to be premature more often than White infants, they were, on the other hand, more advanced in postnatal ossification development (Garn and Clark). From a national policy point of view, improving the educational and occupational correlates of socio-economic status and defining race specific standards will provide action programs a headstart in reducing the prevalence of prematurity.☆

298.   Shelton, J. 1975. Induced Abortion: Georgia. Paper Presented at the 24th Annual Epidemic Intelligence Service Conference, Center for Disease Control, Atlanta, Georgia, April 21-25, 1975. 15 pp.

Induced abortion in Georgia in 1973 is discussed. Following the U.S. Supreme Court decision of January 1973, the number of abortions increased drastically (p < .001). In 1972 there was approximately 1 abortion for every 7 live births. By 1973, there was virtually no difference in the abortion to live birth ratio. The accessibility to abortions was increased markedly as evidenced by women no longer leaving the state to get abortions, women outside the state coming to the state to receive abortions, and the rural women getting a more equitable share of their abortions. Rural women still have limited access to abortions, particularly rural black women. The data indicate that illegal abortion deaths have been prevented in Georgia by the legalization of abortion.☆

299. Stevenson, C.S., and C.C. Yang. 1962. Septic Abortion with Shock. Obstetrics and Gynecology 83 (9): 1229-1239.

A notable increase in the incidence of infected abortion at a Detroit hospital is reported, emphasizing its relationship to increased criminal abortion and its increased morbidity and mortality due to development of antibiotic-resistant strains of pathogenic bacteria responsible for the pelvic inflammatory disease (PID). Because of this new resistance trend, this paper advocates more aggressive treatment of PID. The increased incidence of PID and infected abortion is also related to a 3-fold increase in the Black population of Detroit in the past 10 years and also to an apparently decreased incidence of sterility among men and women in the medically indigent group (perhaps a result of decreased incidence of gonorrhea). Morbidity among patients with septic abortion admitted to the Detroit Receiving Hospital is more than 3 times as high as the 20-25% usually reported for a series of cases of abortion in 1 hospital. During the past 2 years, 662 cases of infected abortion were seen and treated, and during that time, there were 12 with shock (primarily septic). Of these 12 cases, all were incomplete abortions; all were aged 17-25 years, and all were Blacks, except for 1 Mexican. For all, massive antibiotic therapy was instituted immediately. Since the shock was due to sepsis rather than blood loss, the danger of overtransfusion was reiterated. And it was pointed out that cardiac decompensation is a greater danger than might be expected because such sepsis also confers actual instability of the patient's apparatus for maintaining blood pressure. Dilation of the cervix and evacuation of the uterus should be performed after 24 hours of antibiotic therapy in all cases, unless specifically contraindicated. ☆

300. Swartz, D.P. 1973. The Harlem Hospital Center Experience. In: The Abortion Experience: Psychological and Medical Impact. H.J. Osofsky and J.D. Osofsky (eds.). Hagerstown, Maryland: Harper and Row. Pp. 94-121.

The director of the Harlem Hospital Center describes the establishment of patient-requested abortion services at his hospital when the new liberal New York abortion law went into effect July 1, 1970. It was determined at the outset that abortion was to be regarded as a legitimate health care procedure and as such should be part of the department of obstetrics and gynecology and not a separate unit. Nevertheless, there were severe problems in understaffing and rather extensive psychological and functional "blocking" on the part of much of the staff when dealing with abortion patients. A routing system was devised for walk-in patients to expedite services. A maximum of 5 patients of 10 weeks or less gestation were managed in an "ambulatory" manner. The patients checked in at 8 a.m. and were generally able to return home in the late afternoon or evening. patients with pregnancies of 11 to 12 weeks' duration were admitted to the hospital the evening before the procedure was done and could return home later on the day of the operation. Abortions were not done between 13 and 15 weeks unless they were combined with abdominal sterilizing operations. After 16 weeks, abortions were done by saline instillation. If this failed, the patient was discharged and readmitted a week later. Complications were recorded in 8.7% of vacuum pregnancy termination cases and 26.5% of saline instillation patients during a 10-month period studied in depth. There were 6 established uterine perforations--only 1 of which required a hysterectomy--and 1 mortality. The woman who died had a history of severe hemolytic crises due to sickle cell disease. Since the program was begun, there has been a reduction in the number of patients admitted with incomplete abortions and an abrupt decline in neonatal mortality, which was probably related to nonmedical community abortion practices. The strong, hospital-provided contraceptive services have increased since the abortion program began, much to the surprise of many staff workers. *

301.   Tietze, C. 1977. **Legal Abortions in the United States: Rates and Ratios by Race and Age, 1972-1974.** Family Planning Perspectives 9 (1): 12-15.

Legal abortion was more widely utilized as a method of fertility control by nonwhite (mainly blacks) women in the United States in the 1972-74 period. The abortion rate per 1,000 women 15-44 was 2.2 times higher and the abortion ratio, owing to the higher birth rate of the nonwhite population, was 1.5 times higher in 1972-1974. The higher abortion rates and ratios among nonwhites were certainly associated with less effctive use of contraception leading to more unwanted or mistimed pregnancies; but this observation cannot explain to what extent less effective use reflected attitudinal differences concerning contraception among blacks, and to what extent contraceptive services were less available or accessible to members of minority groups. The age pattern of abortion ratios by race suggests that legal abortion was less acceptable, available or accessable to black teenagers and to older black women than to blacks in the prime repoductive ages. If the pattern of age-specific abortion ratios had been the same among nonwhite women as it was among white women, with the abortion ratio at age 25-29 and all age-specific pregnancy rates remained the same, the number of legal abortions among nonwhites would have been 60 percent higher than it actually was during the 1972-1974 period. Conversely, if nonwhite women had been as successful as white women in preventing unwanted or mistimed pregnancies, without any change in the numbers of wanted or accepted pregnancies, a much smaller number of abortions among nonwhite women would have been required than was actually obtained.*

302.   Treadwell, Mary. 1972. **Is Abortion Black Genocide?.** Family Planning Perspectives 4 (1): 4-5.

This is a plea by Treadwell for the repeal of all restrictive abortion laws, as well as for fertility control in general. Mary Treadwell, a black activist leader and the then Executive Director of Pride, Inc., a self-help agency in Washington, D.C. providing rehabilitation services and job training for disadvantaged blacks, issued a statement on October 14, 1972 in connection with an abortion law repeal demonstration sponsored by the Women's National Abortion Action Coalition. The article consists of excerpts from that statement. The gist of the article is that the decision to get an abortion must be made by the woman (who has the right to control her own body) and her physician.*

303. U.S. Center for Disease Control, Family Planning Evaluation Division. 1974. **Abortion Surveillance.** Atlanta, Georgia: Center for Disease Control, Family Planning Evaluation Division. 35 pp.

In 1969 the Center for Disease Control (CDC) began to collect data on legal abortions. During 1969-1972, 17 states adopted more liberal abortion laws, the number of states reporting to the CDC increased from 10 to 28, the annual number of reported legal abortions increased from 22,000 to 586,000 and the number of legal abortions/1000 live births increased from 6.3 to 180.1. Analysis of the reported legal abortions for 1972 revealed 1/3 of the abortions were preformed on women less than 20 years of age, and 30.8% of the abortions were preformed on married women. The number of abortions/1000 live births was generally higher for women with no children or with 3 or more children. The number of legal abortions/1000 live births for white was 161 and 225 for blacks. 84.1% of the abortions were performed by suction or sharp curettage and 79.1% were obtained during the 1st trimester. For those states for which information was available, 93.0% of the reported abortions were performed for mental health reasons. The number of deaths/100,000 legal abortions was 3.2. Abstracts of 6 abortion studies were also included. One study reported higher complication rates for super coil abortion procedures compared for saline amniotic fluid exchange abortions. 2 studies demonstrated the importance of Rh-immune globulin utilization. The 4th study reported that the death rate was 6.5/100,000 abortions in New York from July 1970 to July 1971. The risk of death associated with saline amniotic fluid exchange abortions was 7-9 times greater and the risk associated with hysterectomy was 100 times greater than the risk associated with suction or sharp curettage. The 5th study described 2 cases of maternal death attributed to the use of para-cervical block during suction curettage. In the 6th study an effort was made to ascertain the optimal time to remove retained placenta, a problem frequently encountered in saline amniotic fluid exchange. Findings indicated the placenta should be removed during the 1st hour following delivery of the fetus. Tables describing 1972 for selected states include 1) number of abortions, live births and abortions/1000 live births; 2) age distribution of aborters; 3) age-specific abortion ratios; 4) abortion ratios by race; 5) % of total abortions performed on married women; and 6) abortion to live birth ratios by

number of previous births. Additional tables, presenting 1972 data
for selected states, show the number and % of abortion 1) by race; 2)
by marital status; 3) by family size; 4) by type of procedure; 5) by
gestation duration; 6) by reason for abortion; and 7) performed on
out of state residents. Other tables present data on 1) abortion
reporting statistic; 2) % increases in abortions for 1969-1972 for
selected states; 3) number and % of abortions performed in state and
out of state on the residents of each of the 50 states for 1972; and
4) annual % of total abortions performed prior to the 13th gestation
week for selected states for 1970-1972.☆

304.   Vincent, C.E., et. al. 1970. **Abortion Attitudes of Poverty-level
Blacks.** Seminars in Psychiatry 2 (3): 309-317.

The preliminary examination of frequency distributions of the attitudes about abortion expressed by a sample of 776 poverty level
(PL) and 215 lower middle income (LMI) black females, ages 15 to 39,
revealed no association of their attitudes with age, parity, marital
status, and "miscarriages" (spontaneous and induced). Much higher
proportions (80-87 per cent) of these two groups of black females, as
well as of 500 of their husbands and/or current sexual partners, were
found to be opposed to abortion than has been found for predominantly
white respondents (20-35 per cent). The positive and consistent association between education and favorable attitudes about abortion,
which we found for both groups of black females and for the black
males, is consistent with similar findings by others for whites. The
trend of our findings that favorable attitudes of blacks about abortion were positively related to church membership and to frequency of
church attendance was in the opposite direction from previous
findings for whites. Rossi, for example, found that for whites frequent church attendance was strongly associated with conservative
views on abortion. However, our findings are consistent with those of
Reiss who found higher frequency of church attendance for blacks (but
not for whites) to be associated with permissive premarital sexual
attitudes. The unexpected proportion of blacks in our study who expressed highly conservative views on abortion is contrary to the
general consensus of the existing literature that Blacks' sexual
behavior and attitudes are more permissive than those of whites.
Whether these more conservative views are limited to abortion, or are
also present in regards to other sexually-related behavior for our
study groups will be explored in subsequent analyses of the data.
Further exploration of the initial finding of a directional trend
between increased frequency of church attendance and more liberal attitudes about abortion may reveal this seemingly contrary trend to be
related to the educational level of frequent church attenders. The
preliminary stage of our data analysis at this time, however, has
precluded other than descriptive reporting of the results of initial
data runs and frequency distributions on selected items.*

305.   Westoff, Charles F., and Norman B. Ryder. 1969. **The Structure of
Attitudes Toward Abortion.** Milbank Memorial Fund Quarterly 47 (1,

Part 1): 11-37.

In view of the recent surge of interest and legislative activity concerning abortion in the United States, an analysis of the structure and social correlates of women's attitudes toward abortion is especially pertinent. The data are derived from a series of questions in the 1965 National Fertility study asked of a national probability sample of 5,516 (4,332 whites and 1,184 blacks) currently married women under the age of 55. Following an open-end question on feelings about interrupting a pregnancy, each woman was asked whether she would endorse the practice under the following circumstances: if her health were seriously endangered, if the woman were not married, if the couple could not afford another child, if they did not want any more children, if the woman had been raped. As of late 1965, married women in the United States were overwhelmingly in favor of abortion if the mother's health is threatened; they are about evenly divided in the case of deformity or rape, and they are overwhelmingly opposed if the woman is not married, cannot afford another child, or simply does not want any more children. The two most common combinations of responses are a rejection of all reasons except health, and acceptance on the grounds of deformity, rape and health, but a rejection of the other three reasons. Nine per cent reject all six reasons; five per cent appear to endorse the principle of abortion on demand by accepting all six reasons for abortion. More favorable attitudes toward abortion are held by older women who either have or hope they have completed childbearing. As expected, Catholic women are most opposed to abortion and Jewish women least opposed. Among protestant women, those from fundamentalist sects are least favorable. Attitude toward abortion varies strongly with the amount of education the woman has received. In general, except among Catholics, the higher the level of education the more favorable the attitude toward abortion. Nonwhite women are consistently less favorable than white women toward abortion, a difference that does not appear reducible to educational differences. Other variables revealing some relation to attitudes toward abortion are region and size of place of residence, income and occupational status, wife's work history, religiousness, fertility and attitudes toward contraception and sterilization. The article concludes with a series of multivariate analyses in which some 15 to 20 variables are explored in their connections with attitude toward abortion.**

C. STERILIZATION

306. Anonymous. 1973. Genocide: Sterilization of Welfare Mothers in S.C. Draws Fire. Jet 44 (20): 24-25.

Spreading as rapidly as cancer, the wangling mess involving the sterilization of Blacks multiplied last week, diverging upon welfare mothers in South Carolina.*

307. Anonymous. 1973. Alabama Halts Sterilization of Retarded Youngsters.
      Jet 44 (21): 23.

      This essay discusses the controversies surrounding the involuntary
      sterilization of poor and retarded black youngsters in Alabama, South
      Carolina, and involuntary sterilization of a 13-year-old black girl
      in the State of Texas. The essay reports that Federal District Court
      Judge Frank M. Johnson has ordered involuntary sterilizations to be
      stopped in Alabama. It is expected that other states may follow suit*

308. Anonymous. 1973. Genocide: Cash-or-Sterilization Plan Comes Under
      Fire. Jet 44 (22): 14.

      Doctors in Aiken, South Carolina, have reportedly forced welfare
      mothers to undergo sterilization. Discusses the controversy sur-
      rounding the issue that girls age 17 and up (and possibly as young as
      14 years) are told that they must either give up their right to have
      children in the future, or else the children that they are carrying
      will not be delivered. The essay also discusses the ruling by a
      federal judge in Alabama ordering no sterilization be performed
      solely for birth control purposes on any minor or any individual who
      is not in a position to give legal consent.*

309. Anonymous. 1973. Rules Will Not Stop Sterilization: HEW. Jet 44 (23):
      5.

      Despite the recently issued guidelines by the U.S. government pro-
      hibiting the forced sterilization of persons receiving federal medi-
      cal care, the government admits that sterilization will probably
      continue. This is because the rules by themselves cannot mean a thing
      unless they can be policed.*

310. Anonymous. 1973. Poor Should have Option for Sterilization: Expert.
      Jet 45 (6): 15.

      The controversy over sterilization which has led to the development
      of tighter restrictions on the use of federal money for sterilization
      may close an option to the poor which is always available to the
      rich.*

311. Anonymous. 1974. Federal Judge Sets Rules for Alabama Sterilizations.
      Jet 45 (18): 5.

      Judge Frank M. Johnson, Jr. ruled recently that sterilizations could
      be performed "only when the full (range) of constitutional protec-
      tions has been accorded to the individuals involved."*

312. Anonymous. 1974. Sterilization of Females to Resume in Alabama. Jet
      46 (25): 5.

After a $6-million damage suit was filed charging that two black
teenagers in Montgomery were sterilized without the consent of their
parents, sterilization operations were suspended. However, these
federally supported operations have resumed, reportedly because
federal guidelines protecting the constitutional rights of the
patients have become available.*

313.   Berry, William Earl. 1973. Furor Mounts Over Sterilization of Blacks.
        Jet 44 (19): 20-21.

        In this article Berry discusses the furor and the law suits over
        involuntary sterilization of black girls in the states of Alabama,
        Texas, and North Carolina.*

314.   Bumpass, Larry L., and Harriet B. Presser. 1972. Contraceptive
        Sterilization in the U. S.: 1965 and 1970. Demography 9 (4): 531-548.

        The authors show that there was a significant increase in the
        prevalence of contraceptive sterilization in the United States
        between 1965 and 1970. This increase accelerated in the later years
        of the period and was shared in by virtually all subgroups
        examined--whites and nonwhites. As to differential sterilization by
        race, the authors show there was a marked difference by race in the
        life cycle characteristics of the couples who were recently (1970 or
        a year or two earlier) sterilized. They found that black couples were
        generally older, were married considerably longer, and had more
        births at the time of sterilization as compared to white couples. It
        was found that more than one half of the black couples were
        sterilized after having 6 or more births. The authors point out that
        the later sterilization for black, with respect to various aspects of
        timing, may be the result of lesser awareness of the operation
        earlier in the life cycle, or is due to a greater reluctance on the
        part of blacks to be sterilized, which serves to delay its timing. It
        was also found that about one half of all sterilizations were
        vasectomies, but vasectomies have outnumbered tubal ligations in
        recent years.*

315.   Bronstein, E. S., and D. Lentz. 1973. Characteristics of Vasectomy
        Patients Utilizing a Mobile Unit in Georgia. Journal of the Medical
        Association of Georgia 62 (April): 110-113.

        A mobile vasectomy service begun in June 1971 in Richmond County,
        Georgia, is described. The equipment is in a Winnebago mobile family
        planning unit. Services are provided for patients using the service
        during its first year of operation, June 1, 1971 to June 1, 1972, is
        reported. 28.6% of the wives were 30-34 years old. 94.14% were white
        and 2.2% were non-white. 73.25% resided in Richmond County, 14.28%
        were from Columbia County, and 3.66% were from Burke County. 22% of
        the patients were US Army Employees, 15% blue collar, and 15.52% were
        white collar workers. The mean number of children of the marriage
        sample was 2.3. 6 patients have had follow-up sperm counts which

remain positive (2.2%). 5 of these patients have had a repeat
operation with 3 negative sperm counts and 2 waiting results. 1
pateint refused the second operation. Comparative data are presented
from other studies throughout the world.*

316. Butts, June Dubbs. 1969. Perceptions of the Experience of Tubal
Ligation: An Exploratory Study in Fertility Control Among Twenty Low
Income, Black Women. Unpublished Ph. D. Dissertation. Columbia
University.

The investigator made a survey of the literature to determine types
of follow-up studies previously made of women who had undergone tubal
ligation--i.e., surgery involving cutting and tying off the Fallopian
tubes--for the purpose of permanent fertility control. This exploratory study was designed to ascertain perceived changes either in
attitude or behavior on the part of twenty low income, black women.
Assessment was made in three basic areas: self-perception, sexual
functioning, and maternal functioning. The investigator focused on
the subject's perception of the experience of tubal ligation in an
interview which utilized an original questionnaire to assess the
results of this operation at least one year post-operatively. The
subjects' perceptions were made explicit when they were asked to make
an anatomical sketch of the internal female reproductive organs. The
subject was asked to diagram where and how the tubes were cut and
tied on a standardized form. The purpose of this task was two-fold:
to correct any misconceptions concerning the operation, and to assess
the meaningfulness   of body imagery. Seventy-nine subjects were
ligated at the Harlem Hospital Center during the first two years of
its Tubal Ligation Program. Twenty-two successful interviews were
completed. They represent a self-selected sample because they chose
to participate in this follow-up effort whereas fifty-seven did not.
Two interviews were conducted in Spanish, and later discarded from
this sample, thus leaving a more cohesive group of subjects. These
women were ligated on the basis of multiparity, according to the
ratio established by the American Medical Association: a woman is
eligible for this operation if she has had five children by the age
of twenty-five, four by age thirty, or three by age thirty-five.
Married women must have the husband's written consent. The
questionnaire examined the subject's ability to perceive changes in
her life which she may have attributed to the "freeing-up" effects of
the operation. Whereas these twenty subjects reflected uniformly good
adjustments, a larger sampling of the possible group (the fifty-seven
other ligatees) may have changed the results considerably. Subjects
expressed more satisfaction in their roles as mothers than as wives;
however, those scoring either high or low on one scale tended to be
consistent on all. The investigator elucidated several factors which
distinguish this study as a descriptive rather than a statistical
one. She related these findings to possible future avenues of
research. The role of the investigator is delineated according to its
components: sex, race, and class (educational and/or cultural aspects
of this particular investigator) and the ways in which she felt each

of these factors affected rapport.*

317. Darity, W.A., and C.B. Turner. 1974. **Research Findings Related to Sterilization: Attitudes of Black Americans.** Paper presented at the Fifty-First Annual Meetings of the American Orthpsychiatric Association, San Francisco, California, April 8-12, 1974. 10 pp.

In a study of 1890 black respondents from both a northern and a southern city (Philadelphia and Charlotte, North Carolina) sterilization was found to be among the least preferred methods of birth control. Due to the history of sterilization in the U.S. and recent attempts to use sterilization as a means of social control, many blacks feel sterilization is "a white plot to eliminate blacks." More than 70% indicated they would not accept sterilization even if they had all the children they wanted. However, 90% do support strong local programs on birth control education.☆

318. Ferster, Elyce Z. 1966. **Eliminating the Unfit: Is Sterilization the Answer?** Ohio State Law Journal 27 (4): 591-633.

Recent lower court decisions in California and Ohio have focused public attention on the use of sterilization as an instrument of social policy. The author traces the history of sterilization in the United States and analyzes current legislation and practices. The scientific premise upon which eugenic sterilization is based is now subject to considerable doubt. Nonetheless, sterilization has found questionable new support among those seeking to reduce welfare rolls.*

319. Hicks, Nancy. 1973. **Sterilization of Black Mother of 3 Stirs Aiken, S.C.** The New York Times, August 1. P. 27.

This is the story of a 20 year old black mother whose Fallopian tubes were snipped and tied by one of the doctors in town after she had given birth to her third child. The purpose of the involuntary sterilization has been to reduce the welfare rolls. Hicks indicated that this has not been the only case in Aiken, or in the South. This has been the third case disclosed in just one month which has been performed on poor black women on welfare. The disclosures have caused outrage, and have prompted several law suits, and has caused the (HEW) to issue new guidelines for involuntary sterilizations. Hicks discusses similar cases in Alabama, and the surrounding legal and public controversies relative to involuntary sterilizations of poor black women.★

320. Hodson, Cora B. 1933. **An Instrument in Race Progress.** Birth Control Review 17 (4) : 105-16.

This is a call by an Englishwoman for the need for eugenic steriliza- tion in America as an instrument in race progress. Hodson, however, emphasizes that recruitment of patients for sterilization must be entirely voluntary, for voluntary system has and will work very well.*

321.   Kennard, Gail. 1974. **Sterilization Abuse.** Essence 5 (October): 66-67, 85-86.

Katie (not a real name), an 18-year old black woman on welfare, had been admitted to the city hospital in Baltimore, Maryland, with a ruptured membrane; her baby had to be delivered by cesarean section. A nurse had talked to her and had asked her to sign two papers: (1) an operation permit; (2) a consent form for tubal ligation. In this essay, Gail Kennard asserts that although Katie had consented to her sterilization, she had done so under physical and emotional stress of child birth. In other words, she "was a victim of the type of abuse tens of thousands of women are exposed to in hospitals throughout the country. "The author expands on this issue by provding several examples from different parts of the nation.*

322.   Morrison, Joseph L. 1965. **Illegitimacy, Sterilization, and Racism: A North Carolina Case History.** The Social Service Review 39 (1): 1-10.

Compulsory sterilization of unwedmothers (mostly poor blacks on welfare) has been a subject for serious debates in two consecutive North Carolina's National Assemblies, known to be among the more progressive in the South. Viewing the debate as a sign of the importance attached to the issue, Morrison attempts to study the forces underlying this punitive proposal. In doing so, among other things, he examines the history of sterilization and black illegitimacy in North Carolina. Disclaiming that he is attempting to establish a causal relationship between welfare debate, the civil rights struggle, and North Carolina's flirting with compulsory sterilization for illegitimacy, he concludes that those who sincerely favor the enactment of such a law nonetheless do not operate in a vacuum, rather in a climate of opinion that favors certain punitive action.*

323.   Pratt, W. F. 1975. **Sterilization in the United States: Preliminary Findings from the National Survey of Family Growth, 1973.** Paper Presented at the Annual Meetings of the Population Association of America, Seattle, Washington, April 17-19. 13 pp.

Data on the frequency and distribution of sterility in the United States was collected, examined, and compared with prior years for the period July 1973 to January 1974. Almost 25% of the 30 million women surveyed were sterile or married to sterile men. Of the 25%, 5% represent sterility from nonsurgical causes. Of the remaining 95%, 4.5 million or 70% were female surgical sterilizations. A majority of sterilizing operations were reported to be for contraceptive reasons. In comparing this data with that collected for 1965 and 1970, the proportions of currently married sterile couples rose 2% from 1965 to 1970, and less than 1/2% between 1970 and 1973. Over the same period while the proportions contraceptively sterile doubled from 8% to 16%, they were matched by a decline in noncontraceptive operations. The

documented shift in attitudes toward sterilization since 1970 may be
an important element in why total sterility among currently married
women has increased very little since 1965 despite marked increases
in contraceptive operations. Prospectively, as many as 36% of currently married women may opt for contraceptive sterilization before
age 45.☆

324.   Presser, H. B., and L. L. Bumpass. 1972. Demographic and Social
        Aspects of Contraceptive Sterilization in the United States:
        1965-1970. In: Demographic and Social Aspects of Population Growth.
        Commission on Population and the American Future Research Reports,
        Volume 1. Washington, D.C.: Government Printing Office. Pp. 505-568.

        The attitudes toward sterilization and its practice among American
        couples in 1965 and 1970 are examined. The basis for the data are the
        National Fertility Studies for 1965 and 1970. Married women under the
        age of 45 and living with their husbands make up the sample. The
        analysis shows a change in women's attitudes toward both male and
        female sterilization. An attitude of majority disapproval in 1965 had
        changed to 1 of majority approval in 1970. In 1965, 8% of American
        couples had practiced contraceptive sterilization; this increased to
        11% in 1970. There was an increase from 13% to 19% in the practice of
        contraceptive sterilization when only those couples desiring no more
        children were considered. About 1/2 of all contraceptive procedures
        were elected by women in 1970 and about 1/2 were elected by men.
        Among white couples, it appears that the potential demand for
        sterilization is greater among wives. There is considerable interest
        in female sterilization among black couples but little interest in
        male sterilization. A significant finding was that the age of the
        wife was inversely related to serious consideration of both female
        and male sterilization with younger couples more receptive to steri-
        lization. For white and black women who have had difficulty control-
        ling their fertility, the potential demand for female sterilization
        is greatest. Religion does not seem to be related to the potential
        demand for sterilization. ☆

325.   Rochat, R. W. 1976. Regional Variation in Sterility, United States:
        1970. Advances in Planned Parenthood 11: 1-11.

        The degree to which regional differences in the prevalence of
        different types of sterilization operations were due to variations in
        the demographic characteristics of the populations living in those
        regions was assessed using data obtained from 5,981 currently married
        women included in the National Fertility Study undertaken in the
        U.S. in 1970. Respondents and their husbands were each assigned to 1
        of 5 sterility status categories. These categories included 1) fe-
        males, sterilized for contraceptive reasons; 2) males, sterilized for
        contraceptive purposes; 3) males or females, sterilized for non-
        contraceptive reasons; 4) fecund individuals; and 5) subfecund indi-
        viduals. 76% of the female sterilizations, performed for contracep-
        tive purposes, were tubal ligations, and 73.6% of those performed for

noncontraceptive reasons were hysterectomies. The prevalence of female contraceptive sterilizations was highest in the southern states
and the prevalence of male contraceptive sterilizations, or vasectomies, was highest in the western regions of the country. The prevalence of noncontraceptive sterilizations was high in both the
southern and western sections of the country. Most of the regional
differences were attributable to variations in the demographic
characteristics of the populations living in these areas. Women
sterilized for contraceptive purposes tended to have high parity,
non-Catholic religious affiliation, and to have given birth to an
unwanted child. Men who had vasectomies tended to be white, non-
Catholic, educated, and married to women with high parity. Women who
had noncontraceptive sterilizations tended to be non-Catholic and to
have little education. Tables providing data on these couples show 1)
% of the population in each sterility status category by region and
by community size; 2) % distribution of couples by demographic
characteristics and sterility status; 3) % distribution of couples by
religion of wife and sterility status; 4) prevalence of male and
female contraceptive operations by wanted or unwanted status of
previous births; 5) % of fecund couples by age and by region; and 6)
% distribution of couples with low incomes by region and
contraceptive status.☆

326.   Ruzek, S. B. 1978. Sterilization. In: The Women's Health Movement:
Feminist Alternatives to Medical Control, by S. B. Ruzek. New York:
Praeger. Pp. 46-47.

Feminists did not become involved with the issue of forced
sterilization until recently. While black women in the south were
fighting against forced sterilization, women in the feminist movement
were concerned primarily with obtaining the right to be sterilized on
demand. Feminists fought to remove the age, parity, and spouse
consent requirements which frequently prevented women from obtaining
sterilizations. In the south, poor black women have frequently been
sterilized without their consent. The issue has now been brought to
the public's attention. In Alabama a 1 million dollar lawsuit has
been filed against a gynecologist who sterilized 2 black girls
without proper consent while working in a federally funded family
planning program, and the Department of Health, Education, and
Welfare has revised its sterilization guidelines. Despite the public
outcry against forced sterilization, 94% of the gynecologists in 4
major cities, who were surveyed in a recent study, said that they
favored mandatory sterilization of welfare women with 3 or more
illegitimate children. Since 1970 there has been a rapid increase in
female sterilizations among minorities. 20% of all black married
women are sterilized and 14% of all Native American women are
sterilized while only 7% of all white married women are sterilized.☆

327.   Sardon, J. P. 1976. La Progression de la Sterilization aux Etats-Unis
[The Advancement of Sterilization in the United States]. Population
31 (2): 492-498.

The preliminary findings of the 1973 National Survey of Family Growth are reported and discussed. The findings are summarized in 7 tables, showing the incidence of sterilization by age of the woman in a couple, by sex, by religion, and by ethnic group. The findings are insufficient to determine the role of sterilization among other contraceptive methods, e.g., whether its rapid increase is among people who used or would otherwise use oral contraceptives or whether it attracts couples who would not use other methods, notably oral contraceptives. Its influence on American fertility is also unknown, although it appears to be one of the causes of the present lower fertility.*

328.   Slater, Jack. 1973. Sterilization: Newest Threat to the Poor. Ebony 28 (12): 150-156.

This article discusses the nature and the consequences of forced involuntary sterilization of poor black women on welfare by the federally supported family planning clinics for the purpose of controlling the U.S. black population by force. According to Slater the majority of women sterilized in this country are poor black women. For example, he maintains that about 65% of women sterilized in North Carolina since 1964 were blacks. Involuntary sterlization in North Carolina involves racism--"and beyond racism some unspeakable wish to control black population growth by force." Slater cites evidence that the birth rate among poor people in recent years have voluntarily fallen more rapidly than among the middle class, and calls on the authorities to stop the crime of involuntary sterilization and not use it as a measure of controlling the growth of the black population.*

329.   Thompson, M. Cordwell. 1973. Genocide: Black Youngsters Sterilized by Alabama Agency. Jet 44 (17): 12-15.

Other than cities such as Atlanta, Tuskegee or Birmingham, in much of the rural South the white man still tells blacks what they should or should not do, Thompson asserts. This being the case, the author discusses the sterilization of two black girls of the Relf family. The white doctor had asked the illiterate Mrs. Relf to sign tubal ligation papers for her daughters. Mrs. Relf had done only what the white man had asked her to do without understanding the meanings of sterilization and/or tubal ligation. Thompson concludes that the Relf family case is only one example of what is happening to many poor and illiterate blacks in the United States.*

330.   Weisbord, R. G. 1975. Coercion and Society's Parasites. In: Genocide? Birth Control and the Black American, by R. G. Weisbord. Westport, Connecticut: Greenwood Press. Pp. 137-157.

It was not until 1942 that procreation was recognized as a basic right in the U.S. Lawbreakers, recipients of public assistance, and blacks have been the major candidates for coercive, punitive sterilization. Blacks are no longer valued for the cheap labor they provide but viewed increasingly as a public welfare expense. Nazi Germany is cited as the precedent for racist-motivated genocide programs. Blacks are represented on welfare rolls out of proportion to their total in the population; any attempt to impose sterilization as a condition for continued welfare is veiled racism. The practice will probably continue because it offers a simple and easy solution to a complex problem. Sterilization of welfare women or as a condition for abortion provides practice in surgery for beginning doctors.✰

331. Woodside, Moya. 1950. Sterilization in North Carolina: A Sociological and Psychological Study. Chapel Hill: University of North Carolina Press.

Throughout this book there are numerous references to sterilization and fertility control among black population in North Carolina. Topics covered include: black attitudes toward childbearing; lack of black doctors in the North Carolina hospitals; number of castrations performed at Goldsboro State Hospital; contraception among black women; North Carolina's Eugenics Board policy towards blacks; blacks and illegitimacy; infant mortality among blacks in N. C.; black maternal health; ratio of sterilizations performed on blacks; and, sterilization and race prejudice. Relative to the ratio of sterilization among blacks Woodside reports that of a total of 1,901 sterilizations, 1,437 were performed on whites and 464 on blacks, a proportion which corresponded closely to their ratio of 27.5 percent in the general population of the State. However, this correspondence was not maintained by sex, for black females were found to be sterilized about half as often as would be expected, while black males, on the contrary, 2 1/2 times more often than whites. Castrations were also found to be proportionately higher among blacks than whites (28 blacks; 30 whites). The major conclusion of the author is that North Carolina provides a "most interesting experiment in the changing social attitudes. Through the public health and welfare services, up-to-date measures of fertility control have been made widely available to a rural conservative people, of whom almost a third are Negroes, and encouragement given to their use. If, in this culture, education and propaganda can bring about in a comparatively short time the desired modification in thought and behavior, there will be fresh hope for those who still believe that persuasion, not compulsion, is the road to human betterment."★

D. GENOCIDE OR BIRTH CONTROL?

332. Allen, J.E. 1977. An appearance of Genocide: A Review of Governmental Family Planning Program Policies. Perspectives in Biology and Medicine 20 (2): 300-306.

An increasing number of newspaper and magazine articles in the black community are charging U.S. government family planning programs with genocide, largly due to the insensitivity of program administrators. A large reason for this is the fact that abortions are free but medicines cost money. Much of this is due to the fact that the pharmaceutical industry is a profit-making venture in the U.S., but the appearance is still given that officials are more interested in stopping black babies than in curing black children. The Report of the Commission on Population Growth and the American Future recommended spending 10 times as much on birth control as on maternal and child health services. Title 10 of the Public Health Services Act also focuses on low-income families as does Title 4-A of the Social Security Act. In the early 1970s many Office of Economic Opportunity centers asked for family planning funds, which were freely available, and used them for maternal and child health, which is what the poor really wanted. The poor also report they feel a subtle coercion when on welfare and are afraid voluntary abortion will be followed by compulsory sterilization. State and local family-planning policies, including a number of bills which would have required compulsory sterilization after a welfare mother had a certain number of illegitimate children have fueled concern. Fortunately none of these bills ever became law, but their very introduction raises genocide charges. A 1968 study of 10 counties in North Carolina revealed that discriminatory attitudes were directed toward disadvantaged, public assistance women regardless of color. It is recommended that family planning services be merged with maternal and child health services, which might result in increased use in a less emotionally charged atmosphere, and a sharp curtailment in use of public funds to sterilize minors. Abortion policy can be retained because, unlike sterilization, abortion respects the right of program participants to decide when and how many children should be born.☆

333.   Anonymous. 1971. **Blacks View Limitations on Number in Family as Genocide Effort by U.S.** Jet 40 (August 5): 20-21.

Briefly discusses the findings of some studies showing that blacks in the United States oppose any government-imposed attempt to control their population. By introducing family planning into the poor communities (mostly black communities) the U.S. officials have attempted to reduce the number of poor people on the welfare roll. This has led some black militants/activists to proclaim that family planning program is aimed at black genocide. The essay concludes by stating that: "At a time in history when Blacks are making significant political gains, many Blacks feel that proposed national population control measures are calculated attempts to neutralize the rapidly-increasing Black political power." ★

334.   Anonymous. 1973. **Genocide: Sterilization of Welfare Mothers in S.C. Draws Fire.** Jet 44 (20): 24-25.

Spreading as rapidly as a cancer, the wangling mess involving the sterilization of Blacks multiplied last week, diverging upon welfare mothers in South Carolina.*

335.   Anonymous. 1973. Genocide: Cash-or-Sterilization Plan Comes Under Fire. Jet 44 (22): 14.

Doctors in Aiken, South Carolina, have reportedly forced welfare mothers to undergo sterilization. Discusses the controversy surrounding the issue that girls age 17 and up (and possibly as young as 14 years) are told that they must either give up their right to have children in the future, or else the children that they are carrying will not be delivered. The essay also discusses the ruling by a federal judge in Alabama ordering no sterilization be performed solely for birth control purposes on any minor or any individual who is not in a position to give legal consent.*

336.   Anonymous. 1973. Strict Sterilization Rules Proposed by HEW Officials. Jet 45 (3): 68.

In the interest of protecting the civil rights of the more than 100,000 persons (mostly poor and/or black) sterilized each year, the Department of Health, Education and Welfare (HEW) has proposed strict new regulations, which requires the written consent by each patient and judicial review of patients under age 21. The proposal has grown out of the Montgomery, Alabama, and Aiken, South Carolina cases, where allegedly minor black girls were either sterilized without the consent of their parents, or were refused medical care during their pregnancy period until they had consented to sterilization.*

337.   Anonymous. 1973. ZPG for Blacks Without Health Care Plan is Termed Genocidal. Ob. Gyn. News 8 (9): 5.

A zero population growth rate would constitute genocide for Negroes in the U.S. because perinatal and adult mortality is higher for blacks than that of Caucasians, Dr. Henry W. Foster said at the annual convention and scientific assembly of the National Medical Association. "The black birth rate still needs to decline, but not all the way to a zero growth rate," said Dr. Foster, Chairman of the Department of Obstetrics and Gynecology at Tuskegee Institute, Tuskegee, Alabama. This is why black people are opposed to family planning when it is not linked with a program of comprehensive health care.   Dr. Foster said he is "incensed" when he travels across Alabama and finds expensive modern facilities for performing tubal sterilization and well-staffed birth control clinics, but substandard maternal care facilities. He has seen clinics where IUDs can be inserted, but they have no funds for hospitalization of the few patients who suffer complications of the insertion. "As doctors we know the positive aspects of family planning, but as blacks we feel that other things are more important," Dr. Foster said. The birthrate of black people last year was about 19/1000 compared with 14.5/1000 for white people. Family planning is applicable to Negroes, but not to the same degree that it is to Caucasians. The assumption that family planning should apply to the entire population equally is based on the false assumption that all Americans share the same middle-class life style, Dr. Foster said.*(Full text).

338. Bradley, Valerie Jo. 1970. Black Caucus Raps About Planned Genocide of Blacks. Jet 38 (18): 14-18.

The gist of this essay is that birth control program in the United States is a plan to kill blacks. ★

339. Cade, Toni. 1970. The Pill: Genocide or Liberation. In: The Black Woman: An Anthology. Toni Cade (ed.). New York: Signet Books. Pp. 162-169.

Cade, herself a black woman, talks about birth control pills from the point of view of a group of black women in the liberation movement. Before joining the group she had thought that women in the movement will be heavy pill users, because pill was regarded as a liberator. But after joining the group she finds the opposite. That is, the "Sisters" (the members of the group) believed that the abandonment of birth controls will result in less "cruising, less make-out, less mutually exploitive sexual makeups, and more warmth in the man-woman relationship." In this essay, Cade tries to answer questions such as: What about the pill? Does it liberate or does it not? Will it help the members of the group to forge new relationships or not? Does it make the group accomplices in the genocidal plot engineered by the man or does it not? Does nonuse of contraceptives necessarily guarantee the production of warriors? Should all or only some of the Sisters dump the pill? What are the Brothers' responsibilities in all of this? Who said that the pill means you are never going to have children? And, do the Sisters need to talk about communes, day-care centers, and pregnancy stipends? Cade does not believe that pill really helps to liberate women.★

340. Craven, Erma C. 1972. Abortion, Poverty and Black Genocide: Gifts to the Poor? In: Abortion and Social Justice. Thomas W. Hilgers, and Dennis J. Horan (eds.). New York: Sheed and Ward. Pp. 231-243.

Poverty and Black genocide are realities in the United States. The introduction of abortion has poignantly brought this into clear perspective. IT MUST NOT BE ALLOWED TO GO FURTHER! If we are truly a nation who speak of civil human rights, then we must prove that we carry no prejudices. The abortion issue, with its gnawing ability to make one honest, may very well be the ultimate test. if we can openly admit our prejudice, then perhaps we can begin to move forward. If we cannot, then we will move one step further down into the valley of death. The blood-and-guts problem is our lack of compassion and our lack of concern. More and more, women are being seen as wombs to be deactivated rather than human beings with lives to be fulfilled. Only when this impoverishment is eliminated can we fully expect to enter the new frontier.*

341. Darity, W.A., C.B. Turner, and H.J. Thiebaux. 1972. An Exploratory Study on Barriers to Family Planning: Race Consciousness and Fears of Black Genocide as a Basis. Advances in Plannned Parenthood 7: 20-32.

Many black leaders have expressed strong feelings that family planning programs are forms of genocide. This paper aims at exploring some of the historical and general aspects of the problem, reviews some contemporary thoughts, and reports on parts of a research project comparing the 30-and-under age group with the over 30 age group of a random sample of black males and black females. This study is conducted among a random sample of 159 black households to determine the extent of this feeling. It was found that although 68% of the total sample agreed that birth control projects are aimed at low-income people, 72% disagreed with the statement: "Encouraging blacks to use birth control is comparable to trying to eliminate this group from society;" 44% of the females under 30 and 36% over 30 had received birth control information from a clinic or a doctor. On the other hand, 84% of the total would not be sterilized even if they had all the children they wanted. Sixty-two percent agreed that blacks should operate birth control clinics in black neighborhoods. Only 28% felt that blacks should not limit their family size. However, among males 30 and under 47% opposed family limitation.★

342. Darity, William A., C.B. Turner, and H.J. Thiebaux. 1975. Race Consciousness and Fears of Black Genocide as Barriers to Family Planning. In: Population Studies: Selected Essays and Research. K.C.W. Kammeyer (ed.). Chicago, Illinois: Rand McNally. Pp. 433-447.

As part of a larger project a pilot study interviewed 159 households in a New England city to determine relationships between race consciousness and attitudes toward family planning. It was found that 84% of respondents under 30, both male and female, preferred the terms "black" or "Afro-American" compared with 61% over age 30. This was used as an indicator of degree of race consciousness. 73% of males over 30, 59% of females under 30, and 71% of females over 30 felt birth control clinics were aimed at low income people. 29% of the men under 30 but none of the men over 30 felt all forms of birth control are designed to eliminate black Americans. 5% of women under 30 and 18% of women over 30 agreed to this statement. 47% of men under 30 also felt encouraging blacks to use birth control is comparable to trying to eliminate this group from society. 27% of men over 30 and about 20% of women in both age groups agreed. 34% of males under 30 felt abortions are part of a white plot to eliminate blacks compred to 19% of men over 30, 15% of women under 30, and 21% of women over 30. 28% of males under 30 felt sterilization is a white plot to eliminate blacks, compared with 6% of men over 30, 8% of women under 30, and 21% of women over 30. Since males under 30 have the greatest suspicions about family planning, they should be involved in any clinic planning and administration. In additon, they have had the least direct experience with family planning clinics (15% compared to 44% of women under 30). Also, 53% of men under 30 said neither they nor their spouse had ever used any method to control family size while 91% of the women under 30 said they had used some method. Both men and women in both age groups felt blacks should be in control of clinics and businesses in black areas. This argues for greater black control of clinics, more effort to make sure the clinics are seen as available to all, and greater sensitivity to preferences of method in the black community. Abortion and sterilization are not highly acceptable. 84% of respondents rejected sterilization, 94% of males rejecting. 78% rejected abortion, 88% of males under 30. ☆

343.   Farrel, W.C., and M.P. Dawkins. 1979. **Determinants of Genocide Fear in a Rural Texas Community: A Research Note.** American Journal of Public Health 69 (6): 605-607.

Most studies of the fears of American blacks about genocide have been done among urban populations. The present study explores the relative importance of social background factors as predictors of genocide fears among rural blacks. The study was done among a 7% stratified random sample (104 households) of women aged 15-44 and their most significant male partner in a southeastern Texas county in which over 1/2 the population is black. An interview schedule consisted of precoded and openended items and was administered by a team matched for sex and race. Various indicators of genocide fear were shown to be related to selected background characteristics, including family planning practice, sex, age, racial identification and education. Further analysis revealed these 5 variables combined explained 19% of the variance in race genocide fear, the most important predictors being sex and education. The present study suggests that the same conditions that lead to fears of genocide in urban conditions exist in rural areas, which may serve as an obstacle to creating meaningful family planning strategies (in that family planning itself may be viewed as an act to perpetrate genocide). Future research should continue to monitor social factors and include psychological and economic predictors in terms of their influence on genocide fears and resultant family planning behavior among American blacks. ★

344.   Gregory, Dick. 1971. **My Answer to Genocide: Bitter Comic Prescribes Big Families as Effective Black Protest.** Ebony 26 (October): 66-72.

This is a one-man opinion on black fertility control which is best expressed in the opening sentences of the article. "My answer to genocide, quite simply, is eight black kids--and another baby on the way. Now I know that statement is going to upset a whole lot of white folks, and even some black folks." Using the conventional academic standards, this essay is highly subjective, impressionistic, and journalistic at best. Nevertheless, it is an interesting article to read, for it may provide some clues to the social-psychological barriers that must be overcome before blacks can accept fertility control without the feeling that it is a white conspiracy against them. ★

345.   Hudgins, John. 1972. Is Birth Control Genocide? The Black Scholar 4 (3): 34-37.

The issue of birth control-genocide is one of the most controversal issues in the black community. Of all, the most crucial issue at hand is to examine the conditions of the black community. Hudgins addresses himself to the questions: Can the black commuity afford the unlimited reproduction? If blacks are going to advocate family planning, what kind should be advocated? And when birth-control genocide charge is leveled against the other group, and at the same time we see a large number of unwed mothers and the resulting no-dad children in the black community, it must be asked what is meant by genocide. Hudgins' main point is that the genocide charge has not been accompanied by a sense of seriousness of purpose, for if black people sincerely believe that they are being gradually wiped out, they must mount a serious defense against it. Appearing frustrated on the issue, as a whole, Hudgins' article is a be-quiet-or else-rise-up and defend your baby-making in tone.★

346.   Johnson, Robert E. 1973. Legal Abortion: Is It Genocide or Blessing in Disguise?. Jet 43 (26, March 22): 12-19.

In this essay Johnson examines a discussion of abortion by a teacher and his class of teenage girls; discusses legalization of abortion in Illinois and other states in the union, and reviews the issue of legal abortion from a disguised genocidal point of view. He points out that while black women, who regard legalized abortion as a "blessing in disguise", took their burdens to the Friendship Medical Center in Chicago and left them there, the black men, who saw legal abortion as white racist genocide, demonstrated in front of the medical facility trying to persuade the black women not to terminate their unwanted pregnancies. The author talks about the director of the above mentioned medical facility as a "lunch hour" abortionist. Himself an anti-abortionist, the author attempts to convince his readers to believe in his views.★

347.   Littlewood, T.B. 1977. Black Genocide and Homewood-Brushton. In: The Politics of Population Control, by T.B. Littlewood. Notre Dame, Indiana: University of Notre Dame Press. Pp. 69-87.

The conflict between black leaders who view birth control clinics as genocide efforts by the white community and black women who feel the need to limit individual families became a crisis when Family Plan-ning opened a clinic in the Homewood-Brushton area of Pittsburgh. The statements of various black leaders, ranging from the extreme rhetoric of the Black Panthers to more moderate statements by the National Association for the Advancement of Colored People, all agree that an increase in population is essential for black people to become a controlling force in the nation's economy; birth control clinics are seen as a white reaction to black increases in number. Since few blacks are on the boards of directors of family planning agencies, the suspicions increase. The black community also wants to know why there are not volunteers pushing health services and making sure welfare checks and food stamps are distributed. Lack of attention to these basic health and welfare needs is a valid objection. On the other side a health official in the District of Columbia pointed out that in the previous 5 years 54 women lost their lives in childbirth in the District, 2 of them white--"so if I was really interested in something genocidal, I'd tell all the black women to go out and get pregnant." The coalition of black organizations that forced the closing of the Homewood-Brushton family planning clinics was faced by a counterorganization of black women. The clinic was reopened in better facilities. The fight then shifted to unauthorized sterilizations which were routine among black women in southern hospitals. It is pointed out that high birthrates have not prevented Catholics from achieving political power. By concentrating in a few large states and becoming active in politics, their economic standing has advanced in spite of higher birthrates.☆

348. Patterson, William L. (ed.). 1970. **We Charge Genocide: The Crime of Government Against the Negro People.** New York: International Publishers. 238 pp.

This book consists of the reprint of a petition first presented to the United Nations in 1951, with a new foreword by William L. Patterson. The petition presented what was called "various acts of genocides" by the U.S. government against the black population of the United States from January 1, 1945 to June 1951, arranged under the articles and provisions of the United Nations Genocide Convention. The document attempts to provide a full picture of acts of genocide against black population, and asks "that the General Assembly of the United Nation find and declare by resolution that the Government of the United States is guilty of the crime of Genocide against the Negro population of the United States and that it further demands that the government of the United States stop and prevent the crime of genocide".★

349. Sarvis, B., and H. Rodman. 1974. **Black Genocide.** In: The Abortion Controversy, by B. Sarvis and H. Rodman. New York: Columbia University Press. Pp. 173-187.

This chapter (chapter 9) addresses the charge that blacks became the major target of birth control as a part of racial oppression; that making sterilization a precondition for providing abortion service, or making population control program a precondition for giving financial aid to the third-world countries, has genocidal implications. Some social scientists and black activists believe that black genocide is possible. These discussions are carried out under the headings: (1) The Population Controllers; (2) Compulsory Sterilization; (3) Power in Numbers; and, (4) Will Birth Control Eliminate Poverty?.★

350.   Schulder, Diane, and F. Kennedy. 1971. Black Genocide. In: Abortion Rap, by Diane Schulder and Floryne Kennedy. New York: McGraw Hill Book, Company. Pp. 151-161.

On several radio programs blacks have denounced abortion as racist genocide directed at Blacks. An emphatic statement was issued by the Black Panther Party just a few days after the new New York State abortion law became effective. This position was very much reminiscent of the position taken at the Black Power Conference in 1967, in Newark, N.J., where there was a consensus among the participants that birth control and abortion were both forms of black genocide. Despite the position taken by the more radical groups in the black community, the authors cite several opposing views taken by some notable blacks. The chapter also discusses some of the reasons for back suspicion--for instance, blacks believe that some of the people active in population control and family planning have a bad stench of racism. Some of the ironies associated with black genocide position are examined. The chapter concludes that the black genocide charge is losing momentum, and in fact some black women have publicly opposed the black genocide position.★

351.   Sinnette, Calvin H. 1972. Genocide and Black Ecology. Freedomways 12 (1): 4-46.

When blacks level the charge of birth control genocide against the dominant group in the society, the whites not only dismiss the charge as unfounded, but go on to say that the blacks' accusation is no more than an extrimist rhetoric by militant blacks, or ascribe such charges to black paranoia. This essay, a library review of literature on black genocide, examines the many dimensions of this hotly debated issue in the black community. The author provides many statements in support of the position held by the blacks. The author maintains that blacks continue to be denied a living wage (employment), they suffer from malnutrition, and are unable to obtain decent housing or medical care; instead, they see a consortium of governmental/private groups who mount a rigorous campaign to curb the so-presented evils of overpopulation. Sinnette concludes his essay by emphasizing that previous generations of blacks were aware of the dominant society's conspiracy against them in the name of fertility control. The question still figures prominantly in contemporary discussion of the plight of black population not only in the United States, but worldwide. What is missing, however, is the serious study of the real problem in its many dimensions, which is the study of health, socioeconomic, moral, and ethical aspects of the genocide issue from a black point of view and providing blacks with those instruments with which it can ensure its survival and its unequivocal liberation.★

352. Stewart, D.E. 1969. Questions and Answers About the Charge of "Genocide" as it Relates to Planned Parenthood-World Population, its Affiliates, and the Provision and Expansion of Private and Publicly Sponsored Family Planning Program in the U.S. New York: Planned Parenthood-World Population. 12 pp.

A small minority in the black community has adopted a pro-natalist position, and charged that family planning is a racist plan to keep non-whites weak in number. On the premise that both sides on this question must keep communication open and non-defensive in an effort to understand each other, the author attempts to answer these charges directly. He offers a brief history of the subject, summarizes medical, scientific and factual answers to the charges and, in question-and-answer format, suggests how these charges might be dealt with by family planning personnel.☆

353. Thompson, M. Cordell. 1973. Genocide: Black Youngsters Sterilized by Alabama Agency. Jet 4 (17): 12-15.

Other than cities such as Atlanta, Tuskegee or Birmingham, in much of the rural south the white man still tells blacks what they should or should not do, Thompson asserts. This being the case, the author discusses the sterilization of two black girls of the Relf family. The white doctor had asked the illiterate Mrs. Relf to sign tubal ligation papers for her daughters. Mrs. Relf had done only what the white man had asked her to do without understanding the meanings of sterilization and/or tubal ligation. Thompson concludes that the Relf family case is only one example of what is happening to many poor and illiterate blacks in the United States.★

354. Treadwell, Mary. 1972. Is Abortion Black Genocide? Family Planning Perspectives 4 (1): 4-5.

This is a plea by Treadwell for the repeal of all restrictive abortion laws, as well as for fertility control in general. Mary Treadwell, a black activist leader and the then Executive Director of Pride, Inc., a self-help agency in Washington, D.C. providing rehabilitation services and job training for disadvantaged blacks, issued a statement on October 14, 1972 in connection with an abortion law repeal demonstration sponsored by the Women's National Abortion Action Coalition. The article consists of excerpts from that statement. The gist of the article is that the decision to get an abortion must be made by the woman (who has the right to control her own body) and her physician.★

355. Turner, C., and W. A. Darity. 1973. Fears of Genocide Among Black Americans as Related to Age, Sex, and Region. American Journal of Public Health 63 (12): 1029-1034.

In recent years there has been increasing concern in the black community that birth control and/or family planning programs may be a method of perpetuating black genocide. This fear is based on historical and contemporary realities, for black Americans have been subjected to a long period of brutality. The increasing number of punitive and compulsory sterilization is often given as example of such racism. In this paper, the authors try to determine the extent of genocide fears among a sample of black Americans and attempt to explore the relationship of this fear to demographic variables such as age, sex, education as well as region. The analysis is based on a sample of 1,890 black Americans living in either Philadelphia, Pennsylvania, or Charlotte, North Carolina.   Three null hypotheses tested are: (1) There is no difference in genocide fears between younger as compared to older blacks.   (2) There is no difference in genocide fears between black males as compared to females. And, (3) There is no difference in genocide fears between northern blacks as compared to southern blacks. The data for testing these hypotheses are collected through an interview technique. The major finding of the study is that genocidal fears are widely held in the black population and that the variables age, sex, region, and level of education are related to the prevalence of these fears--that is, all three null hypotheses are rejected. The authors conclude that genocide fears of blacks continue to create barriers to the effective use of family planning methods, and that this dilemma will remain unresolved till the life circumstances of black Americans improve.★

356.   Weisbord, R. G. 1973. Birth Control and the Black American: A Matter of Genocide? Demography 10 (4): 571-590.

During the 1960s and continuing into the 1970s, the charge that birth control and abortion are integral elements of a white genocidal conspiracy directed against Afro-Americans has been heard with increasing frequency and stridency in black communities. The genocide theory finds greatest acceptance among spokesmen for black nationalist and black revolutionary groups, but suspicion of family planning programs is not limited to them. An analysis of black leadership opinion on birth control is provided in this paper. The black debate over the desirability of population limitation is traced back approximately fifty years. It began with a dispute between those blacks who believed that in sheer numbers there was strength and those blacks, such as W. E. B. DuBois, who argued that among human races, as among vegetables, quality and not quantity counted. An appreciation of the sexual exploitation of the chattel slave in the ante-bellum period, which did not end with emancipation, is also essential to an understanding of the roots and rationale of the genocide notion which are the foci of this paper.*

357.   Weisbord, R. G. 1975. Birth Control as Black Genocide: Fact or Paranoia?. In: Genocide? Birth Control and the Black American, by R. G. Weisbord. Westport, Connecticut: Greenwood Press. Pp. 3-10.

Recent worldwide concern about overpopulation has led to the general respectability of birth control. The history of the family planning movement, including the medical, legal, and psychological barriers to its development, is reviewed. Many blacks, especially those associated with black nationalist or black revoluntionary organizations, fear birth control as a form of black genocide. Most black leaders who favor birth control at all want the services to be made available to all people but not forced on any group.★

358.   Weisbord, R. G. 1975. **The Meaning of Genocide.** In: Genocide? Birth Control and the Black American, by R. G. Weisbord. Westport, Connecticut: Greenwood Press. Pp. 11-24.

Negative black attitudes toward planned parenthood grow out of American black history and the pervasive racism blacks have suffered. The history of blacks in America is reviewed. The brutality of the slave trade and the institution of slavery, the mob violence which has been directed against blacks, and the persistent discrimination are discussed.★

359.   Weisbord, R. G. 1975. **Black Sexuality and the Racial Threat.** In: Genocide? Birth Control and the Black American, by R. G. Weisbord. Westport, Connecticut: Greenwood Press. Pp. 25-40.

White manipulation of black sexuality throughout American history has led to the present-day black nervousness regarding publicly sponsored family planning programs. Western civilization has historically believed a racial mythology which teaches that blacks, both male and female, are more passionate and primitive in their sexual instincts. The history of slave-breeding and punitive castration is cited. The early twentieth century movement to sterilize unfit persons also had a racist overcast.★

360.   Weisbord, R. G. 1975. **Concluding Thoughts.** In: Genocide? Birth Control and the Black American, by R. G. Weisbord. Westport, Connecticut: Greenwood Press. Pp. 176-187.

Concluding thoughts on birth control and whether it represents genocide to the black American, deals with the public statements of black American opinion makers. There is a large body of evidence to demonstrate that while there is paranoia on the part of many blacks concerning racial genocide and historical evidence to sustain such fears, the vast majority of blacks approve of birth control and practice it. While some pronatalists view increased black population as a means of bettering opportunity, helter-skelter black propagation for political purposes is misguided strategy. Government appears to place a high priority on making birth control information available to poor blacks while less effort is made to provide indigents with jobs, housing or medical care. Black and white allies have reacted strongly to coercive sterilization as an infringement of human rights. Indeed, the Census Bureau statistics indicate that the poor have reduced their birth rate sharply in recent years. However, it is better opportunity which will provide the necessary motivation to control births.☆

361. Weisbord, R. G. 1975. Sterilization, Genocide, and the Black
      American. In: Genocide? Birth Control and the Black American, by R.
      G. Weisbord. Westport, Connecticut: Greenwood Press. Pp. 158-175.

      Several celebrated cases of forced sterilization are described. The
      nature of these cases of coercive sterilization has led to cries of
      racial genocidal extermination. The case of the Relf sisters in which
      an illiterate mother signed a consent for her minor daughters'
      sterilization, and which was investigated by Senator Edward Kennedy's
      U.S. Senate Health Subcommittee has raised questions of the motives
      of the Community Action Agency of Montgomery which treated the girls.
      Federal guidelines designed to protect the rights of individuals
      undergoing federally funded sterilizations remained undistributed to
      local agencies such as this, probably for political reasons. In
      response to the case, the Council of Negro Women and ZPG jointly
      asked that the use of federal monies for sterilization of minors be
      terminated. Judge Gerhard Gesell of the U.S. District Court for the
      District of Columbia found that the Secretary of Health, Education
      and Welfare was without statutory authority to fund the sterilization
      of persons incompetent under state law to consent to an operation.★

                        ------O✼O✼O✼O✼O------

Chapter 4
Black Health and Mortality

362. Anderson, S.G., F.C. Greiss, and W.J. May. 1972. **Maternal Mortality in North Carolina, 1966-1970.** North Carolina Medical Journal 33 (11): 949-952.

Three hundred and fourteen (314) reported maternal deaths (those occurring during pregnancy or 90 days postpartum) in North Carolina in 1966-1970 were studied in an effort to determine progress made in the care of pregnant women and to pinpoint areas of concern. The leading causes of direct obstetric death were toxemia, hemorrhage, vascular accidents, infection, and anesthesia. The vascular accident rate has continued to increase since 1956-1960. Rates from all other causes were down, although the decrease in toxemia was not as great as in the recent past. Lack of adequate antenatal supervision and delay in hospitalization are cited as identifiable factors in the toxemic deaths, emanating, it is suspected, from the cost of obstetric care. To remedy this, obstetric care should be made available to all parturients regardless of economic state. Among the causes of indirect obstetric deaths are cardiac, vascular disease, urinary, hepatic, pulmonary, and diabetes. 4 of the 16 deaths from vascular diseases were attributed to pulmonary embolus occurring late in the puerperium. Women with severe varicosities, marked obsesity, grand multiparity, and a past history of thrombophlebitis, or women who have undergone surgery, such as caesarian section or sterilization, are more likely to experience a thromboembolic event. The increase in amniotic fluid emoblism is undoubtly due in part to increased awareness. However, the injudicious use of oxytocin can bring on this condition. Indirect obstetric deaths have become

relatively more important because of the decline in direct obstetric
deaths. The maternal mortality rate for blacks is nearly 3 times that
for whites. Improving health care for blacks would lead to an
immediate reduction in maternal mortality rates. If black rates could
be lowered to that of whites, maternal mortality rates would decrease
by 30%.☆

363. Anonymous. 1977. Expectation of Life Among Nonwhites. Metropolitan
      Life Insurance Company Statistical Bulletin (March): 5-7.

      Life expectancy for the nonwhite population in the U.S. has improved
      in recent years. It reached a record high of 67.9 in 1975. Tables are
      presented to show the pattern of change in the life expectancy for
      the nonwhite population between 1959 and 1975. Fluctuations in life
      expectancy are discussed.★

364. Armstrong, Robert J. 1972. A Study of Infant Mortality From Linked
      Records by Birth Weight, Period of Gestation, and Other Variables.
      HEW, National Center for Health Statistics, DHEW Publication No.
      (PHS) 79-1055. Washington, D.C.: Government Printing Office. 90 pp.

      Mortality experience of the 1960 live-birth cohort duringg the first
      year of life, by birth weight, period of gestation, age of mother,
      color, sex, plurality, and age at death. One of the author's
      findings is that infant mortality rate varied greatly by birth
      weight, being highest for the lightest babies and lowest for infants
      weighing between 3,001 and 4,500 grams at births. The rate also
      varied by color, and sex, but the variation was much less than that
      observed among the various weight groups.★

365. Bleiweis, P.R., R.C. Reynolds, L.D. Cohen, and N.A. Butler 1977.
      Health Care Characteristics of Migrant Agricultural Workers in Three
      North Florida Counties. Journal of Community Health 3 (1): 32-43.

      [This is a study based on a sample of 291 migrant heads of households
      interviewed, of whom 222 or more than 91 percent, were blacks. The
      study considers health care differentials by demographic variables
      such as age, sex, marital status, education, occupation, residence,
      and income]. Farm workers, representing 65% of the migrant work
      force in the St. Johns River basin agricultural area of north
      Florida, were questioned in 1973-1974 about their own and their
      families' health status and about their use of professional health
      care services and facilities. The facilities available for use by
      this population included 22 physicians in private practice, two
      hospitals, three public health clinics, and two health clinics
      operated for migrants. Most contacts made by the migrant farm workers
      were with the health care professionals in the public facilities,
      primarily those in the migrant health clinics. The average number of
      visits made by migrant farm worker heads of households to a physician
      each year was 3.5 visits. In 1971, the National Health Survey
      reported an average of 4.9 physician visits for all U.S. citizens.

The major factors that affected utilization were the presence of an acute medical condition and the perception of being in poor health. The factors that generally have been thought of as impediments to seeking health care, such as transportation, the presence of children in the household, and a lack of education, were found to be of little import. The acute disease conditions that were most frequently reported by these migrant workers as the reason for their contacts included respiratory illness, digestive system problems, injuries, and musculoskeletal problems. The chronic conditions included heart disease and hypertension, musculoskeletal disorder, digestive system problems, and genitourinary problems. Little use was made of dental services, except for tooth extractions.*

366.   Bourne, J.P., and R.W. Rochat. 1975. Association Between Perinatal/ Infant Mortality and Family Planning in Rural Georgia. Paper Presented at the Thirteenth Annual Meetings of the Association of Planned Parenthood Physicians, Los Angeles, California, April 17, 1975. 4 pp.

Tables are presented showing the association between perinatal/infant mortality and family planning in Georgia. Table 1 shows that black females comprise 29.3% of all females in Georgia. 44.7% are rural women, 9.0% completed median school years by the time they were 24 years old, 35.6% had families with annual incomes of less than $3000. The age of fertile black females ranged from 10-44. Table 2 shows that the general fertility rate in Georgia was 156.6, 24.2% of the black births were from unwed mothers and 24.1 were delivered at home by a midwife. The perinatal death rate was 43.6 and the infant rate was 45.5. Between 1960 and 1971 the number of black out-of-wedlock births of a study area in Georgia had decreased from 746 to 488. Between 1960 and 1968 more babies were delivered by mothers between the ages of 20-39 in the study areas. Table 5 shows that the black live births by birth order was lower in 1965 than in 1960, and Table 6 shows that black perinatal and infant mortality did decrease between 1960 and 1971. A study and control group were used in each table.☆

367.   Carter, Elmer A. 1932. Eugenics for the Black. Birth Control Review 16 (6): 169-170.

In this paper, Carter discusses blacks' misconceptions about family plannning as a conspiracy against them. Carter emphasizes that the poor blacks who either do not have reliable family planning information or under the influence of anti-family planning statements radiating from the black community do not practice birth control may eventually under economic pressures end up with illegal abortions and thus endangering their own health and even lives. Carter concludes by stating that "...the race problem in America is infinitely aggravated by the presence of too many unhappily born, sub-normals, morons, and imbeciles of both races. It will be a tremendous misfortune if those who are fighting the battle for birth control should remain unmindful or indifferent to the plight of the Negro. For at present the practice is confined to those whose offspring would be best fitted to carry the lance of racial progress."★

368.   Chabot, Marion J., J. Garfinkel, and M.W. Pratt. 1975. Urbanization and Differentials in White and Nonwhite Infant Mortality. Pediatrics 56 (5): 777-781.

This study analyzes infant deaths in the United States, 1962 to 1967, by place of residence, to determine to what degree variations in age at death are related to degree of urbanization and race. Results of the study indicate that: (1) after one day of life infant mortality increases progressively as degree of urbanization decreases; (2) the differences between urban and rural death rates are greatest in the posthebdomadal (1 week or older) period; (3) in all age groups at all levels of urbanization, the nonwhite infant is at a marked disadvantage relative to the white infant; (4) the older the infant, the greater the disadvantage for nonwhite infants in rural areas; (5) had the white infant mortality rate prevailed among the nonwhite population over the six-year period from 1962 to 1967 an estimated annual total of 11,597 nonwhite infants would have survived their first year of life; (6) 40% of the excess deaths are in infants under 7 days and 60% in the posthebdomadal period; (7) fetal death rates increase progressively as degree of urbanization decreases, complementing a direct relationship between under 1 day mortality and urbanization resulting in a level trend for perinatal mortality.*

369.   Chase, Helen C. 1969. Registration Completeness and International Comparisons of Infant Mortality. Demography 6 (4): 425-433.

The physical development of the live born infant is the single most important variable governing its survival: infant mortality among those weighing 2,500 grams (5 1/2 pounds) or less at birth is 17 times the mortality among those weighing more than 2,500 grams at birth. The variation in mortality according to birth weight (or gestation) is greater than for subclasses of color, sex, maternal age, or birth order. Infant mortality in the United States is significantly higher than in a number of other countries e.g., Sweden, Netherlands, Norway. The difference is thought, by some, to be due to underregistration of low birth weight infants in other countries. In this paper, distributions of live births by birth weight for Denmark, England and Wales, New Zealand, and the United States, and infant mortality data for Denmark and the United States are examined. The data do not support a hypothesis of gross underregistration of live born infants in other countries. The results indicate that some index of physical development (birth weight, gestation, or a combination of both) should be included in any appraisal of infant mortality.*

370.   Chase, Helen C. 1972. A Study of Infant Mortality From Linked Records: Comparison of Neonatal Mortality from Two Cohort Studies,

United States, January-March 1950 and 1960. Washington, D.C.: U.S. Department of Health, Education, and Welfare, DHEW Publication No. (HSM)72-1056. 99 pp.

This comparative study of neonatal mortality in the U.S. based on two cohorts of infants born alive during January-March 1950 and 1960 includes consideration of color, sex, plurality, birth weight, gestation, age of mother, total birth order, cause of death, and age at death. The results have added much information regarding differences between infants born to different socioeconomic groups. Among the outstanding differences are those between white infants and all other infants. According to Chase, the risk of neonatal death for white infants was 18.9 per 1,000 live births in the 1950 cohort, and 16.9 in the 1960 cohort. For all other infants the rate remained unchanged at 26.7 per 1,000 live births. Lower rates in the later cohort were evident for males and for females, and for single but not for plural births. Chase examines a number of factors which are known to be associated with neonatal mortality. The method selected is that of cohort rates derived from linked infant-death and live-birth records. Because the study is based on official vital records, a number of important variables such as family income, housing, etc. have not been available for analysis. In spite of this limitation, this publication provides substantial guidance for future studies of neonatal infant mortality, and its variation along the racial and socioeconomic lines.★

371.   Chase, Helen C., and F.G. Nelson. 1973. Education of Mother, Medical Care and Condition of Infant. American Journal of Public Health 63 (Supplement): 27-40.

This paper presented some findings from a study of live births and linked infant death records for infants born in New York City in 1968. The study group was a heterogeneous one consisting of a sizable group of white infants delivered of foreign-born mothers (13.3 per cent), of mothers born in Puerto Rico (15.8 per cent), and of mothers who were native-born Negroes (22.6 per cent) in addition to the largest group of white infants whose mothers were native-born (42.9 per cent). The residual category (5.4 per cent) included small groups of foreign-born Negroes, Chinese, Japanese and other ethnic groups. Of the total group, 35.7 per cent of the mothers had at most 1-3 years of high school education. The proportions varied from 15.9 per cent for the white native-born group to 71.6 per cent for the Puerto Rican group. The Negro group had a more favorable educational pattern than the Puerto Rican group, and one that was more similar to that of the white foreign-born group. Of the entire cohort, 18.5 per cent of the infants were born out-of-wedlock, and the proportion declined with increasing level of education. This relationship persisted irrespective of ethnic group and despite their different levels of educational attainment. According to the birth certificates, about 8.9 per cent of the mothers appeared to have had no prenatal care. On the average, the white native-born and foreign-born groups started

care earlier and had more prenatal visits than the Puerto Rican or
Negro groups. Similar differences were noted with regard to the type
of hospital and type of service. The white native-born and foreign-
born groups used predominantly private service in proprietary and
voluntary hospitals while the Puerto Rican and Negro groups used
predominantly general service in voluntary and municipal hospitals.
Infant mortality and the proportion of infants who were of low birth
weight were inversely related to education for all ethnic groups.
Infant mortality and the proportion of low birth weight infants among
those with an elementary school education or 1-3 years of high school
were about double that of infants whose mothers had some college
education. Similar differentials were noted between illegitimate and
legitimate births, and according to risks. Infant   mortality   was
associated with prenatal care as well. When only those live births
with 36-43 completed weeks of gestation were considered, infant
mortality increased as the interval to the first prenatal visit was
delayed, and decreased as the number of visits increased. The   data
are useful for background information for health planning and
considering health education and prenatal care programs in
relationship to the educational level of mothers. However, they
cannot be interpreted too narrowly as a cause-and-effect relationship
because of other correlated characteristics such as income,
nutrition, and cultural factors.*

372. Damon, Albert. 1969. **Race, Ethnic Group, and Disease.** Social Biology
      16 (2): 69-80.

      This paper examines the association between race and disease. Dis-
      cusses several examples of race-ethnic group-specific diseases. It
      concludes that "distinctive racial or ethnic patterns of disease can
      be profitably applied by the public health official to the detection
      and prevention of disease and by the clinician in diagnosis and
      treatment. The Anthropologist can gain insight into human origins,
      relationships, distribution, and adaptation. The geneticist has new
      material for the study of heredity in human populations. And finally
      the epidemiologist gains clues to the cause of some of man's major
      diseases, with the ultimate hope of eradication."★

373. Davis, R., Jr. 1975. **A Statistical Analysis of the Current Reported
      Increase in the Black Suicide Rate.** Unpublished Ph.D. Dissertation.
      Washington State University. 119 pp.

      The purpose of this investigation was to re-evaluate Henry and
      Short's external restraint theory, in light of a reportedly
      increasing Black suicide rate. Specific attention was focused on
      accounting for the increasing Black suicide rate through an analysis
      of five structural variables deemed important by external restraint
      theory. These variables (sex, age, strength of the relational system,
      social status and community integration) were integrated into one
      theoretical model. The data for this analysis were taken from copies
      of death certificates and day records made available by the Orleans

Parish Coroner's Office, New Orleans, Louisiana. The sample consists of 779 death certificates. This number constitutes 206 suicides and 573 non-suicides. The non-suicides are made up of homicides, accidental deaths, and natural deaths. Path analysis in the form of our theoretical model was used to determine the conditional probability of dying by suicide for our sample of New Orleans' Blacks. The model also allows us to determine the net effects (when all other variables are held constant) of each independent variable on suicide for the twenty-year period 1954 through 1973. Our model indicated that the conditional probability of dying by suicide in the first decade (54-63) of our sample was 3.5 percentage points less than the conditional probability of committing suicide in the latter decade (64-73). The increase in New Orleans Black suicides occurred late in the 64-73 decade, primarily among the young (25-34) and old (55-64). The ratio of male to female suicides during our twenty-year sample was 3.3 to 1. The modal Black who committed suicide during this period was found to be a 39 year old male laborer, who was unmarried and lived in either the Desire or Carrollton area of the city. Black females were found to opt for less lethal methods for their suicide attempts than Black males. While men preferred the highly lethal methods of firearms, women preferred the far less lethal method of poison. Over-all, the method of committing suicide for Blacks roughly resembles that of whites for our sample. In our evaluation of Henry and Short's external restraint theory, we found that at the zero order level of analysis, the assumptions Henry and Short make about the relationship between external restraints and suicide are not valid for our population. However, when other variables are held constant, the inverse relationship between status and suicide found at the zero order level is reversed, lending support to Henry and Short's cliam of a direct relationship between status and suicide. Consequently, the assumptions about external restraints and suicide were found to be valid for our population when using multiple regression analysis.*

374. Davis, R. 1981. The Significance of the Black Population Undercount in the Production and Use of Health and Mortality Rates. In: Black People and the 1980 Census. Volume 1: Proceedings from a Conference on the Population Undercount. Chicago, Illinois: Illinois Council for Black Studies. Pp. 630-640.

Data from the National Reporting System for Family Planning Services showed that 33% of the 3.8 million women in the United States who visited organized family planning clinics in 1978 were teenagers. The data in this report are based on information obtained from observation, medical records, or from personal interviews. A descriptive analysis of the teenagers under study is presented and both sociodemographic characteristics and the types of services the teenagers received are examined. Most of the patients, both black and white teenagers were under age 16. Most of the teenagers who visited the clinics were new patients. More than 1/2 of the teenagers had never been pregnant; more than 3/4 had never had a live birth.

About 40% of the teenagers had never used a contraceptive method regularly prior to the clinic visit. For those who had ever used a method, the largest proportion--48.8%--had used the oral contraceptive (OC). The general pattern was that teenagers whose previous method was medical, i.e., OC, IUD, or diaphragm, continued that method or chose another medical method. Most teenagers who used less effective methods switched to the more effective methods during the visit. The proportion of teenagers who adopted or continued OC use was significantly larger than that of women age 20 years and older. The proportion of teenagers who had had at least 1 abortion since 1973 (almost 12%) represented 34% of the teenagers who had had at least 1 pregnancy. A higher proportion of the older women than of the teenagers had had at least 1 abortion since 1973.☆

375.   Demeny, Paul, and Paul Gingrich. 1967. A Reconstruction of Negro-- White Mortality Differentials in the United States. Demography 4 (2): 820-837.

This paper summarizes the results of an investigation of the validity of Negro-white mortality differentials as reflected in the series of official United States life tables since the turn of the century. Pertinent excerpts from these often-quoted tables are reproduced in Appendix Table A-1 for convenient reference. The paper divides into two main parts. First, mortality levels and differentials beyond early childhood are derived, without use of the existing vital records, by interpreting the series of ten-year cumulative survival rates implicit in the census records for native whites and for Negroes. The results are in general agreement with the official figures, particularly for males. Second, mortality levels and differentials in early childhood are estimated by extrapolating the official e_5° values via model life tables; that is, by the analytical procedure that would be followed in the absence of direct information on early childhood mortality. Unless it is assumed that age patterns of death for United States Negroes were extremely deviant from those found in populations with reliable census and vital statistics, one must conclude that the official figures grossly underestimate early childhood mortality for Negroes, at least for the period, 1910-40. It follows that, during those decades, Negro-white mortality differentials in terms of expectation of life at birth were also substantially higher than is suggested by the official estimates.*

376.   Dott, A.B., and A.T. Fort. 1975. The Effect of Maternal Demographic Factors on Infant Mortality Rates: Summary of the Findings of the Louisiana Infant Mortality Study, Part I. American Journal of Obstetrics and Gynecology 13 (8): 847-853.

69,556 birth and 1541 death certificates for infants in Louisiana during 1972 were matched and reviewed to identify groups needing special medical care. This, the 1st of 3 reports, analyzes the effect of intrinsic patient factors such as age, child spacing, legitimacy, education, socioeconomic status, and race on infant mortality rates.

In general, nonwhites have higher infant mortality than whites (24.5 vs. 15.8). This pattern is unchanged when controlled by education, legitimacy status, age (except under age 15), number of children, or place of delivery. Only white patients who delivered in state charity hospitals, or who had fewer than 9 prenatal visits, or infants weighting less than 5 1/2 pounds at birth had greater rates. Rates were higher for illegitimate babies than for those born in wedlock (22.8 vs. 15.5) and for babies born to women under age 15 (41.1 for white women, 29.9 for black women). Very old mothers also had higher infant death rates; for women over 40 infant death rates were 25.1 for white women, 32.9 for black and neonatal death rates were 20.1 for white and 30.4 for black. When parity is examined in relationship to maternal age, the old dictum that "too many children too soon leads to greater risk" is upheld. Infant mortality rates for the 2nd child or a mother aged 15-19 is 30.1; for her 3rd child, 68.3; for a 5th child of a mother aged 20-24, 50. There is a steady decline in infant mortality, both neonatal and postnatal, with increased education regardless of race. There was almost a 75% drop between the rate for women with less than 8th grade education and those who had completed high school (6.8 to 1.9). These data show the less educated, middle-class black woman delivering in a private hospital fares about as well as the comparable white patient. The health professional must continue to try to improve education, nutrition, medical care, and support of community welfare programs.☆

377. Dunn, J.E., and D.F. Austin. 1977. Cancer Epidemiology in the San Francisco Bay Area. In: Epidemiology and Cancer Registries in the Pacific Basin: National Cancer Institute Monograph 47. Washington, D.C.: Government Printing Office. Pp. 93-98.

Approximately 12,000 annual cases of cancer are registered with the San Francisco Bay Area Resource for Cancer Epidemiology. The study population of 3 million individuals is composed of Whites, Blacks, American Indians, Chinese, Japanese, Filipinos, and other ethnic groups. This resource is a data base for epidemiologic studies such as those in progress on the relationship of cancer of the breast, the ovary and the cervix to such factors as childbearing, fertility, and exogenous hormone use. Other ongoing studies proposed include the role of diet in the etiology of breast and colorectal cancer; a sociomedical assessment of childhood cancer; work on melanoma in relation to phenotypic, behavioral, and occupational factors; and an assessment of the cytologic history of clinical cervical cancer patients. As an example, a brief description is given of the study method and preliminary findings for the research on colorectal cancer. In addition, the cooperation of local craft unions is being sought in order to monitor cancer incidence among different occupations.☆

378. Erhardt, Carl L., and Helen C. Chase. 1973. Ethnic Group, Education of Mother, and Birth Weight. American Journal of Public Health 63 (Supplement): 17-26.

Using the data relative to 3,115 infant deaths from 142,017 live birth cohort in New York City in 1968, the authors describe the variations in birth weight with respect to ethnic (White, Black, Chinese, Japanese, Others) differences and educational attainment of the mother and duration of gestation in addition to the effect of birth weight on infant loss. It is the finding of this paper that the proportion of low weight babies, in general, decreased with advancing educational attainment of the mothers. This pattern, however, is not found to be uniform for all ethnic groups. Relative to blacks, a regular and marked reduction in the proportion of low birth weight infants with increased education of the black native-born group. The authors argue that the differentials between ethnic groups in the proportion of low birth weight and its association with the education of mother shed some doubts on the validity of the hypothesis that birth weight is genetically determined. Determinants of low birth weight (e.g., short duration of gestation, and prenatal care) are also discussed.*

379.   Farley, Reynolds. 1972. **Fertility and Mortality Trends Among Blacks in the United States.** In: Demographic and Social Aspects of Population Growth and the American Future, Research Reports, Volume 1. Charles F. Westoff and Robert Parke, Jr. (eds.). Pp. 111-118.

The vital rates of blacks in the United States are at a higher level than those of whites. The racial difference in crude rates is greater for fertility than for mortality and, as a result, the black population is growing more rapidly than the white. In 1969, the rate of natural increase approximated 1.7 percent annually among blacks; 0.7 percent among whites. Since the late 1950's, birth rates have decreased among both blacks and whites but the racial difference in fertility persists. Apparently many couples adopted more effective techniques of birth control during the 1960's but the incidence of unplanned or accidental pregnancies remains greater among blacks than among whites. Although actual fertility rates are higher among blacks, desired family size is smaller among blacks than among whites. Racial differentials in mortality have traditionally favored whites. The racial gap in life expectation has narrowed a bit during the last 30 years. Nevertheless, impressive differences are evident. The current life expectation of nonwhites equals that of whites in 1940 while the current infant mortality rate of nonwhites is at the same level as that of whites in 1945. This paper summarizes racial trends and differentials with regard to fertility and mortality. Certain population projections are then presented.*

380.   Freeman, M.G., W.L. Graves, and R.L. Thompson. 1970. **Indigent Negro and Caucasian Birth Weight-Gestational Age Tables.** Pediatrics 46 (1): 9-15.

A study of indigent Caucasian and Negro birth weight-gestational age data has been presented. A total of 7,547 Caucasian and 9,800 Negro deliveries are included. Race and sex are important variables in birth weight percentiles. Criteria for similar future studies are suggested.*

381. Garn, S.M., H.A. Shaw, and K.D. McCabe. 1977. **No Ifs, Ands, or Buts, an Essay On the Maternal Smoking Effect.** Paper Presented at the Symposium in Honor of Dr. Olaf Mickelson, East Lansing, Michigan, June 17, 1977.

In a study of more than 18,000 normal term infants, the % of low birth weight infants, of short length infants, and of infants with small head circumferences was markedly higher for mothers who smoked than for mothers who did not smoke. Furthermore, the % of small infants increased as maternal smoking increased. The smoking effect persisted into the 3rd and 4th year of the child's life for low weight and into the 7th year for short length and for small head circumference. In examining the smoking habits of mothers with small normal term infants, it was found that infants of low weight, of short length and with small head circumferences had an excess of smoking mothers and an even greater excess of mothers who smoked heavily. Prematurity is also associated with maternal smoking. When the frequency of premature births for smokers and for nonsmokers was compared separately for whites, Puerto Ricans, and blacks, and within each group by educational level, the relationship between prematurity and smoking held for each group and for each educational level. The mechanism by which smoking reduces infant size is unknown, but we do know that it is a nutritional variable and that it is probably the single largest cause of prematurity and small normal term infants. Most importantly, we know how to prevent it. Bar graphs depict 1) the % of low birth weight infants by maternal smoking habits for white normal term infants and 2) the % of premature infants by level of maternal education for whites, Puerto Ricans, and blacks. Line graphs show the % of smoking mothers with short length children, with low weight infants, and with small head circumference children by age of child for blacks and for whites. Tables present 1) the % of short length, low weight, small head circumference infants by maternal smoking habits and by age of child and 2) the proportion of short length, low weight, and small head circumference children, grouped by age, by maternal smoking habits to the total sample.☆

382. Geerken, Michael, and Walter R. Gove. 1974. **Race, Sex, and Marital Status: Their Effect on Mortality.** Social Problems 21 (April): 567-579.

This study has investigated racial differences in marital roles by looking at particular patterns in types of mortality apt to be affected by psychological factors. The data clearly suggest that there are not sharp differences in the nature of the marital roles occupied by blacks and whites. However, the differences that do occur are consistent with the traditional race literature,which suggest a greater tendency toward female dominance in black families than in white families. Thus, the data support the view that marriage is slightly more advantageous for white men than for black men, while being unmarried is slightly more disadvantageous for white men than for black men. In contrast, married black women appear to be slightly better off than married white women. Furthermore, the data are consistent with the view that black women who are heads of households are more able than their white counterparts to cope with the burden of raising children by themselves.*

383. Glass, Leonard, et al. 1974. **Effects of Legalized Abortion on Neonatal Mortality and Obstetrical Morbidity at Harlem Hospital Center.** American Journal of Public Health 64: 717-718.

Studies have shown that as a result of the 1970 New York abortion law, leaving the termination of pregnancy at the discretion of patient and her physician prior to the 24th week of gestation, there has been a significant decline in the maternal and neonatal mortality rates, as well as a decline in the number of illegitimate births in New York State. This study examines these effects relative to the patients--mostly blacks--using the Harlem Hospital Center. More specifically, it deals with an examination of the effects of the new abortion law on perinatal, neonatal, and maternal mortality rates as well as maternal morbidity at the Harlem Hospital Center, with a predominantly poor black patients. The Hospital's neonatal and obstetrical data for 1966 through 1971 were analyzed. The major findings of this study were: (1) the in-hospital neonatal mortality rate declined from an average of 33.9/1,000 live births during the 1966-69 period to 18.9/1,000 live births in 1971; (2) the frequency of admissions for incomplete abortions in relation to the annual number of deliveries was found to be significantly lower in 1971 than during the 1966-69 period; (3) from July 1970 through 1971 only two maternal death had occurred--one of these had occurred in a women with sickle cell anemia who died as a result of complications of her primary illness; (4) the neonatal mortality rates at Harlem Hospital Center which prior to 1970 far exceeded those of both the white and nonwhite population of the United States declined following the legalization of abortion.★

384. Hale, C.B., K. Kirk, R.L. Shiller, and S. Schaffer. 1979. **Infant Mortality Differentials in Alabama, 1976-1978.** Paper Presented at the American Public Health Association Annual Meetings, New York, November 1979. 6 pp.

A data file containing selected items from birth and death certificates of 2575 singletons who died in Alabama from January 1976 to December 1978 was subjected to secondary analysis. Cross tabulation and multivariate techniques were used to develop information on which policy and program decisions could be based; the analysis focused on characteristics of mothers whose infants died. The study asked the general question: within the universe of infants who died, is it possible to identify 1 or more characteristics that occur more frequently than might be expected by chance. Part of the answer was already known: being black puts an infant at almost twice the risk of death as being white. Therefore the research question was asked separately for whites and blacks, within Health Services Administration geographic areas designed as planning units. Results show areas which have disproportionate infant mortality for each component and racial group. The findings suggest infant mortality, but interracial and inter-area differences illustrate the difficulties of reaching both black and white risk groups with a single statewide program. Data are presented in tables, with a brief descriptive abstract.**

385.   Hecht, P.K., and P. Cutright. 1979. Racial Differences in Infant Mortality Rates: United States, 1969. Social Forces 57 (4): 1180-1193.

Using multiple regression analysis, we measured the effects of demographic, health, and socioeconomic variables on race-specific neonatal and postneonatal infant mortality rates. The racial difference in rates in 1969 is due to 1) effects of mean differences in black and white population characteristics, 2) differences in the impact of independent variables, and 3) differences from other causes. Higher black than white infant mortality is the result of unfavorable black means on birthweight, age of mothers at birth, education, and marital stability. Black mortality is also higher because mothers age at birth, marital stability, and education have more favorable impact on mortality for whites than blacks.*

386.   Hendershot, G.E. 1979. Work During Pregnancy and Subsequent Hospitalization of Mothers and Infants: Evidence From the National Survey of Family Growth. Public Health Reports 94 (5): 425-431.

Data on ever-married primiparas from the National Survey of Family Growth conducted by the National Center for Health Statistics were used to investigate the relationship between working in the last trimester of pregnancy and 2 indicators of illness--hospitalization of women for complications of pregnancy and hospitalization of their infants during the first year of life. These indicators are more likely to occur among women who work during the last few months of their first pregnancy than among women who stop working earlier. Moreover, this association is greater among black than white women: for black women who work in the last 3 months of their first pregnancy, the rates of hospitalization of the mother or infant are more than twice as high as for white women who do not work that late. Among women who are provided prenatal care by a private physician and among women who have insurance that pays for all or part of the hospital bill, working in the last trimester is not associated with higher rates of hospitalization. Hospitalization of the mother or child occurred for 1% of the primiparas. Among those who worked in the last trimester the percentage was slightly higher--17.1%. The author concludes that the association of working late in pregnancy with higher rates of hospitalization does not mean, necessarily, that working is a cause of hospitalization. It does indicate, however, the need for epidemiologic and medical research on the relationship.☆

387. Henson, D., and R. Tarone. 1977. An Epidemiologic Study of Cancer of the Cervix, Vagina, and Vuvla. American Journal of Obstetrics and Gynecology 129 (5): 525-532.

The survey was conducted from 1969 through 1971 in 7 metropolitan areas and in 2 states. The population surveyed represented 10% of the total population in the U.S. The incidence rates of in situ and of invasive squamous carcinoma of the cervix were greater in black than in white women; the risk being twice as great for black women (p less than .001). A high risk was associated with early onset of sexual activity. Cancer in situ preceded invasive cancer. For white women, rates for invasive carcinoma of the cervix remained constant after age 45 but for black women rates increased after 45. The rates for adenocarcinoma of the cervix showed patterns similar to those of intraductal breast carcinoma. Adenocarcinoma of the cervix and squamous cell carcinoma of the cervix seem to have different etiologies. Multifocal cancer sometimes also developed in the vagina or vulva in association with carcinoma of the cervix. The highest incidence for carcinoma in situ of the vagina and vulva occurred after age 60. The highest rates of insitu carcinoma of the cervix occurred between 25-35 years of age. The relative numbers of white and black women having Papanicolaou tests may have influenced the rates for in situ carcinoma. With increasing age, fewer women have this test. Older women should be more frequently screened. The age-adjusted incidence rates for invasive cervical carcinoma in England and in the U.S. were similar.☆

388. Jakobovits, Antal, W. Westlake, L. Iffy, M. Wingate, H. Caterini, R. Chatterton, and M. Lavenhar. 1976. Early Intrautrine Development: II. The Rate of Growth in Black and Central American Populations Between 10 and 20 Week's Gestation. Pediatrics 58 (6): 833-841.

The application of the growth-rate standards, established for Caucasian embryos and fetuses in a previous report, to Black and Central American racial groups has been investigated. Comparison between menstrual age and crown-to-rump length indicated differences in the 10 to 15 weeks gestation range. However, growth rates for the same groups were practically identical between the 15th and 20th weeks pregnancy. This finding suggests that the actual rate of growth is closely similar in the respective ethnic groups and that apparent discrepancies reflect erroneous, or purposefully false, menstrual histories rather than dissimilar growth patterns. Largely identical rates of development were suggested by the crown-rump length to foot length to body weight interrelations among the various racial groups. A moderate, but rather predictable, deviation from the earlier established standards was noted in the crown-rump length versus foot length ratios of Black American fetuses, providing the only exception to what appears to be a practically identical rate of growth for the investigated ethnic groups in the first half of gestation. The evaluation of the results was extended to involve the effect of educational and social factors on currently available data of embryonic and fetal growth. It is suggested that heretofore uncon- sidered factors may affect the validity of widely quoted standards of intrauterine growth.*

389.   Jiobu, Robert M. 1972. Urban Determinants of Racial Differentiation in Infant Mortality. Demography 9 (4): 603-615.

This study relates differential socioeconomic status between blacks and whites to racial differentiation in infant mortality rates. The basic assumption is that decreases in socioeconomic differentiation and related variables lead to decreases in the black-white infant mortality differential. A comparative approach based on aggregate measures of socioeconomic differentiation is utilized to compare sixty-one United States urban places. Path Analysis shows that neonatal mortality differentiation is virtually unaffected by socioeconomic differentials while decreased racial differences in hospital births tend to increase neonatal mortality differentiation. In contrast, postneonatal differentiation is affected by socioeconomic differentiation. It is concluded that despite some suggestions that infant mortality is no longer responsive to socioeconomic factors, postneonatal differentiation is affected by socioeconomic differentials when comparison is based on city units.*

390.   Johnson, Charles S. 1932. A Question of Negro Health. Birth Control Review 16 (6): 167-169.

Johnson discusses black health in relation to birth control, family planning, fertility, and veneral diseases and the resulting dangers to childbearing and maternal mortality among blacks. He also examines the part played by economics. Johnson concludes that inaccessibility of reliable information, inability of blacks to secure high priced professional advice, and reliance upon dangerous folk measures constitute three major problems in the black population.*

391.   Kitagawa, Evelyn M., and P.M. Hauser. 1973. Differential Mortality by Race, Nativity, Country of Origin, Marital Status, and Parity. In: Differential Mortality in the United States: A Study in Socioeconomic Epidemiology, by Evelyn M. Kitagawa and Philip M. Hauser. Cambridge, Massachusetts: Harvard University Press. pp. 93-113. (Chapter 6).

This chapter summarizes mortality differentials by a number of "social" characteristics which, though related to socioeconomic status, are not generally considered a component of socioeconomic status as such. Death statistics by race, country of birth, and marital status are readily available because these items are reported on the legal death records. However, death rates calculated by relating deaths (tabulated by characteristics as reported on census records) have been viewed with suspicion because of potential errors resulting from discrepancies in the reporting of these items on death certificates and census schedules. The analyses of mortality by race, country of origin, and marital status in this chapter utilize the tabulations of deaths compiled by the National Center for Health Statistics for the three-year period 1959-61, supplemented by cross classifications (compiled from the 1960 Matched Records Study) which compare responses to these questions on 1960 death certificates and 1960 census schedules. The latter permits correction of the death rates for discrepancies in reporting on the two records and, incidentally, also provides some indication of the extent of error involved in using uncorrected rates. The mortality ratios for ever-married women by parity (number of children ever borne) were derived from the 1960 Matched Records Study.*

392. Klebba, A. Joan, J.D. Maurer, and E.J. Glass. 1973. **Mortality Trends: Age, Color, Sex, United States 1950-1969.** HEW, National Center for Health Statistics. DHEW Publication No. (HRA)74-1852. Washington, D.C.: Government Printing Office.

This is an analysis of countervailing changes in components of the nearly stable crude death rate during 1950-69, trends of age-adjusted and age-specific death rates by color and sex, and changes in sex and color differentials for mortality by age. Important trends include the rise in the death rate for young people 15-24 years of age, the fall in the death rate for older Americans 45 years and over, and the upturn in the level of excess mortality for young men, particularly for nonwhite men.★

393. Kovar, Mary Grace. 1977. **Mortality of Black Infants in the United States.** Phylon 38 (December): 370-397.

This paper does not attempt to discuss the clinical factors involved in infant mortality. I have instead taken a demographic and public health approach and attempted to document the changes and components of change in the mortality rates of black infants in the United States over the time periods where the data are reasonably reliable, to identify some of the high risk population groups,and to look at the geographic variation of black infant mortality in the United States. There are several approaches which can be taken if we really want to reduce the number of black infants who die in this country each year. I hope that the data I have presented here will be useful in selecting an effective approach. My own bias is that I would like to see the efforts targeted where they would prevent the most deaths. Programs targeted to reduce infant mortality rates in Northern suburbs, for example, will not prevent many deaths of black infants. That's not where many black babies are born and that's not where they die.*

394. Macri, J.M., et al. 1978. **Maternal Serum Alpha-Fetoprotein and Low Birth Weight (Letter).** Lancet 1 (8065): 660.

An association between raised maternal serum alpha fetoprotein (AFP) and low birth weight has been noted in a mass screening for neural tube defects underway since 1976 in Nassau County, New York. During 1975 and 1976, the number of births averaged 12,882. 6.9% of babies weighed less than 2500 gm at birth; 5.9% were white and 14.9% were black. A retrospective analysis of 1364 screened pregnancies confirmed that low birth weight was associated with maternal serum AFP levels above the 95th centile (P<.001). Additionally, the low birth weight trend was confirmed in data on 152 pregnancies with known outcomes. Within these 152 pregnancies, 22 multiple gestations, 1 multiple congenital anomaly, 10 elective terminations of pregnancy, and 24 spontaneous abortions, still births, and intrauterine fetal deaths were observed. 95 normal fetal outcomes yielded 11 with birth weights below 2500 gm (12%): 77 white mothers delivered 7 babies below 2500 gm (9%), whereas 12 black mothers delivered 4 babies below 2500 gm (33%). These 3 series indicate that a segment of the population exists at high risk of low birth weight; this segment might benefit from AFP testing at different times during pregnancy to enhance prediction of low birth rate, providing suitable indices are developed.☆

395. Madans, J.H., J.C. Kleinman, and S.T. Machlin. 1981. **Differences Among Hospitals as a Source of Excess Neonatal Mortality: The District of Columbia, 1970-1978.** Journal of Community Health 7 (2): 103-117.

Between 1970 and 1978 the neonatal mortality rate for black infants in the District of Columbia remained essentially constant while the national rate declined steadily. This report examines adjusted hospital specific neonatal mortality rates in order to determine the extent to which the District's lack of improvement can be explained by excess mortality in a few hospitals. The indirect method of adjustment utilizing standardized mortality ratios (SMRs) is used to control for the effect of the birth weight distribution on hospital-specific neonatal mortality rates. A generalized least squares approach is used to model the changes in the SMRs for any hospital between 1970-72 and 1973-75, and four hospitals experienced no change in the 1973-75 to 1976-78 period (although one of these hospitals had very low SMRs initially). The remaining four hospitals experienced a 37% decline in their SMR's during the second interval (1973-75 to 1976-78). If the three hospitals that had high initial rates and showed no change in mortality rates from 1973-75 to 1976-78 had experienced the 37% decline, the District's SMR in 1976-78 would have been reduced by 20%.*

396. Mare, R.D., and S.K. Matsumoto. 1980. **Socio-economic Effects on Child Mortality in the United States.** Paper Presented at the Annual Meetings of the Population Association of America, Denver, Colorado, April 10-12.

This collection of 7 tables and 1 figure examine a number of

socioeconomic variables as they affect child mortality in the U.S.
The first table examines the 5 of deaths from major causes in the
U.S. (1975) as compared with England and Wales (1970-72) and adds the
factor of class differences in mortality for England and Wales.
Table 2 connects mother's schooling with the % of children dead and
breaks those deaths down by race and sex.   Table 3 utilizes the
variable of annual family income with the same aforementioned factors
and Table 4 combines the 2 variables to arrive at a total figure.
Table 5 examines the goodness of fit statistics for the effects of
the 2 variables on child mortality by age and sex for whites. Table 6
deals with the estimated probabilities of dying between schooling and
mortality for U.S. whites.   The final table compares survival
percentages from life tables based on vital statistics to June 1975
CPS estimates. The included figure diagrams the relationship between
the % of deaths due to accidents and its association between mother's
schooling and child mortality for certain age-race-sex groups.☆

397. May, W.H., J.B. Miller, and F.C. Greiss. 1978. Maternal Deaths from
      Ectopic Pregnancy in the South Atlantic Region, 1960 Through 1976.
      American Journal of Obstetrics and Gynecology 132 (2): 140-147.

      Using statistics from the National Center for Health Statistics for
      the South Atlantic states for 1960-1975, maternal mortality rates
      from ectopic pregacy were determined. The ectopic pregnancy death
      rate for the entire period was 0.29/10,000 live births, but the rate
      for blacks was markedly higher than the rate for whites. The rate
      decreased 40% from 1960-1965 to 1971-1975; however, when the rates
      were examined by race, it was found that the rate for whites had
      remained almost constant while the rate for blacks had decreased
      considerably. Apparently the decrease is related to improved living
      conditions and health care for blacks and not to any general
      improvement in the level of diagnosis and treatment of ectopic
      pregnancy. In a more detailed analysis of maternal death records from
      the North Carolina Medical Society for 1961-1976, the rate of ectopic
      pregnancy death was 6 times higher for blacks than for whites. The
      rate for all groups combined remained relatively constant, with a
      possible upward trend in the 1973-1976 period, and the proportion of
      direct obstetric deaths and of hemorrhage deaths accounted for by
      ectopic pregnancy deaths increased considerably from 1961-1964 to
      1973-1976. An analysis of the 24 ectopic pregnancy deaths recorded in
      the North Carolina data, revealed that in 2/3 of the cases, the delay
      in diagnosis was attributable solely to physician delay. Both sets of
      data indicate a lack of progress in the early diagnosis of ectopic
      pregnancy and point to a need for doctors to be taught to "think
      ectopic." A recommendation is made that in the future maternal
      mortality rates for ectopic pregnancy be computed in reference to the
      number of conceptions instead of the number of live births as the
      recent increase in abortion tends to bias the computation. Tables for
      the South Atlantic states and for the District of Columbia show the
      rates for ectopic pregnancy deaths, number of live births, and number
      of ectopic pregnancy deaths by race and by state for 1960-1965,

1966-1970, 1971-1975, and the total for 1960-1975. A graph compares the ectopic pregnancy rates for whites and for blacks in each 5 year period for the South Atlantic Region. Graphs depicting the North Carolina data for the 1961-1964, 1965-1968, 1969-1972, and 1973-1976 show the rates for direct obstetric death, hemorrhage deaths, and ectopic pregnancy deaths as well as the % of these deaths attributable to ectopic pregnancy. Other tables for North Carolina show 1) the age, race, and parity characteristics of ectopic pregnancy victims and 2) % of cases by symptoms, type of diagnostic confirmation, site of pregnancy, and by person responsible for diagnostic delay.☆

398. Meeker, Edward. 1976. **Mortality Trends of Southern Blacks, 1850-1910:** Some Preliminary Findings. Explorations in Economic History 13 (1): 13-42.

In this study new estimates of indices of levels of health for blacks are presented for the decade 1850-1860, the year 1880, and the decade 1900-1910. The new results are compared with those of past studies and it is argued that the revised figures make better use of existing data. For the last decade of slavery, and for the year 1880, stable population analysis and model life tables are used. For the years following 1880 the estimation relies on both model life tables and an indirect scheme which makes use of information on rates of population growth and new estimates of changes in fertility.*

399. Michielutte, R., et al. 1973. **Early Sexual Experiences and Pregnancy Wastage in Two Cultures.** Journal of Comparative Family Studies 4 (2): 225-238.

Data from 2 different cultures were compared in order to examine the relationship between female early sexual experiences and eventual pregnancy wastage. The comparison was made between a North Carolina group of low-income blacks, assumed to be sexually permissive, and a Costa Rican sampling of primarily low-income white and Indian women, a sexually restricted group. It was found that age at first marriage, age at first intercourse, and age the women first learned about contraception had little relationship with an eventual level of pregnancy wastage. Only the age of first conception correlated with pregnancy wastage. In the United States sampling age at first conception related to pregnancy , but the differences were small. The Costa Rican sampling showed this same relationship only for the youngest women in the sampling. High levels of pregnancy wastage, which correlate with early ages of first conception, are also thought to eventuate in higher fertility levels. Even the small relationships found between age at first conception and pregnancy wastage would lend support for providing better contraceptive services to young women, married and unmarried, with the goal of postponing this first pregnancy.*

400. Morris, N.M., J.R. Udry, and C.L. Chase. 1977. **Reduction of Low Birth**

Weight Rates by the Prevention of Unwanted Pregancies. Family Planning Resume 1 (1): 252-253.

It has been claimed that a direct relationship exists between the occurrences of low-birth-weight births and unwanted pregnancies. A strong correlation has been shown between the incidence of low birth weight and the infant mortality rate. Therefore, a reduction in unwanted pregnancies should lead to a reduction in the infant mortality rate. This study was based on interviews with 3030 black and 4891 white postpartum mothers at 60 major hospitals in 17 U.S. cities. Women were questioned about the wantedness of the pregnancy at the time of conception. Low birth weights were 10.6 of black and 5% of white births. Among both groups there was no definite relation between low-birth-weight and unwanted pregnancies. An exception was that, among women with some college education, unwanted births were more prone to have more frequent low-birth-weight births than women who had wanted the pregnancy. It is concluded that the prevention of unwanted pregnancies will not contribute to the reduction in the occurrence of low-birth-weight births. These results cast doubt on some planning claims.☆

401.   Pick, J.B. 1977. Correlates of Fertility and Mortality in Low-Migration Standard Metropolitan Statistical Areas. Social Biology 24 (1): 69-83.

Significant determinants of fertility and mortality were looked for among 17 demographic and socioeconomic variables characterizing the populations of 29 low-migration standard metropolitan statistical areas (SMSAs). Regression analysis showed density to be correlated negatively with life expectancy of white females and positively with the gross reproduction rate (GRR) of nonwhites. The GRR of whites was inversely related to the level of medical care, but the GRR of nonwhites was most closely linked to the percent of nonwhites in an area, with higher percentages lowering the GRR. Greater white income increased nonwhite infant female mortality because of competition for medical services.★

402.   Phillips, J.H., and G.E. Burch. 1960. A Review of Cardiovascular Diseases in the White and Negro Races. Medicine 39: 241-288.

Although many of the statistics and comments noted in this review seem rather inconclusive, there are enough significant cardiovascular differences between the white and negro races to justify recording such racial data in all studies. These show the Negro to differ from the white in many ways other than skin color and physical or anatomic features. Therefore, by careful recording and analysis of data the important factor of racial differences can be more completely clarified.*

403.   Rahbar, F., L. Westney, and J. Momeni. 1982. Prenatal Factors Affecting Perinatal Mortality in Blacks. Journal of the National

Medical Association 74 (10): 949-952.

A study of 222 black mothers who gave birth to low-birth-weight infants in a tertiary care center showed that prenatal care plays a significant role in perinatal outcome; the effect of prenatal care was especially dramatic in the infants weighing less than 1,500 grams. In addition, maternal age is an important factor when less than 17 years. When a teenage pregnancy is associated with a lack of, or irregular, prenatal care, fetal outcome is compromised.*

404.   Rao, S.L.N. 1973. On Long-Term Mortality Trends in the United States, 1850-1968. Deomgraphy 10 (3): 405-419.

This study of United States life tables analyzes the process of mortality transition during 1850-1968. Special features of the study are (1) a phase-specific, rather than an age-specific, analysis of mortality and (2) use of measures based on person-years of life (nLx) in phase-intervals, rather than survival rates (nPx) or expectation of life at given ages (e$_5^o$). The analysis suggests that the historical transition of mortality in the United States can be described as a three-stage process: an initial stage of slow improvement during 1850-1900, a second stage of rapid improvement during 1900-1950, and a third stage of slower improvement since 1950. Quantitative measures of rapidity of mortality decline in the several phases indicate that they are not identical for all phases and in all stages.   The analysis also suggests that there have been rapid changes in the components of overall mortality differentials by sex and race in the United States. The paper draws attention to the need for studies of factors in variations of mortality at ages beyond 50 in the United States population subgroups.*

405.   Rochat, R.W. 1977. Pap Smear Screening: Has it Lowered Cervical Cancer Mortality Among Black Americans? Phylon 38 (4): 429-447.

Cervical cancer screening through the Pap test has become more widely and frequently used since the 1950s, and during that time the cervical cancer mortality rate has declined; however, the author argues, no studies have been able to measure the influences of other possible factors in the decline or to examine potentially harmful effects of screening such as inappropriate hysterectomies due to false positive diagnoses. The prevalence of cervical cancer among various U.S. minorities is outlined and data illustrating the steady decline in the mortality rates from cervical cancer of black women (who had the greater incidence of cancer) are presented. Factors that may contribute to this decline are cited, and the increased prevalence of total hysterectomies for reasons other than cancer is considered significant. Utilization and reliability of the Pap test are discussed, and a study revealing the variability of interpretation of biopsies by pathologists is reported, with data. Calculations from the data indicate that the predictive value of the Pap test increases with the prevalence of cervical cancer; therefore the

author suggests that screening efforts be taken or a second
interpretation be solicited in the event of a positive diagnosis of
cervical cancer.☆

406.   Rush, D., and E.H. Kass. 1972. **Maternal Smoking: A Reassessment of
the Association of Perinatal Mortality.** American Journal of
Epidemiology 96 (3): 183-196.

A prospective study of pregnant women of a Boston hospital was
undertaken in 1961-1962 to assess the relationship of smoking with
perinatal mortality and with other differences found in the study
population of 490 white and 530 black women. The analysis of
perinatal mortality was heightened by the addition of data on 2256
additonal patients who fulfilled the same criteria as the study
population. More than twice as many whites smoked cigarettes than
blacks. White multigravidae who experienced a loss of the observed
pregnancy had a history of excessive loss (34.2%) which was
accentuated among the smokers (52.8%). Birth weights were higher in
whites and nonsmokers and rose linearly with time for gestation over
40 weeks in nonsmokers whereas diminished birth weights were
associated with long gestations in smokers. The average length of
gestation among blacks was substantially lower than among whites, and
whites had higher hematocrits. Social differences, including place of
birth and marital status, were found between smokers and nonsmokers,
but differences in birth weights were not related to social factors.
Perinatal mortality was almost double among black smokers, with loss
occuring frequently early in pregnancy. The stillbirth/neonatal death
ratio was found to be independent of race, smoking, or parity. A
review of the English language literature shows an impressive
association between maternal smoking and perinatal loss when the
figures are aggregated. As would be expected, this loss is greater
among women of lower economic status where differences may be
accentuated (as they may also be in late pregnancy).☆

407.   Rush, D. 1974. **Respiratory Symtoms in a Group of American Secondary
School Students: The Overwhelming Association With Cigarette Smoking.**
International Journal of Epidemiology 3 (2): 153-165.

In order to ascertain the magnitude and consistency of the
association between cigarette smoking and respiratory symtoms, 12,595
Rochester, New York, public high school students completed questionnaires in the spring of 1968. Boys reported more smoking than
girls, whites more than blacks, and older children more than younger
children. The amount of smoking reported reflected parental smoking,
especially among girls. Among boys, there was a negative relationship
between socioeconomic status and reported smoking, but there was no
comparable gradient among girls. There was school by school variation
in reported smoking unexplained by age or socioeconomic status,
especially among girls. Current smoking was strongly associated with
reported respiratory symptoms. Younger smokers had generally higher
rates of symtoms, but there were only minor differences between the

sexes. Those with a past history of pneumonia reported an excess of recent lengthy chest illness. Among those not currently smoking, blacks had much higher rates of symptoms than whites and children of lower socioeconomic status, especially girls, also reported a somewhat higher rate of some symptoms.☆

408.   Ryan, G.M., and J.M. Schneider. 1978. **Teenage Obstetric Complications.** Clinical Obstetrics and Gynecology 21 (4): 1191-1197.

The mother and her baby which may be mitigated by good prenatal care, intensive nutritional counseling, and attention to social problems. A study of 222 predominately black, single adolescents who delivered at the University of Tennessee Center for the Health Sciences during the 2-month period between December 1977 and February 1978 revealed an increased incidence of hypertension and convulsive disorders as well as a high rate of toxemia and fetal distress during labor and delivery. Birth weights of less than 2500 gm were associated with a 12% incidence of prematurity, and nearly 15% of the newborns required intensive care (23 had high-risk Apgar scores at 1 minute and 18 at 5 minutes). Perinatal mortality was 54/1000. In this population, teenage pregnancy is viewed as an accepted and even welcome occurrence, supporting the finding that poor neonatal care is a prime cause of the increased complications of adolescent pregnancy. Comprehensive personal services are required to achieve patient compliance with prenatal medical care.☆

409.   Schottenfeld, D. 1981. **The** Epidemiology of Cancer: An Overview. Cancer 47 (5, Supplement): 1095-1108.

This is a general discussion of cancer epidemiolgy in the U.S. Mortality, incidence, and survival trends over the 25-year period from 1950 to 1974 are traced for 12 possible cancer sites in males and females. Patterns of occurrence are specified for blacks, children, and young adults. A brief discussion is devoted to cross-national occurrences and migrational trends in different types of cancer. Cancer epidemiology can contribute to cancer prevention by increasing understanding of the risk factors and etiologic mechanisms. Total cancer mortality increased over the period for males, both white and black, while it decreased for females, both white and black. In 1974, the age-adjusted cancer mortality rate per 100,000 was 219.7 for black males, 177.3 for white males, 135.3 for black females, and 118.2 for white females. The contribution of each type of cancer to this total must be identified by sex, race, ethnicity, social class, and place of residence. Cancer sites for which tobacco and alcohol are major determinants in the U.S. occur more often among men, blacks, lower socioeconomic groups, and with increasing urbanization and increasing age. Cigarette smoking contributes to 30-35% of all cancer deaths occuring among males in the U.S.☆

410.   Salisbury, L., and A.G. Blackwell. 1981. **Petition to Alleviate**

Domestic Infant Formula Misuse and Provide Informed Infant Feeding Choice: An Administrative Petition to the United States Food and Drug Administration and Department of Health and Human Services. Unpublished. San Francisco California: Public Advocates, Inc.

This rulemaking petition to the United States Food and Drug Administration and Department of Health and Human Services was filed on June 17, 1981. To date, the various agencies named as respondents have acknowledged receipt of the petition, but they have not yet made any decisions regarding the procedures they will follow for its consideration. This document presents the following information: 1) trends--the increasing use of infant formula among the poor while educated and higher income women are choosing to breast feed; 2) medical harms--documentation of the incidence of infant morbidity and mortality resulting from proper and improper use of infant formula; 3) factors which discourage breast feeding--the impact of hospital practices, professional attitudes, and promotional practices on the mother's feeding choice and ability to breast feed successfully; 4) institutional role models--descriptions of the key ingredients of several programs that have successfully increased the incidence of breast feeding among low income women; 5) the parties that are being petitioned and their legal authority and obligation to respond; 6) remedies/relief--proposals for government action that can provide low income families with the information and support needed to make informed feeding choices and safely nourish their children. The facts, figures, and information presented in this petition demonstrate that any delay in remedying the current situation is costly not only in terms of the human suffering caused by unnecessary illness, but in the ever-increasing burden of expenditures borne by taxpayers for easily preventable hospital visits and medical treatment.☆

411. Siegel, J.S. 1953. **Natality, Mortality, and Growth Prospects of the Negro Population of the United States.** Journal of Negro Education 22 (3): 255-279.

Siegel seeks to summarize the more significant data bearing upon black-white differences in natality and mortality levels and trends, and to evaluate them in terms of the relative growth prospects of the two population groups. He examines the changes that are expected to occur in the age and sex composition of the black population, as well as its total size. Siegel concludes that with respect to the relative growth prospects of the two population groups, the relative proportion of blacks and whites in the U.S. are expected to maintain their present balance for some time to come, though the proportion of blacks may increase slightly. Reasons for this are discussed.★

412. Siegel, J.S. 1978. **Prospective Trends in the Size and Structure of the Elderly Population, Impact of Mortality Trends, and Some Immplications.** In: United States Congress. House of Representatives. Select Committee on Aging. Consequences of Changing U.S. Population:

Demographics of Aging. Volume 1. Hearings, May 24, 1978. Washington, D.C.: Government Printing Office. Pp. 76-121.

The number of people who are 65 and older will increase by nearly 40% between now and the year 2000, the rise in the number of births up to the early 1920s being the principal factor for the prospected increase. If fertility moves toward replacement level, about 12% of the population will be 65 and over by the year 2000; if fertility continues at current levels a sharp rise will occur in the 2010s-2025s because of the baby-boom of the 1945-1960s. Rates of increase are expected to be greater for females than for males, without, however, the tremendous differences in the growth rates of the sexes seen in the last few decades: there were 69 males for every 100 females in the U.S. in the age group 65 and over in 1976. Male mortality has been higher than female mortality at each age in life, and the basis for this gap rests on social, genetic, and biological factors. Due to the decline in death rates, life expectancy for both males and females has been climbing: it was estimated at 70.2 years in 1968; it was 73.5 years in 1977. Death rates for blacks are higher than for whites below age 65, and then there is a crossover at ages 75-79. There is little basis for anticipating major increases in life expectancy in the U.S. in the next several decades. Cardiovascular and cerebrovascular diseases, and malignant neoplasma accounted for 3/4 of elderly deaths in 1976. Mortality trends are not only difficult to predict, but must be closely related to projected fertility trends: the percentage of the population 65 and over projected today for the year 2000 is higher than that projected for this group in past years. These demographic changes will have important social and socioeconomic implications; the ratio of elderly persons to working age persons will increase, and will relegate elderly people in a situation of societal and familial dependency, and will force the government into playing a bigger part in providing health services for the elderly. Both these problems will become very serious after 2010. ★

413. Selig, Suzanne Mae. 1976. Selected Characteristics of Cities and the Difference in Mortality Between Urban Blacks and Whites. Unpublished Ph.D. Dissertation. University of Cincinnati.

This dissertation investigates the relationship between selected characteristics of 144 large U.S. cities and the difference in mortality between white and black males. Eighteen causes of death are examined for white and black males for the years 1959-1961. It is hypothesized that a set of city characteristics, commonly employed to explain differential mortality, will be related to the difference between white male and black male urban mortality rates. Eight characteristics of cities are measured: the difference between white and black "poverty"; the difference between white and black "rich"; the difference between white and black "unskilled"; the difference between white and black professionals; the degree of residential segregation of the black population; the amount of available "adequate" housing; the amount of per capita municipal health expenditures; and the severity of the climate of the city. It is hypothesized that cities wherein blacks and whites have relatively similar resources (measured as the independent variables) will also have similar white and black cause-specific mortality rates. Four types of analyses are performed: computation of a zero-order correlation matrix of each of the eight independent variables and each of the eighteen causes of death; stepwise regression in which a small set of independent variables is sought to predict the dependent variable; as well as two additional techniques which involve a re-classification of the eighteen causes of death. None of these analyses offers any support for the hypotheses. Explanation as to the lack of support for these hypotheses included a discussion of the nature of the methodological and statistical procedures used, the nature of the data itself, as well as a discussion of additional variables which could account for the difference between white and black mortality rates. It is concluded that additional variables must be important to explain this difference. Among these are diet and nutrition, as well as societal discrimination. As these factors do not readily lend themselves to be studied at this level of analysis, it is possible that although differences exist between cities in differential mortality cities might not be the most appropriate units to explain differential mortality.*

414.   Shin, Eui Hang. 1975. Black-White Differentials in Infant Mortality in the South, 1940-1970. Demography 12 (1): 1-19.

This paper examines the trends and variations in the black-white differentials in infant mortality in ten selected Southern states during the 1940-1970 period. The patterns observed from the Southern states are compared with those observed from seven selected Northern states and the country as a whole. The ratios of black to white infant mortality rates and Fein's "time-lag" statistics are used as measures of the extent of black-white differentials. The gaps between blacks and whites in both neonatal and postneonatal mortality rates have widened in the Southern states between 1940 and 1970. No significant differences between the Southern states and the Northern states in the extent of black-white differentials in infant mortality were observed. A positive association between variations among the Southern states in postneonatal mortality differentials had a weak inverse relationship with income inequality. A series of general explanations of the observed trends and variations have been presented. Also, a detailed methodological consideration of the possible influence of artifacts of the data trends and variations has been made.*

415.   Spiers, P.S. 1972. Father's Age and Infant Mortality. Social Biology 19 (3): 275-284.

The role of the father's age on infant mortality is examined through 1960 data gathered by the National Center for Health Statistics, which linked 100,000 death and birth certificates. The information on these matched certificates was used to obtain various distributions of infant deaths by mother's and father's age. Causes were separated by race and by whether or not deaths were caused by congenital malformations. For each mother's age group among whites and nonwhites, there was a distinct tendency for the death rate to fall and then rise again as the father's age increased. The lowest rate generally occured when the mother's and father's age were about the same. For deaths from congenital malformations, the sample pattern is suggestively present among white death rates but not among nonwhite rates. Data from births registered in North Carolina in 1968, which included information on parent's education, were examined to see if variations in infant mortality rates with the father's age result from irregular social circumstances, such as the practice of less educated men to marry much younger women. The education level among both whites and nonwhites of older fathers and younger mothers were lower in every mother's age group than for couples roughly the same age. With these figures, mortality associated with younger fathers tended to increase; with older fathers it tended to decrease. Deaths from congenital malformations showed no tendency toward this trend, which contrasted sharply with trends from the 1st study. The conclusion is reached that some support is found for the hypothesis that infant mortality increases as either the father's age or the span between the mother's and father's age increases, and that, except in the case of congenital malformations, this results in part from socioeconomic factors.☆

416.   Sutton, G.F. 1971. Assessing Mortality and Morbidity Disadvantages of the Black Population of the United States. Social Biology 18: 369-383.

A review of recent data concerning morbidity and mortality differences between the white and black population is presented to reflect upon the contribution of these data to the relative well-being of the black population. Crude death rates and even age-adjusted mortality rates obscure important mortality differences between blacks and whites. These differences are found particularly at those ages which are of most significance in considering the problem of the social welfare of the population. The black-white differentials are greatest where they have the greatest impact. Morbidity data do not demonstrate such effects; however, it is apparent that mortality and morbidity experiences are closely interdependent and that an integration of these effects, which has not yet been successfully carried out, would be of considerable utility. Data currently published which are illustrated here do not lend themselves to simple interpretation of black-white differences related to welfare implications. The size of the mortality differential by race in the working ages is more appropriate to the concerns of the social welfare of blacks as a population in the aggregate than differentials taken more broadly as to general mortality. Even so, once we have established the relative level, the question remains: What is the calculus of well-being such that it is possible to sort out significant gains in the analysis of trends in the well-being of blacks in the United Stated?*

417.   Sutton, G.F. 1977. Measuring the Effects of Race Differentials in Mortality Upon Surviving Family Members. Demography 14 (4): 419-430.

A model is developed to use marital history data from the U.S. Current Population Survey and mortality statistics from the federal registration system to estimate color differences in (a) the risk of widowhood among women in the working ages and (b) the cumulative duration of widowhood. Color differentials in mortality among married males are thereby translated into person-years of dependent survivorship among women, in anticipation of our later estimating average and cumulative lifetime income losses for the survivors. Initial results of this model, dealing with the demographic aspects of survivorship, are presented.*

418.   Sutton, Gordon F. 1978. Mortality Differences by Race and Sex: Consequences for Families. In: The Demography of Racial and Ethnic Groups. Frank D. Bean and W.P. Frisbie (eds.). New York: Academic Press. pp. 301-314.

Color differentials in mortality are commonly studied with an eye to group differences in health conditions and well-being in the population. Another aspect of color differentials in mortality is that concerned with the consequences of premature death of adult males upon surviving and dependent family members. Measures of widowhood and paternal orphanhood for differentials are computed and are shown to exceed the values of mortality differentials as to the extent of the disadvantage of the nonwhite population. The color differentials are influenced by sex differentials in mortality by color but do not predominate in the outcomes. Although such demographic measures illuminate the matter at hand, the next steps in the study of the burden of mortality upon surivors is the calculation of measures of economic loss and color differentials in such losses for use in the consideration of national social policy.*

419.   Thompson, S.J. 1979. Change in Maternal Attitudes During Pregnancy. Paper Presented at the American Public Health Association Annual Meetings, New York, November 1979. 16 pp.

This study attempts to determine whether pregnant women who have experienced complications experience different maternal attitudes than women with normal previous pregnancies, and to assess changes in maternal attitudes during the gestational period. The subjects were 112 Black women attending a maternity clinic who were in good health, 17 through 34 years of age, within the first 20 weeks of their 2nd, 3rd, or 4th pregnancy, and with no known elective abortions. Subjects were interviewed between 10-20 weeks for demographic variables and maternal attitudes and at 36 weeks for symptoms and maternal attitudes. The 18-item pregnancy questionnaire, developed in 1971, contains scales which represent a level of anxiety state. The 112 women were divided into 2 groups of 65 women with normal pregnancy histories and 47 with prior complications to determine whether the attitude items would discriminate between women with and without previous pregnancy complications. Although a discrimination using a reduced set of 4 variables was statistically sifnificant, the variables fail to separate the 2 groups clearly. The attitude varibles may fail to discriminate between the groups because prior experience is not important in the formation of maternal attitudes or because the instrument may not measure attitudes related to spontaneous abortions, which were the major previous complication among the women. The assessment of change in maternal attitudes during pregnancy was hampered by an attrition rate of 29% between the first and second interviews. The data failed to support the hypothesis that attitudes toward pregnancy change as the pregnancy progresses. Mean changes in 17 of the 18 items in the scale indicated that attitudes tended to become more negative as pregnancy progressed, but they were not statistically significant. The findings in this sample are only partially consistent with other studies.☆

420. Valanis, B.M., and D. Rush. 1979. A Partial Explanation of Superior Birth Weights Among Foreign-Born Women. Social Biology 26 (3): 198-210.

This study of 766 black women reexamined the issue of advantage in birthweight and length of gestation in foreign-born women and confirms the reported higher birthweights among that group. Subjects were new registrants for prenatal care at a public clinic in Harlem, New York City, 1971-1973, and were part of a randomized trial of nutritional supplementation during pregnancy. 3 nativity groups were represented: New York City, southern United States, and foreign countries. Despite the standard selection of all subjects for high risk for low birthweight, foreign-born women had only 3.8% of births under 2500 grams in contrast to 15.6% among the southern women, and 18% among New York city natives. 6 sets of variables were examined in relation to birthweight outcome. An average birthweight advantage of 218 grams for the foreign-born was found to be associated with higher childhood social status and more positive health behaviors.**

421. Valien, Preston. 1970. Overview of Demographic Trends and Characteristics by Color. Milbank Memorial Fund Quarterly 48 (2, Part 2): 21-37.

The growth and changing distribution of the Negro population have important social implications for the Nation. The percentage of Negroes in the total population has changed little since 1890, when it was 11.9 per cent. For several decades after 1890, the Negro population declined as a proportion of the total population until 1930, when it was 9.7 per cent. Since 1930, however, lower Negro mortality, relatively higher Negro birth rates and the restriction of

European immigration in the 1920's combined to reverse the declining trend. In 1960, the Negro population was 10.5 per cent of the total population and in 1970 it is estimated to be slightly above 11 per cent. The great change in Negro population has not been in numbers or in relative proportion, but in regional and urban distribution. The movement of Negroes away from the South has reduced the percentage of the Negro population living in the South from 90 percent in 1910 to slightly over 50 percent in the late 1960's. The movement of Negroes has been to the cities and especially to the central cities of metropolitan areas. In 1960, the six cities with the largest Negro population were all outside the South (New York, Chicago, Philadelphia, Detroit, Washington and Los Angeles). These six cities with Negro populations ranging from over one million in New York City to over 300,000 in Los Angeles, had almost a fifth of all Negroes in the United States. It is the concentration of Negroes in the central cities that heightens the visibility of Negroes in the cities and creates housing problems and pressures on urban resources and services. The metropolitan distribution of the Negro population has implications for other social and economic characteristics. Negroes in metropolitan areas exceed those in nonmetropolitan areas in educational attainment and occupy better-paying and higher-status jobs. It is also well established that the nonwhite to white fertility ratio decreases with increasing income and with urbanization. Finally, voter participation of Negroes in the North and West has been greater than that of whites in the South. As pointed out, Negroes in the North and West voted at a rate seven percentage points higher than that of Southern whites. Where voting participation is combined with the spatial segregation of Negroes in central cities, the increasing political power of Negroes in densely populated urban areas comes as no surprise. This, in turn, will inevitably have long-range effects on the economic, educational, health, family and political status and utlimately upon the level of aspirations of the Negro population.*

422.   Vasantkumar, N.J.C. 1978. **Age Patterns of Mortality of American Blacks, 1940 to 1970.** Unpublished Ph.D. Dissertation. Princeton University.

It is well known that the mortality of the black population of the United States is higher than that of the white population. Less widely known, however, are the differences in age patterns of black and white mortality and the deviations of black mortality patterns from those implied in certain models of mortality. These issues were first discussed by Zelnik (1969). Although some consideration is given to black mortality patterns by cause of death, the focus of this study is on age differences in black and white mortality and the deviations of black mortality from the "West" model life table family of Coale-Demeny model life tables between the years 1940 and 1970. After making adjustments to data, both black and white mortality patterns are compared to those implied in different models of mortality which included the age structure, the cause of death structure, and the age-and-cause structure of mortality. The age, cause and age-cause contributions to the mortality differences between blacks and whites are established. A number of simulations consisting of changes in black cause-specific mortality are then conducted and their effect on Coale-Demeny model life table levels corresponding to black age-specific death rates is observed. Next, black and white age patterns of mortality are compared on a cohort basis and both the cohort and period effects on black mortality are estimated. Finally, an attempt is made to examine the difference in age patterns of mortality between blacks and whites for specific causes of death. A major finding of this study is that black and white age patterns of mortality are similar on a cohort basis. This similarity suggests that the observed "peculiarities" in period data on black mortality are due to cohort and period influences. The causes of death which are largely responsible for the black and white age difference in mortality are not identical in 1940 and 1970. In 1940, almost all the cause of death categories are important in black and white mortality differentials. In 1970, the major differences are due to higher mortality for blacks from cardiovascular diseases, cancer and violence. The cohort and period influences on black age patterns of mortality are not attributable to a single cause of death. Lack of data prevents further analysis of the nature of and specific mechanisms by which cohort and period influences affect black mortality. However, three factors appear to be important: the early morbidity and mortality experience of black cohorts, period changes influencing mortality and the socioeconomic circumstances of blacks in different age groups.*

423. Vavra, Helen M., and Linda J. Querec. 1973. A study of Infant Mortality from Linked Records by Age of Mother, Total-Birth Order, and Other Variables: United States, 1960 Live Birth Cohort. U.S. Department of Health, Education, and Welfare, National Center for Health Statistics, DHEW Publication No. (HRA)74-1851. Washington, D.C.: Government Printing Office.

Infant mortality in the United States, based on a cohort study for infants born alive during 1960, related to age of mother, total-birth order of infant, and other characteristics reported on birth or death records; considers color, sex, and age at death of infants who died during the first year of life. Infant mortality data for this study are based on 107,038 matched death and birth certificates of infants born alive during 1960 who died before age 1. The chances of surviving the first year of life were better for infants born to mothers aged 20-34 years than for those to mothers of other ages, and better for infants of low birth order than for infants of high birth order. The most favorable survival rates were among first births to mothers aged 20-24 and among first and second births to mothers aged 25-29.*

424. Willie, Charles V., and W.B. Rothney. 1962. Racial, Ethnic, and Income Factors in the Epidemiology of Neonatal Mortality. American

Sociological Review 27 (4): 522-526.

Assuming that the evidence on the difference in infant mortality rates between white and nonwhite populations is inconclusive, the authors attempt to determine whether infant mortality rates, particularly neonatal mortality rates, vary by race and ethnicity if socioeconomic status is held constant. This paper also examines the distribution of neonatal mortality in relation to the distribution of families of different income levels by race and ethnicity as well as within the total city. The study is conducted in Syracuse, New York and uses data relative to years 1950 through 1956 limited to the neonatal period. The study includes four racial and ethnic populations in Syracuse--blacks, native whites, Italians, and Polish. The study population consists of 8,626 live births and 197 neonatal deaths. One major finding of this study is that "Negro and Native White populations, though different racially, have similar neonatal mortality rates when socioeconomic status is held constant."★

425.   Wynder, E.L., I.J. Bross, and T. Hirayama. 1960. A Study of the Epidemiology of Cancer of the Breast. Cancer 13 (3): 559-601.

All the factors thought to play a role in development of breast cancer were studied via clinical and interviewing techniques in white American women (632), Negro American women (52), British women (174), Indian women (151), and Japanese women (116). Incidence patterns of breast cancer are summarized; in descending order they are: English women, white American women, Negro American women, and Japanese women. Data suggest lack of nursing has some influence on breast cancer development. There seems to be a significantly higher incidence of breast cancer in mothers, sisters, and aunts of breast cancer victims. Chronic cystic mastitis may predispose women to breast cancer. Breast cancer patients tend to marry later and thus have fewer children. Control Japanese women begin menstruating 2 years later than American women. The complexity of the factors involved in the etiology of breast cancer make statistical analysis difficult. 3 general conclusions are drawn in determining the epidemiological pattern of breast cancer.☆

------O❊O❊O❊O❊O------

Chapter 5
Black Migration, Urbanization, and Ecology

426. Alston, John P. 1971. The Black Population in Urbanized Areas, 1960. Journal of Black Studies 1 (June): 435-442.

The main objective of this paper is to study the socioeconomic profiles of blacks residing in the central cities and the urban fringes of the 213 urbanized areas during 1960. That is, it presents data on a national level representing the black population in the 1960 urbanized areas. The existence of socioeconomic differentiation between the central cities and the suburban (urban fringes) area is noted. According to Alston, on the average, the suburban blacks had higher income, educational, and occupational levels. However, the two population were found not to be completely dissimilar. The suburbs contained large proportions of lower-status blacks which in no way--even taking into account the generally depressed socioeconomic levels of the 1960 blacks--could be defined as middle class. The decade of the 1960's has experienced a migration movement even more pronounced than during earlier decades. ★

427. Bacon, Lloyd. 1973. Migration, Poverty, and the Rural South. Social Forces 51 (3): 348-354.

The 1967 Survey of Economic Opportunity data are employed to test hypotheses about differences in migration selectivity depending on the structural distance traversed in the migration process. Theoretically, the greater the structural distance crossed in the migration process, the more rigorous would be the selectivity. Conversely, where migration involves movement between similar places, little selectivity would be expected. Structural distance was defined as movement across both regional and rural-urban axes. Selectivity was defined by the relative incidence of poverty among the various residence and migration categories. Analysis of movement into and out of the rural South revealed empirical relationships between variables consistent with the theory employed, although important exceptions were found. These exceptions required a modification of the theory.*

428. Beale, Calvin L. 1971. **Rural-Urban Migration of Blacks: Past and Future.** American Journal of Agricultural Economics 53 (2): 302-307.

Most of the current further increase of the urban population is coming from natural increase rather than migration. This point is becoming publicly understood, as is the fact that black urban residents of rural origin were not disproportionately represented in the major riots of late years that stimulated so much belated interest in migration. The period when policy support for programs to benefit rural blacks--and thus perhaps retard migration--could be obtained from urban sources on a self-interest basis was rather brief in its life span. Cutbacks in rural-urban movement now, when the supply of migrants has been somewhat depleted, would be unlikely to have major beneficial effects on efforts to relieve urban congestion or otherwise improve the conditions of urban life.*

429. Bernstein, Irving M. 1968. **The Relationships of Psychiatric Symptoms Among Lower Socioeconomic Post-Hospitalized Negro Schizophrenics to Certain Demographic Variables.** Unpublished Ph. D. Dissertation. New York University. 135 pp.

The problem facing the experimenter was to compare certain symptoms of psychopathology among post-hospitalized Negroes from the lowest socioeconomic level and to determine the relationship of such symptoms to certain demographic variables. The experimental hypotheses were: (1) Lower socioeconomic post-hospitalized Negro schizophrenics with less education have a greater degree of general psychopathology than those with more education. (2) Lower socioeconomic post-hospitalized Negro schizophrenics with less education have different areas and degrees of psychopathology than those with more education. (3) Lower socioeconomic post-hospitalized Negro schizophrenics with less education have poorer role functioning than those with more education. (4) Lower socioeconomic post-hospitalized Negro schizophrenics raised in New York City have a greater degree of general psychopathology than those principally raised outside of New York City. (5) Lower socioeconomic post-hospitalized schizophrenics raised principally in New York City have different areas and degrees of psychopathology from those raised principally outside of New York City. (6) Lower socioeconomic post-hospitalized Negro schizophrenics raised principally in New York City have poorer role functioning than those principally raised outside of New York City. For this investigation "degree of psychopathology" is defined as that score which a patient receives in various areas of psychopathology (aggression, hostility, delusions, and other evidences of psychopathology) from the administration of a psychiatrically structured interview (called the Psychiatric Status

Schedule). The same structured interview also yielded a role functioning score. "Place principally raised" is defined as whether or not a subject was raised in New York City and "education" is defined as the grade a subject has reached in school. Because the experimenter is a research worker in a rehabilitation project at Harlem Hospital, New York City, his entire sample was taken from clinical patients who were eligible for rehabilitation. The measuring instrument used in this study was the Psychiatric Status Schedule developed at the Biometrics Research Unit, Psychiatric Institute, Columbia University. It is an interview consisting of a number of structural questions covering a broad range of psychopathology, including role functioning questions. The interviewer fills in 492 true-false statements about the patient during their session. The experimenter wrote a new analysis of variance computer program having a two-factor design with repeated measures. The new program enabled him to test the overall degree of psychopathology for groups and differences in profiles of psychopathology. The experimenter set out to test (from indices of psychopathology) whether certain Negro schizophrenics in various demographic groups could be thought of (for therapeutic purposes) as one or two groups. In the areas of education (above and below the median education level) and place principally raised (New York City or elsewhere) the experimenter found the two groups very close together in psychopathology sources. Consequently none of the experimental hypotheses were sustained. It was therefore concluded that the groups should not be divided in either variable. In examining a table of intercorrelations, however, experimenter found several significant correlations between age and certain areas of psychopathology, and sex and certain areas of psychopathology. Because of these findings he divided the group at the median by age and by sex. In each case, several highly significant F ratios were obtained. The younger subjects were sicker than the older subjects and the males proved to be sicker than the females. From his research the experimenter concluded that males and females can be thought of as two separate groups for therapeutic purposes. Also older and younger patients can be thus separated. The findings might apply not only to Harlem Hospital but also to other rehabilitation projects.*

430. Blevins, Audie Lee, Jr. 1970. Rural to Urban Migration of Poor Anglos, Mexican Americans, and Negroes. Unpublished Ph.D. Dissertation. The University of Texas at Austin. 202 pp.

Between 1920 and 1965 rural areas lost 30 million persons to urban areas as a result of migration. Explanations of rural-urban migration have focused on "push and pull" factors. In a new approach to push-pull analysis this study concentrated on the migration of poor persons rather than the general population. Too little is known about the poor migrant other than his residence in the urban ghettos. Therefore, the goal of this study was to bolster knowledge of rural-urban migration of poor persons. Emphasis was on the discovery of migrants who were better off after moving and the reasons for returns to the rural areas. The study utilized a unique research design. Three rural areas having heavy outmigration from 1950 to 1960 and low socio-economic levels were selected as points of origin. Each area had an ethnic concentration of Anglos, Mexican Americans, or Negroes. Persons who had once lived in the rural areas but had moved to urban areas were interviewed, and their responses were compared to those of persons still living in the rural areas. The rural sample (454) and the urban sample (407) contained respondents between the ages of 18 and 40. A select number of these, 144, were matched on age and education. Migrants generally moved in response to differential occupation and income opportunities in rural and urban areas. However, other factors such as changes in the life cycle, forced migration, and home ties proved to have unexpected importance in influencing respondents' reasons for migrating. Returnees were prepared to forgo economic benefits in order to live in rural areas. Persons who migrated generally moved directly to the urban area in contradiction to the concept of staged migration. Upon arrival in the urban areas, friends and relatives ameliorated the disruptive aspects of migration by providing job leads, lodging, and information. Migrants scored higher on all objective indices of economic status than rural respondents, with Mexican Americans and Negroes making the greatest relative financial gains. Mexican Americans were the most satisfied with their current urban residence while Negroes were least satisfied. Even though migrants were financially "better off" than their rural counterparts, a majority were ready to change residences--Negroes preferred to move to another city while Anglos desired to return to the rural area. Because many persons bettered themselves by moving to urban areas, it was concluded that no government agency should directly restrict or encourage migration from rural to urban areas or vice versa. However, several indirect policies could ease the disruptive aspects of migration and provide alternatives to migration for rural dwellers. Urban information centers should be established in urban and rural areas; federal funds should be expended to motivate rural residents to stay in school longer, and to improve the quality of the rural schools; and economic development of rural areas should be encouraged. The overall effect of the above policies would be to increase the socio-economic level of rural areas and reduce the net outmigration of poor persons.*

431. Bowles, Gladys K., and J.D. Tarver. 1965. Net Migration of the Population, 1950-60, by Age, Sex, and Color: Population-Migration Report, Volume 1: States, Counties, Economic Areas, and Metropolitan Areas. Washington, D.C.: Economic Research Service, U.S. Department of Agriculture.

"This volume presents net migration estimates by age and sex, and by color where appropriate, for States, Counties, State Economic Areas, Standard Metropolitan Statistical Areas, and Standard Consolidated Areas. These data supplement the intercensus estimates of total net migration for the 1950-60 decade, for all counties of the United States published by the Bureau of the Census in 1962." This volume consists of six parts as follow: Part 1, Northeastern States; Part 2,

North Central States; Part 3, South Atlantic States; Part 4, East
South Central States; Part 5, West South Central States; and , Part
6, Western States.★

432. Cahill, Edward E. 1974. **Migration and the Decline of the Black
      Population in Rural and Non-Metropolitan Areas.** Phylon 35 (3):
      284-292.

      This paper is concerned with some of the facts of rural to urban,
      nonmetropolitan to metropolitan migration of blacks and with
      implications of recent migration trends. Questions addressed are:
      What is the overall trend of the distribution of the black population
      by urban-rural residence? What are the most pronounced trends of
      recent black movement and settlement since 1950? What are the
      demographic effects of migration on the rural population?" ★

433. Campbell, Rex R., D.M. Johnson, and G. Stangler. 1974. **Return
      Migration of Black People to the South.** Rural Sociology 39: 514-528.

      The rising levels of incomes for Black persons, while still lagging
      far behind median incomes for whites, have created a significant
      consumer group. The importance of this market for American business,
      combined with increasing power and involvement in community affairs,
      may encourage further increases in the volume of Black migration back
      to the South.*

434. Campbell, Rex R., et al. 1975. **Counterstream Migration of Black
      People to the South: Data From the 1970 Public Use Sample.** Public
      Data Use 3 (1): 13-21.

      The counterstream of black migrants returning to the South has been
      increasing for many decades. Between 1965 and 1970, there were almost
      one-half as many blacks moving from the North and West to the South
      as there were leaving the South. Between 1970 and 1973, the ratio
      actually reversed to more blacks moving South than North. Most of the
      North to South counterstream is made up of return migrants rather
      than "new" or primary migrants. The data presented in this paper from
      the 1970 1/100 Public Use Sample show that return migrants are likely
      to be younger, better educated, and employed in higher status
      occupations than the total black population in the South.*

435. Clay, Phillip L. 1979. **The Process of Black Suburbanization.** Urban
      Affairs Quarterly 14 (4): 405-424.

      In recent years there has been much discussion in academic and
      popular literature about the increase in the suburbanization of the
      black population. While some of the patterns and trends have been
      documented, no study has analyzed in a disaggregated way the process
      by which black suburbanization takes place, that is, which blacks
      move, to what type neighborhoods they move, and in what patterns they

settle in the metropolitan area. The author analyzes this process in the context of goals for equal opportunity and concludes that the black suburbanization that is occuring represents more of a resegregation of blacks in particular sectors of suburbia than dispersal in an open housing market.*

436.   Coe, Paul F. 1959. The Nonwhite Population Surge to Our Cities. Land Economics 35 (3): 195-210.

The rapid nationwide surge of non-whites from the rural South and into our big, industrial cities of the North and West stands as one of the most significant socio-economic phenomena of our time. In this massive population redistribution, nonwhites increases relatively more than twice as fast as whites in all standard metropolitan areas and five times as fast as whites in the core cities of those SMA's during the past decade. Data available from scattered, current, special censuses suggest that the city-bound stream of nonwhites which was sparked by World War II and the Korean Conflict continues today at an undiminished tempo. While in-migration supplies the bulk of the nonwhite gains in cities, the rate of natural increase among non-whites now sharply surpasses that of the whites. SMA's in the West experienced a much faster rate of nonwhite growth than those of other regions although even in the South nonwhites in SMA's increased at faster rate than they did in the nation at large.*

437.   Connoly, H.X. 1973. Black Movement into the Suburbs: Suburbs Doubling Their Black Populations During the 1960s. Urban Affairs Quarterly 9 (1): 91-111.

In this paper Connolly reports on his study of those surburban communities in the United States that more than doubled their black population during the 1960s, and that blacks constituted at least 10 percent of the total population in 1970. A total of 24 communities are covered by this study. Connolly's major findings are: (1) black surburban growth in the 1960s was selective in character; (2) based on the socioeconomic indices employed, the 1960s black surburbaniza-tion points at a black middle-class penetration of selected suburbs; and, (3) since 1960 the soioeconomic status of blacks in the suburbs has improved to a level where socioeconomic differences among blacks resemble those of whites.*

438.   Cottingham, P.H. 1975. Black Income and Metropolitan Residential Dispersion. Urban Affairs Quarterly 10 (3): 273-196.

In summary, the low level of black residential movement from the central city to the suburban area in the Philadelphia SMSA suggests that black residential decisions are relatively insensitive to income, especially when contrasted with the sensitivity of white residential choices to income. Income is not the only constraint on black residential movement. Similar conclusions have been noted elsewhere with regard to black residential choices in other large

SMSAs. While longitudinal data might permit detection of an upward shift in black suburban selection holding income constant, the poor cross-sectional correlation between black income and suburban selection rates and the obvious gap between black and nonblack rates suggests that any upward shift must have been negligible.*

439. Craigie, D. William. 1977. **Causes and Consequneces of Black-White Residential Differentiation in American Central Cities: A Longitudinal Analysis 1950-1970.** Unpublished Ph.D. Dissertation. The University of Arizona. 172 pp.

This research examines the causal relations between change in racial socioeconomic differentiation and change in racial residential differentiation. Three distinct arguments are summarized: (1) the dominance argument, which asserts that decreases in racial socioeconomic differentiation cause increases in racial residential differentiation; (2) the economic determinism argument, which asserts that increases in racial socioeconomic differentiation cause increases in racial residential differentiation; and, (3) the opportunity restriction argument, which asserts that increases in racial residential differentiation cause increases in racial socioeconomic differentiation. The review of literature pertaining to these arguments reveals that none has been adequately tested. Hence, tests of these three arguments are designed and conducted to assess the explanatory merit of the arguments as they relate to American central cities. Hypotheses developed from the arguments are tested by concomitant change analyses (1960-1970), and lag change analyses (1950-1960 and 1960-1970). Path analytic techniques are used to describe the various relations between measures of change in the racial socioeconomic differentiation variables (education, occupation and income) and measures of change in racial residential differentiation among 34 northern and 40 southern central cities. Concomitant change analyses indicate no causal relation between change in racial residential differentiation and change in any of the socioeconomic variables for northern cities. Among the southern cities, however, concomitant change analyses demonstrate positive associations between the socioeconomic and residential variables, which provide limited support for the economic determinism and opportunity restriction arguments. The question of causal order is assessed by lag change analyses for southern central cities, which provide limited support for each of the three arguments. The findings reveal that (1) changes in racial educational differentiation are positively associated with subsequent changes in racial residential differentiation (economic determinism argument), (2) changes in racial median income differentiation are negatively related to subsequent changes in racial residential differentiation (dominance argument), and (3) changes in racial residential differentiation are positively related to subsequent changes in racial occupational differentiation (opportunity restriction argument). Additional tests control for the effects of migration and various aspects of urban growth on the relations in question. Most significantly, these tests reveal that, among southern central cities, the associations between change in racial socioeconomic differentiation and change in racial residential differentiation among central cities located in SMSA's of 500,000 or more persons (1970) differ drastically from those located in SMSA's of less than 500,000 persons (1970). This research contributes to knowledge of racial differentiation in four major ways. First, the presentation of the data compiled from U.S. census reports provides a detailed description of 1950-1970 change in racial socioeconomic differentiation for 74 cities. Second, this research clearly establishes region as a significant factor affecting all relations between forms of racial differentiation. Third, with reference to the three arguments, this research finds that none is capable of fully explaining how change in racial socioeconomic differentiation and change in racial residential differentiation are related. Fourth, the apparent identification of SMSA size as significant intervening factor provides a point of departure for future research.*

440.   Daymont, Thomas N. 1978. **Parameters of Racial Discrimination in the Late 1960s.** Unpublished Ph.D. Dissertation. The University of Wisconsin, Madison. 292 pp.

This study investigates racial discrimination in the labor market among men in the United States during the late 1960s. Linear and log-linear models were used to calculate two sets of discrimination indicators between 1965 and 1970: (1) indicators of the relative likelihood of black men and white men to obtain different occupational and non-working positions, and (2) an indicators of the relative attainment of occupational status by black men and white men. In addition, we examined the variation of these indicators across levels of selected individual characteristics and across industrial segments of the labor market. Finally, we investigated the relationship between the nature of discrimination and the social organization of labor markets across industries. Our results indicate that during the late 1960s, blacks were less likely than whites with similar characteristics to obtain the more rewarding jobs. Net of a pure rewards dimension, blacks were less likely than whites to obtain jobs (1) which had direct, non-subordinate contact with customers (e.g., sales jobs), (2) in which white workers were successful in establishing a substantial degree of monopoly power in the labor market without uniting with blacks (e.g., craft jobs), (3) for which access was determined more by capital markets than by labor markets (e.g., self-employment), and (4) which tended to be in the private-profit sector rather than in the non-profit or public sectors. Of particular interest was our finding that, contrary to the hypothesis based upon the competitive theory of discrimination, the level of discrimination in competitive industries was as great as it was in those industries in which firms were immune to competitive pressures not to discriminate.*

441.   Deskins, Donald R. 1971. **Residential Mobility of Negro Occupational Groups in** Detroit 1837-1965. Unpublished Ph.D. Dissertation. The University of Michigan. 305 pp.

In this study an attempt is made to assess the residential mobility of the major occupational groups by race in Detroit through time-- 1837-1965. To accomplish this task several hypotheses are posed within a spatial context and tested quantitatively, primarily by employing centrographic techniques. Results are displayed on numerous tables and maps and are found throughout the text and appendices. Hypothesis I tests the proposition that a direct relationship exists between the location of residential neighborhoods defined by major occupational groups and distance from the CBD. The internal structure of Detroit revealed by testing this hypothesis establishes a framework for examining the microcosm notion (Hypothesis II): that the arrangement of neighborhoods within the residentially segregated Negro sub-community is similar to that of the city as a whole. Results from testing Hypothesis I indicate that structurally the city has changed from preindustrial (where workers with high skill occupations resided nearest to the CBD) to an industrial structure (where those with the least occupational skill are found at the city's center). Similar structural changes for the Negro sub-community are revealed by testing Hypothesis II. The tests of these hypotheses also furnish the data necessary to determine residential mobility by occupation and race as well as providing insights on social distance are related to white racial attitudes and neighborhood quality. Whites were found to be residentially more mobile than Negroes while the within group residential mobility for both races positively favored those occupational groups with the highest level skills. Through time social distance between racial groups has remained constant as have racial attitudes and differences in neighborhood quality.*

442.   Dillingham, Harry C., and D.F. Sly. 1966. The Mechanical Cotton-Picker, Negro Migration, and the Integration Movement. Human Organization 25 (4): 344-351.

The authors expand and discuss their major theme that modern cotton technology has had a significant impact on black migration and unemployment rate. What does this mean to the blacks? They conclude that the future looks very bleak for blacks to obtain new employments.★

443.   Dlugacz, Yosef D. 1979. The Propensity to Move: A Sociological Analysis of the Process of Moving Among Whites and Blacks. Unpublished Ph.D. Dissertation. City University of New York. 269 pp.

This study is an examination of the racial and nonracial determinants of residential mobility from New York City. It explores a number of hypotheses currently used to explain or justify apparently high levels of "white flight". In part it introduces research on the factors determining the intention to move and explores the complex issues that are pushing people out of or repelling them from New York City. An important objective of this study is to determine the degree to which race and race prejudice influence mobility. It is quite likely that prejudice has been overrated as an explanation of urban relocation at the expense of economic issues, family composition, neighborhood and demographic factors. Six New York City neighborhoods that are experiencing various degrees of racial transition were studied. 621 Interviews were conducted in these neighborhoods in the spring and summer of 1976. The characteristics of the sample are as follows; 80 percent is white, 18 percent is black and 2 percent is Puerto Rican. 60 percent are married, 18 percent are divorced, widowed or separated and 22 percent are single. The average length of residence in the neighborhood is 12 years, with a range from one to 72 years. The median family income is $14,321, the average level of education is 12 years and 45 percent are employed. 301 Respondents rent their dwelling units and 38 percent of them live in rent controlled apartments. 319 are homeowners of which 35 percent own single-family housing and 25 percent own two-family houses. Five major factors are introduced here to explain the determinants of mobility: 1) Family composition which includes marital status, age, family size, and sex; 2) Housing conditions which consist of housing types, tenure status, and respondent's satisfaction with their home; 3) Neighborhood including length of residence, attitude towards neighborhood, neighborhood social and physical conditions; 4) Prejudice of whites towards blacks; and, 5) social economic status. A brief summary of the results is as follows: non-white respondents were found to have a somewhat greater tendency to relocate within the city's boundaries than whites. Prejudice seems not to have any effect on the intention to move among whites. The majority of whites state that they will accept blacks and Puerto Ricans moving to their blocks. However, in some instances whites who stated that they live in neighborhoods where a large number of non-white live, want to move. Also, whites as well as non-white respondents intend to move from neighborhoods that have experienced a great deal of racial trouble. The decision to move was expressed in general as a function of dissatisfaction with space and housing conditions among large households. Crime, physical deterioration and lack of social ties were found to be correlated with the intent to move. Families with children are sensitive to the social and physical environment provided by the neighborhood. Social economic status was found to differently affect respondents of each race. Occupation is the only factor that correlates with the intention to move among non-whites. Whites were found to be influenced by education, income and occupation. This study concentrated on the first phase of residential mobility--the intention to move, thus adding to a greater understanding of the high rates of residential mobility in New York City.*

444.   Duncan, O.D. 1968. Patterns of Occupational Mobility Among Negro Men. Demography 5 (1): 11-22.

The survey of "Occupational Changes in a Generation," conducted by the United States Bureau of the Census in March, 1962, gives tables on intergenerational mobility (father's occupation to first job and father's occupation to 1962 occupation) and on intragenerational mobility (first job to 1962 occupation). The mobility tables for

Negro and non-Negro men aged 25-64 years reveal pronounced contrasts. The majority of Negro men, regardless of their social origins, found themselves in lower manual jobs (operatives, services workers, or laborers) in 1962. For them, it was only a slight advantage to have grown up in a family whose head was a higher white-collar (professional, managerial, proprietor) worker. For the majority of non-Negro men (overwhelmingly white), by contrast, such favorable origins meant that they remained at the higher white-collar level, and a near majority of white men who originated at the lower white-color level moved up to the higher level. Negro men who originated at the lower levels were likely to remain there; white men were likely to move up. Negro men who originated at the higher levels were likely to move down; white men were likely to stay there. Although Negro social origins are not as favorable as those of whites, this is the lesser part of the explanation of racial differences in occupation achievement. The greater part of the explanation lies in inequalities within the process of mobility itself.*

445.   Edwards, Ozzle L. 1970. Patterns of Residential Segregation Within a Metropolitan Ghetto. Demography 7 (2): 185-192.

The residential segregation of families by income and by state of the family life cycle within Milwaukee's black community resembles in both pattern and degree that in the white community. The greater the difference in income, the more dissimilar are the distributions by census tract. Dissimilarity is greater between younger couples without children and older couples with children than between any other pair of family types defined by husband's age and presence of children. However, segregation by income was substantially greater than by family type in 1960. The bases of selectivity of blacks in "changing" areas of the city, where the proportion black is still relatively low, and of whites in the "suburban" areas adjoining the city are similar. Families in the higher income groups and couples with children are over-represented in these areas. It would appear that given the pressures of limited housing space in the inner core of the black community, given the fact that certain amenities are not available in that area, and given the economic and social barriers which restrict the movement of blacks into the suburbs, the changing areas must function as "suburbs" for the black community.*

446.   Farley, Reynolds. 1968. The Urbanization of Negroes in the United States. Journal of Social History 1 (3): 241-258.

The distribution of the black population with regard to urban or rural residence has followed a curious pattern in the United States. Farley examines the process of urbanization of blacks and attempts to elucidate some of the factors responsible for this process. He shows that blacks began to migrate from the South during the years following the Civil War, and this out-migration became substantial after 1900. Practically all those who left the South migrated to cities in the North and West. Economic factors are cited as the main reason for blacks to leave the South. As a consequence of the shifts in black population, today blacks are more urbanized than the white population. Rates of population change since 1960 suggest a continuing movement of blacks from rural areas to cities. Since the Southern black population is still large and rapidly growing, we may expect a continuation of these trends in the foreseeable future. In brief, the author surveys broad trends from the latter part of the 17th century to the present (1968) time.★

447. Fligstein, Neil David. 1978. Migration From Counties of the South, 1900-1950: A Social, Historical, and Demographic Account. Unpublished Ph.D. Dissertation. The Univeristy of Wisconsin, Madison. 182 pp.

This study attempts to provide a causal account of the migrations of blacks and whites from counties of the South from 1900 to 1950. In order to do this it is necessary to establish how the major social relationships in the South evolved from 1865 to 1900 and their implications for the migrations that occurred in the 20th century. Once this is achieved, each decade from 1900 to 1950 is considered in terms of the relative class positions of blacks and whites, the expansion and contraction of cotton cultivation, and the patterns of urbanization and industrialization of the South and North. This consideration results in the construction of multivariate models which attempt to assess the relative effects of these various factors on the net migration rates of whites and blacks. The data analysis uses counties of the South as units of analysis and data is gleaned from census and other historical sources. The two major arguments in the literature put forward about the migrations that occurred suggest 1) people left the South mainly in response to wage rate differentials, i.e., higher wages elsewhere, and 2) the introduction of tractors and cotton pickers mechanized cotton production and reduced the need for labor thereby supplying a "push" to the migration. The results of this study suggest that both of these explanations are mainly wrong. This study emphasizes the economic conditions within the South and argues that the "pull" of the North is only operative because conditions are so bad in the South. Before 1930, the migrations of blacks and whites are highly responsive to changes in cotton cultivation and opportunities to become owners and tenants, as well as the urbanization and industrialization of the South. The boll weevil infestation appears to have caused a fair amount of out-migration particularly among blacks. As blacks tended to be tenants, they were more vulnerable to the ups and downs of the cotton economy and their patterns of migration reflect this. After 1930, the major cause of black and white migration was the transformation of cotton agriculture from a labor intensive tenant economy to a capitalist machine-oriented economy. This was achieved by the self-conscious political activity of the organized farm owners who benefited from the Agricultural Adjustment Act of 1933. This Act paid farm owners to restrict cotton acreage. Farm owners restricted acreage, released their tenants, and invested their subsidy payments in machines, thereby reducing their need for their tenants even further. Therefore, it was not mechanization per se that forced blacks and whites off the land. Rather, it was acreage reduction and the concomitant intensification of production that caused the out-migrations. From 1930 on, the acreage reduction, along with the Second World War, and the urbanization and industrialization of the South and North were the major impetuses to black and white migration. The study ends by noting that it was the federal government in alliance with large cash crop producers who produced the migrations from 1933 on that resulted in the formation of ghettos in the North. It is suggested that there is irony in the fact that the federal government discovers the urban poor in the early 1960s and does not recognize its role in the creation of that underclass.*

448.   Frazier, E. Franklin. 1937. Negro Harlem: An Ecological Study. American Journal of Sociology 43 (July): 72-88.

In contrast to the Negro community in Chicago with a spatial pattern determined almost entirely by the ecological organization of the larger community, the radial expansion of the Harlem Negro community from its center, the area in which Negroes first settled, can be represented by five zones, similar to the pattern of zones of a self-contained city. The expansion of the Negro population coincides with the degree of physical deterioration in these Zones as indicated by the proportion of nonresidential structures and lodging-houses, and by the type, age, and condition of residential structures. The ecological organization of the Negro community was indicated in the significant increases in the proportion of women, children, and married men and women in the population and in the ratio of children to women of child-bearing age of the successive zones marking the outward expansion of the community. Family desertion and the proportion of families on Home Relief declined in the successive zones. The distribution of crime and delinquency did not reveal significant variations from zone to zone. While the concentration of economic, political, and cultural institutions in the first zone distinguished this area as the center of community life, the dispersion of recreational institutions revealed the extent to which the main arteries of travel and the "satellite loops" marred the symmetry of the general pattern. This study indicates that a local community inhabited by a segregated racial or cultural group may develop the same pattern of zones as the larger urban community.*

449.   Frazier, E. Franklin. 1937. The Impact of Urban Civilization Upon Negro Family Life. American Sociological Review 2 (5): 609-618. Reprinted in: E. Franklin Frazier on Race Relations: Selected Writings (1968). G. Franklin Edwards (ed.). Chicago and London: University of Chicago Press.

Asserting that urbanization of the black population during the present century "has effected the most momentous change in the life of the Negro since his emancipation", Frazier assesses the impacts of urban living on the black families who have migrated to the cities.★

450.   Frey, William H. 1978. Black Movement to the Suburbs: Potentials and
       Prospects for Metropolitan-Wide Integration. In: The Demography of
       Racial and Ethnic Groups. Frank K. Bean and W.P. Frisbie (eds.). New
       York: Academic Press. Pp. 79-117.

       This study was undertaken to enable urban scholars and policymakers
       to estimate how much metropolitan-wide residential integration could
       be accomplished in the short run if successful open suburbs programs
       were to be implemented. Although recent studies have indicated that
       the economic potential now exists to bring about a high degree of
       residential integration, the aggregate migration and redistribution
       processes that are constantly at work in large metropolitan areas
       tend to dictate the pace with which this potential can be realized.
       Through the analysis of migration and residential mobility data from
       24 large SMSAs, I have examined the pace of recent residential inte-
       gration as it has been mediated by these demographic processes in the
       past. I have also looked at the prospects for future changes in this
       pace that would accompany a substantial "opening" of the suburbs to
       blacks. In each part of the study, I focused exclusively on one
       dimension of racial integration--the suburbanization of metropolitan
       blacks.**

451.   Furstenberg, F.F., Jr., T. Hershberg, and J. Modell. 1975. The Origins
       of the Female-Headed Black Family: The Impact of the Urban Experi-
       ence. Journal of Interdisciplinary History 6 (2): 211-233.

       The authors assert that the relation between family structure and
       mobility has been a topic of great sociological interest. In this
       paper they, thus, attempt to examine how family structure and family
       composition differ among different ethnic groups in the second half
       of the nineteenth century in Philadelphia. Their analysis is based on
       a sample drawn from the decennial Federal population manuscript
       schedules for 1850 to 1880. The black sample consists of all black
       households; the white ethnic samples are drawn systematically from
       the whole number of households headed by immigrants from Ireland,
       Germany, and by native white Americans. None includes fewer than
       2,000 households for each census year. Section headings are: The
       Structure of the Household; Changes in the Household Structure Over
       Time; Ethnicity and Family Composition; Family Composition and
       Economic Conditions; Family Composition and Mortality; and, Variant
       Patterns in Family Composition. The impact of urban life on family
       structure is also examined.*

452.   Gaston, Juanita. 1977. The Changing Residential Pattern of Blacks in
       Battle Creek, Michigan: A Study in Historical Geography. Unpublished
       Ph.D. Dissertation. Michigan State University.

       In recent years, the number of geographical studies on black
       Americans has increased tremendously. However, few studies have
       focused on the spatial development and formation of black
       communities, with even fewer on the development of black communities

in small sized cities of 50,000 or less. This study examines the changing residential pattern of blacks in Battle Creek, Michigan. The genesis, growth, and migration of blacks to Battle Creek as reflected in the changing residential patterns are examined over a 90 year period. This, in turn, involves tracing the social and economic forces behind the migration and settlement patterns in different periods. The "Dagwood Sandwich" approach in historical geography is utilized in an attempt to describe and explain the spatial distribution of the black population. The first step in the approach was to establish a history of change by mapping the residential location of black families for the nine decades between 1850 and 1930. The second step was to describe the patterns and analyze the processes creating the patterns. The study relied heavily upon manuscript censuses and city directories to identify black households. Because of changes in social and economic conditions in Battle Creek, the residential patterns were temporarily divided into three parts: the 1850 to 1870 period--an era of rapid in-migration of blacks, mainly from the border states to the pioneer village; the 1880 to 1900 period--an era of marked increase in economic growth and low in-migration of blacks; and 1900 to 1930--an era of rapid urbanization and concomitant heavy in-migration of sourthern blacks to Battle Creek. Cartographic analysis reveals that the residential patterns of blacks were dispersed during the three periods. However, in the 1900 to 1930 period, the patterns were becoming increasingly clustered. Spatial assimilation, seemingly, was the process by which the spatial patterns were formed. The principal factors working to produce the spatial distribution of blacks in Battle Creek were accessibility to sources of jobs, low income housing, and to a lesser degree, kinship and friendship ties, and group identification. After 1910, racial discrimination became an important factor in the residential pattern of blacks. While no formal restrictive covenants were imposed, it became increasingly difficult for blacks to purchase housing outside of certain areas. The data indicate that the forces which created and changed the residential patterns of blacks in Battle Creek, a small sized city, as opposed to metropolitan cities, were different in degree rather than kind. Because of the low magnitude of blacks in the city from 1850 to World War I, blacks were widely dispersed throughout the city; later residential clustering intensified in response to rapid in-migration. These stages in the development of residential areas were experienced in other cities, e.g., Lansing, Michigan, Chicago, Detroit, and Seattle, Washington, to mention a few, at a much earlier period in the development of these cities, depending on the size of the city and the magnitude of the black population. In fact, with the exception of Lansing and Seattle which developed black areas a few years later, a ghetto pattern had emerged by 1930, and the process of "invasion and succession" had been clearly identified as the mode of expansion of the black residential areas. Battle Creek was in the embryonic stage of the ghetto development during the last decade of this study.*

453. Geruson, Richard Thomas. 1973. **Migration in the New York City Area**

Since the Civil War: A Descriptive, Analytical and Comparative Study. Unpublished Ph.D. Dissertation. University of Pennsylvania. 773 pp.

This dissertation describes, analyzes, and compares, within an economic framework, the patterns of migration in the New York area since 1870. These flows are a function of the forces producing excess labor demand in the areas of destination and the excess labor supply in the areas of origin. New York's experience not only continued trends apparent before the Civil War but reflected more generally the impact of population and labor changes unleashed by the growth of modernization in the United States urban areas and its spread to rural and urban areas elsewhere. The Census of Population yields decadal time series estimates for migration and population by sex and color-nativity, cross-classified by age; and, labor force by sex and color-nativity, cross-classified by occupation and industry. After a description of the trends and long swings of the series, the interrelations among these variables are analyzed. Shifts in net migration, labor force participation, and aging and mortality serve as measures of labor supply components and changes in occupational work force distribution illuminate the demand for labor. Industrial changes generate much of the occupational shift. The four main in-migrant groups are Italians from the southern provinces, Jews from the Pale region of eastern Europe, Negroes from the four southeastern states, North Carolina, South Carolina, Virginia, and Georgia, and Puerto Ricans from the island. These migrants were typically more concentrated in non-farm jobs, more skilled occupationally, more educated and urbanized than the mother stocks from which they came. The timing of the beginnings and terminations of each sub-stream is a function of the general modernization process in the wider origin areas, their respective nation states. One hypothesis suggests that the threshold levels in the stock characteristics may be necessary before mass migration will take place. A second hypothesis, called economic blockages, suggests that the specific source groups were cut off from a full sharing in the economic and social progress incident to their area's economic development in the decades prior to and during mass migration. These blockages were exacerbated by non-economic factors and demographic pressures on the labor supply side but were affected mainly by economic stagnation on the labor demand side. This latter was caused by the slow and uneven diffusion of the industrialization process, continued technical backwardness, institutional rigidities, and declining terms of trade in the agricultural sector. New York was the prime receiving area. Its specific industrial mix generated large numbers of non-skilled jobs and an extraordinary amount of skilled jobs which matched the abilities of the migrant groups. This growth and development was made possible by the interaction of external economies in service industries, downward shifts in the long run cost curves, and innovations in new products and services with high price and income elasticities of demand. The reduction in real labor costs attendant to the upgrading in skills and education of her large and versatile labor force, of which the non-native while immigrant was a key component, maintained her a dominant national position.*

454.   Gill, Flora Davidov. 1975. Economics and the Black Exoduse: An
        Analysis of Negro Emigration from the Southern United States,
        1910-1970. Unpublished Ph.D. Dissertation. Stanford University. 191
        pp.

        Black emigration from the South is considered as an example of long-
        distance migration of poor, unskilled workers. It has been character-
        ized by large oscillations of the rate of flow over time as well as
        by considerable differences between the various states. In addition,
        migration rates vary markedly among age groups. The main purpose of
        this study is to develop a conceptual framework within which the
        temporal, spatial and demographic variations all are explained simul-
        taneously. Perhaps as important is the methodological purpose of the
        study: to deal explicitly with the problems of testing microlevel
        hypotheses by using aggregated (i.e., macro-level) data. Such
        problems are to be found in many empirical studies. Yet, they are not
        widely acknowledged, as many be seen from the survey of the economic
        literature on internal migration in Chapter One. The theoretical
        model of this dissertation starts with an hypothesis specifying the
        individual's decision to migrate, and then proceeds to derive the
        corresponding macro-level relationship by explicit aggregation across
        individuals. The specification at the micro level is relatively
        simple: labor migration is viewed as an action involving a choice of
        the geographical area that offers the maximal income stream. This
        choice, however, is subject to constraints which can effectively bar
        the individual from attaining his best choice. He then must settle
        for the second, or nth, best destination, or even decide not to
        migrate at all. These constraints arise from an imperfect capital
        market and from paucity of information on job opportunities. Another
        consideration is the various transfer costs involved in migration.
        Hence, for migration to occur the expected income (utility) in the
        destination areas has to exceed that in the state of origin by at
        least the amount of the transfer costs involved. It is postulated
        that psychic costs are by far the most variable component of the
        transfer costs within a given population. Thus, while some people
        would require only small income differential in order to migrate,
        others would not move unless a much larger additional income is to be
        gained. Three new features appear in this specification. The first is
        the treatment of the decision to emigrate and the choice of specific
        destination as simultaneous decisions. The second is the notion of
        constraints and the specific nature of their impact, while the third
        is the concept of variability of psychic costs, or the notion of
        heterogenous tastes. Observations of migration rates of Black males
        from eleven Southern states to seventeen Northern states were used to
        estimate the regression model derived from this theoretical specific-
        ation. The measurement of the relevant variables of the regression
        model is discussed in Chapter Three. Among other problems, it was
        necessary to make allowances for the difference between gross and net
        migration flows, and to adjust the income variables for geographical

differences in the cost of living. Both problems have been neglected by previous studies of internal migration. Six separate regressions were estimated from cross-section observations, one for each of the decades during the period 1910-1970. The results provide strong support for the hypothesis that the finance and information constraints greatly reduce the set of accessible locales of destination. When such constraints are not binding, in periods of low unemployment, spatial earnings differences elicit significant migration responses. The findings are consistent with the hypothesis that in regard to migration the tastes of members of a given population are stable, but such attitudes vary significantly from one individual to the next.*

455. Gottlieb, Peter. 1977. **Making Their Own Way: Southern Blacks' Migration to Pittsburgh, 1916-30.** Unpublished Ph.D. Dissertation. University of Pittsburgh. 330 pp.

During the years from 1916 to 1930 southern blacks moved to the North in unprecedented numbers. While many authorities have referred to this population shift as one of the most important episodes in Afro-American history, few of them have analyzed it in depth. More importantly, the treatments of black migration to date have emphasized the economic and social effects of the northward movement while glossing over the actual experiences of the migrants themselves. This study examines the migration of southern blacks to Pittsburgh, Pennsylvania from 1916 to 1930, with particular attention to the origins of geographic movement, migration patterns, occupations, and work experiences. The over-all analysis presents migration as an evolving process by which blacks gradually transferred their homes from the South to the North. Drawing on oral histories of Pittsburgh migrants and employment records of southern black males hired at a Pittsburgh industrial firm, the study focuses on the kinds of changes the migrants faced in their day-to-day lives. Three major themes are developed in the thesis. The first is the migrants' capacity of initiating geographic movement and adapting to the conditions of urban industrial society. Chapter three shows the migration to Pittsburgh grew out of rural blacks' long-established practice of migrating seasonally between farm and non-farm work within the South. When southern blacks learned of job opportunities in the steel industry after 1915, they already possessed the knowledge and experience necessary to begin long-distance migration. Pittsburgh migrants relied mainly on their own social and economic resources to reach their northern destination. They often received assistance from friends and relatives already in the city in the form of housing and job information. A second theme in the dissertation concerns southern blacks' transiency during their earliest period of residence in Pittsburgh. Transiency resulted from the migrants' goals as well as from their assessment of urban opportunities. Chapter five discusses black workers' low job status at a Pittsburgh iron mill and their tendency to quit their positions soon after they were hired. Chapter six demonstrates that male migrants' initial objective in Pittsburgh was to earn as much money as possible in a short period of time. Dissatisfaction with inferior jobs, coupled with the goal of accumulating a cash reserve as quickly as possible, underlay the migrants' initial transiency in Pittsburgh. In addition to these primary factors, however, the migrants' emotional attachment to family, friends, and community institutions in their places of origin caused many of them to return to the South either permanently or on frequent visits. Chapter seven treats the final theme in the dissertation: the impact of southern migration on social relationships in Pittsburgh's black community Differences of culture and occupational status between the migrants and black residents of the city increased the social distance between the black upper and lower-class. This is seen both in the efforts by the Pittsburgh Urban League to make the southern newcomers efficient employees and thrifty, sober citizens as well as the hostility toward the migrants expressed by upper-class blacks generally. Migration also affected black institutions in the city. A comparison of two black Baptist churches in one neighborhood reveals that, while the churches differed in the wealth and education of their members during the migration years, they also diverged in the kind of migrant they attracted. Blacks from the upper South joined the more affluent congregation, while those from the deep South joined the poorer one. Thus the migration, by creating clearer demarcations between the upper and lower levels in Pittsburgh's black community, provided the migrants distinct social groups with which to identify when they settled in the city.*

456. Gray, Willia Bowser. 1975. Residential Pattern and Associated Socio-Economic Characteristics of Black Populations of Varying City-Suburban Locations Within the San Francisco Area: A Census Based Analysis with Emphasis on Black Suburbanized Populations of 1970. Unpublished D.SW. Dissertation. University of California, Berkeley.

Black and white population movements since 1940 have drastically altered racial compositions of central cities of the United States. Blacks have migrated in large numbers from the rural South to such cities within the last three decades; concurrently, whites have made inner metropolitan shifts to "outer rings" or suburbs of these central cities. These racial residential shifts had created as of 1970 a national central city black population of 28 per cent with a suburban black population of 5 per cent. Further, the central city populations get "blacker" with each census report; the suburban rings retain their predominant "whiteness". Specific social, economic and physical malfunctions of metropolitan areas are seen by many as resulting from such racial population imbalance between central cities and their suburbs. Those who theorize such racial cleavage as a major "cause" of metropolitan maladies have begun in prescribing a specific remedy--black suburbanization. Acceleration of the rather recently begun black suburban thrust is recommended as partial remedy for city-suburban fiscal imbalance, level of central city physical blight and troubled race relationships. It is further conjectured

that black suburban movement will "help" blacks specifically, in addition to address of mentioned general problems of metropolitan areas.
Comparative analysis of total populations as divided by city and suburban residence reveals a suburban population with higher median income, improved housing quality, higher educational level, improved
neighborhood amenities in terms of the physical environment. Those
encouraging black suburbanization on the basis of specific benefits
for that racial group assume a black suburbanization process similar
to total population processes. The suburbanization of the black population will sort out that socio-economic "cream" of stated population; the cream will be further enriched by improved housing and job
opportunities blossoming in suburbia. Central city blacks will share
in the benefits in that the outmovement of suburbanized blacks will
allow a less impacted city population of the group. The purpose of
this study is addition of empirical perspective to existing
theoretical perspectives addressing the pros and cons of encouraging
black suburbanization by policies and instrumentation of programs.
The study addresses the issues of the specific benefits to the black
subsegment of the total population. This will be accomplished by
socio-economic comparisons of central city and suburban black
populations within the San Francisco-Oakland Metropolitan Statistical
Area of the 1970 Census. We question the belief that black suburbanization is following in similar pattern to total population pattern;
a number of hypotheses are formulated relating to spatial patterning
and associated socio-economic characteristics of varying geographical
black populations of the Bay Area. Such hypotheses testing is
instrumentalized to make the suspected dissimilarities explicit. In
our belief that the black suburbanization process differs significantly from total processes is substantiated by this effort, one part
of the two prong basis for encouraging such process is put to
question within this specific area. However, it is further our
opinion that black suburbanization is alive and healthy--and will
continue without regard to theoretical or empirical discussions
generated. Blacks within the Bay Area are suburbanizing, though from
depressed numerical bases, at a ratio substantially higher than that
of total populations. Thus the study may most significantly provide
the basis for an understanding prerequisite to wise decision making
and actions relating to the emerging black suburban movement.*

457.   Greenwood, Michael J., and P.J. Gormely. 1971. A Comparison of the
        Determinants of White and Nonwhite Interstate Migration. Demography 8
        (1) 141-155.

        The primary objective of this study is to present an explanation of
        the interstate migratory movements of white and nonwhite persons
        which occurred over the period 1955-1960. The study is similar to
        several other recent studies in that we estimate the magnitudes in
        which various factors have influenced interstate or interregional
        migration in the United States. It differs from earlier studies in
        two important respects. First, we estimate and compare the magnitudes
        in which certain factors have influenced both white and nonwhite

interstate migration. Second, unlike previous studies, many of which
have made "country-wide" estimates of the determinants of migration,
we have disaggregated data to the state level and obtained white and
nonwhite "migration elasticities" for every state. These elasticities
are in turn used to test several additional hypotheses relating to
racial and regional differences in the elasticities themselves. We
argue that discrimination against nonwhites and/or differences in
"social milieu" between South and nonsouth provide a unifying explanation for most of the observed differences in white and nonwhite
migration elasticities.*

458.   Grindstaff, Carl Forest. 1970. **Migration and Mississippi.** Unpublished
Ph.D. Dissertation. University of Massachusetts. 361 pp.

The purpose of this thesis is to study Mississippi as a state of
origin and as a state of destination of migrants. Specifically, the
study is concerned with (1) state-of-birth migrants, (2) population
characteristics of migrants, and (3) State Economic Area migrants.
The data used in the study were gathered from census reports compiled
by the United States Bureau of the Census. Mississippi had been a net
state-of-birth in-migration state for both whites and blacks until
the Civil War. Since 1900, the state has been an out-migration state
for both races. The black state-of-birth out-migration has been increasing at an increasing rate since World War I, while in-migration
is very small. The white migration has stablized since 1920. That is,
the proportionate increases in out-migration have been matched by
similar proportionate increases of in-migration. The state-of-birth
migration has taken place historically within well defined streams
and counterstreams. White in-migrants came to Mississippi from the
South Atlantic Regions of the United States and from contiguous
states. White migrants from Mississippi historically moved to the
West South Central Region. Since 1950, the origins and destinations
have been more diverse. Black migration involving Mississippi is
almost totally out-migration, generally to the North Central Region,
specifically to Illinois. Streams and counterstreams of migration
between Mississippi and other areas vary according to age, sex, race,
occupational skills, education and employment status of migrants.
Black and white out-migrants from Mississippi are generally attracted
to urban areas in other states, regardless of whether or not their
origins were rural or urban. The shorter the distance of the move,
the more likely the migrants are in the dependent ages and the less
likely they are to be young adults. However, all migration is age
selective, with young adults aged 20 to 44 proportionately over-
represented in migration streams when compared to nonmigrants.
Migrants who are in professional or related occupations are more
likely to move longer distances than non-professional migrants. However, migrants are more likely to be unemployed than nonmigrants.
Females predominate in short distance moves and males predominate in
long distance moves. Professionals are among the most migratory and
operatives and laborers among the least migratory in comparison to
nonmigrants, and, in general, migrants have more years of schooling

than nonmigrants. Whites in Mississippi are more likely to make intra-state moves while blacks, in comparison to whites, are more likely to make inter-state moves. The State Economic Area analysis indicates that the migration of blacks is more directed than the migration of whites. Specifically, the number of alternative destinations are fewer for Negroes, and the major proportion of the Negro migrants go to relatively few, quite specific areas. These data also show that migrants who leave relatively poor socio-economic areas are usually of a higher socio-economic standing in terms of demographic indicators than the nonmigrant population of these areas. However, the destinations of these migrants are usually characterized by a population which ranks higher in terms of these indicators than in the in-coming migrants. Thus, such migration tends to lower the socio-economic "quality" of the population at both the points of origin and destination. Current trends indicate that Mississippi will continue to be a net out-migration state for blacks. There will be also substantial white out-migration, but white in-migration is on the increase, coming mainly from other states of the deep South, but with significant numbers moving from states in the North and in the West.*

459. Hamilton, Horace C. 1964. **The Negro Leaves the South.** Demography 1: 273-295.

The purpose of this study has been to review and analyze the most recent available demographic facts of the movement of blacks out of the South. Contending that the migration of black population from rural to urban communities, from southern states to the metropolitan centers of the nation, has been and will continue for many years "to be a major cause of human misery, social maladjustment and inter-racial misunderstanding", Hamilton hypothesizes that population increase and migration have been and will continue to be important contributing causal factors in race conflict and in the kind, magnitude, and rate of the adjustments between the races needed to be made. Hamilton attributes the movement of blacks from the south to the high rate of natural increase in the South, mechanization of southern agriculture, shift of cotton production to some other regions of nation, governmental programs limiting agricultural production, and rapid economic development in nonsouthern states. The author draws the general conclusion that as a result of this massive migration from the south, the time tables of interracial adjustment must be speeded up.★

460. Hare, Nathan. 1965. **Recent Trends in the Occupational Mobility of Negroes, 1930-1960: An Intracohort Analysis.** Social Forces 44 (December): 166-173.

An intracohort analysis of occupational trends produced more consistent results than did conventional approaches to the study of labor force change. There was a trend of convergence between the occupational distributions of white and Negro males from 1930 to 1940 and, especially, from 1940 to 1950, which did not hold, however, during the fifties. Figures for the South showed a trend of convergence similar to that of the country as a whole during the 1940s; but, in contrast to popular opinion, the Negro lost notable occupational ground in the South during the fifties. The factor of education was found to be of special importance for the Negro's mobility during periods of substantial occupational change.*

461. Harris, LeRoy E. 1974. **The Other Side of the Freeway: A Study of Setttlement Patterns of Negroes and Mexican Americans in San Diego, California.** Unpublished Ph.D. Dissertation. 343 pp.

This dissertation deals with the migrations of Negroes and Mexican Americans to San Diego, California and the housing patterns which resulted from the influx of these groups. The study concentrates on the period 1950 to 1970, but traces migration and housing trends back to 1890. San Diego is a moderately large city of 700,000 residents (1970). In spite of its urban nature, however, this city contains numerically and proportionately smaller numbers of Negroes and Mexican Americans than most other urban areas of the country. This can generally be explained by the absence of a strong industrial base of employment in the city. Although San Diego is located next to an excellent harbor, it is isolated from the east by ranges of steep mountains and early railroads were built to Los Angeles rather than San Diego. Moreover, many early residents of San Diego preferred to keep the city as a tourist and retired mecca and did not actively encourage industry. During the twentieth century, then, industry grew much more rapidly in Los Angeles than in San Diego and with the growth of industry came greater employment opportunities for large numbers of unskilled workers. Many more Negro migrants from the South thus settled in Los Angeles than in San Diego. The same was true for Mexican migrants to California. Political, social and economic upheavals in Mexico drove many Mexicans north in search of a better life, and they settled in those cities with unskilled employment opportunities. Even the growth of the aircraft industry in San Diego did not provide much inducement for Negroes and Mexican Americans to settle here. Employment in such industries usually required skills not possessed by these migrants. Employment in the service fields and in government related occupations provided most of the job opportunities for Negro and Mexican migrants and these two fields were not broad based enough to attract large numbers of such persons. Once in San Diego, Negroes and Mexican Americans were generally confined to areas of the city considered less desirable by white residents. As early as 1926, whites were moving out of residential areas which had been built in the 1880's seeking homes in new tract developments. The housing thus vacated was often occupied by Negro and Mexican residents. By the 1920's, then, a pattern of movement of Negroes and Mexican Americans into the southeast sections of the city had been established. This pattern continued in the same direction until 1970. Although the neighborhood occupied by these groups expanded into contiguous areas of the city, it did not become diffused into the city as a whole. The extent to which Negroes and Mexican Americans are segregated from the larger community is very typical of the degree of segregation found in other cities as measured by the Taeuber scale and by indexes developed by the author of this study. Using these indexes it is possible to conclude that Negroes in San Diego are segregated from the rest of the community to fully twice the extent that Mexican Americans are so segregated. Moreover, Mexican Americans made more progress toward integrated housing in recent decades than did Negroes. Several forces were found to account for the segregated housing patterns in San Diego. Survey data indicate that to some extent segregation was voluntary and that people prefer to live in neighborhoods with other persons of similar ethnic and cultural backgrounds. Higher housing costs outside the Negro and Mexican American neighborhoods was also a factor discouraging persons of these groups from moving into other neighborhoods, but data in this study show that equally low cost housing is also available in many other parts of the city. A very strong force contributing to segregated housing was found to be the widespread use of restrictive covenants covered most property in the city from 1910 to 1950. Also, available evidence suggests that real estate agents contributed to the formation of segretated housing patterns in the period 1910-1965. None of these forces explains segregation entirely. In reality, housing patterns probably resulted from an interaction of all these factors. Recent trends indicate that the degree of segregation of Negroes and Mexican Americans in San Digeo is decreasing. This trend is best explained by the passage of applicable state and federal legislation during the 1960's.*

462. Hauser, Robert M., and D.L. Featherman. 1974. White-Nonwhite Differentials in Occupational Mobility Among Men in the United States, 1962-1972. Demography 11 (2): 247-266.

Intercohort shifts between 1962 and 1972 in the occupation distributions of white and nonwhite men are analyzed and compared at ages 35-44, 45-54, and 55-64. Both white and nonwhite occupation distributions were upgraded over the decade, but among nonwhites the shifts away from the lowest-status occupations were expressed partly in increasing rates of absence from the labor force. There are indications of especially rapid shifts in the occupation distributions of nonwhite men at ages 35-44. Among whites and nonwhites intercohort shifts in the occupation distribution can be attributed primarily to changing patterns of movement from first full-time civilian jobs to current occupations, rather than to changing occupational origin distributions or patterns of movement to first jobs. The white and nonwhite occupation distributions did not show a clear pattern of convergence over the decade. They became less similar at ages 35-44 and more similar at older ages. White and nonwhite distributions were most likely to converge in those occupation groups where the share of whites was stable or declining, rather than in groups whose share of the occupation distribution was increasing. Later cohorts of nonwhites would have a much more favorable occupational distribution if they had enjoyed the mobility patterns of whites in earlier cohorts. In 1972, the inferior occupational chances of nonwhites are due primarily to their disadvantageous patterns of occupational mobility, rather than to impoverished social origins.*

463.   Hawkins, C. Homer. 1973. Trends in the Black Migration from 1863 to 1960. Phylon 34 (June): 140-152.

Traces the migration of blacks in the United States from their emancipation until 1960. The migration is broken into the following time periods: (1) from 1863 to 1900; (2) from 910 to 1930, with attention to the conditions which prompted the mass exodus that begun in 1910; (3) from 1930 to 1950; (4) from 1950 to 1960; (5) attention is also given to the changing character of black migration, and (6) the future migration of blacks. In conclusion, it is predicted that black migrants will be free to go to any part of a city to settle. This points to the idea that the cities of the future will not have a black core encircled by white rings. Though they may remain predominantly black, the encircling rings will show an increasing proportion of blacks. This prediction is based on the belief that the trends that were in existence during the period 1955-60 will continue.*

464.   Henderson, Donald H. 1921. The Negro Migration of 1916-1918. Journal of Negro History 6 (October): 383-499.

In accordance with its title, in this long essay Henderson attempts to interpret the massive 1916-1918 black migration in the United States. Henderson's main objective is to sift-out from the mass of literature the most salient facts regarding black movements. Blacks could not overcome economic and social barriers of race prejudice in the South. This caused them to flee to another locality. Henderson also discusses many other motives for black migration, new opportunities, the problems migrants faced, and the effect of migration on the black family. He asserts that black migration is not any different from movements by other human groups, and that like any other group, black movement follows certain economic, political, social, and religious forces operating in the environment of the migrants.*

465.   Hershberg, Theodore, A.N. Burstein, E.P. Ericksen, S. Greenberg, and W.L. Yancy. 1979. A Tale of Three Cities: Blacks and Immigrants in Philadelphia: 1850-1880, 1930 and 1970. Annals of the American Association of Political Science 441 (January): 55-81.

Determining whether the black experience was unique, or similar to that of earlier white immigrant groups, is central to the debate over whether blacks should be the beneficiaries of special compensatory legislation in the present. To answer this question requires interdisciplinary research that combines a comparative ethnic, an urban, and a historical perspective. Thus we observe the experience of three waves of immigrants to Philadelphia: the Irish and Germans who settled in the "Industrializing City" of the mid-to-late nineteenth centry; the Italians, Poles and Russian Jews who came to the "Industrial City" at the turn of the twentieth centry; and blacks who arrived in the "Post-Industrial City" in their greatest numbers after World War II. Analysis of the city's changing opportunity structure and ecological form, and the racial discrimination encountered shows the black experience to be unique in kind and degree. Significant changes in the structures that characterized each of the "three cities" call into question our standing notion of the assimilation process.*

466.   Hill, Herbert. 1966. Demographic Change and Racial Ghettoes: The Crisis of American Cities. Journal of Urban Law 44 (Winter): 231-285.

Hill asserts that "current civil rights struggles are rooted in three major demographic developments of the American Negro community: accelerated growth, increasing mobility, and rapid urbanization. Almost half of the Negro population now lives in the North, but the response of American cities to this development has been a vast increase and rigidity in the pattern of residential segregation. Thus the Negro finds that he has left the segregated South for the segregated northern slum... The violent outburst in the ghettoes of Harlem, Chicago, Philadelphia, Cleveland, Rochester, Jersey City, Watts, and elsewhere must be understood as the revolt of the powerless against the hopelessness and despair of their lives. The same destructive social forces that exist in Watts exist in every Negro ghetto throughout the United States. As long as these conditions are permitted to continue, as long as the ghettoes are permitted to exist, there will be the increasing danger of widespread disorders and of the potential disruption of the entire society. Eliminating the ghetto from American society must become the first priority for all the basic institutions of our society. At stake is not only the future of our most important cities or the welfare of the Negro population, at the very heart of this matter is the future of the nation."★

467.   Himes, Joseph S. 1971. Some Characteristics of the Migration of Blacks in the United States. Social Biology 18 (4): 359-366.

Himes briefly examines some trends of the migration of blacks within the U.S. in recent years. His analysis is based on the most recent census data. Shows that although the black population has continued to increase throughout the present century, the rate of growth varied, peaking in the 1950-60 decade at about 2.5% per annum and declining thereafter. All regions gained population from black in-migration from the South. The proportion of blacks residing in cities of all sizes, and especially in metropolitan areas, continue to grow, though at varying and declining rates. As a consequence, by 1967 blacks constituted over half the population of one city and

MIGRATION, URBANIZATION, AND ECOLOGY   261

almost half in several others.The proportion of blacks in the center cities of metropolitan areas increased more from natural increase than from in-migration, and the rate of in-migration was on the decline. The youngest sector of the central city black populations of the largest metropolitan areas tended to grow fastest, mainly from natural increase. Black in-migrants were found to be younger, better educated, and more likely to be employed in white-collar occupations. The sex ratio of males to females tended to be similar in both the migrant and non-migrant populations. Followed by a two page discussion by Daniel O. Price.★

468. Ibom, Godfrey Gamali. 1973. A Dynamic Quasi-Stochastic Model for Forecasting Population Distribution of Residential Black Pupils in Suburbia. Unpublished Ph.D. Dissertation.The Ohio State University. 115 pp.

The primary purpose of this study was to generate a predictive mathematical model to forecast the migration of blacks out of the ghettos into the once-forbidden white suburbs. A thorough identification of the variables (both endogenous and exogenous) related to residential shifts within a metropolitan area were made. These residential mobility determinants were modified and extended in order to build a conceptual model that would properly depict the mobility behavior of the black households who are "escaping" from the ghetto. The basic approach in deriving the mathematical model was the Expansion Method in which Gale and Moore's linear framework model predicting migration flows was used as the "initial" model. The migration process was described by a Semi-Markov Process in order to incorporate the Axiom of Cumulative Inertia and Luce's Axiom of Choice. A modified Poisson Distribution and a Gamma Distribution were used to compute the matrix of transition probabilities.*

469. Johnson, Daniel M. 1973. Black Return Migration to a Southern Metropolitan Community: Birmingham, Alabama. Unpublished Ph.D. Dissertation. University of Missouri at Columbia. 157 pp.

This study was designed to investigate black return migration to a Southern metropolitan community, Birmingham, Alabama. Returnees were analyzed in terms of their volume, demographic characteristics, reasons for moving back, and their satisfaction with the destination community. Theoretical propositions and generalizations relating to the characteristics of migrants were tested to determine the extent to which they were supported with data on black return migration to the South. The research procedure consisted of selecting 30 black groups using a stratified area probability sample controlling for race and socio-economic status and screen interviewing each resident to determine migrant status. From the 4,657 households screened, 101 returnees were found eligible for a focused interview to secure household characteristics, migration histories, reasons for moving and community satisfaction. A control group of 55 non-migrants with similar demographic characteristics were also interviewed. The major

findings indicated that the volume of black return migration to
Birmingham, Alabama, was small. Approximately 2.2 percent of the
black population consisted of returnees. Return migration was shown
to be selective in terms of age and sex but less so with respect to
marital status, education, occupation, and income when compared with
the non-migrant control group and the total black population of
Birmingham. Returnees were largely motivated by non-economic reasons.
The most frequently stated reasons for returning to the South related
to family matters. Finally, returnees and non-migrants were found to
exhibit similar levels of community satisfaction as measured by an
18-item Likert-type scale eliciting responses to the institutions,
agencies, and services common to most metropolitan areas. Among the
conclusions was the need for more research of a comparative nature to
distinguish more clearly between return migrants and migrants in
general.*

470.   Johnson, Daniel M., and R.R. Campbell. 1981. **Black Migration in
America.** Durham, N.C.: Duke University Press. 190 pp.

This book is the most recent treaty on historical black migratin.
Starting with the slave trade, the authors trace the forced and free
black migration through ante-bellum period into the 1970s, when the
long-term trend of black migration out of the south has started to
reverse itself. The study is based primarily on census data. But,
other demographic data as well as economic and historical sources are
also utilzied. The major causes of black migration are discussed. The
chapter headings are: 1, Introduction; 2, The Atlantic Slave Trade: A
Forced Migration; 3, The Domestic Slave Trade; 4, The Civil War and
Reconstruction; 5, The Turn of the Century; 6, The Great Migration
and the Post World War I Era; 7, The Depression Years; 8, World War
II; 9, The Aftermath of World War II; 10, The Fifties: The Relocation
of Black America; 11, The Sixties: A Decade of Social Change; 12,
Epilogue: The 1970s.★

471.   Jones, Eugene Kinckle. 1926. **Negro Migration in New York State.**
Opportunity 4 (January): 7-11.

Study of Blacks in the North, what led them to migrate to New York,
and the social complexion of the black population in New York.
Because blacks migrated to New York, political power is strengthened,
church and social service organizations providing better programs and
New York became the center of intellectual and cultural life among
blacks in America.*

472.   Jones, Marcus Earl. 1978. **Black Migration in the United States with
Emphasis on Selected Central Cities.** Unpublished Ph.D. Dissertation.
Southern Illinois University at Carbondale.

This investigation attempts to examine the black migration process in
the United States from the Antebellum period in the South up through
the mid-1970s. An historical geographic methodology is utilized to

analyze the problem. The use of descriptive and analytical techniques aid in understanding the problem. The investigation of the problem involves a description and analysis of the historical antecedents underlying the behavioral process of black migration. Black migration in the United States is a function of various factors operating in their places of origin and destination. Changes in the social and economic organizations of rural and urban structures has pushed and pulled blacks out of a rural society into an urban one. The net effect has been the redistribution of the black population in the United States, with consequential changes in their social and economic status. Modernization and industrialization are two concomitant processes which attracted blacks to the social and economic opportunities in urban America. The impact of technological innovations, wars, and public policy are analyzed in terms of their impact on the historical geography of black migration. Black migration is analyzed through a framework which reflects various environmental, social, economic, and political forces operating in the United States, within a particular decade or phase of time. Primary emphasis is on historical factors, central city characteristics, and the characteristics of black migrants. Central cities with a population of 50,000 or more black in 1970 are analyzed in terms of their relationships with selected social, economic, demographic, and spatial characteristics. The characteristics of black migrants and their migration streams are examined with respect to understanding the underlying motivations of this behavioral process. A regional (South and Nonsouth) comparison is made of black and white migration patterns in order to understand their past and present trends. Also, the various ideas, concepts, and theories on migration in general and black migration in particular are analyzed in this investigation. The selected economic characteristics of 1970 central cities are: the percent increase in employment of selected industries, 1958-63; the median income of nonwhite families and unrelated individuals in 1960; the percentage of the total labor force involved in manufacturing in 1960; and the mean income of female-headed Negro families in 1969. The social characteristics of central cities are: median education of nonwhites 25 years old and over in 1960, and the percentage of nonwhites, 25 years old and over with less than five years of education in 1960. The development and trends in black intermetropolitan migration are examined with respect to the following characteristics: age, sex, occupation, residence, poverty status, and receipt of public assistance. The emergence of black counterstream migration into the South is noted as a new major migration stream. The spatial characteristics such as regional location of central cities and residential status of black migrants both are very important in explaining black migration behavior. Black migration rates related to the following characteristics of central cities: changes in employment, welfare income, median education, population size, and proportion of adults with less than five years of education. Black males were found to be more mobile than black females, especially those in semiskilled and skilled occupations. However, black females were more mobile in white collar occupations

than black males. The black migration process has undergone many
changes since its beginning during the Antebellum era. It has changed
in its directions, trends, and development, and thus has been
influenced by many social, economic, technical, environmental, and
political factors in America.*

473. Koren, Barry. 1978. Residential Mobility in a Potentially Changing
Neighborhood: A Study of Household Moving and Staying in the
Aftermath of a School Conflict. Unpublished Ph.D. Dissertation.
University of Wisconsin, Madison.

I tested two leading theories of residential mobility in a
neighborhood that had been struck by a school crisis. Both school and
neighborhood were vulnerable to racial succession. One theory,
traditionally offered in racially changing neighborhoods, is that
those fearful of status and personal loss will be driven out. (The
variables I tested were income and occupational status, complaints
about the social milieu, proximity to Blacks, and advice one would
give to a friend about buying a home in the neighborhood.) The second
theory, frequently used in racially stable neighborhoods, is that
people move when their stage of life is one in which their housing
needs are changing and complaints stemming from these changes arise.
(The variables that I tested were age, tenure status and preference,
years in the home, size of household, and complaints about ordinary
aspects of their home and neighborhood--such as the closets being too
small).I used randomly generated telephone numbers in order to insure
that my sample was representative of the neighborhood population.
These numbers included unlisted as well as listed telephone numbers.
Additionally, provisions were made so that men and women had an equal
opportunity for inclusion. There were 270 standardized telephone
interviews completed during the summer of 1973, five months after the
school conflict ended. The response rate was 80%. To test the fear
and life cycle hypotheses, I randomly divided the sample into two
half-samples, stored the second half-sample, and applied
multivariate discriminant analysis to the first half-sample.
Discriminant analysis produced one formula using the fear variables
and another using the life cycle variables. Each formula told me how
to mechanically predict whether a household would move or stay. I
then compared (by means of chi-square tests of independence)
predicted behavior with actual household moving and staying behavior
in the two-year period after the school crisis. I repeated this
process ten different times for ten different payoffs for correctly
predicting a mover. After sparkling results on the first
half-sample--surpassing those of Peter Rossi's classic 1955 study,
Why Families Move--neither the life cycle nor the fear hypothesis
results achieved even statistical significance on the important fresh
second half-sample. (The only way that I found of predicting
individual household moving and staying behavior was to ask people
their plans, and that worked remarkably well.) I conclude that
failure of the two theories to be supported was due to either of two
causes (or a combination of them): failure of the methodology or

weaknesses in the fear and life cycle hypotheses. My analysis and intuition suggest that the latter is the case and that there is a troubling question still before us--how is it that people move from a potentially changing neighborhood? A related and more far-reaching question is also raised--could it be that the results published by Rossi and others were overly optimistic, or dead-wrong? (After all, I could have stopped with my excellent first-half-sample results, as I think my predecessors have). My recommendation to those interested in the neighborhood that I studied is to engage in positive experimentation. It appears to be foolish to devote large amounts of resources in any one direction (such as tenant patrols or magnet schools). When I venture beyond my data the path that I find inviting both from the theory-building and action-oriented perspectives is to effect mobility and neighborhood stabilization by strengthening the everyday, shared social life in the community.*

474. Landon, Fred. 1920. The Negro Migration to Canada After the Passing of the Fugitive Slave Act. Journal of Negro History 5: 22-36.

President Fillmore signed the Fugitive Slave Bill on September 18, 1850. This started a black migration that continued up to the start of the Civil War, causing thousands of black people to cross into Canada and resulting in many thousands more to move from one state into another in order to find safety from their pursuers. Landon describes these movements, citing several uglier incidences associated with pursuers attempting to prevent the blacks to gain their freedom; he also documents the important role played by Canada in providing safe home for the immigrants and thus determining the course of slavery issue in the United States. ★

475. Lee, E. 1967. Migration and the Convergence of White and Negro Rates of Mental Disease. In: Proceedings of the World Population Conference, Belgrade, August 30 to September 10, 1965. Volume 2: Selected Papers and Summaries: Fertility, Family Planning, Mortality. New York: United Nations. Department of Economic and Social Affairs. Pp. 410-413.

Improved social and economic status of the Negro, plus migration, have contributed to the rapid convergence of Negro and white rates of mortality, as measured in terms of the absolute differences in rates, regardless of cause of death. Migration was a contributing factor as redistribution of the Negro has been from areas with high mortality into areas with low mortality. However, due to inadequate data, it is not known whether or not the convergence has been accompanied by a convergence in morbidity rates. Morbidity comparison, such as that of relative rates of mental disorder and role played by migration, is nevertheless possible due to the excellence of admissions data to hospitals for mental disease in New York state. This study shows that the difference between rates of first admission for whites and nonwhites in New York have been diminishing throughout the periods

1939-41 through 1959-61 and this was because Negroes form the overwhelming bulk of the nonwhite population of this state. Rate for white males increased by 14% from 1939-41 to 1959-61 while that of nonwhite males fell by an equal proportion. Rates for white females increased by more than a fifth while those for nonwhites fell by more than a tenth. Sex differentials within races were also affected, with rates for nonwhite males being 40% higher than for nonwhite females. By 1950, overall differences by sex had become unimportant among whites. The convergence of rates between whites and nonwhites was mostly attributed to the sharp decreases in rates for migrants as compared with increasing or approximately stable rates for non-migrants. The importance of migration in health studies is briefly explored.★

476.   Lee, Anne S., and G.K. Bowles. 1974. Policy Implications of the Movement of Blacks Out of the Rural South. Phylon 35 (3): 332-339.

The authors examine the effects of various governmental actions (urban renewal, rural development programs, agricultural policies, growth and relocation of industries, etc.) on population distribution and relocation. They discuss black migration from the rural South, the urban non-South, the urban South, policy implications and related service needs. The authors maintain that in the past, policies were conducive to migration out of rural areas, with concomitant shifts in service needs. In the future the movement out will be slowed down and may even be reversed. The service needs of rural blacks in cities are almost the same as those of other urban blacks. This study suggests improvement as possibilities for rural South, and assumes that if these improvements and new innovations for rural development are instituted, the service needs of rural blacks can be reduced so that they more closely approximate those of other Americans.★

477.   Lee, Anne S., and G.K. Bowles. 1974. Contributions of Rural Migrants to the Urban Occupational Structure. Agricultural Economic Research 26 (2): 25-32.

Lee and Bowles examine the contribution of rural to urban migrants to lower-status urban occupations in the United States in 1967. Differentials are noted in occupations of rural-urban migrants for race and sex groups and for southern as compared with non-southern groups.★

478.   Lewis, L. Thomas. 1971. Some Migration Models: Their Applicability to Negro Urban Migration. Unpublished Ph.D. Dissertion. Clark University.

The gravity (distance) model and three derivatives, the intervening opportunities model and two multivariate models are tested upon United States Negro urban migration. Data for three stratified, random samples for each of two different time periods, 1935-40 and 1955-60, are employed in the study. The three movements sampled are:

migration from the South to the major Negro urban areas; inter-regional migration and intraregional migration. The distance and intervening opportunities models are transformed to their log linear equivalents, and estimates of migration flows are determined by regression analysis. Six separate tests of the models are undertaken. The multivariate models are multiple regression extensions of the gravity model. These models represent an exploratory attempt to replace the mass function of the gravity model with variables which might better explain migration than do the usual elements of the gravity model. The two multivariate models differ in the form of their variables. Most of the variables in the first model are compound variables formed by dividing values associated with characteristics at the migration destinations by values for the same characteristics at the migration origins. In the second multivariate model most of the elements employed are separate variables for each migration origin and destination. Stepwise multiple regression analysis is utilized in determining the exact composition of both these models. Each multivariate model is tested upon the same three sets of 1955-60 migration flows that are used in testing the distance and intervening opportunities models. The multivariate models are not applied to 1935-40 data because of less satisfactory ancillary data for that period. After the models are processed, their residuals reveal that some additional variables may be influential in explaining migration. Several of the suspected factors can only be represented by nominal scaling. Therefore, when the models are reprocessed the influence of some of the new variables is incorporated through the use of dummy and interaction variables. Some rather satisfactory results are achieved by these alterations. Among the pertinent conclusions derived from this study are: (1) The intervening opportunities model, in most instances, performs only slightly more satisfactorily than the other models. (2) The application of these models to an ethnic form of migration does reveal a tendency for more improved outcomes from these models than from similar studies where group homogeneity was not considered. (3) One of the basic elements of the so-called intervening opportunities model, the intervening opportunities variable, generally does not play a statistically significant role in the model. (4) There is some indication, although it is not conclusive, that the efficiency of the models will vary with the type of migration flows to which they are applied, (5) Although positive proof is lacking, this study does reveal some evidence that the various forms of the migration flows may exert an influence upon the constituent variables of all the models, especially those of the multivariate models. (6) There is a strong relationship between the number of migrants between two places and the amount of personal contact between them; a surrogate variable for this factor proved generally to be a highly importannt ingredient in the multivariate models. (7) It appears that Negro migration is affected by socio-economic factors at the migration origins and destinations in a sort of push-pull relationship, although the "pull" of factors at the destinations may be more influential than the "push" of conditions at the origins. (8) It has long been thought that Negro Migration in the United States tends to follow established migration channels. Through the use of dummy and interaction variables this assumption is clearly established.*

479.   Lieberson, Stanley. 1978. Selective Black Migration from the South: A Historical View. In: The Demography of Racial and Ethnic Groups. Frank D. Bean, and W.P. Frisbie (eds.). New York: Academic Press. Pp. 119-141.

The question considered in this study is a simple but important one: Was the position of blacks in the North and West undermined by the massive out-migration from the South through the years as well as by the numerically important flow in the opposite direction? In particular, did this great migration stream bring blacks to the North and West whose potential did not compare with those already there as well as generate greater white hostility and resistance to blacks generally? (Note that the changes in black-white relations caused simply by the growing number of blacks in the North is a separate question that is not addressed here). The educational characteristics of adult blacks provides an indicator that was probably not greatly altered after migration to the North, and, hence, unlike employment or occuaption, is largely a fixed attribute. Assuming that the Census Survival Ratios accurately portray the life chances of various segments of the northern black population, analysis of the educational composition of adult blacks in the North and West with what would have occurred if there had been no migration into or out of the South indicates that net migration had only a moderate impact on the educational distribution of blacks in the North. In most instances it lowered this distribution, but not severly. Hence, based on the data available here, it is extremely unlikely that any deterioration in the position of blacks in the North could be attributed to the changing quality of the black migration stream. Although gains in the educational level of black adults in the North was slowed down slightly in many decades because of migration, the upward thrust was still considerable in each period because of mortality among the older and less educated blacks, coupled with the addition of new and more educated cohorts reaching adulthood. In short, the new migrants had a minimal impact.*

480.   Lieberson, Stanley. 1978. A Reconsideration of the Income Differences Found Between Migrants and Northern-Born Blacks. American Journal of Sociology 83: 940-966.

Southern-born blacks living in the North differ from northern-born blacks in income, labor force participation, and occupation. These economic gaps cannot be explained by differences in age and education between the birthplace groups. Currently the two main interpretations are: (1) a highly selective migration of blacks from the South involving more than age and education and/or (2) the existence of some fundamental differences between the two birthplace groups. The evidence gathered indicates that a substantial part of the selective migration process is not really taken into account when the controls normally available for age, sex, and education are applied. Further, it indicates that return migration of southern-born blacks is both numerically sizable and largely selective of blacks who did not fare well in the North. Hence, there are important selective processes involved in determining which southern blacks remain in the North as well as in determining their initial migration from the South. Based on certain assumptions about regional differences in the opportunity structure for education, ridits are used in lieu of actual attainment to control for education's influence on North-South differences in income. When selective migration is also taken into account, the results are radically different such that the southern income advantage disappears completely. The usual procedures for dealing with educational differences can generate totally misleading results. The approach to educational attainment used here may be applied to a wide variety of empirical questions involving education and similar types of variables.*

481.   Lief, T. Parrish. 1970. The Decision to Migrate: Black College Graduates and Their Tendency to Leave New Orleans. Unpublished Ph. D. Dissertattion. Tulane University. 399 pp.

This study was about a migratory-prone category of people. They possessed a combination of factors associated with migratory proneness for they were young adult, urban Negroes recently graduated from deep South universities. Because of differential influences, as anticipated, some migrated and some did not. It was hypothesized that migratory decisions are affected both by the multiple positions that the individual occupies in the social system and by the dynamics of his interpersonal experiences. The investigation sought to uncover those possible areas where social positions and interpersonal influences are associated with migratory behavior. While the dimension of social positions, both ascribed and achieved, has had considerable attention in studies concerned with internal migration, the interpersonal dimension has received less analysis. The present study's aim was to demonstrate the importance of interpersonal influences as they related to migratory behavior. The sample was composed of 125 respondents-approximately 1/5 of the 1964 and 1965 graduating classes of the predominantly Negro universities in the New Orleans area. The study was conducted in two stages: the initial interview within a few months after graduation and a follow-up. A standardized interview schedule with open-ended questions was used and qualitative as well as quantitative findings were recorded. The qualitative data provided information which was not reported by several large scale mailed surveys conducted about the same time of this study. The review of literature concentrated on: 1) the migratory proneness of similar populations, 2) positional and motivational findings, and 3) interpersonal findings. This investigation's findings were reported in two sections. The first analyzed the variables of sex, status and occupation and the respondents' migratory intentions and motivations. It found that their migratory intentions strongly correlated with their subsequent behavior. Especially migratory-prone were those males who came from white-collar homes. School teaching was the only occupational choice significantly associated with this sample's mobility behavior: females who selected school teaching as their career tended to remain. As anticipated, occupational causes were associated with most of the moves. On the other hand, family reasons and causes were also observed, more so with the females. The reasons for remaining followed a similar pattern. Because the central goal was to underscore the contribution of interpersonality, the research examined a number of areas hypothesized to be associated with migratory behavior. The second section concentrated on: 1) the family, 2) campus and community involvement and the attempt to sever local ties, and 3) pre- and post-migratory experiences in the forms of travel, communications and peer group dynamics. Some of the findings were as follows. The father was identified as a figure of work and the mother a figure of the home by most of the respondents with attachments to the mother being significantly important for the non-migratory females. Migrants, in contrast to non-migrants tended to perceive parental encouragement of migration. Parental influences were important not only prior to the moves, but they also affected subsequent migratory adjustments including the return of some females. The desire to be with other people, to sustain family ties, and to be involved in the local area significantly differentiated the non-migrants from the migrants. The migrants, on the other hand, felt more autonomous, had more distant orientations, were more involved in campus life and civil rights activities, were higher achievers and had less community roots. Migrants had more prior travel experiences, discussed migration more, saw their friends as migratory-prone, had more personal contacts, more sources of information about the North and West, had a higher evaluation of these areas and, as some of the cases indicated, were exposed to persistent enticements from potential employers. Peers played important pivotal roles in the decision to migrate, and, for some, the decision to make the journey North, living arrangements, and returning. The study concluded with a sugested migrant typology derived from the different migrant and non-migrant types discovered in the findings. The study also suggested stages in a migratory process, stages in which the person has been influenced by other people responding to his social position, his role orientations and occupational considerations; his degrees of volition, his migratory plans and his actual migratory behavior. The appendix included a historical survey of Negro migratory flows to and within the United States.*

482. Long, Larry H. 1975. How the Racial Composition of Cities Change. Land Economics 51 (3): 258-267.

The increasing percent blacks in central cities of metropolitan areas is a subject of widespread comment and is typically identified as arising from (1) higher natural increase among blacks, (2) continued black inmigration, and (3) white outmigration to suburbs. But no one has ever calculated the relative importance of these three variables in increasing the percent black in large cities, nor has anyone considered whether the relative importance of the three variables in bringing about the increase has been changing. This paper uses available data on components of population change (natural increase and net migration) to answer the above questions.*

483. Long, Larry, and Diana DeAre. 1981. The Suburbanization of Blacks. American Demographics 3 (8): 16-21, 44.

At least two important transitions characterized the black population in the 1970s. One was that a declining proportion of America's black population was living in the central cities. Another was that the long-standing flow of blacks to the North was halted. After increasing for many decades the percent of the nation's blacks living in the Northeast and North Central regions fell from 39.5 percent in 1970 to 38.5 percent in 1980; the percent living in the South held steady at 53.0 percent in 1970 and 1980. Pending final confirmation with migration data from the 1980 census, the present findings suggest that for blacks the long exodus from the South is over, and a new exodus from cities has begun.*

484. Long, Larry H., and Daphne Spain. 1978. Racial Succession in Individual Housing Units. U. S. Bureau of the Census, Current Population Reports, Series p-23, No. 71. Washington, D.C. : Government Printing Office. 19 pp.

The data support the idea that Black husband-wife couples with children lead the way in replacing White households.... In terms of income, the Black households moving in tend to resemble closely the White households moving out, suggesting that changes in the socio-economic composition of the neighborhoods result primarily from same race successions. But perhaps this conclusion is not too surprising in view of the fact that about 94 percent of all housing successions during the period under study (1967 to 1971) were same-race successions (Whites replacing Whites or Blacks replacing Blacks).* [Part of author's summary and conclusions].

485. Long, Larry H., and K.A. Hansen. 1977. Selectivity of Black Migration to the South. Rural Sociology 42: 317-331.

The probability of blacks moving from the South has been directly related to years of school completed. Of those who leave, the most highly educated are the most likely to return. This and other evidence fails to support the hypothesis that return of the least capable migrants accounts for why southern-born blacks in the North earn more than northern-born blacks. Other implications are explored. The rate of black migration from the South appears to be declining at almost every educational level, and return migration seems to be rising at almost every educational level. The degree of selectivity of black outmigration and return migration did not appreciably change between the 1950's and the 1960's.*

486.   Long, Larry H., and L.R. Heltman. 1975. Migration and Income
Differences Between Black and White Men in the North. American
Journal of Sociology 80: 1391-1409.

Blacks moving from the South to the North have had lower levels of
education and have taken lower status jobs than northern-born blacks.
Nevertheless, data from the 1970 census indicate that after a few
years residence in the North the southern-born blacks are able to
earn higher incomes than northern-born blacks, apparently due in part
to higher labor force participation rates. For these reasons, controlling for age and education reduces the income difference between
blacks and whites, but controlling for age and region of birth
increases it. Southern-born whites in the North and West have tended
to have lower levels of education, higher unemployment rates, and
lower incomes than whites of similar age in the North and West
who are not interregional migrants. Interpretations, explanations,
and uses of these findings are suggested, especially with regard to
past and future changes in the black-white income ratio.*

487.   Lundgren, Terry Dennis. 1976. Comparative Study of All Negro Ghettoes
in the United States. Unpublished Ph. D. Dissertation. The Ohio State
University. 176 pp.

This dissertation integrates two lines of ecological research to
identify the nature of the internal differentiation of black ghettoes
in the United States and to compare their ecological structure to the
SMSA's in which they are located. The Classical ecological formula-
tions with respect to the formation and characteristics of urban subareas form the theoretical orientation for the definition of the
black ghetto, while the methodology of the factorial ecologists is
used to define the internal structures of ghettoes and SMSA's. Since
the Classical emphasis is on territoriality and its relationship to
cultural homogeneity, the black ghetto is defined in spatial and
demographic terms by contiguity and percent Negro. In order to insure
sufficient cases for analysis, the author chose the cluster of at
least fourteen contiguous census tracts for operationalization of
ghetto, each containing at least 50% Negro. Empirical evidence from
the literature shows that such a measure is conceptually meaningful
and procedurally feasible. Analysis of the methodology of the
factorial ecologists shows that the best factor method to obtain
meaningful results with ecological data is Image analysis. This
method is approximated by a principal factor direct solution with
iterations to improve the communality estimates. Constraints are
illustrated to be applied to the data set to improve the fit to
the factor model. An oblique solution is chosen for rotation as the
most general case. The units of analysis are the 1970 SMSA's in the
United States. Definitionally, 47 black ghettoes are located within
36 SMSA's. Seven SMSA's contained multiple ghettoes with New York
containing five distinct ghettoes. Following previous factorial
studies, thirteen variables are selected which are available on
tape from the Bureau of the Census across the 36 SMSA's. The rather

involved procedure necessary to obtain the data in a form suitable
for analysis is given in the Appendix. The analysis was carried out
on a twelve variable subset which showed the best fit to the
factor model across the 36 SMSA's. Consistent with previous factorial
studies, the 36 SMSA's are described by four factors named urbanism,
familism, social rank and black. There is an inverse correlation
between the urbanism and black factors and the other factor
relationships are orthogonal. A four factor solution of the ghettoes
yielded the four SMSA factors plus two additional factors, one
defined by a fertility measure and the other defined by sex ratio and
poverty measures. Differences in the obliquely rotated solutions
between ghettoes and their surrounding SMSA's are relatively minor. A
factor-by-factor comparison of each SMSA and its included ghetto(es)
indicated a high degree of similarity between their structures. A
canonical analysis of the direct solutions of ghettoes and SMSA's
showed that an average of over 98% of the variance in one matrix can
be explained by the variance in the other. Thus, the major finding of
this research is that ghettoes are very similar ecologically to the
SMSA's within which they reside.*

488.   Malone, Erwin Lionel. 1957. The Phenomenon of Increasing Uniformity
in Unrelated Areas of the United States: An Investigation into
Industrial and Sociological Patterns and Trends in Certain States of
the United States, 1870 to 1950. Ph.D. Dissertation. Columbia
University. 383 pp.

Though much is known of the national attributes in various fields,
knowledge remains limited concerning the contributions made to the
national patterns by the different sections. Early historical patterns reviewed herein from 1607 to 1860, indicated marked industrial
and cultural differences between the sections, each of which pursued
specialized habits of work and thought. To test the thesis of a trend
toward increasing sectional uniformity, four separate areas differentiated by specific attributes were selected from four different
sections of the United States, and their patterns studied for the
period 1870-1950. The areas chosen for investigation: California, a
state in the Far West, in which there had been rapid industrialization of an original agricultural economy; Iowa, an outstanding
farm state in the agricultural Mid-West; Pennsylvania, a highly
industrialized state in the East, with the greatest industry diversi-
fication, and South Carolina, a state in the old agricultural
South. Occupation distribution data of the United States Censuses
were used for determination of the industrial patterns. Because
occupation data as reported at the various censuses were not directly
comparable, comparability was achieved for the first time by
analyzing, coding and reassembling each of the national and state
censuses according to the listing used by the Census Bureau when
reporting the Occupation Census of 1900. From the reassembled data,
charts were drawn and tables compiled to illustrate the decennial
national and state patterns in the major industrial divisions,
1870-1950, the changes which had occurred, and the short and long

term trends in these divisions. In the four widely separated and industrially different areas there was found a marked trend toward increasing homogeneity. Differences which in 1870 had existed between the United States and the separate areas, and between the areas themselves in each industrial division: Agricultural Pursuits; Professional Service; Domestic and Personal Service; Trade and Transportation; Manufacturing and Mechanical Pursuits; and Mining and Quarrying, had greatly diminished by 1950. Similar trends toward increasing homogeneity among the different areas were found to exist in each of the sociological fields examined: Urbanization, Nativeborn Migrants, Percent Negro Population, Median Age of the Population, Females Married, Differential Fertility, Educational Costs, and Per Capita Incomes. The findings indicate further lessening of the differences which remained between the areas in 1950. The trend toward increasing industrial and cultural likenesses probably will continue. An appendix provides details of procedures; the similarities between the selected states and the regions in which they are situated; the percent of the working populations in the United States, California, Iowa, Pennsylvania and South Carolina, which was employed in each major occupation division at each occupation census, 1870-1950; the number of people in each main occupation division in the states studied; the gainfully occupied males and females in the states at each occupation census from 1870 to 1950, reclassified according to the listing used to report the 1900 Census of Occupations.*

489.   McAllister, Ronald J., E.J. Kaiser, and E.W. Butler. 1971. Residential Mobility of Blacks and Whites: A National Longitudinal Survey. American Journal of Sociology 77 (3): 445-457.

A limited literature suggests that blacks move more often than whites but that their mobility is more local. In testing this double hypothesis with interviews from a national panel of 1,500 households, we find that greater black mobility is largely explained by blacks' tendency to be renters. Black renters are less likely to move, and black owners are about as stable residentially. Furthermore, blacks are more likely to move only within their neighborhoods or communities and much less likely to move elsewhere in the metropolitan area or to migrate out of it. Not only do different racial categories move differently, but they apparently do so for different reasons.*

490.   Meade, A. Carl, Sr. 1971. The Residential Segregation of Population Characteristics in the Atlanta Metropolitan Statistical Area: 1960. Unpublished Ph. D. Dissertation. The University of Tennessee. 132 pp.

The Atlanta standard metropolitan statistical area, in 1960, was an increasingly urbanized area characterized by population growth, expansion, and economic dominance. It is in precisely such a context that ecological theory proposes a greater amount of residential segregation in the inner zones of the metropolitan area than in the outer zones. This proposition was empirically tested over seven socioeconomic indicators. Census tracts were classified into eight concentric zones emanating from the metropolitan center, with the intraclass correlation coefficient employed as a measure of segregation. Observed results strongly support the hypothesis. Despite evidence of segregation distributions in the predicted direction, segregation scores were found to be relatively low, especially in the extreme zones. Hence, the census tract, because it may lack any homogeneous demographic referent, may not be an exacting enough unit for much sociological work. The census tract unit was, however, found to be relatively homogeneous for at least one of the socioeconomic indicators. The race characteristic demonstrated relatively high segregation values. The fact that race was found to be the most segregated of the indicators is significant, in that race segregation scores were found to influence the segregation distributions of other socioeconomic indicators. Thus though all but one of the indicators demonstrated low segregation values that characteristic which did show high values was found to be one of primary importance. An inverse association was found between distance from the metropolitan center and population density. Distance was also found to directly influence, in an inverse manner, residential segregation. Partial correlation analysis revealed that the original positive correlation between density and segregation disappears, when controlling on distance. The population composition of a zone was found to have a small, but direct, influence upon residential segregation. Findings regarding the existence of the direct effect of distance upon population composition, however, were inconclusive.*

491.   Miller, A.R. 1974. The Black Migrant: Changing Origins, Changing Characteristics. In: Papers on the Demography of Black Americans. Atlanta, Georgia: Atlanta University. W.E.B. Dubois Institute for the Study of the American Black.

This paper consists of two major parts: (1) Recent Migration to Metropolitan Areas; this section includes discussions on the origins of recent migrants and their demographic characteristics such as age, education, activity status and occupation. (2) Interstate Migration and "Multiple Movers".★

492.   Miller, Brenda Kaye. 1979. Racial Change in an Urban Residential Area: A Geographical Analysis of Wilkinsburg, Pennsylvania. Unpublished Ph. D. Dissertation. University of Pittsburgh. 197 pp.

Settlement by blacks into predominantly white urban neighborhoods has become an important feature for researchers in studying trends in American cities. Prior to the 1960's, geographers who studied the settlement of blacks into urban areas centered their attention on the black ghetto. Since the 1960's geographers have begun to study the mobility of blacks into white urban neighborhoods. Wilkinsburg, Pennsylvania was chosen as an appropriate study area in the Pittsburgh Metropolitan area because it has shown a dramatic change in its racial composition. Wilkinsburg has changed from a predominantly white community with a black population of only 2.4 percent in 1960, to a racially changing area with a black population of approximately 35.0 percent in 1977, according to Mr. James Huff, Borough Manager. The findings indicate that: (1) People who move into better neighborhoods compared to those who move into worse neighborhoods will expect more from public schools and will tend to be more critical if public schools do not meet the desired expectations, (2) People, regardless of income, occupation, and lifestyle, judge the quality of their neighborhood more by what they believe to be the desirability of their neighbors than by the physical condition (beauty, safety, greenery, neighborhood resources, and so forth) of the neighborhood, (3) Dwelling units will house more blacks than the previous number of whites, where blacks have replaced whites in racially changing areas, (4) The households who migrate to Wilkinsburg have comparable incomes, occupational status, and educational attainments to whites presently living in Wilkinsburg and all households who have relocated to Wilkinsburg indicate a trend in residential status from rentorship to homeownership, (5) People, in general, with similar socioeconomic status tend to hold similar values which may be manifest in like behavior patterns.*

493.   Moorhead, James William. 1971. **Negro Suburban Migration: 1955-1960.** Unpublished Ph. D. Dissertation. Brown University. 226 pp.

This study analyzes the migration of the Negro population in the United States from the central cities of metropolitan areas to the surrounding rings and Negro migration to the ring from areas outside the immediate metropolitan area. The general question explored is the extent to which the suburban movement of Negroes is similar to that of whites. Mobility data from the 1960 federal census provide the basis for the investigation. In the census mobility was measured by comparison of an individual's residence on April 1, 1955 with his residence at the time of the census in April, 1960. For purposes of this study, a migrant is an individual who reported a 1955 residence outside the immediate metropolitan area, and who in 1960, was recorded as residing in the suburban ring of a metropolitan area. The analysis shows that Negroes move from central cities to rings in much smaller numbers and at much lower rates than whites. This pattern is not changed when Negro rates of movement are adjusted for age, occupation, education and income, indication that differentials in the socio-economic composition of the Negro and white populations do not account for the large difference between the Negro and white rates of mobility from central city to ring. There is some variation in this pattern by size and regional location of the metropolitan area. While the central city is an important source of migrants to the ring, slightly more than half of the Negro and white in-migrants to the ring part of SMSAs originate from places outside the immediate SMSA. Of those Negroes and whites who migrate from outside the SMSA about half originate in other metropolitan areas, although whites show a greater propensity than Negroes to migrate from other metropolitan areas into the suburban ring. Both Negro and white migration from the central

city to the ring was generally selective of those with a higher
socio-economic level than those remaining in the central city.
However, the socio-economic difference between the Negro central city
population and the Negro migrants to the ring was considerably less
than the comparable difference for whites. Predictably, the
socio-economic level of Negro migrants was lower than the level for
white migrants. The Negro ring population has a lower socio-economic
level than the Negro central city population, a pattern which is in
contrast to that of whites. The higher socio-economic level of the
Negro migrants could increase the socio-economic level of the Negro
ring population. However, Negro migrants from outside the SMSA have a
lower socio-economic level than migrants from the central
city, offsetting some of the gain in socio-economic level for the
ring population as a consequence of migration from the central
city. The limited number of Negro migrants to the ring tend to move
into suburbs having a lower socio-economic level than the suburbs
which are almost entirely white. The analysis leads to the conclusion
that the suburbanization of Negroes is in fact an outward extension
of the Ghetto.*

494.   Pick, J.B. 1977. Correlates of Fertility and Mortality in
Low-Migration Standard Metropolitan Statistical Areas. Social Biology
24 (1): 69-83.

Significant determinants of fertility and mortality were looked for
among 17 demographic and socioeconomic variables characterizing the
populations of 29 low-migration standard metropolitan statistical
areas (SMSAs). Regression analysis showed density to be correlated
negatively with the gross reproduction rate (GRR) of nonwhites. The
GRR of whites was inversely related to the level of medical care, but
the GRR of nonwhites was most closely linked to the percent of nonwhites in an area, with higher percentages lowering the GRR. Greater
white income increased nonwhite infant female mortality, possibly
because of competition for medical services. ★

495.   Pleck, Elizabeth H. 1974. Black Migration to Boston in the Late
Nineteeth Century. Published Ph.D. Dissertation. Brandeis University.
260 pp. [For published version see the next item].

This thesis described black migration to one Northern city in the
late-nineteenth century. It weighted the impact of two variables,
migrant status and length of residence in a metropolis, on the
conditions of blacks in Boston, 1870-1900. The major sources for the
study were the federal manuscript census schedules--3445 blacks in
1870 and 5854 in 1880. The history of black migrants began in their
birthplaces--for some of them, as slaves on Virginia plantations.
Chapter I examined in detail the histories of two large groups of
former slaves who arrived in Boston before and after the Civil War.
Many of the migrants did not settle in Boston but left the city for
other parts of Massachusetts and the Northeast. Chapter II examined
the transient patterns of movement among Boston blacks. Chapters

III-V described the impact of migration and transiency on three aspects of black society--the black occupational situation, family composition, and associational life. These three chapters described differences between migrants and city-bred blacks in their assimilation to city life. To the extent that there were differences, city-bred blacks experienced more difficulties than migrants from the South. Long residence in the city increased the number of female-headed households, changes in marital partners, and "abandonment" of children. It decreased the attempts of blacks to escape from poverty by establishing small business. The study concluded that "the city did not solve the problems" of black migrants. In fact, extended contact with the city created problems unknown to Southern blacks, and offered no escape from conditions of poverty.*

496.   Pleck, Elizabeth H. 1979. Black Migration and Poverty: Boston, 1865-1900. New York: Academic Press. 239 pp.

This book is a demographic analysis of economic and social conditions of poor Southern black migrants to the North, using Boston as an example. The study is primarily based on longitudinal studies of manuscript census schedules. But, Pleck also utilizes documents such as widow's pension requests to the city directories, dissertations and other available literatures. The book consists of seven chapters and four appendices. The chapter headings are: (1) Introduction; (2) Black Boston; (3) Southern Migrants; (4) Children of the North; (5) Employment; (6) Families; and, (7) Conclusion. The headings for the appendices are: (A) Selected Tables; (B) Occupational Classification; (C) Reliability of the Census; and (D) Black Female-Headed Households, 1850-1925. The book also contains a "Bibliographic Essay".★

497.   Price, Daniel O. 1970. Urbanization of the Blacks. Milbank Memorial Fund Quarterly 48 (2, Part 2): 47-58.

Writing in 1970, Price examines the pattern of out-migration of blacks from the South during the past 100 years (1870-1970). Discusses the socioeconomic characteristics of the migrants. The author contends that the black population of the U.S. has redistributed itself beginning with the situation in which over 80% resided in the rural South. According to Price, by 1970 only about 25% still resided in rural areas of the South; about 5% in rural areas in other parts of the country and the remaining evenly distributed between urban areas in the South and urban areas outside of the South. He also finds a low concentration of blacks in small cities outside of the South. ★

498.   Price, Daniel O. 1971. Rural to Urban Migration of Mexican Americans, Negroes and Anglos. International Migration Review 5: 281-291.

This study compares rural to urban Mexican-American, Negro and Anglo migrants with non-migrants continuing to live in the areas from which the migrants came. Virtually all of the migrants were better off financially than they had been before migration and better off than the non-migrants in the rural areas. The migrants also had better levels of living as measured by several indicators. The Anglos maintained the closest ties to the rural area from which they came, but the Negroes had the highest proportion sending money back. Expressed happiness in the urban areas did not show much association with improvements in financial status, but most members of each group reported feeling happier in the urban than in the rural area.*

499.   Reid, John D. 1974. Black Urbanization of the South. Phylon 35 (3): 259-267.

Although black migration continues to be directed out of the rural South, it is directed not only to other regions in the United States but to Southern urban areas as well. Overall urban growth of 22 percent for blacks in the region was witnessed in the largest urban centers in the South, places having in excess of 250,000 inhabitants in 1960. Declines in the black Southern rural population from heavy out-migration over many decades has left a population with proportionately larger numbers of children and aged and proportionately fewer persons of working age. This has placed a heavy burden on both those who remain and work in rural areas and has created a demand for services beyond what most rural counties which have suffered high rates of out-migration's selective effects on this variables. Therefore, those who are left are frequently faced with only menial low-paying occupations. With increasing urbanization in the South, however, much of the potential loss of talented black youth from the South may be averted. Although one in three blacks residing outside the South in 1970 was Southern born, the proportion has dropped considerably from the post World War II figure of one in two. Furthermore, in 1950 only two percent of native Southern blacks were born outside the South. In 1970, almost one in ten had been born in other regions of the country. This increase in proportion born outside the South may well be indicative of return movements into the region, in-migrations directed not to rural and farm areas, but to the South's rapidly growing urban centers. As economic and educational differentials gradually disappear between black and non-black in the South and as greater proportions of black females aspire to labor force status, the South may well regain substantial black population lost to other regions over many decades in the past.*

500.   Reischaner, Robert Danton. 1971. The Impact of the Welfare System on Black Migration and Marital Stability. Unpublished Ph.D. Dissertation. Columbia University.

Welfare system has been accused of being counter productive. Results of this study found that migration from the South was unrelated to welfare opportunities elsewhere, patterns of migration somewhat influenced by welfare opportunities in areas of destination and avail-

ability of welfare has little to do with rate at which low income persons leave cities. Welfare related instability arises because
public assistance lowers both the benefits of marriage and the costs
of disruption to the poor by providing subsidized alimony payments.★

501.   Samdani, Ghulam Mohammad. 1970. Migration and Modernization: A Study
of Changing Values and Behavior Among Former Migrants From the Rural
South to Upstate New York. Unpublished Ph.D. Dissertation. Cornell
University. 240 pp.

The study focusses its attention on rural settlements (referred to as
staygrant communities), consisting of families (referred to as
staygrant families) of southern Negro, former migratory laborers, who
have "dropped out" of the migrant stream to settle in the North. The
research examines the processes of migration and modernization of the
staygrant families. The analysis is based upon survey data collected
from 186 families in nine staygrant communities in Wayne County, New
York, in the summer of 1968. Only 31 percent of the staygrants have
been regular migratory farm workers prior to migration to the North,
the remaining 69 percent are not regular migratory workers. They have
used the migratory stream as a channel of geographical and occupational mobility. Although the size of the migratory farm labor force
has been declining over the last decade, it still constitutes a sizeable proportion (about one-fifth) of the annual seasonal hired labor
of over half a million workers in the country, and about 60 percent of
over 30,000 seasonal workers in New York States. The data indicate
that the phenomenon of the "migrant dropout" is likely to continue in
the future. The staygrant families, in general, show a higher educational attainment, income, and employment in urban-type occupations,
compared to the migratory farm worker families who remain in the
stream. Economic motives are largely responsible for the migration of
staygrants from the South to New York State. More than 40 percent
cite economic reasons for migration. A desire to improve living
conditions is also an important factor in their migration. About 20
percent cite this as a reason for migration. Other reasons such as
"have to follow rest of the family" are cited, but by a much smaller
number. The staygrant families have, in most of the cases, improved
their financial condition since their migration to New York State.
This is evidenced from about 70 percent of the respondents who
indicated this directly, 85 percent who indicated an improvement in
their overall living conditions and, finally, a proportion who
indicated a general upward occupational mobility. The living conditions, however, are unsatisfactory as reported by about three-
forths of the respondents, undoubtedly the result of a median income
of only $357.00 per month. Poor housing and lack of basic facilities
such as running water are largely responsible for the staygrants
dissatisfaction with living conditions. The staygrants might well be
expected to acquire urban traits as a result of living in the urban
North. This is partially confirmed by the relationship of length of
residence and occupational mobility with higher modernity scores. In
addition, level of education, urban-type of place of origin, satis-

faction with the community, higher level of social participation, and home-ownership, each tend to relate to higher modernity score. Attention is given to four policy alternatives regarding social planning for the staygrant families. These are: health, economics, modernity, and assimilation. Health is considered to be the most important of these. Improvement in housing and neighborhood is suggested as a necessary course of action. From the standpoint of economics, provision of employment facilities is emphasized, since it is likely to increase the income of the families (which, in turn, may alleviate many of their social problems). Need for modernization of values, as a first step toward effective participation in urban life, is emphasized. It is suggested that attention may be given to factors such as education and social participation, instrumental to the modernization of values from traditional to modern. Based on the indications that the staygrants are willing to assimilate into the urban Northern society, better housing arrangements are suggested as a possible action that might be taken to facilitate the process of assimilation.*

502. Scott, E. Jay. 1920. **Negro Migration During the War.** New York: Oxford University Press. 189 pp.

In this book Scott examines the movement of black population during the war, and studies the causes and effects of this population movement both in the North and the South. In the introductory chapter, Scott compares black movement during the war with earlier migrations of similar characteristics. Chapter headings are: Causes of Migration; Stimulation of the Movement; The Spread of the Movement; The Call of the Self-sufficient North; The Draining of the Black Belt; Efforts to Check the Movement; Effects of the Movement on the South; The Situation in St. Louis; Chicago and Its Environs; The Situation at Points in the Middle West; The Situation at Points in the East; Remedies for Relief by National Organizations; and, Public Opinion Regarding the Migration. This book also contains a 9-page bibliography followed by an index. ★

503. Scroggs, W.O. 1917. **Interstate Migration of Negro Population.** Journal of Political Economy 25 (December): 1034-1043.

The years 1916 and 1917 witnessed heavy black migration to the North. To better understand this phenomenon, Scroggs reviews the movement of the black population since 1865 (when the 1863 Emancipation Proclamation decreed by President Abraham Lincoln took full effect with the end of the Civil War). Scroggs concludes his study by a pessimistic note: "...that the mere removal of the Negro to another environment is not the ultimate solution of what we call the 'race problem'; at the most it can only modify the problem. As the European peasant does not escape all his economic ills when he stands for the first time under the Stars and Stripes, so the Negro will still have troubles after crossing the Mason and Dixon line." ★

504.   Shannon, Lyle W., and Magdaline Shannon. 1973. **Minority Migrants in the Urban Community: Mexican American and Negro Adjustment to Industrial Society.** Beverly Hills: Sage Publications. 352 pp.

This book is based on a study conducted in the Northern Industrial City of Racine, Wisconsin. Its focus is on the adjustment problems facing immigrant Mexican-Americans who have moved into Racine from the Southwest, and black immigrants from the deep South. A large portion of the book is devoted to a comparison of blacks, Mexican-Americans, and Anglos in Racine with those who have remained in the community of their origin. That is, the communities from which the migrants came.★

505.   Sharp, Harry, and Leo F. Schnore. 1962. **The Changing Color Composition of Metropolitan Areas.** Land Economics 38 (2): 169-185.

The 1960s growth of the nonwhite population of cities in the United States was described as one of the outstanding sociological phenomenon. In this study Sharp and Schnore document this trend and attempt to answer these questions: "What are the reasons for these massive shifts? How long will the major cities of the country continue to lose population? Will we eventually have core areas that are faced with acute depopulation? How far will the population redistribution by race continue? Will our largest SMSA's eventually consist of white rings surrounding nonwhite cities? And, for the cities themselves, what are the implications of these major changes in population composition?" Their analysis is limited to the twelve largest Standards Metropolitan Statistical Areas (SMSA's). The authors conclude that "...the twelve largest SMSA's have experienced very similar population shifts between the central city and the ring over the last thirty years....For a variety of reasons the central cities, particularly their innermost cores, are falling short of compensating for the residents they are losing to the suburbs. Some observers have claimed that new public housing and other redevelopments in the inner city have begun to slow the general suburban drift and may eventually reverse it. While this may occur in the future, the available data for large cities do not yet provide much support for this contention."★

506.   Sherman, Richard B. (ed.). 1970. **The Negro and the City.** Englewood Cliffs, N.J.: Prentice Hall. 192 pp.

This book consists of a collection of articles written by distinguished black authors. The subjects covered range from economic conditions to education, to migration and social protests. The period covered is from 1920 to 1970. One chapter entitled "Urbanization and Negro Family", deals directly with black migration and urbanization. In this chapter Sherman points out that urban life is having adverse effects on the black family.★

507.   Shin, Eui Hang. 1971. **Migration Differentials of the Nonwhite Popu-**

lation: United States, 1955-1960. Unpublished Ph.D. Dissertation. University of Pennsylvania.

This thesis is primarily based on analysis of the characteristics of nonwhite migration in the United States from the data of the 1960 Census of Population on migration during the five-year interval of 1955 to 1960. The present study attempts to define the patterns of differentials and selectivities of nonwhite migration by age, sex, marital status, family status, fertility status, labor force status, employment status, occupation, and educational attainment. The primary objectives are to describe the various aspects of migration differentials and selectivities and to analyze their concomitant effects on the prospective developments of the characteristics of nonwhite population. The analysis is focused on the differences in the characteristics not only between migrants and nonmigrants in general but also among the subgroups with respect to mobility status, such as nonmovers, intracounty movers, migrants within the same state, migrants between contiguous states, and migrants between noncontiguous states. Since the data on the characteristics of migrants are based on their characteristics at the time of the census (not at the time of migration), we have encountered a serious problem in interpreting the differences in the characteristics of the population by mobility status. We have attempted, however, to view the observed differentials from the standpoint of both pre- and post-migration differentials, depending upon which seemed most appropriate in the specific context. The patterns of nonwhite migration differentials and selectivities are heavily influenced by the regional differences in the social and economic status of the nonwhite population, particularly between the South and the non-South. Therefore, the characteristics of migrants are analyzed in each specific migration stream whenever the proper data are available. Two different types of migration streams are considered in this study: first, those between two geographic areas, such as interdivisional and interregional migration streams, second, those between two different types of areas, such as intermetropolitan migration streams and nonmetropolitan to metropolitan migration streams. A special attention is given to the analysis of the characteristics of nonwhite migrants to and from the large metropolitan areas. In particular, the 53 Standard Metropolitan Statistical Areas with a total population of 500,000 or more in 1960 have been selected for this consideration. On the whole, there is a strong indication that the social and economic statuses of nonwhite migrants to large metropolitan areas have been considerably improved. This is, in part due to the convergence of such statuses between the South and the non-South and in part due to the increasing importance of intermetropolitan streams in the total nonwhite migration. However, as the major source of net migration for most of the large metropolitan areas is still of Southern nonmetropolitan origin, (i.e., of lower socio-economic statuses) the overall net effect of nonwhite migration to and from the large metropolitan areas is therefore found to be negative.*

508.   Shin, Eui Hang. 1978. Effects of Migration on the Educational Level
       of the Black Resident Population at the Origin and Destination,
       1955-1960, and 1965-1970. Demography 15 (1): 41-56.

       Using the 1960 and 1970 census data, this paper analyzes the net
       effects of the interregional migration of black males on the
       educational levels of the resident black male population at the
       regions of origin and destination. Significant variations are
       observed in the educational selectivity of out-migrants from each
       region, by region of destination. Comparing the educational levels of
       the return migrants to the South with those of the resident popula-
       tion in the nonsouthern regions provides no evidence that the return
       migrants are "failed" migrants. The net effect of interregional mi-
       gration on the educational levels of the black male resident popu-
       lation at the regions of origin and destination is insignificant in
       most age groups, for both the 1955-1960 and 1965-1970 periods. In
       particular, in-migration from the South to nonsouthern regions has
       little effect on the educational levels of the resident population in
       most age groups. In fact, for nonsouthern regions, out-migration is
       more detrimental to the educational level of the resident black male
       population than is in-migration from the South. Furthermore, the net
       effect of interregional migration has declined from the 1955-1960
       period to the 1965-1970 period.*

509.   Shin, Eui Hang. 1979. Correlates of Intercounty Variations in Net
       Migration Rates of Blacks in the Deep South, 1960-1970. Rural
       Sociology 44 (Spring): 39-55.

       From the theoretical notion of ecological complex a multistage path
       model of black migration is constructed. This model is used to test a
       series of hypotheses on the causal relationships between the net
       migration rates and environmental, sustenance organization for 405
       selected counties in the deep South. The independent variables in the
       model jointly account for about 52 percent of the variance in net
       migration rates for the 1960-70 period. Among the independent vari-
       ables considered, the personal income variable has the largest effect
       on net migration rate, followed by percent of the labor force in
       agriculture and percent black population. A detailed comparison
       between the findings of previous studies and the present study is
       presented.*

510.   Social Science Institute. 1943. Negro Internal Migration, 1940-1943:
       An Estimate. Social Science Institute, Fisk University. A Monthly
       Summary of Events and Trends in Race Relations 1 (2): 10-12.

       Examines steady influx of blacks into urban war centers from 1940 to
       1942 when blacks constituted less than 5 percent of the total in-
       migrants, and the 1942-43 period when a sharp rise in black migration
       was observed. Study is based on employment records, ration book

registrations, United States Employment service Data, enumeration of migrants at railroad centers, applications for housing, and local observers. The study includes 41 cities. It provides tables showing population increase for some 11 cities. The study concludes that black migration had not reached its peak. Predicts that black in-migration will slow down only after some relaxation for labor demands.★

511.   Sohardjo, Sri P. 1981. Toward a Socioeconomic Model of Migration and Fertility. Unpublished Ph.D. Dissertation. The Florida State University. 147 pp.

Three objectives were identified to explore the relationships between migration and fertility. First, to examine migrant-native fertility differentials within the context of traditional assimilation and social mobility models. Second, to explore the relationship between relative income and fertility in order to draw-out its potential theoretical and empirical implications for the study of migrant-native fertility differentials. Third, to develop an alternative model drawing on some assumptions of the assimilation and social mobility models and incorporating ideas developed in studies of the relationship between relative income and fertility and relative income and migration. The data used were derived from the Second Stage Indonesian Intercensal Population Survey (SUPAS 11). The results indicate that longer term (early) migrants were more assimilated to the norms of the urban native population than the shorter term (late) migrants as suggested by the similarity of their fertility and that of the urban native. The data on migrants' backgound showed that early urban migrants had similar fertility to the urban natives. On the other hand, early rural migrants had slightly lower fertility rates than the urban natives which suggested that the motivation for upward social mobility accounted for the migrants' fertility behavior. When recent migrants were compared to urban natives, the former showed lower fertility than the urban natives even after age had been controlled. This supported the social mobility assumptions. Further tests on the social mobility model found that female characteristics such as education, employment, family planning participation, and age at first marriage had stronger effects than male characteristics. The results of these test imply that the longer the migrants lived in urban centers, the closer the convergence of fertility behavior with that of urban natives. The findings on the relationship between relative income and fertility are inconclusive, although a clear positive association emerged. The alternative model needs to be further studied by improving measurements on relative income, probability of obtaining a job, perceived income differential, and mobility which should include all types of individuals in the population. The alternative model was developed on the assumptions proposed by assimilation and social mobility models by introducing relative income as the budget constraint for individuals to attain their aspirations.*

512. Spain, Daphne G. 1977. The Effects of Intrametropolitan Mobility on Racial Residential Segregation. Unpublished Ph.D. Dissertation. University of Massachusetts. 184 pp.

Intrametropolitan mobility was introduced as a new variable into the current research on racial residential segregation. Because mobility is a mechanism of change in urban structure, and residential segregation is one aspect of that structure, the inclusion of intrametropolitan mobility into causal models of residential segregation was expected to increase the amount of variance explained in segregation scores. Using 1970 Census data for 230 SMSAs, total intrametropolitan mobility did prove to be a statistically significant positive indicator of residential segregation. And mobility broken down by race, in some instances, significantly increased the variance explained over models using only total mobility. On the national level, population size had the strongest effect on segregation, while total or white mobility had the second strongest effect. Since population size represents a whole array of unmeasured variables (e.g., age, political structure, and economic base of the city), it is understandable that it carries the greatest weight in affecting segregation. For mobility to consistently be second in strength speaks to its importance as an explatory variable in residential segregation research. Region of the country and unit of analysis affect the relative importance of mobility and the other independent variables (population size, percent black, and income inequality). Among northern SMSAs, percent black and white mobility showed the greatest effects on segregation, while among southern SMSAs population size and black mobility proved strongest. Patterns varied for the central city analysis: northern central cities replicated the northern SMSAs, but in southern central cities mobility dropped out as a statistically significant indictor of segregation. The models which applied equally well to central city and SMSA proved inappropriate to ring analysis. There are three basic conclusions to be drawn from this research. (1) Intrametropolitan mobility is an important variable in the study of residential segregation. The greater the mobility rate of a metropolitan area, the greater its racial residential segregation. Aggregate decisions to move particularly among the white population, result in greater, not less segregation. (2) Region of the county is a salient consideration in residential segregation research. Regional differences still exist, enough so to make a national model of segregation inadequate to explaining the phenomenon. (3) Not surprisingly, unit of analysis affects the results of the model. The SMSA was chosen as appropriate for this research because the larger-bounded unit incorporates the effects of all internal mobility on the entire metropolitan area.*

513. Spear, Allan H. 1967. Black Chicago: The Making of a Negro Ghetto, 1890-1920. Chicago: University of Chicago Press.

Various references are made throughout the book to black migration and the impact of migration on black community life in Chicago. Why

did ghettoes develop in Chicago? The role of migration in the
formation of ghettoes is discussed. Spear delineates the means used
in Chicago to prevent blacks from establishing a decent community,
except ghettoes. The analysis is mainly based on data from report by
the Chicago Commission on race Relations entitled: **The Negro in
Chicago, 1922.**★

514.   Stinner, William, and G.F. DeYong. 1969. **Southern Negro Migration:
Social and Economic Components of an Ecological Model.** Demography 6
(4): 455-471.

This paper considers social and economic correlates of age-specific
1950-1960 net migration of Negro males from a sample of 150 southern
counties. A model is developed with five components: (1) economic
activity and urbanization, (2) white traditionalism, (3) demographic
and ecological pressure, (4) nonwhite poverty, and (5) nonwhite home
ownership. The dominant migration forces, as evidenced by correlations with component indicator variables, are the "pull" factor of
change in non-primary industrial employment, the "push" factor of
population pressure in the nonwhite rural-farm sector, and the "push"
of white traditionalism. However, the significance of model components varied when analyzed along age and industrial development
continua. In the younger age groupings, industrial employment growth,
population pressure, and white traditionalism were dominant migratory
forces while in the older age groupings, industrial employment growth
and non-home ownership were most significant. For Negro males in
agricultural counties, the major migration propellents appeared to be
the "push" of population pressure in the rural farm sector and
non-ownership of homes. On the other hand the statistical explanation
for Negro migration in more industrialized southern counties rests
primarily with the "pull" of increased employment in non-primary
industries along with population pressure. The importance of the
findings for migration theory is discussed.*

515.   Taeuber, Conrad. 1974. **The Growth of the Black Metropolitan
Population.** In: Papers on the Demography of Black Americans. Atlanta,
Georgia: Atlanta University. W.E. B. Dubios Institute for the Study
of the American Black. 12 pp., plus one table.

"Covering such topics as proportion of black population in central
cities, increase in that proportion due to natural increase or to
migration, age composition of the black urban population, and origins
of black migrants to metropolitan areas." ★

516.   Taeuber, Karl E., and Alma F. Taeuber. 1965. **The Changing Character
of Negro Migration.** American Journal of Sociology 70 (4): 429-441.

Recently published data on migration during the 1955-60 period reveal
that, contrary to the popular stereotype, Negro in-migrants to a
number of large cities, despite the presence of a socioeconomically
depressed group of non-metropolitan origin, were not of lower average

socioeconomic status than the resident Negro population. Indeed, in educational attainment Negro in-migrants to northern cities were equal to or slightly higher than the resident white population. Comparisons with limited data for earlier periods suggest that, as the Negro population has changed from a disadvantaged rural population to a metropolitan one of increasing socioeconomic levels, its patterns of migration have changed to become very much like those of the white population.*

517. Taeuber, Karl E., and Alma F. Taeuber. 1965. **Negroes in Cities.** Chicago: Aldine Publishing Company.

By largely utilizing the census statistics, as well as their own measuring tools, this work deals mainly with a scientific, objective and exhaustive investigation of residential segregation and neighborhood change as it impacts blacks in different U.S. cities. The study is demographic, historical, and comparative emphasizing the process of segregation. It includes an analysis of the characteristics of black families that migrated from the South between 1940 and 1960, and points out the socioeconomic impacts that this migration had on them. The authors conclude that the continuing changes in patterns of the black population distribution have profoundly altered the character of race relations in the U.S.*

518. Thomas, Wesley Wyman. 1975. **Intra-urban Migration and the Racial Transition of Residential Areas: A Behavioral Approach.** Unpublished Ph.D. Dissertation. University of Cincinnati. 312 pp.

The changing racial composition of an intra-urban residential area is the result of biases in the racial character of migration streams to and from the community. This research used a conceptual model of migration decision-making to analyze the stages of migration for black migrants moving within or into an area of racial transition as well as white migrants moving within or out of such an area. The community of Bond Hill-Cincinnati, Ohio was the study area with randomly selected migrants to and from the area over the period from 1968 to 1974. Household heads were interviewed to obtain information concerning their reasons for moving, search criteria, and family characteristics. Hypotheses were proposed concerning the reasons for moving, search criteria, and migration patterns for subgroups of migrants. The black migrants moving within or to the study area were divided according to their past housing tenure. A hypothesis that they would have previously occupied rental housing with the move being from renter to owner housing was shown to be valid. The hypothesized reasons for moving for renter versus owner were also shown to be valid through the use of certain analytical procedures. Renters moved for reasons pertaining to housing needs while owners moved because of dissatisfaction with the neighborhood environment. A discriminant analysis showed a significant difference between the groups according to housing and life cycle status reasons for moving. Similar procedures were used to examine the hypothesized search criteria of black migrant subgroups delimited according to their change in housing tenure. For the renter moving to rental housing, the quality of housing was the core of their search criteria. The primary group moving from renter to owner had search criteria centered on housing and neighborhood qualities with the neighborhood environment forming the basis of the search priorities. The hypothesized trend toward neighborhood criteria, when the household remained in the owner market, was shown to be valid. The realtor was shown to play an active role in the search for a new residence. Although the realtor was involved in the search, he was not shown to be instrumental in guiding the areas chosen as possible areas of residence. In looking for a residence, the black migrant centered its search in areas outside the previous area of residence. The search included areas with middle income populations adjacent the primary ghetto core or in scattered clusters of black population. The migration was from the ghetto community between the Central Business District and the study area. The division of the white out-migrant homeowners according to their stage in the life cycle was a useful means of examining their reasons for moving. Contrary to what was hypothesized, the late life cycle group's primary reason for moving related to their feelings about the status of the neighborhood. Housing status was a secondary dimension of move reasons. The middle and early life cycle group moved due to perceived changes in neighborhood status. Housing need was secondary. A discriminant analysis showed future housing need as being the significant discriminator of the reasons for moving between the two groups. Remaining in the owner market the younger life cycle group had search criteria representing their need for an environment for raising children. In contrast the late life cycle group saw housing convenience as important. A significant difference between groups was shown on the priority of an environment for children. As the white migrant homeowner looked for an alternative residence, the area of origin was not considered. Contrary to the hypothesis, the late life cycle group did not search the origin area. Both groups searched adjacent areas in a sectoral configuration extending away from the origin toward the suburban periphery. The migration pattern was also sectoral reflecting the behavioral expression of the search process.*

519. Trigg, Martelle Daisy. 1972. Differential Mobility Among Black and White Physicians in the State of Tennessee. Unpublished Ph.D. Dissertation. The University of Tennessee. 147 pp.

Differential mobility patterns between black and white physicians in Tennessee have been examined in order to isolate certain critical factors associated with their professional mobility. The significance of isolating these factors lies in their potential application by medical schools and hospitals in attracting new physicians to the undeserved areas of our nation. Based on the responses of 848 physicians to a mailed questionnaire, the differential mobility patterns between black and white physicians in Tennessee were examined in light of three different factors suggested by spatial mobility theory. These hypotheses were concerned with: (1) social factors, (2) geographical factors, and (3) practical considerations such as those which potentially contribute to physicians' satisfactions. The findings in these three areas were compared with those of an earlier study by Champion and Olsen (1971). The findings only partially supported the hypotheses. It was concluded that of the factors explored, the most influential in determining physician location are: (1) geographical origins, (2) professional relationships, (3) facilities with which to work, and (4) income expectations.*

520.   Tucker, Jackson, and J. Reid. 1974. **Urban Growth and Redistribution of the Black Urban American by Size of City, 1950 to 1970.** In: Papers on the Demography of Black Americans. Atlanta, Georgia: Atlanta University. W.E.B DuBois Institute for the Study of the American Black. 52 pp.

Section headings include: General Trends of Urban Population Growth Among Blacks Since 1930; Regional Variations in Growth and Distribution, 1950 to 1970; Population Growth by Size of Place; and, Migration to Cities.★

521.   U.S. Area Redevelopment Administration. 1964. **Negro-White Differences in Geographic Mobility.** In: Series in Economic Redevelopment Research. Washington, D.C.: Government Printing Office. 22 pp.

This report ... contrasts the rate and geographic pattern of mobility between Negro and white heads of families, distinguishing between Negroes born in the 11 Southern States which formed the Confederacy and those born elsewhere. After highlighting these differences, it attempts to answer the question--Why are Negro families geographically less mobile now than white families? [Publisher's announcement]. ☆

522.   Veena, Sneh Bebarta. 1979. **The Movement of Blacks From Central Cities to Rings in the Metropolitan Areas of the United States.** Unpublished Ph.D. Dissertation. University of Georgia. 180 pp.

The major objective of this dissertation is to examine the pattern of black mobility from central cities to rings in the metropolitan areas of the United States. Movers from central cities to rings are compared with movers from rings to central cities to see if any differences exist. The movers are also contrasted with nonmovers in central cities and rings. An examination of racial differences in migration is undertaken in an attempt to obtain further understanding of the traditionally low rate of black migration from central cities to rings. Detailed information on the characteristics of migrants is drawn from the 1970 Census publications. Populations are classified by age, sex, race, education, income, employment status, occupation, and size of SMSAs. Data for 1970-78 are obtained from Current Population Reports. The measurements used in the analysis of data are: percent distribution, median, index of dissimilarity, and net mobility rates. After reviewing the literature on black migration and evaluating the demographic theories pertaining to migration, specific hypotheses are advanced. These hypotheses guide the study of various aspects of black migration from central cities to rings in the metropolitan areas of the United States. Findings indicate that black migrants from central cities to rings were higher in socioeconomic characteristics than nonmigrants, particularly at the place of origin. Migrants had more education, higher income, and were more likely to be employed in white collar occupations than the nonmigrants in central cities. Black migrants from central cities to rings were more similar to the migrants from rings to central cities in age and education than they were to the nonmigrants in central cities (place of origin). Migrants were younger and had more education than the nonmigrants. Migration differentials that apply among whites also apply among blacks. Similar to whites, black migrants from central cities to rings had higher median age, higher education, lower unemployment rate, higher median income, and were more likely to be employed in white collar occupations than were the black migrants from rings to central cities. The volume and direction of black migration streams varied with income more than was the case for whites. Among whites the movement was predominantly towards the rings at all income levels, while among blacks the movement of those in lower income levels was towards cities and of those in higher income brackets towards rings. It was also observed that the socioeconomic conditions of ring residents, particularly in the rings of larger SMSAs, was better than those of central cities residents. It was further noted that the most advantageous type of migration was largely restricted to the more educated or to those in more prestigious or economically more rewarding occupations. It was also revealed that black migrants, unlike whites, were drawn to the rings of larger metropolitan areas. Rings of smaller metropolitan areas showed a net loss due to the migration of black population from central cities to rings. Rings of particularly larger SMSAs gained blacks who were young in age, college educated, employed, white collar workers, and in income brackets of $10,000 or more.*

523. Vernarelli, M. Joseph. 1978. Locational Distortion and Black Ghetto Expansion. Unpublished Ph.D Dissertation. State University of New York at Binghamton. 179 pp.

One of the most striking features of urban areas in the United States is racial segregation in housing. One goal of the dissertation was to explain the existence and implications of racial segregation in housing. The second goal of the dissertation was to explain how racial segregation in housing was maintained over time. In order to explain the existence and implications of racial segregation in housing we developed a model of black housing consumption. The model was based on existing monocentric theory with several modifying assumptions. First, we included neighborhood effects as part of the housing bundle available to consumers. Second, because housing is so durable the short run can be quite long. Our model is based on assumption of the short run equilibrium. Third, we considered the spatial location of the black ghetto and the type of housing found there. If we assume that blacks restrict housing choice to the black ghetto, a constraint is placed on the type of housing available for consumption. The black housing consumption model bore two major implications. The first was that blacks face higher prices and consume less housing than comparable whites at every income level. The second implication was that the greatest price and housing consumption differentials occur at the high income levels. We developed a black homeowner expansion model as a first step in explaining how segregation is maintained over time, the second goal of the dissertation. One implication was that when the price of housing in the black ghetto rises, incentives are such to cause the high income blacks to be the first to seek housing in the white community. The second implication of the model was that a differential between the price of housing in the white and black submarkets will persist over time and encourage arbitrage. Speculators, those who engage in arbitrage, play a key role in the process of neighborhood change. The final step in explaining how segregation was maintained over time was the development of a model which explained why certain neighborhoods are more likely to experience black homeowner expansion than others. The implication of the model was that neighborhoods with high quality, low density housing in areas with attractive tax-service provision packages and in areas where it is perceived that racial succession is likely are most likely to experience black homeowner expansion. In the following section we considered empirical findings from the Cleveland SMSA to test the implications of the black housing consumption model and the black homeowner expansion model. Cleveland appeared to be an excellent representative metropolitan area. Cleveland has a large black population which expanded significantly from 1960 to 1970. Racial segregation and animosity was at a high level during the study period creating an atmosphere conducive for speculative activity. In our regression for the value change model we found that, ceteris paribus, value increased faster in changed occupancy blocks than either in all black or all white blocks. This implies that a positive price differential existed between the price of housing in the white submarket and the black submarket for low density, owner occupied housing. In our regression for the black homeowner expansion model we found that more black homeowner expansion occurred in blocks possessing housing characteristics desired by blacks and where residents and buyers perceived racial succession as being likely. We concluded the dissertation with the presentation of policy recommendations aimed at breaking down racial segregation over time.*

524.   Wadley, Janet K., and Everett S. Lee. 1974. The Disappearance of the Black Farmer. Phylon 35 (3): 276-283.

Our conclusions can be brief. The black farmer in the United States has nearly disappeared and the black population in rural farm areas may soon follow. On the average, black farms are small and concentrated in areas where cotton and tobacco are still the chief crops. Their operators are old and there is a marked exodus of young farmers. Farming in the United States will soon be an occupation relegated to whites. Prospects for revival of black farming are very slight. In retrospect it appears that World War II and the social and technological changes that came with it sounded the knell for the small farmer. Among these the black is simply the first to go.*

525. Watson, Ora Vesta Russell. 1956. A Comparative Demographic Analysis of Two Louisiana Cities: Baton Rouge and Shreveport. Ph.D. Dissertation. Louisiana State University. 347 pp.

The objective of this demographic analysis is to compare the populations of two Louisiana cities, Baton Rouge and Shreveport, with reference to number and distribution, race and nativity, age composition, the balance between the sexes, martial condition, educational status, religious affiliation and population change. For the greater part the data utilized in the study were obtained from United States Government Census and Vital Statistics publications. When deemed reliable and useful, however, other sources of information were consulted. Each of these urban centers is located on a river: Baton Rouge on the Mississippi River in south-central Louisiana and Shreveport on the Red River in the extreme northwestern part of the state. In 1950, Shreveport ranked as the second city in size in Louisiana, with 127,206 residents, and Baton Rouge was third with a population of 125,629. Whites constitute more than two-thirds of the population of both cities, with Shreveport's proportion of nonwhites slightly exceeding that of the Capital City. The nonwhites of both metropolitan centers consist almost entirely of Negroes, who live generally in definitely segregated areas, particularly in Shreveport. The foreign-born whites are of minor importance, constituting only a fraction of one per cent in each city. The population of Baton Rouge is younger and more masculine than that of Shreveport, which is characterized by relatively higher proportions of females and aging persons. In both cities the greatest concentration of persons is in the productive ages, and sex ratios under 100 prevail. Among Baton Rouge inhabitants a higher ratio of males to females prevails than among the residents of Shreveport. In 1950 more than two-thirds of the adults in both cities were married, but this was the case for relatively more males in Shreveport and for more females in Baton Rouge. The median school year completed and the proportion of persons having completed four or more years of college are higher in Baton Rouge, but relatively more persons within the school ages are in attendance at school in Shreveport. The educational status of the population of both of these cities is higher than that of any other substantial component of Louisiana's population. In the two cities, as would be expected, whites have a higher educational attainment than nonwhites and females higher than males. The most important occupational category in both cities is that of "private wage and salary workers." Baton Rouge workers are primarily engaged in physical-production activities in blue-collar categories, while in Shreveport service-production activities of the white-collar variety predominate. The majority of church-affiliated persons are Protestant, with Baptists ranking first in importance. Catholics rank second numerically in Baton Rouge and third in Shreveport. Indexes of fertility indicate that some of the recent rapid population increase in both cities is due to relatively high birth rates. However, in-migration seems to be by far the more important factor. Recent reports indicate that more than 50 per cent of the population of Baton Rouge has lived there less than 15 years, and similarly that the newcomers to Shreveport number over 300 families per month.*

526. Weiss, Leonard, and J.G. Williamson. 1972. Black Education, Earnings, and Inter-regional Migration: Some New Evidence. American Economic Review 62: 372-383.

Using data from the 1967 Survey of Economic Opportunity, the authors study the relations between black male income and age, education, residence, and geographic source of education. Results are compared with previous studies based on the 1960 census data. Parameter shifts which occurred during the 1960s are reported. One of the major conclusion of this study is "...that the inferiority of southern black schools (especially rural schools), alleged by the Coleman Report to account for the poverty of black migrants to the North, can be discounted. Indeed, the overall effect of a northern or large southern urban ghetto environment appears to be more harmful to black economic progress than is a rural southern origin."★

527. West, Herbert Lee, Jr. 1974. Urban Life and Spatial Distribution of Blacks in Baltimore, Maryland. Unpublished Ph.D. Dissertation. University of Minnesota. 149 pp.

This study is concerned with the migration of black people from the rural areas of Maryland and other southern states to the city of Baltimore, Maryland, covering the years 1940 through 1970. It follows blacks primarily from the areas of Virginia, North and South Carolina to an urban area, their adjustment to a new environment, the formation of the black ghetto in Baltimore, and the mutual inter-action between the ghetto and the city. A description of motivating factors for out-migration from the rural South is included, documented with statistical tables. The contrast between an urban city and a rural environment is given, describing urban life in Baltimore and the adjustment problems faced by southern blacks. Some of the sociological factors involved in the movement from the South to Baltimore are indicated. The intra-urban migration of blacks is discussed extensively, as well as the out-migration of whites to the suburbs. A sample was selected from among the thousands of lower and middle black residents to gather data concerning economic, social, and educational aspects of life in Baltimore. Some attention is focused on the bourgeois blacks of Baltimore also. Finally, a discussion of some alternatives to the urban crisis of Baltimore's ghetto, and a look at Baltimore in an urban perspective are included. This study does not pretend to be an exhaustive analysis of conditions in all cities to which black migrants have gone. It is specialized rather than comprehensive in its scope, dealing with the situation of migrants from the rural South relocated in a particular urban center.*

528. Wienker, Curtis Wakefield. 1975. The Influences of Culture and Demography on the Population Biology of a Non-isolate: The Colored People of McNary, Arizona. Unpublished Ph.D. Dissertation. The University of Arizona. 242 pp.

This is a processual study of physical anthropology as anthropology, formulating and testing hypotheses of biological significance from ecological, historical, sociocultural, and demographic data pertinent to the Black population of of McNary, Arizona. The Black residents of McNary are a small and atypical group of Black Americans. They live at a moderately high altitude, 2200 meters, in a relatively cold environment on an Indian Reservation in a company town that is geographically isolated by modern American standards. An unstable economic history has caused McNary's Black population to fluctuate drastically in size. Immigration and emigration have shuffled and reshuffled the population. Today McNary's adult Black population is overwhelmingly derived from a "caste" of Southern Black sawmill workers. The present population pyramid is hourglass shaped. Effective population size and isolation indices are low. These data suggest three major hypotheses of biological and evolutionary significance: (1) the potential for the operation of genetic drift, (2) morphological divergence from other U.S. Blacks due to "caste" isolation and millwork occupations, and (3) biological response to the moderately high altitude, cold environment. These hypotheses are tested with ABO, Rh, Hb, skin reflectometry, birthweight, and anthropometric data collected primarily from 49 adult Black males from McNary. At the ABO and Hb loci and in skin reflectometry Black McNary is very similar to West African Yorubans. At the Rh locus, McNary has a uniquely high frequency of the Rh allele, .533. Anthropometrically, Black McNary appears to be more "African" than a typical U.S. Black population. Black McNary birthweight is lower than other U.S. Black populations, subscapular adiposity is higher. Moreover, the Rh data and perhaps the Hb and ABO data indicate the operation of genetic drift. "Caste" isolation, a lack of significant European admixture, and the nature of millwork adequately explain Black McNary male morphological divergence. Low birthweight and high adiposity appear to be responses of a basically "African" population to the environment of McNary. Each of the three major hypotheses is partially or totally supported by the biological data. In demonstrating the inter-relationships of ecological, historical, sociocultural, demographic, and biological parameters, this is a processual case study of physical anthropology as anthropology, demonstrating that no gap exists between the social and biological sciences.*

529. Wilkie, Jane Riblett. 1976. Urbanization and De-urbanization of the
      Black Population Before the Civil War. Demography 13 (3): 311-328.

      Pre-Civil War black urbanization is examined using data from federal
      census records, 1790 to 1860. The black population is found to be as
      urban as the white population initially, but its urbanization
      underwent relative decline in the last two decades before the Civil
      War. Foreshadowing current patterns, the northern black population
      was heavily concentrated in the largest cities, and the free black
      population was the most urban of all groups. The timing of black
      urban decline in the North, as well as regional and size of the place
      differences in that decline, suggest that both competition with
      immigrants in major eastern seaboard cities and the passage of the
      Fugitive Slave Law in 1850 contributed to black de-urbanization. For
      the South the explanations of black urban decline proposed by Wade
      Conrad and Meyer Goldin, and Bonacich are evaluated, and Bonacich's
      split labor market theory is judged to be most consistent with the
      demographic trends.*

530. Willie, Charles Vert. 1957. Socio-Economic and Ethnic Areas of
      Syracuse, New York. Unpublished Ph.D. Dissertation. Syracuse
      University. 327 pp.

      This analysis tests three major theories of urban organization. The
      ecological organization of Syracuse in 1950 is analyzed according to
      the concentric circle, the sector, and the multiple nuclei theories
      of urban structure. Also an analysis is made of the distribution of
      occupational, educational, and age characteristics throughout the
      city. Census tabulations are the chief source of data and census
      tracts are the basic units of analysis. Socio-economic and ethnic
      areas are delineated. Then population and housing characteristics are
      analyzed according to their distribution within these areas.
      Socio-economic areas are obtained by grouping tracts with similar
      index scores. The composite index consists of rental, home value,
      house type, occupation, and education measures. Ethnic areas are
      obtained by grouping those tracts in which the observed percentage of
      an ethnic group is three or more times greater than the expected.
      Six socio-economic areas are delineated, and areas for six
      ethnic groups are outlined--Irish, German, Russian, Polish, Italian,
      and Negro. The present area of the city--approximately 25 square
      miles--was about 40 percent settled at the close of the nineteenth
      century. Growth and expansion of Syracuse have been closely
      associated with four factors: (1) topographical features, (2) periods
      of economic prosperity, (3) periods of economic depression, and (4)
      major world wars. Most rapid expansion of this city occurred during
      the decade of 1920, reaching a peak in 1927. The city is dichotomized
      into old and new halves--the old consisting of pre-twentieth century
      dwellings and the new mostly consisting of post 1920 structures. Age
      of dwelling structure, land use and land evaluation (listed in order

of their importance) appear to have an association with level of status. The modest association between socio-economic status and land evaluation is a significant finding of this study. Three socio-economic areas extend from the center of the city to its periphery. All six areas touch the periphery in one or more census tracts. Syracuse, therefore, has grown into a pattern of sectors. Instead of encircling the city, each socio-economic area is associated with one or more geographic directional sectors. For example, the highest area is primarily an East Side development. The multiple nuclei of populations present at the beginning of the city diffused into a single unit as Syracuse expanded between 1825 and 1850, resulting in a single hub around which the city has grown. The population by occupational and educational characteristics is unequally distributed throughout the city. This kind of distribution was anticipated. Also population by age is unequally distributed throughout the city. For example, there are fewer persons than expected in all adult age intervals below 35 to 40 years in the two highest socio-economic areas. Socio-economic area of residence and age hold a predictable correlation with each other. Most of the ethnic areas are located in the older half of the city, excepting one of the Russian foreign-born (Jewish) neighborhoods. There are more white collar workers and more home owners in the Jewish, Irish, and German areas. Their family income is also higher than that of families in Italian, Polish, and Negro areas. The fact that Russian, Irish, and German groups--different in national heritage and in religious background--are similar in the behavior of home buying when occupation and income are similar suggests that ethnicity may be less specifically related to the behavior of home ownership than occupation and income. How general is the applicability of this principle is not determined. It is concluded that the urban community should be viewed as an organization of physical, social and cultural systems, each system having several components.*

531. Woodson, C. Godwin. 1969. A Century of Negro Migration. New York: Russell and Russell.

This is a historical and descriptive analysis of black migration. The book contains nine chapters with the following headings: (1) Finding a Place of Refuge; (2) A Transplantation to the North; (3) Fighting it out on Free Soil; (4) Colonization as a Remedy for Migration; (5) The Successful Migrant; (6) The Confusing Movement; (7) The Exodus to the West; (8) The Migration of the Talented Tenth; and (9) The Exodus During the World War.*

532. Woofter, Thomas Jackson. 1920. Negro Migration, Changes in Rural Organization and Population of the Cotton Belt. New York: W.D. Gray. 195 pp.

In the first part the author examines the system of agriculture from agricultural regime of slavery (including its breakdown) to the tenant system and its advantages and disadvantages. The second part deals with the effects of changes in the agricultural system on population problems and movements. The author shows that prior to 1910 population movement was from one rural area to another rural area. But, after 1910 industrial development (which has been partly responsible for the breakdown of the agricultural system) has acted as the main magnet pulling the rural population to the indsutrial centers. ★

533.   Zodgekar, A.V., and K.S. Seetharam. 1972. Interdivisional Migration Differentials by Education for Groups of Selected SMSA's, United States, 1960. Demography 9 (4): 683-699.

An attempt is made to investigate the educational differentials between various types of interdivisional migrants and nonmigrants in selected Standard Metropolitan Statistical Areas (SMSA's) of the United States. The analysis is carried out for four color-sex groups standardized for age. We have been able to identify three distinct patterns of migration differentials by education, that is, the J-shaped, the U-shaped, and the reverse J-shaped distributions. The tendency for migrants to be better educated than nonmigrants, by and large, has received support from the data we have analyzed. Wherever this tendency has not been confirmed, the main factors which, we believe, have influenced the differentials are the proportion of foreign-born whites, the geographic location of the places of origin and destination, and the differences in levels of educational attainment.*

- - - - - -O❋O❋O❋O❋O- - - - - -

Chapter 6
Black Population Growth, Composition, Spatial Distribution and Vital Rates

534. Agresti, B. F. 1978. The First Decades of Freedom: Black Families in a Southern County, 1870-1885. Journal of Marriage and the Family 40 (November): 697-706.

Data on family residential patterns for blacks in a Southern farming county in 1870 and 1885 are presented. The 1870 data show high percentages of black families in nonfamily or non-nuclear family households, which lends support to traditional sociological beliefs. In 1885, however, the two-parent family was the norm and there were no important family structural differences between blacks and whites in the county. The findings are related to other recent writings on black family history, to changes in the social and economic environment, and to the prevailing system of agriculture which, it is argued, affected the relationship of blacks to whites and the structure of black families. The analyses include an analysis of the age and sex distribution of black population of Walton county, 1870 and 1885.*

535. Attah, E.B. 1973. Racial Aspects of Zero Population Growth. Science 80 (4091): 1143-1151.

One of the recommendations of the Commission on Population and the American Future is that the nation should welcome and must plan for an eventual stabilization of the U.S. population. The purpose of this paper is to examine the "consequences of different rates of approach to zero growth. Specifically, what would be the effects of different rates on the short-and long-term growth of the respective segments of the population? How long would it take the population to stabilize, and how much would the population have increased by then? What intermediate trends would appear in the proportion of nonwhites in the population, and what would be the relative sizes of the white and nonwhite segments in the long run? ... To what extent are the different groups willing to undertake measures such as rapid fertility reduction for the purpose of benefiting the society as a whole? These and several related questions are examined, and it is suggested that the answers to these questions are far from being predetermined.*

536.   Bailer, Lloyd H. 1953. The Negro in the Labor Force of the United States. Journal of Negro Education 22 (3): 297-306.

The author outlines some general demographic characteristics of the black breadwiners.*

537.   Baird, J.T., and L.G. Quinlivan. 1972. Parity and Hypertension. Vital and Health Statistics Series 11, No. 38. Washington, D.C.: Government Printing Office.

To determine whether parity is a factor in the etiology of hypertension, data obtained in a national survey of adults aged 18-79 years, were analyzed. The total sample of 7710 included 4211 females of which 3581 were examined. Of these, 146 were found to be pregnant. These were excluded from the data leaving 3435 to be reported on. It has been reported that 30.2-50.9% of women who have preeclamptic toxemia are left with a residual hypertension following pregnancy. In women who have had a previous preeclamptic toxemia, recurrent preeclamptic toxemia has a reported incidence of 13-65%. Diastolic blood pressure was found to increase consistently with age through the age group 55-64 and then decline for both white and black women. Systolic blood pressure increased with age at a greater rate over all age groups, with the exception of 75-79 years. After parity 3, a consistent increase for diastolic pressure occurs at each succeeding parity level with a similar trend for systolic blood pressure. At lower parities mean systolic pressures for black women were higher than those for white women. Women of gravidity 6 and over had higher blood pressures than those with fewer pregnancies. The moderate but significant association of gravidity with systolic blood pressure rise almost vanishes when the effects of age and body weight are accounted for. It is concluded that neither parity nor gravidity played an important part in the etiology of cardiovascular hypertension. 9 tables give details of findings. An appendix gives mathematical equations used in computing results.☆

538.   Basu, Ramala. 1978. The Effects of Aging on Residential Changes and Mobility of the Low Income Elderly: A Case Study From Allegheny County, Pennsylvania. Unpublished Ph.D. Dissertation. University of Pittsburgh. 172 pp.

The major objective of this research was to learn if the frequencies of residential changes and if mobility declined with increasing age, especially after 65. Another objective was to determine if the frequency of mobility varied between high density areas and low density areas. The focus was on a group of urban, low income elderly (65 years old and over). Many studies have examined the spatial behavior of the elderly and concluded that the frequencies of residential changes and of mobility declined after 65. On this basis, it was hypothesized that there would be a decline in mobility after 65 and there would also be fewer changes in residence after 65. It would be different in terms of sex, marital status, and race of the elderly, and the frequencies of trips would be different among elderly living in high density and low density areas. The primary data were obtained through a questionnaire survey of one hundred elderly of age 65 and over, who were selected through a simple random sample. Regression Analysis of Variance were used to analyze the data. The research revealed that the frequency of residential changes declined significantly with increasing age, but this frequency did not vary significantly in terms of sex, marital status, and race. The frequency of trips for maintenance needs, such as trips to grocery stores, other stores, banks, and post offices, declined significantly with increasing age after 65. For healthcare needs, the frequency of trips increased for all elderly, but this increase was not constant with increasing age. Divorced elderly tended to show more decline in the frequency of trips than the marital groups. The frequencies of trips did not vary significantly between high density and low density areas. The topography (i.e., the steep slopes) of Allegheny County was cited by the elderly as a major factor limiting their mobility, and it is interesting to note that fear of crime was not mentioned by them as a significant factor limiting their mobility. The findings have implications for further research of samples from different social and economic classes to obtain the subgroup differences in terms of sex, marital status, and race.*

539. Blalock, H.M., Jr. 1957. **Percent Non-White and Discrimination in the South.** American Sociological Review 22 (6): 677-682.

This study was designed to test certain hypotheses concerning the relationships between various indices of discrimination and rate of non-white increase and percent non-white. Moderate positive correlations were obtained between rate of non-white increase and income and educational differentials, but correlations with other indices of discrimination were non-significant. On the basis of these findings and those of a previous study, the writer concludes that the relationship between discrimination and rate of minority increase is at most a relatively weak one. Correlations between per cent non-white and all indices except occupational differentials were moderately high. These relationships were remarkably linear except for counties with less than 5 per cent non-whites that had substantially lower discrimination scores than other counties. In view of the fact that comparable correlations for non-Southern S.M.A.'s were considerably lower than those obtained in the present study, the conclusion is

that the relationship between these two variables is by no means a
necessary one, but is dependent upon other variables. An increase in
the relative size of the minority may directly increase the total
amount of competition with the majority, but this competition need
not be defined along group lines and therefore may not result in
increased discrimination. There may be a threshold below which
discrimination and minority percentage are only slightly related. The
exact level of the threshold may be determined by such factors as the
amount of prejudice toward the minority, the degree to which the
minority is easily visible, and the presence of group norms
sanctioning discrimination. Further study is needed to determine
whether or not such thresholds do in fact exist and to investigate
the exact nature of the relationships among the variables involved.*

540.   Bogue, Donald J., et al. 1964. A New Estimate of the Negro Population
       and Negro Vital Rates in the United States, 1930-60. Demography 1
       (1): 339-358.

It is said that the black population of the United States has been
underenumerated by a sizable percentage at all the censuses since
1790, and the registration of vital events relative to the black
population is thought to have been very incomplete, especially prior
to 1950. Consequently, demographers have tended to regard black
statistics so inadequate as to be untrustworthy for refined demographic analysis. For this reason, demographic study of the black
population has lagged behind. In this paper, Bogue et al. report on
findings and techniques employed in making new estimates based on
census data and registration of death by age, using the 1960 census
figures as the basis for backward reconstruction of cohorts, by sex
and single year of age, on four alternative assumptions of general
underenumeration. The authors make comparison of the indicated errors
of enumeration with earlier estimates of census errors by Akers for
1960 and by Coale for 1950 census. They also compare the reported and
estimated births and deaths by single years, 1930-1960, yielding
implied rates of completeness of enumeration and corrected crude
birth and death rates.*

541.   Bressler, Tobia, and N. R. McKenney. 1965. Negro Population: March
       1964. U. S. Bureau of the Census, Current Population Reports,
       Population Characteristics, Series P-20, No. 142. Washington, D.C.:
       Government Printing Office. 34 pp.

This is a demographic, social, and economic profile of the black
population in the United States. The report is based on a national
sample statistics collected by the Bureau of the Census in the March
1964 Current Population Survey.*

542.   Brotman, Herman B. 1971. Facts and Figures on Older Americans.
       Washington, D. C.: Administration on Aging (2): 3.

Brotman discusses the facts and figures on black aged and compares it with whites. According to Brotman, the shorter life expectancy for blacks results in a smaller proportion of older black Americans. The 22.7 million blacks of all ages represent 11.2 percent of the total population. The older black population increased from 1.2 million in 1960 to 1.6 million in 1970. This is a higher rate of growth than that of the total black population. It makes up 6.9 percent of all blacks as compared with 6.2 percent in 1960. As is also the case among the white population, older black women outnumber the older black men and the difference is increasing. The ratio of women per 100 men among blacks 65 years or older rose from 115.0 in 1960 to 131.0 in 1970. While this ratio is not as large as it is for whites, the ratio for blacks of all ages is over 110 as compared with only 105 for whites.★

543.   Brotman, Herman B. 1972. **Facts and Figures on Older Americans.** Washington, D. C.: Administration on Aging (5): 3.

Brotman surmises that based on the first counts, the 1970 census data show a total of 22.7 million blacks of all ages, or 11.27 percent of the total U. S. population. That is, an increase of about 3.8 million since 1960 when the figure was 18.9 million, or 10.5 percent of the total population. As a result of a lower life expectancy among blacks, as compared with whites, the black aged in 1970 numbered 1.6 million or 7.8 percent of all of the aged. This was still an improvement over the 1960 figures when the 1.2 million black aged represented only 7.1 percent of all of the aged in the United States. In other words, only 6.9 percent of the total black population is aged 65 and over as compared with over 10 percent whites.★

544.   Brotman, Herman B. 1974. **Facts and Figures on Older Americans: State Trends, 1960-1970.** Washington, D. C.: Administration on Aging (6): 4-5.

According to Brotman between 1960 and 1970 the number of blacks 65 years of age or older grew faster than the total black population. The 65+ age group grew from 1.2 million in 1960 to 1.6 million in 1970. This is a higher rate of growth than that for the total black population. The black population aged 65 and over in 1970 accounted for 6.9 percent of the total black population as compared to 6.2 percent in 1960. Against this national average for the aged black population, the trend in numbers and percent of this population varied considerably among the states. Brotman indicates that in terms of rates of change between 1960 and 1970, six states had substantial growth of 100 percent (i.e., doubling) or higher in their aged black population: North Dakota, 175 percent; Alaska, 142.2 percent: Nevada, 122.7 percent; Hawaii, 108.8 percent; Main, 107.3 percent; and, Wisconsin, 104.2 percent. These increases, however, were based on very small base numbers in 1960, ranging from a low of 8 to a high of 2,051. In 1970, percent aged in all states differed from the national average of 6.9 percent. There were 16 states with larger proportions than the national average. The remaining states had a smaller percentage of aged black population than the national average. Eight of these states were within one percentage point lower than the national average. Thirteen states were within two percentage points, and the remaining were more than two percentage points lower than the national average.★

545. Calef, Wesley C., and Howard J. Nelson. 1956. Distribution of Negro Population in the United States. Geographical Review 46 (January): 82-97.

The geographical distribution of Negroes is slowly becoming more like that of the rest of the population. But even if present trends continue, it will probably take several more decades to complete a proportionate distribution of Negroes. Negroes have been much less urbanized than the remainder of the population, but recently they have been migrating to cities at a rate faster than the national rate, so that they are now about as urbanized as the white population. The geographical sections of the United States , and they are extremely large, that have not yet absorbed anything approaching their proportionate numbers of Negroes are the rural and semirural areas outside the Southeast. Since Negroes have settled in rural and small-town areas in Ohio, southern Illinois, and southern Michigan, there appears to be no insuperable hurdle to Negro dispersion into similar areas elsewhere outside the Southeast. However, the strong trend toward increasing urbanization of the general population and the increasing capital requirements of farming may cause Negro migration to bypass these areas.*

546. Clemence, Theodore G. 1967. Residential Segregation in the Mid-Sixties. Demography 4 (2): 562-568.

Special censuses conducted by the Bureau of the Census at the request and expense of local governments provide current statistics for many large cities which are compared with corresponding data from the 1960 Census. An analysis was made of the changes in the racial composition of the cities, and of the areas within the cities (defined by census tracts) which had a high concentration of Negro population in 1960 for ten cities of 100,000 or more population at mid-decade. As in the 1950-60 period, Negroes continue to move into the central cities of metropolitan areas while white persons continue to move out to the suburbs at a faster rate, and this results in net declines in the populations of the cities. The proportion of nonwhite persons living in areas of high Negro concentration has remained about the same or increased slightly in a majority of the cities, while in a few (such as Cleveland, Rochester, and Raleigh) this proportion has declined; that is, relatively more Negroes in these cities now live outside the ghetto neighborhoods. When the racial composition of the ghettos is examined, however, a higher proportion of the residents are now Negro when compared to 1960 in each of the ten cities. Thus, the concentration of Negroes in ghetto areas has shown little change, but the trend of white persons moving away from the Negro neighborhoods, either to other parts of the cities or to the suburbs, has increased sharply, and this has tended to polarize the Negro and white populations within large cities.*

547. Coale, A., and N.W. Rives, Jr. 1973. A Statistical Reconstruction of the Black Population of the United States 1880-1970: Estimates of True Numbers by Age and Sex, Birth Rates, and Total Fertility. Population Index 39: 3-36.

This paper describes new procedures...used to reconstruct the black population, distributed by age and sex, from 1880 to 1970. The article is divided into two parts: the first describes the several steps of successive approximination used in the construction and then discusses the resultant estimates of undercounts by age and sex in the decenial censuses; the second explains how fertility of the black population is estimated, presents the estimates, and compares black and white fertility trends since early in the nineteenth century.*

548. Coe, Paul F. 1955. Nonwhite Population Increases in Metropolitan Areas. Journal of the American Statistical Association 50 (June): 283-308.

This analysis is devoted primarily to nonwhite population changes which have occurred in Standard Metropolitan Areas (SMA's) from 1940 to 1950. However, a helpful backdrop against which to evaluate the percent SMA nonwhite changes is the long-term growth pattern of nonwhites in the United States total. The need for this orientation is the greater, since the recent trend runs noticeably counter to that which obtained for over a century.*

549. Cooney, Rosemary S. 1979. Demographic Components of Growth in White, Black, and Puerto Rican Female-Headed Families: Comparison of the Cutright and Ross/Sawhill Methodologies. Social Science Research 8 (June): 144-158.

This study examines the methodological differences between Cutright's (1974, Journal of Marriage and the Family 36, 714-721) and Ross and Sawhill's (1975, Time of Transition: The Growth of Families Headed by Women. The Urban Institute, Washington, D.C.) analyses of demographic components of growth in the number of female-headed families and replicates their procedures within a comparable time/age framework in order to resolve their contradictory findings. The analysis suggests that while changes in living arrangements and population are the two major factors accounting for changes in the number of White female--headed families between 1940 and 1970, marital instability is the major factor responsible for the increase in the number of White female-headed families between 1960 and 1970. Cutright's analysis of long-term changes for nonwhites is debatable. The relative importance of demographic factors in explaining the absolute increase in female--headed families between 1960 and 1970 clearly varies by ethnic/racial group. One of the major implications of this study is that if we had better historical data we would expect to find that the relative importance of demographic components affecting the growth of female-headed families differs for White and non-White women. Both the Cutright and Ross/Sawhill methodologies show differences in the demographic components of the growth of female-headed families between 1960 and 1970 for Puerto Ricans, Blacks, and non-Spanish Whites in the Middle Atlantic Region.**

550. Cooper, A.J., et al. 1963. Biochemical Polymorphic Traits in a U.S. White and Negro Population. American Journal of Human Genetics 15 (4): 420-428.

Report on field study of cardiovascular disease in the white and black populations of Evans County and part of Bullock County, Georgia, in 1960, in which 1,287 blacks and 2,090 whites were compared as to 15 polymorphic traits. The field study was preceded by a special census.*

551. Cortese, C.F., and J.E. Leftwitch. 1975. A Technique for Measuring the Effects of Economic Base on Opportunity for Blacks. Demography 12 (2): 325-329.

An assessment of the occupational opportunities for selected groups of in-migrants (i.e., Negroes) requires a technique which controls for effects of both national and local employment patterns. We suggest a measure based upon the location quotient and referred to as the "differential opportunity ratio" as a method which provides the necessary controls. It is applicable in the comparative studies of cities and in analyses of other population groups for which data are available.*

552. Cowhig, James D. 1967. The Negro Population of the United States, March 1967. Welfare in Review 7 (January-February): 14-16.

Cowhig contends that the geographic distribution of the population of the United States as well as their age distribution, family size, composition, and income have important consequences for the nation's welfare. This paper consists of a brief examination of these demographic variables on the welfare of the black population.*

553. Cowhig, James D., and Clavin Beale. 1964. Socioeconomic Differences Between White and Nonwhite Farm Populations of the South. Social Forces 42 (3): 354-362.

Data from the Censuses of Agriculture and Censuses of Population and Housing are used to compare the socioeconomic status of the white and nonwhite farm population of 14 southern states in 1950 and 1960. The farm operator level-of-living index, and measures of income, educational attainment, and housing are used as indicators of socioeconomic status.*

554.   Cox, Oliver C. 1940. Sex Ratio and Marital Status Among Negroes.
        American Sociological Review 5 (fall): 937-947.

        In advanced societies, the effect of variations in the sex ratio on
        marital status is hardly perceived; so much less is the understanding
        of its effect among racial and ethnic groups. According to Cox
        marriage among black men is influenced less by changes in the sex
        ratio than among white men; the percentage of urban black females   .
        married, for given changes in the sex ratio, varies about 13 times as
        much as that of males. For native whites, the variation was found to
        be somewhat less than twice as great for females as for males. This
        racial difference of greater variations for white males and black
        females may be attributed to the employment conditions of females. As
        the sex ratio increases, white men may have to face greater problems
        than black men in obtaining wives because of favorable employment
        among white women. Employment being more rare among black women, the
        sex ratio may operate more nearly as if gainful employment did not
        exist among them. According to Cox's calculations, the total
        percentage married among blacks increased two percent in the South
        and one percent in the North for every ten percent increase in the
        sex ratio. ★

555.   Cummings, John. 1918. Negro Population: 1790-1915. Washington, D.C.,
        U.S. Bureau of the Census: Government Printing Office. 844 pp.

        This is the most comprehensive volume of statistics on demographic,
        social and economic profile of the black population covering a period
        of 125 years from 1790 to 1915. The volume consists of seven parts:
        Part I, Growth and Geographic Distribution: 1790-1910; Part II,
        Migratory Displacement and Segregation; Part III, Physical Character-
        istics; Part IV, Vital Statistics; Part V, Education and Social
        Statistics; Part VI, Economic Statistics; and, Part VII, General
        Tables. ★

556.   Dhaliwal, Manmohan S. 1970. Preferences in the Size of Family Among
        Senior Girls in Black Segregated High Schools in South, Central, and
        Western Parts of Mississippi. Unpublished Ph.D. Dissertation. Utah
        State University. 116 pp.

        This study seeks to discover the attitudes of the young black senior
        high school girls of South, Central, and Western parts of Mississippi
        regarding their preferences for the ideal and desired family sizes.
        This study attempted to determine the ideal family size, to identify
        the socio-economic factors that influence family size preferences,
        to determine the norms of expected and desired family size and to
        provide guidelines and delineate important information to plan
        further research in this area. In order to achieve these objectives
        the hypotheses were formulated and tested. The following relationship
        were found: (1) The girls whose parents have either the lowest or the
        highest levels of education have indicated the larger family size as
        compared to those whose parents have slightly less than a high school

education. (2) The group of respondents belonging to the Catholic faith have indicated the largest desired and the ideal family size. (3) The females with a longer rural background have indicated larger desired and ideal family size. (4) Those respondents who have belief in birth-control have indicated a smaller desired and ideal family size as compared to those who do not believe in birth control.(5) There is a slight tendency to prefer larger ideal and desired family size among respondents who desire to marry at relatively young ages compared to those who desire to marry after 25 years of age. (6) A strong positive relationship between the grade point average and the desired and ideal family size exists; the higher the grade point average, the larger the preferred size of the family. (7) The findings of this study regarding the spacing interval between the successive births indicated that those females who prefer a shorter period of spacing indicate a larger desired and ideal family size.*

557. DuBois, W.E.B. 1967. The Philadelphia Negro: A Social Study. New York: Shocken Books. 520 pp.

Several chapters of this book, originally published in 1899, deal with the demographic characteristics of some 40,000+ strong black population of Philadelphia in late 1890s. Chapter 5 discusses the size, age and sex composition of the black population of Philadelphia county; chapter 6 discusses the conjugal conditions; Chapter 7 considers the source of the black population; Chapters 8, 9, 10, and 11 examine education and illiteracy, occupation, health, and black family, respectively. DuBois's demographic analyses include comparisons with whites in Philadelphia county.*

558. Duncan, Otis Dudley, and Beverly Duncan. 1957. The Negro Population of Chicago. Chicago: University of Chicago Press. 330 pp., + Tables.

The Duncans intensively analyze demographic statistics on the Chicago's black population. The study is based on census data from 1910 to 1950. The authors pay special attention to the relative contribution of natural increase and of net migration to the growth, distribution, and the composition of the black population in Chicago. One major finding of this study is that despite its rapid rate of growth, the pattern of black's population distribution did not change significantly during the 40 years studied.*

559. Eblen, Jack E. 1972. Growth of the Black Population in Ante Bellum America, 1820-1860. Population Studies 26: 273-289.

The period between 1820 and 1860 is one of the most interesting and critical in the history of black Americans. These 40 years saw the revitalization of the institution of slavery, and following the War of 1812, its rapid expansion across the South....This study attempts to improve our knowledge and understanding of both the period and the black population. It offers a reconstruction of the ante bellum black population and a discussion of its vital rates and parameters of growth.*

560.   Eblen, Jack Ericson. 1974. New Estimates of the Vital Rates of the United States Black Population During the Nineteenth Centruy. Demography 11 (2): 301-319.

The difficulties of obtaining credible estimates of vital rates for the black population throughout the entire nineteenth century are overcome in this study. The methodology employed the notion of deviating networks of mortality rates for each general mortality level, which was taken from the United States study the Concept of a Stable Population. Period life tables and vital rates for intercensal period were generated from the new estimates of the black population at each census date. The results of this study are highly compatible both with the life tables for the death-registration states in the twentieth century and the recent Coale and Rives reconstruction for the period from 1880 to 1970 and with several estimates of vital rates previously made for the mid-nineteenth century. This study places the mean life expectancy at birth for the black population during the nineteenth century at about 33.7 years for both sexes. The infant death rate (1000 m_O) is shown to have varied between 222 and 237 for females and between 266 and 278 for males. The intrinsic crude death rate centered on 30.4 per thousand during the century, while the birth rate declined from 53.2 early in the century to about 43.8 at the end.*

561.   Elifson, K.W., and J. Irwin. 1977. Black Ministers' Attitudes Toward Population Size and Birth Control. Sociological Analysis 38 (3): 252-257.

The attempt was made to explain the various influences upon a black minister's stance toward the issue of population control. Attitudes toward ideal black population size and genocidal efforts by whites were assessed in conjunction with a larger study of 154 black ministers in Nashville, Tennessee. A variety of demographic and experiential indicators which hypothetically should serve as predictors of the stance taken by the ministers were considered. A consistent and sharp linkage was identified between the extent to which a person is disenchanted with the general relationship between blacks and whites and the manner in which he perceives a crucial population issue. This was demonstrated in terms of attitudes and in 2 behavioral measures. The more rhetorically active men were at the quantitative end of the contimuum. If the black minister is in fact effective in influencing the members of his congregation, a shift toward the quantitative approach on the part of churchgoing laymen might be anticipated. Those who were rhetorically inactive and qualitatively oriented should have little if any influence.**

562.   Erickson, J. D. 1976. The Secondary Sex Ratio in the United States 1969-71: Association with Race, Parental Ages, Birth Order, Paternal

Education and Legitimacy. Annals of Human Genetics 40 (Part 2): 205-212.

An analysis of the secondary sex ratio, using recent and extensive U.S. data, in which the simultaneous effects of several variables were investigated, was conducted. Computer tapes containing information derived from birth certificates of live-born infants were made available by the U.S. National Center for Health Statistics. The data contained in the tapes used here comprise a 50% sample of all live births in the U.S. for the years 1969-1971. For the present analysis, the following information, in addition to sex, was ascertained for each of 5,349,446 births: race of mother, age of mother, age of father, total birth order (includes live births and fetal deaths), legitimacy, and paternal education. Analyses of the effects of these factors on the sex ratio were made using the Mantel-Haenszel approach and weighted linear regressions. It was learned that the overall sex ratio for whites is 1.058 while that for blacks is 1.027. However, the patterns on the various independent variables are similar for both races. The previously described negative association of birth order and sex ratio has been confirmed. For legitimate and illegitimate births combined, maternal age and paternal age are unimportant factors once account is made of birth order. This pattern obtains for both blacks and whites. The sex ratio for legitimate and illegitimate births is equivalent, but the fact of legitimacy or illegitimacy may affect the association of the ratio with birth order and parental ages. Paternal education is not significantly related to the ratio, but the highest probability of a male birth is found among fathers with intermediate levels of attainment. Although the association between sex ratio and order of birth is highly significant in the statistical sense, the proportion of male births changes less than 2% over the extreme values of birth order.☆

563. Farley, Reynolds. 1965. The Demographic Rates and Social Institutions of the Nineteenth-Century Negro Population: A Stable Population Analysis. Demography 2: 386-398.

A study assuming that "the Negro population of the United States was a closed one after the end of slaving in 1808, and the growth that did occur must have been due to natural increase." Estimates, obtained for 1830-50 and 1850-80, include: life expectation at birth; life expectation at age 10; infant mortality rate; crude birth rate; crude death rate; rate of natural increase; general fertility rate; percent under age 15; dependency ratio. Consideration of "whether the demographic patterns indicated by the population models are congruent with the living conditions and institutional arrangements of the Negro population of the last century."★

564. Farley, Reynolds. 1968. The Quality of Demographic Data for Nonwhites. Demography 5 (1): 1-10.

Demographic data for nonwhites in the United States are often assumed to be of low quality. Problems arise because of undercount and under-registration and because individuals included in the census do not always provide accurate information. This paper describes some of the major errors which confound data for nonwhites and attempts to measure the impact that these errors have for various demographic rates.*

565.   Farley, Reynolds. 1970. Growth of the Black Population. Chicago: Markham Publishing Company.

Farley describes the varying rates of black population growth by analyzing trends in fertility and mortality. Farley gives an account for the changes in these demographic rates. In explaining the growth of the black population, Farley concentrates on the effects of factors such as marital status, birth control, ecological and economic factors, as well as the health conditions of the black population. The book consists of nine chapters and an appendix. Some of the chapters are cited separately in this volume.*

566.   Farley, Reynolds. 1970. The Changing Distribution of Negroes Within Metropolitan Areas: The Emergence of Black Suburbs. American Journal of Sociology 75: 512-529.

Several studies have indicated that central cities and their suburban rings are coming to have dissimilar racial composition. A closer examination of the data reveals that suburban rings do not have an exclusively white population. There are now, and always have been, suburban communities of blacks. In recent years, the growth of the Negro suburban population has accelerated. This growth appears concentrated in three types of areas: older suburbs which are experiencing population succession, new developments designed for Negro occupancy, and some impoverished suburban enclaves. Despite this growth, city-suburban differences in the proportion of black population are increasing, and patterns of residential segregation by race within suburbs are emerging which are similar to those found within central cities. In the past, city-suburban differences in socioeconomic status were different among whites and Negroes. Unlike whites, the blacks who lived in the suburbs were typically lower in socioeconomic status than the blacks who lived in central cities. The recent migration to the suburbs, however, is apparently selective of higher status blacks, and it is likely the census of 1970 will reveal that the socioeconomic status of suburban blacks exceeds that of central city blacks.*

567.   Farley, Reynolds. 1971. Indications of Recent Demographic Change Among Blacks. Social Biology 18 (4): 341-357.

On the basis of figures displayed in this paper, we conclude that the federal policies and activities of the 1960's have failed to eliminate racial differences in education, occupation, or income. In every comparison, blacks were at a disadvantage in both 1970 and

1960. We might speculate that the programs of this decade would have
their greatest impact upon young people who recently were attending
school and who joined the labor force within the last few years. Even
if we limit our comparisons to these age groups, we observe that
blacks have finished fewer years of school, earn less, and hold
proportionally fewer prestigious jobs than do whites of identical
ages. Apparently, some progress was made between 1960 and 1970 just
as it was in the score of years preceding 1960. Among both races,
educational attainment increased, the occupational distribution was
upgraded, and real purchasing power rose substantially. In almost
every comparison, the gains were somewhat greater among blacks than
among whites and most indicators of racial differentiation declined.
With regard to education, racial differences in median attainment
were sharply reduced. The number of blacks employed as craftsmen or
white collar workers went up rapidly and the median income of nonwhites increased faster than that of whites. Nevertheless,   as   we
mentioned previously, very large racial differences remain. For
instance, at the end of the decade, one-third of all blacks were
classed as impoverished compared to 10% of the whites, and the median
family income of Negroes was but three-fifths that of whites... These
differences, and similar differences in occupation and education,
suggest that even if blacks make progress during the 1970's as they
did during the 1960's, there will still be large racial differences
when the next decennial census is taken, and blacks will still be at
a disadvantage.*

568.   Farley, Reynolds. 1977. Residential Segregation in Urbanized Areas of
the United States in 1970: An Analysis of Social Class and Racial
Difference. Demography 14 (4): 497-518.

Sociologists and urban commentators often portray metropolitan areas
as highly segregated by social class and race. We measured the extent
of socioeconomic residential segregation in urbanized areas of the
United States in 1970, determined whether cities were as segregated
as surburban rings, and compared levels of socioeconomic and racial
residential segregation. We found moderate levels of residential
segregation of socioeconomic groups. Levels of social class
segregation varied little from one urbanized areas to another and
were about the same in central cities and suburban rings. Racial
residential segregation was much greater than the segregation of
social classes within either the black or white communities. The
extent of racial residential segregation does not vary by educational
attainment, occupation, or income.*

569.   Farley, Reynolds, and Albert Hermalin. 1972. The 1960s: A Decade of
Progress for Blacks? Demography 9 (2): 353-370.

Between 1960 and 1970 blacks, as well as whites, improved their
socioeconmic status. Among both races, educational attainment
increased, the occupational distribution was upgraded, and real
purchasing power rose markedly. In almost every comparison, the gains

were somewhat greater among blacks than among whites and thus most indicators of racial differentiation declined. Nevertheless, the changes of this decade failed to eliminate racial differences with regard to socioeconomic status. In all comparisons, except for the income of certain groups of women, blacks were at a disadvantage when compared to whites both at the start and at the end of this decade, and very large racial differences remain. Further socioeconomic progress by blacks during the 1970s will probably not eliminate racial differences. The article concludes by relating the socio-economic trends to such other aspects of race relations as integration, governmental policy, and the attitudes of whites and blacks.*

570.   Frisbie, W. Parker, and Lisa Neidert. 1977. Inequality and the Relative Size of Minority Populations: A Comparative Analysis. American Journal of Sociology 82 (5): 1007-1030.

Socioeconomic differentials separating whites and blacks have been shown to correlate positively with percentage of blacks in a population. However, in multiracial or multiethnic populations, it is necessary to take into account the effects of the relative size of each minority present in nonnegligible numbers. In the research reported here, the relationship between socioeconomic inequality and the proportion of Mexican Americans and blacks in the population of metropolitan areas was decomposed through path-analytic techniques. Analysis of a model incorporating the impact of the size of both minorities indicates that minority income levels are inversely related to minority size and that disparities between majority and minority income and occupation tend to grow as relative minority size increases. Mexican American Occupational levels vary positively with the percentage of blacks, but black occupational status was found to be virtually unrelated to the proportional representation of Mexican Americans in metropolitan areas. Finally, the positive relationship between minority percentage and inequalities of income and occupation persists net of the effects of a number of plausible alternative explanations. The data employed in this analysis are drawn from 1970 U.S. census tabulations on 40 of the 46 Standard Metropolitan Statistical Areas (SMSAs) Located in the Southern U.S.*

571.   Glenn, Norval D. 1964. The Relative Size of the Negro Population and Negro Occupational Status. Social Forces 43: 42-49.

The hypothesis that the relative size of the Negro population and Negro occupational status are inversely related was not supported by a study of the populations of the 151 SMA's that had 100,000 or more people in 1950. However, this finding was not construed as a refuta-tion of the widely held belief that discrimination against a minority varies directly with the relative size of the minority population. Rather, it was concluded that "overflow" of Negroes into intermediate level occupations offsets any greater discrimination in those localities where the relative number of Negroes is large.*

572. Green, D.S., and E.D. Driver (eds.). 1978. **W.E.B. Dubois on Sociology and the Black Community.** Chicago and London: The University of Chicago Press. 320 pp.

Throughout this book there are repeated references to demographic characteristics of the black population. The most relevant sections are chapters six and nine.★

573. Hart, John Fraser. 1960. **The Changing Distribution of the American Negro.** Annals of the Association of American Geographers 50 (3): 242-266.

The changing distribution of its black population has been one of the most dramatic aspects of population geography of the United States over the last half century. The objective of this paper is to examine and describe the changing patterns of black population distribution in the United States. Patterns are analyzed and interpreted, both temporally and areally. The author concludes that the American black population is becoming increasingly urbanized, and largely as a result of migration from the rural South to metropolitan areas outside the South. In light of the information here presented, the three major streams of Negro migration in the United States can be defined more precisely. Natural increase data indicate that the great majority of Negro migrants from the South Atlantic states come from the Inner Costal Plain and the Piedmont of Georgia, the Carolinas, and Virginia; state of birth data show the vast majority of migrants from these states move to the Northeast; and the natural increase data indicate that migrants to the Northeast settle almost entirely in the metropolitan area of Megalopolis. In the same fashion, we may conclude that the second major stream consists of migrants from the Delta, the Black Belt, and virtually the entire state of Mississippi who are moving toward Chicago, Detroit, and the other urban centers from Cleveland to St. Louis. This stream, like the first, is fed partially from the Georgia-Alabama Coastal Plain, which also appears to send migrants to peninsular Florida. The third stream of Negro migration originates in the sandy lands of southern Arkansas, northern Louisiana, and eastern Texas, and flows westward toward Los Angeles, San Francisco, and Seattle; some migrants from the Delta also appear to join this stream. Examination of Negro population trends by regions shows a reciprocity between regions which would seem to indicate that these streams of migration have existed for at least half a century, although their volume was not so great in the earlier years. Migration has nonetheless decimated the Negro population of many areas, as is revealed by the study of peak years. First, Negroes left the hills, which had reached their peak by 1900; then they left the South Atlantic states, where 1910-20 peaks are most common; next came heavy migration from the central South, where most counties have peaks between 1910 and 1940; more recently heavy migration from the trans-Mississippi South has been associated with peaks in 1930 and in 1940. But the cities--the major magnets for Negro migrants--had more Negroes in 1950 than they had ever had

before, and are increasing their share of the nation's increasing
Negro population. Urbanization for the American Negro has come more
belatedly than it came for his white neighbor, but now that it has
started it is proceeding with a rush. Negroes have almost disappeared
in some rural areas where once they were numerous. Virtually every
nonmetropolitan county in the South had fewer Negroes in 1950 than in
some previous year, whereas metropolitan areas throughout the nation
had their maximum Negro population in 1950. But Negro migrants are
attracted mainly to cities outside the South. In short, the American
Negro, who was a rural Southerner two generations ago, is rapidly
becoming an urban Northerner or Westerner.*

574.   Hauser, Philip M. 1965. Demographic Factors in the Integration of the
        Negro. Daedalus 94: 847-877.

        The size, rate of growth, distribution, and composition of the black
        population both influence integration and provide some indications of
        the extent to which it has been achieved. The precise way in which
        these demographic factors affect integration is not definitely
        studied. This paper attempts to summarize the characteristics of the
        black population and examines how the changes in the black population
        affect integration.*

575.   Hauser, Philip M. 1966. Demographic and Social Factors in the Poverty
        of the Negro. In: The Disadvantaged Poor: Education and Employment.
        Washington, D.C.: Chamber of Commerce of the United States. Task
        Force on Economic Growth and Opportunity. Pp. 229-261.

        The Negro American constitutes the largest and most visible minority
        group in the United States. In 1960, the Negro population, at 18.9
        million, made up over a tenth of the total population of the nation.
        In 1963, the 4.8 million non-white households made up about 10
        percent of all households in the country. But the 2.3 million
        non-white households steeped in poverty, according to the official
        definition of the Federal Government...constituted almost one-third
        of all poor families in the nation. The disproportionate incidence of
        poverty among Negro Americans can be understood only against the
        background of their demographic and social history in the United
        States. Moreover, policy and programs designed to eradicate poverty
        among Negroes must necessarily be developed on the basis of such an
        understanding. It is the purpose of this working paper to summarize
        relevant aspects of the demographic and social history of the Negro
        in his residence in this nation and to consider the implications of
        the data for the war against poverty.*

576.   Hillery, George A., Jr. 1957. The Negro in New Orleans: A Functional
        Analysis of Demographic Data. American Sociological Review 22 (2):
        183-188.

        This paper is based on a chapter of Hillery's unpublished Ph.D.
        Dissertation, The Negro In New Orleans: A Demographic Analysis,

Lousiana State University, 1954. The major objective of this paper is to investigate the relationship between population characteristics and processes and social values. The author attempts to achieve his goal through an explanation of observed demographic differentials by race, using a sociological theory. More specifically, he formulates and attempts to test the hypothesis that: "One function of the white man's definition of the racial situation is to create demographic differentials between his own and the Negro population." The lack of adequate data leaves the testing of this hypothesis inconclusive.★

577.   Hope, John II. 1953. The Employment of Negroes in the United States by Major Occupation and Industry. Journal of Negro Education 22 (3): 307-321.

Examines the distribution of non-agricultural employed black population groups in the United States during the 1940-50 decade. Compares with the white population. Analysis is based on the 1940 and 1950 census data.★

578.   Hout, Michael. 1979. Age Structure, Unwanted Fertility, and the Association Between Racial Composition and Family Planning Programs: A Comment on Wright. Social Forces 57 (4): 1387-1392.

This analysis has shown that Wright's (for abstract see Gerald C. Wright, Jr. in the section on family planning in this bibliography) charge of racism in the provision of family planning services is unfounded. Although he considers the political climate of an area important, the cornerstone of his charge is the observed correlation between racial composition and the availability of family planning services. Without that correlation, no charge of racism can be made. This analysis has shown that the correlation he reports is spurious. Net of controls for need for family planning services in the construction of the measure of family planning availability and controls for socioeconomic conditions in the multiple regression, the effect of racial composition on the availability of family planning services is not significantly different from zero.*

579.   Huyck, Earl E. 1966. White-Nonwhite Differentials: Overview and Implications. Demography 3 (2): 548-565.

This paper reviews the arguments for maintaining a separate series of statistics for the white and nonwhite populations of the United States; only by maintaining factual data will it be possible to document inequality and discrimination. It then summarizes some white-nonwhite differentials: fertility, life expectancy, health, school attendance, educational attainment, and income. The human, social, and polictical implications are then reviewed.*

580.   Illinois Council for Black Studies. 1980. Black People and the 1980 Census. Volume 1: Proceedings from a Conference on the Population

Undercount. Chicago, Illinois: Illinois Council for Black Studies.

This book contains the proceedings of a conference on the population undercount held at the University of Chicago, November 30-December 1, 1979. The main focus of the conference was on the anticipated undercount of black and other minority groups in the 1980 U.S. census and on steps needed to rectify the consequences of the undercount, particularly the need to use adjusted census figures that include those people missed when deciding such matters as the allocation of federal funds and the apportionment of political representation. Some specific papers in this book are as follows: G.A. McWorter. Racism and the Numbers Game: A Critique of the Census Underenumeration of Black People and a Proposal for Action. Pp. 87-170; H. Kirksey. The Black Undercount and Political Issues. Pp. 233-271; A. Vann. The Census and Black Elected Officials. Pp. 305-319; N.R. McKenney. Studying the Black Experience with the 1980 Census. Pp. 517-533; R.W. Bailey. The New Disenfranchisement: The Census, the Undercount, and Black Power in Electoral Politics. Pp. 536-600; L. William. Census Data in Research, Teaching, and Studying the Conditions of Black Women. Pp. 601-625.★

581. Jones, Barbara A. 1979. Utilization of Black Human Resources in the United States. The Review of Black Political Economy 10 (1): 79-96.

In this paper Jones assesses the state of the black economy by describing the socio-demographic characteristics of blacks in terms of labor force participation rates, unemployment rates, patterns of occupational distribution, and some other factors that affect blacks' manpower. This paper can best be described as a study in economic demography of blacks.★

582. Jones, C. 1974. Population Issues and the Black Community.   In: Political Issues in U.S. Population Policy. V. Gray and E. Bergman (eds.). Lexington, Massachusetts: D.C. Heath. Pp. 151-166.

Black reactions to population issues in the United States are generally negative. This is a reaction to white-formulated policies. Black nationalists are more militantly opposed to population control proposals than either civil rightists or black radicals. Black nationalists believe racial differences to be natural, racial separateness to be necessary, and racial struggles to be inevitable. For the struggle, blacks will need as large a population as possible. Civil rightists and black radicals might support population control policies if white policy-makers would also support social justice for blacks. Suspicion of the motives of whites might be lessened if blacks were given a chance to participate in the decision-making process. It is unknown how closely leadership views correlate with those of the general black population.★

583. Katz, William L. (ed.). 1968. The American Negro: His History and Literature: The Atlanta University Publications Nos. 1, 2, 4, 8, 9,

11, 13, 14, 15, 16, 17, 18. New York: Arno Press and the New York Times.

Several of the publications included in this volume deal with the demographic characteristics of black population in the United States. Publication No. 1, entitled "Mortality Among Negroes in Cities", is the proceedings of the Conference for Investigation of City Problems, held at Atlanta University, May 26-27, 1896. Publication No. 2, entitled "Social and Physical Conditions of Negroes in Cities", is the proceedings of the same conference held at Atlanta University, May 25-26, 1897. Publications Nos. 11 and 13, also demographic in nature, are proceedings of the same conference held at Atlanta University in subsequent years.★

584. King, Allan G., and R. White. 1976. Demographic Influences on Labor Force Rates of Black Males. Monthly Labor Review 99 (November): 42-43.

Frederic B. Siskind in a 1975 article entitled: "Labor Force Participation of Men, 25-54, by Race" (Monthly Labor Review, July 1975, Pp. 40-42) called attention to a marked decline in labor force participation rates among prime age black males. According to his analysis, Siskind concluded that some 26 percent of the decline was attributable to increased eligibility for disability payments between 1955 and 1972. Siskind attributed large residual component of the trend to the joint influence of changes in demographic variables, marital status and place of residence on the labor force participation of black males. In the present article, King and White using the method of direct standardization present data which cast doubts on the validity of Siskind's conclusion. King and White conclude that there is no strong support for the idea that changes in marital status and residence contributed significantly to the decline in the labor force participation rates of prime age black males between 1950 and 1970.★

585. Lieberson, Stanley. 1973. Generational Differences Among Blacks in the North. American Journal of Sociology 79: 550-565.

A generational classification is virtually a standard procedure for research on European and Asian migrants and their descendants in the United States. An analogous distinction is rarely applied to the southern- and northern-born components of the black population living in the North. Analysis of educational attainment among northern black residents indicates the existence of substantial differences between these two generations with respect to this important characteristic. Likewise, decomposition of the effect of population increase on changes in urban racial segregation indicates that growth in the northern- and southern-born generations has opposite consequences. Therefore, changes in the southern-born proportion among the black population of the North may greatly distort inferences about the causes of long-term shifts in the conditions of blacks living in that region. There are certain implicit theoretical assumptions made when generation is overlooked in research on blacks or any other racial or ethnic group. Although these assumptions may be valid in some contact settings--particularly for later generations--their validity can usually be resolved through empirical research.*

586. Lieberson, S., and C.A. Wilkinson. 1976. A Comparison Between Northern and Southern Blacks Residing in the North. Demography 13 (2): 199-224.

Differences between Southern and non-Southern blacks living in the North and West are considered for a wide variety of attributes such as employment, occupation, income, marital stability, and offspring's performance in school. Migrant blacks have generally more favorable rates than their Northern- and Western-born compatriots after standard demographic controls are applied to an unusually detailed set of cross-tabulations based on the One-Percent Sample Tapes for 1960. Perhaps the sharpest gap exists with respect to marital condition; Southern blacks of both sexes are more likely to marry and, among those ever married, live more frequently with their spouses. Some of the results reported by earlier investigators require considerable modification. For example, the fact that Northern black men are less often at work than migrants has led to speculations about regional differences in work orientation among blacks, but a detailed analysis of labor force activity indicates this pattern does not hold for women. Likewise, the migrant income advantage is found to vary by education such that it is confined to those with low educational attainment. The use of sample tapes permits a novel analysis of differences between Northern-born blacks classified by whether they are second or at least third generation residents of the North (children of Southern- or Northern-born parents, respectively). For the attribute measured, school per-formance, the gap is essentially nil. Finally, an alternative is suggested to the existing causal interpretations of North-South gaps among black residents of the North. Reconsidered in particular are the higher labor force rates of migrant men and their more frequent employment in blue collar jobs.*

587. Lorimer, Frank, and Dorothy S. Jones. 1953. The Demographic Characteristics of the Negro Population in the United States. Journal of Negro Education 22 (3): 250-254.

This is a brief examination of age structure, sex ratio, urban-rural distribution, and farm-nonfarm distribution of the black population of the United States based on the 1950 census data.*

588. Marshall, Harvey, and John Stahura. 1979. Black and White Population Growth in American Suburbs: Transition or Parallel Development?. Social Forces 58 (1): 305-328.

This study examines the impact of black population size and rate of increase on white population change in American suburbs between 1960 and 1970. The data indicate that there is no tipping point. In small suburbs the black population variables interact, while in medium and large suburbs percent black has a moderate additive effect on white population growth and black population increase is unimportant. These patterns persist even when variables causally prior to the white and black population variables are controlled. Finally, in only a few instances within the observed range of percent black or rate of black population increase, or any combination of these variables, was there any absolute decline in the white population.*

589. Marston, Wilfred George. 1966. Population Redistribution and Socioeconomic Differentiation Within Negro Areas of American Cities: A Comparative Analysis. Unpublished Ph.D. Dissertation. University of Washington. 259 pp.

The basic purpose of this dissertation is to examine the patterns and processes of (1) socioeconomic differentiation and (2) population redistribution within Negro communities of nineteen American cities. Moreover, certain demographic characteristics of the cities are analyzed with particular emphasis on how the characteristics are associated with these patterns and processes. Another purpose is to test the applicability of existing models of urban spatial structure for use in the analysis of Negro communities. The cities selected range in size from approximately 900,000 to slightly over 100,000. Data are from census tract publications for both 1950 and 1960; detailed characteristics reported for "nonwhites" for those tracts with 250 or more nonwhites in 1950 and those tracts with 400 or more in 1960 were the primary data used. Simple proportions, socioeconomic status scores, an index of residential dissimilarity, and Spearman's rank order correlation are the statistical techniques used. The Negro community of each city is divided into the older established area and the emerging area. This is somewhat analogous to the distinction between central city and suburb and is designed to test the proposition that spatial structure and growth are patterned basically the same way in the Negro community as in the larger urban complex. More specifically, the analysis consists of (1) measurement of change in socioeconomic status and social class segregation in established areas during the 1950-60 decade, (2) a comparison of established and emerging areas with respect to socioeconomic status, social class segregation and mobility status, (3) an intra-zonal comparison of established and emerging areas, and (4) an assessment of structural characteristics with respect to their influence on the patterns and processes within the Negro community. The level of socioeconomic status and the amount of segregation increased slightly within established areas during the 1950-60 decade. This is particularly significant when compared to the fact that the white population in established area census tracts experienced a reduction in the level of socioeconomic status and little change in the amount of social class segregation during the decade. In general, differences between established and emerging areas were in the expected direction.

Emerging areas (1) were higher in socioeconomic status, (2) were marked by more social class segregtion, and (3) received a greater proportion of new residents than did established areas. Within both established and emerging areas, the concentric pattern was evident with respect to socioeconomic differentiation and even in cases where the concentric pattern was weak, significant differences still existed between zones. Population size of the urban area, Negro population size, and rate of suburbanization of the total population were each negatively associated with the level of socioeconomic status in established areas and positively associated with established-emerging area status differentials. On a general level, the over-all findings are consistent with the existing model of urban areal structure and growth. However, the frequent and sometimes persistent deviations suggest that the model is over-simplified and inadequate to account for the specific patterns and processes of socioeconomic differentiation and population distribution within the Negro community and a revision is needed. For example, a substantial amount of the areal expansion of the Negro community is taking place "horizontally" (sideways) and toward the center of the city and most of the expansion is into relatively old residential neighborhoods. The results of this study support the contention that the distinction between the established and emerging areas of the Negro community is both theoretically and methodologically sound.*

590.   Mayo, Selz C., and C.H. Hamilton. 1963. Current Population Trends in the South. Social Forces 42 (1): 77-88.

A study of census data, 1940-1960, on population growth and redistribution. Change in the population by color, changing residential distribution; population processes, changing functional roles, and the future population. ★

591.   Mayo, Selz C., and C.H. Hamilton. 1963. The Rural Negro Population of the South in Transition. Phylon 24 (2): 160-171.

A study based largely on U.S. censuses 1940-1960, of changes in the Southeast in the black population's size and distribution, residential composition, fertility and migration status, and functional roles. ★

592.   McKenney, N.R. 1967. Negro Population: March 1966. U.S. Bureau of the Census, Current Population Reports, Series P-20, No. 168. Washington, D.C.: Government Printing Office. 38 pp.

This is a study of demographic, social, and economic characteristics of black population compared with whites. It consists of two main parts: descriptive (the first 14 pages) and tabular (the remaining 24 pages).★

593.   McKenney, N.R., et al. 1972. The Social and Economic Status of the Black Population in the United States, 1971. U.S. Bureau of the

Census, Current Population Reports, Series P-23, No. 42. Washington, D.C.: Government Printing Office. 164 pp.

This is a descriptive analysis of demographic, social and economic conditions of the black population in the United States in 1971. "The majority of the statistics in this report are from the Bureau of the Census, but some are from other government and private agencies." In addition to seven pages of introductory remarks, sections include: I, Population Distribution; II, Income; III, Employment; IV, Education; V, Housing; VI, The Family; VII, Voting; VIII, Selected Areas, followd by an appendix.*

594.   McKenney, N.R., et al. 1973. The Social and Economic Status of the Black Population in the United States, 1972. U.S. Bureau of the Census, Current Population Reports, Series P-23, No. 46. Washington, D.C.: Government Printing Office. 116 pp.

Statistics describing the general, social, and economic character-istics of the black population in the United States are presented in this report, which is the sixth in a series on the subject. In general, the report focuses on the changes which have occurred within the last five years in income, employment, education, housing, and other major aspects of life. The most current data available are presented here.*

595.   McKenney, N.R., et al. 1974. The Social and Economic Status of the Black Population in the United States, 1973. U.S. Bureau of the Census, Current Population Reports, Series P-23, No. 48. Washington, D.C.: Government Printing Office. 146 pp.

A statistical description of the current social and economic status of black Americans is presented in this report, which is the seventh in a series on the subject. The particular focus of this report is on the changes which have occurred in the 1970's in population distri-bution, income, education, employment, family composition, health, voting, and other major aspects of life. Comparisons are made with the mid- and late 1960's. Comparable data on blacks are not always available so the time period used varies in the report; however, the most current data available are always presented.*

596.   McKenney, N.R., et al. 1975. The Social and Economic Status of the Black Population in the United States, 1974. U.S. Bureau of the Census, Current Population Reports, Series P-23, No. 54. Washington, D.C.: Government Printing Office. 195 pp.

A statistical overview of the demographic, social, and economic characteristics of the black population in the United States is presented in this report, which is the eighth in the series on the subject. This study brings together the relevant data from the Census Bureau as well as from other government and private agencies.*

597. McKinney, John C., and L.B. Bourgue. 1971. The Changing South: National Incorporation of a Region. American Sociological Review 36 (3): 399-412.

The South is herein viewed as a subsystem of a larger, American social system. The paper attempts to demonstrate, using a variety of socioeconomic and demographic indicators, the rapidity with which the South is becoming an integral part of American Society. The analysis is based upon a set of two-way comparisons: the South with itself over time; the non-South with itself over time; and the South with the non-South at specified points in time. The measures used are grouped into five areas: urbanization,industrialization, occupational redistribution, income, and education. The evidence indicates that in these sectors the South has been changing more rapidly than the rest of the nation for the past forty years and moreover is becoming increasingly indistinguishable from the rest of American society.*

598. Murray, R.F.J. 1977. The Ethical and Moral Values of Black Americans and Population Policy. In: Population Policy and Ethics: The American Experience. R.M. Veatch (ed.). New York: Irvington Publishers. Pp. 197-209.

In order to be effective, proposed population policy in the U.S. should be developed with an understanding of black cultural traditions and values. Children and the family unit are of special significance to black Americans because of their West African tribal heritage. Slavery created chaos in the family unit and resulted in poverty and social disorganization for a high percentage of black Americans. Because black Americans have not enjoyed the same cultural stability and affluence as the white segment of the population, many black subcultures insist the proposed population policies focus on limiting their growth. Ethical values of importance to blacks such as security, survival, freedom, truth-telling, and justice contribute to the self-determinism of the race. Many policies proposed by the government will be unsuccessful because they are deliberately restrictive to blacks and ignore their cultural values. Policies to control population can be successful and accepted if they are combined with measures to bring about economic and social reform, and if blacks are permitted to participate in their development and implementation.☆

599. Norton, E.H. 1973. Population Growth and the Future of Black Folk. The Crisis (May): 151-153.

Mrs. Eleanor H. Norton, chairman of the New York City Commission on Human Rights who is also the co-chairman of the Citizens' Commission on Population and the American Future, asserts that at its conception, the Commission on Population Growth and the American Future was viewed with suspicion by many in the minority community, especially blacks. In this article she carefully reviews the objectives of the Commission and the inputs by the minority members of the Commission who proved to be fiercely independent. Norton maintains that suspicions aside, "the real issue for black people and other minorities is how to improve their quality of life. In other words, getting better education, jobs, and social services. We must demand the right of access to better contraceptives and to family planning services so that we can be free to have children when we want them. The ability of individuals to control their own fertility is at the root of controlling their own lives."★

600.   Norton, E.H. 1973. **Population Growth and the Future of Black Folk.** Population Reference Bureau Selection 43: 1-4.

The Commission on Population Growth and the American Future reported that minorities are not responsible for the bulk of population growth, and that they would actually benefit from a slower rate of population growth. A study in 1969, substantiating the first fact, showed that among all women between the ages 35-44, the minority groups only contributed 30 percent of surplus childbearing. Data from the National Fertility Study of 1970 showed unwanted fertility among blacks to be high because of limited access to information and health care services and because of contraceptive failure; the committee urged improved methods of contraception. The commission advocated 1) a policy to reduce unwanted fertility through voluntary fertility control while strongly deploring all forceful measures and all measures which would attempt to control the reproduction of any specific group of people such as welfare recipients, and 2) national programs to improve maternal and child health care to benefit all mothers and children including better day care services. ★

601.   Orshansky, Mollie. 1965. **Counting the Poor: Another Look at the Poverty Profile.** Social Security Bulletin 28 (1): 3-29.

This paper depicts some of the demographic characteristics of the poor many of whom are blacks. The analysis is primarily limited to families of two or more persons. In a separate article, cited as the next entry in this bibliography, Orshansky examines the demographic profile of poverty level individuals by race, age, sex, and employment status in March 1964.★

602.   Orshansky, Mollie. 1965. **Who's Who Among the Poor: A Demographic View of Poverty.** Social Security Bulletin 28 (7): 3-32.

How many are poor in this country, and who are they? An earlier Bulletin article ("Counting the Poor: Another Look at the Poverty Profile," in the January 1965 issue) offered an index of poverty to help answer these questions, in broad terms, for households of different size and type. That article focused largely on the number of families thus defined as poor in terms of 1963 income. The current article spotlights the 35 million individuals in poverty and gives details on their race, age, sex, and employment status in March 1964. Data for the households also appear here, where relevant.*

603. Palen, J.J., and L.F. Schnore. 1965. Color Composition and
      City-Suburban Status Differences: A Replication and Extension. Land
      Economics 41: 87-91.

      Previous research has demonstrated that city-suburban status
      differences in large urbanized areas are just the opposite of those
      seen in smaller areas. Using fresh and more complete data, the
      authors re-examine city-suburban status differences while controlling
      for color. This study partially confirms the hypothesis that non-
      white population would not show the same relationships as the whites.
      The authors discover that there is another important factor (in
      addition to city age and size) to be considered. That factor is the
      regional location of urbanized area. Looking at the non-white data,
      without respect to region, there is practically no relationship
      between size and age on the one hand, and the direction of city-
      suburban variation on the other. When region is controlled, however,
      the study shows that such relationships tend to appear in the North
      and West. City-suburban status differentials among non-whites in the
      North and West are generally similar to those shown by the white
      population in both broad regions. In contrast, the nonwhite data for
      Southern areas do not reveal any clear and consistent associations
      between either (a) the age or (b) the size of the urbanized area and
      (c) the direction of city-suburban status differences.★

604. Pettyjohn, Leonard F. 1976. Factorial Ecology of the Los Angeles -
      Long Beach Black Population. Unpublished Ph.D. Dissertation. The
      University of Wisconsin, Milwaukee. 206 pp.

      The 1970 Black population in the Los Angeles-Long Beach SMSA is
      examined through the use of principal components and principal
      factors analysis to identify internal structural patterns. The
      principal factors model identified six factors, accounting for 66
      percent of the variance among the thirty-five variables under study.
      Although many of the factors are similar to those extracted for
      entire SMSA populations the Black population shows considerable
      variation in spatial patterns compared to the entire SMSA. Oblique
      rotations of the factor matrices reveal that some of the factors are
      correlated and that the commonly used varimax (orthogonal) technique
      would "force" the data into independent descriptors. Cluster analysis
      techniques further indicate that the Black population exhibits
      significant spatial variation in the SMSA. Most of the Black social
      areas that dominate in the central city of Los Angeles also are
      represented in the suburban communities. However, the reverse is not
      true, i.e., most of the higher status areas are only outside the
      city. Classification into social areas shows that status increases
      with distance from the CBD out to about 4 to 5 miles to the west and
      12 to 15 miles to the south. Beyond these distances status begins to
      decrease to more moderate levels.*

605. Pinkney, Alphonso. 1975. Characteristics of the [Black] Population.
      In: Black Americans, by Alphonso Pinkney. Englewood Cliffs, N.J.:

Prentice Hall. Chapter 2.

Pinkney examines various demographic features of the black population in the United States. His analyses include size, growth, fertility, health, mortality, age and sex composition, and distribution (south-nonsouth; rural-urban).*

606.   Price, Daniel O. 1968. Educational Differentials Between Negroes and Whites in the South. Demography 5 (1): 23-33.

This paper examines differences between whites and nonwhites in median years of school completed, by urban and rural areas of southern states. Whites, of course, have higher average levels of education, but the important point is the increasing differential between whites and nonwhites. The differences do not increase in all southern states, but they did increase during the years 1950-60 in seven of the eleven states studied. Only four of the eleven states showed an increase in educational differentials during the years 1940-50. The levels of education in these 11 states were also examined by age and sex and by urban and rural-farm residence, and differences between whites and nonwhites in level of education were examined by cohorts. Each of the states studied had some cohorts in which the educational gap had widened--especially in rural farm areas and more frequently among males than among females. An examination of the education gap among those aged 25-34 years was made for three census periods, 1940, 1950, and 1960. In 1960 the educational gap in this age group in urban areas was less than in either 1950 or 1940. Thus, there is reason to expect decreases in the educational gap in southern urban areas even though specific cohorts show a widening of the gap. Looking at this age group in rural-farm areas, it is seen that the gap in 1960 was greater than in either 1950 or 1940. Thus, in rural farm areas each cohort is starting with a larger differential that tends to increase with increasing age, so that the educational gap in rural farm areas can be expected to continue to increase. The increasing difference in average education between whites and nonwhites is attributed to the higher out-migration rates of the better educated nonwhites. Although survival rates were computed by educational level in order to study this, the sampling variation for those with twelve or more years of education is large because of the small numbers of individuals involved. Analysis of these data is continuing in an effort to associate characteristics of states with patterns of educational selectivity of out-migrants. A recent census report shows that the proportion of nonwhites aged 18-14 years enrolled in school has been falling further behind the proportion of whites in the same age group since 1955. This trend, if continued, will lead to increasing disproportions of whites and nonwhites with college degrees. Unless the gap in educational level between whites and nonwhites is reduced and eventually eliminated there is little hope for the fulfillment of economic expectations on the part of nonwhites.*

607.   Price, Daniel O. 1969. Changing Characteristics of the Negro
       Population: A 1960 Census Monograph. Washington, D.C.: Government
       Printing Office.

       The purpose of this monograph is to examine the major changes that
       have taken place in the Negro population as they are reflected in
       census data since 1870. Because of lack of comparable data, the time
       periods covered vary from chapter to chapter. The 1960 Census of
       Population provides the most recent data used except in chapter VII
       where data for 1965 were available. Some of the data needed were
       available only for nonwhites while other data were available only for
       Negroes. In tabular presentation these two terms are used distinctly,
       but in the textual discussion the terms are used interchangeably
       unless otherwise indicated since 92 percent of nonwhites are Negro.
       In Census Bureau usage, "non-white" includes persons classified as
       Negro, American Indian, Japanese, Chinese, Filipino, Hawaiian,
       part-Hawaiian, Aleut, Eskimo, and "other races." Many people feel
       that the changes taking place in the Negro population in the mid-
       1960's are so great that trends and conditions prior to 1960 are of
       historical interest only, with little relevance to the present and
       future. Although the importance of the changes generated by the Civil
       Rights Act of 1964 and the milieu that produced this legislation are
       not to be underrated, it is doubtful that these changes will be
       reflected in future census data except as minor accelerations of a
       few trends. In most areas of human behavior about which demographic
       data can be collected, the inertia of the past is such that it is
       unreasonable to expect rapid change. Thus, the best guide to a
       picture of the future is a careful look at the past.* [Chapter
       headings are: I. Population Distribution; II. Population
       Redistribution; III. Occupational Change in Cohorts, 1920 to 1960;
       IV. Changes in Broad Occupational Groups; V. Changes in Occupational
       Distribution; VI. Education; VII. Marital Patterns and Household
       Composition; plus Appendix, including statistical tables]. *

608.   Rhee, Jong Mo. 1974. The Redistribution of the Black Work Force in
       the South by Industry. Phylon 35 (3): 293-300.

       Rhee points out that the massive abandonment of farming as a way of
       life and heavy exodus of blacks from the South is one of the most
       stricking demographic developments in the recent history of the U.S.
       This has been accompanied with an increase in the proportion of black
       women in the labor force with a corresponding decline in the
       proportion of black men. "Along with these trends there has been a
       remarkable shift in the redistribution of black workers by industry
       that is much greater than that observed for whites. It is these
       differences in participation in broad industry groups that is the
       subject of this paper." *

609.   Robinson, Henry S. 1969. Some Aspects of the Free Negro Population of
       Washington, D.C., 1800-1862. Maryland Historical Magazine 64: 43-64.

In this article, Robinson takes a historical look at the color composition of the population of Washington, D.C. He asserts that "the Negro has played a prominent role in Washington since the city's early beginnings in the last decade of the eighteenth century....In 1800 there were approximately 14,093 persons living in the District of Columbia....The white population numbered 10,066, free colored-- 783, and slaves--3,244. By 1830 there were 4,604 free colored persons and 4,505 slaves in a total population of 30,261. By 1860 the free colored population had risen to 11,131, while the number of slaves had declined to 3,185 against a total of 75,080....Immediately, prior to the abolition of slavery in the District of Columbia in April, 1862, 78 percent of the colored population was free....It is thus evident that in 1865, when slavery had at last been abolished in the United States... the colored population of Washington was adequately represented by a capable leadership....No longer can it be said that the Negro in Washington at the close of the Civil War was illiterate, poverty-stricken, and without adequate leadership. This survey refutes this theory and attempts to reveal an enlightened group of Negro people who have generally been ignored or overlooked." ★

610. Rubin, E. 1967. **The Sex Ratio at Birth.** American Statistician 21 (4): 45-48.

Several aspects of the disparity in birth ratio of males over females are discussed including variations among different races, variations by order of birth, by age of the parent, and in multiple births. Avenues of statistical exploration are suggested in an attempt to indicate certain peculiarities in nature. The Negro population in the United States has a sex ratio of 102 males to 100 females as opposed to 105:100 for whites, a highly significant difference. Inferences from these statistics are suggested for study of the sex ratios of mixed unions. The group classified as Mulatto show a lower sex ratio and further analysis of this was suggested including examination of slave records. For the white population sex ratio declines from 106.2 to 102.9 between 1st order and 7th order births. This is highly significant. However, nonwhite determinations were more irregular. Data limitations on sex ratio by age of parent prevented conclusive results. Multiple births among whites show a decline from 105.3 for single live births to 103.2 for twins and 86.1 for all other plural deliveries. Among nonwhites these ratios are 102.3, 99.7, and 102.6, respectively. Further information should be developed using the multiple facts relating to the sex ratio at birth.★

611. Saveland, Walt, and Paul C. Glick. 1969. **First-Marriage Decrement Tables by Color and Sex for the United States in 1958-60.** Demography 6 (3): 243-260.

A new set of first-marriage tables is compared with earlier tables that were prepared by Grabill and Jacobson. The new tables show, among other things, the number of first marriages, first-marriage probabilities, and death probabilities for single persons in a stationary (life table) population by color and sex, based on 1960 Census data on marital status and age at first marriage and on general mortality rates for 1959-61. A comparison of the earlier tables with the new tables provides evidence of a decrease of one or two years in the average age at first marriage between 1920-40 and 1958-60 and an increasing tendency for first marriages to be concentrated within a narrower span of years. The prospects for eventual marriage have risen to the point where it is estimated that all but 3 to 5 percent of the young adults are expected eventually to marry. This development has gone so far that the main question remaining is not whether young people will ever marry, but at what age they will marry.*

612. Schmid, Calvin F., and Charles E. Nobbe. 1965. Socioeconomic Differentials Among Nonwhite Races in the State of Washington. Demography 2: 549-566.

Stratification phenomena are of special importance to the field of demography since they are closely related to mortality, fertility, morbidity, occupational characteristics, employment, education, mobility, urbanization, and some other demographic variables. In this paper Schmid and Nobbe are concerned with stratification patterns among nonwhite races in the state of Washington. The general finding of this paper is that there is a relatively consistent and well defined strata hierarchy among the several nonwhite races, as measured by differences in education, occupation, and income. Relative to education and occupation, Japanese ranked highest; blacks ranked 4th; Filipinos, fifth; and, Indians, sixth. With respect to income, white population is found to be in the first place, blacks fourth; Filipinos, fifth; and, Indians sixth. Another finding of this paper is that since 1940 all races have shown upward trends in all three dimensions.★

613. Schnore, Leo F. 1965. Social Class Segregation Among Nonwhite Metropolitan Centers. Demography 2: 126-133.

We have examined 1960 census tract statistics in the areas of heaviest nonwhite concentration within a number of large metropolitan centers. We selected only those tracts which (1) contained at least 400 nonwhites and (2) were contiguous to the main areas of nonwhite concentration, that is, the major ghettos. We then eliminated those tracts with unusual population characteristics, such as those containing large institutional population. Finally, we tabulated the data--for nonwhites only--by combining tracts within radial distance zones, based on a one-mile interval, and (except in New York City) centered on the heart of each central business district. The results are presented in the form of averages for the nonwhite populations of the various distance zones.*

614. Schuyler, George S. 1932. Quantity or Quality. Birth Control Review 16 (6): 165-166.

Many blacks do realize the importance of quality rather than quantity. This is apparent from the profound interest in and strong desire for information on birth control among many blacks. Addressing those who emphasize quantity, Schuyler states: "The question for Negroes is this: Shall they go in for quantity or quality in children? Shall they bring children into the world to enrich the undertakers, the physicians and furnish work for social workers and jailers, or shall they produce children who are going to be an asset to the group and to American society. Most Negroes, especially the women, would go in for quality production if they only knew how."★

615. Simmons, Janet T., and E. S. Lee. 1974. The Extraordinary Composition of Rural Black Population Outside the South. Phylon 35 (3): 313-322.

The point of this paper is very simple. The American black has found little of promise in rural areas outside the South. His presence there is not always--in some areas, not even usually--a matter of choice. To no small degree, the rural non-Southern black lives in institutions or in other types of group quarters. Only in the South do blacks living in households account for the usual great majority, and even there the rural population, one of the last large reservoirs of potential migrants to central cities, is rapidly diminishing. The fall of the birth rate among blacks, coupled with still heavy out-migration of young black adults, may in time reduce the rural black population of the South to the same kind of adventitious population found elsewhere. When that time comes, the black will be most urban of populations, and above all, the most likely to live in the deteriorating central cities, be they Northern or Western, and given present trends, even be they Southern.★

616. Sims, Newell L. 1932. Hostage to the White Man. Birth Control Review 17 (7-8): 214-215.

Neglect, undernourishment, sickness, dependency and delinquency is what the big family is likely to mean for the Negro household. It is this sort of behavior that the white man is coming to resent. Time was when the dominant race was over indulgent, but that is rapidly passing. The Negro can no longer ask indulgence, he must command respect. If he will earn to control his fecundity, he will not have to give hostages to the white man till the white man despises him for his weakness and counts him a social menace.*

617. Smith, T. Lynn. 1957. The Changing Number and Distribution of the Aged Negro Population in the U.S. Phylon 18 (fall): 339-354.

The Negro population of the United States is aging rapidly. During the first half of the Twentieth Century the number of Negroes aged sixty-five and over increased by 229 percent whereas Negroes of all ages gained only 70 percent. Even so, however, the aging of the Negro population was less rapid than that of the total population, for the comparable figures for the latter are almost 300 percent for the aged contingent and just under 100 percent for those of all ages. In 1900 only one Negro out of every thirty-four had passed the sixty-fifth birthday, whereas by 1950 the comparable ratio was one out of every eighteen. There will probably be about 1,150,000 Negroes aged sixty-five and over in 1960, and the number will probably continue to rise until 1990. Then a slight decrease in absolute numbers is likely to take place before the census of the year 2,000. Unless one can forecast the numbers of future births, and this the writer thinks impossible because the birth rate is a variable that is dependent upon other variables we likewise are unable to predict, the proportions of the aged in future years cannot be forecast with any degree of accuracy. Nevertheless it seems unlikely that the proportions of the aged among Negroes will equal that among whites prior to the year 2,000. The larger number of babies born in the years 1875-1884 in comparison with those born in the decades 1865-1874 is the principal cause of the increase in the numbers of aged Negroes between 1940 and 1950. Well over two-thirds of the gain must be attributed to this factor alone. Combined with the decreased mortality in the ages less than fifty-five, the other factor involved in the increased size of the generation, it accounted for 71 percent of the increase. Immigration, almost negligible, was responsible for no more than 2 percent of the gain. Lowered mortality in the ages fifty-five to seventy-four was significant, accounting for about 27 percent of the change. The distribution of the aged Negro population is undergoing some fundamental changes. Among the states the tendency is for the distribution to become even less equitable, in relation to the Negro population in general, than that prevailing in the past. This is in sharp contrast with the tendency of the aged population in general, whose distribution among the various states is becoming more equitable in proportion to population. In general the states with sizable Negro populations in which the proportions of aged Negroes are high and getting higher are located in the heart of the deep South. A heavy exodus of Negroes in the prime of their lives from those states seems to be the principal cause of the rapidly increasing proportions of the Negro aged in those states. Large numbers of aged Negroes are moving from one state to another, with California, Louisiana, Illinois, Michigan, New York, Texas, Florida, Ohio, and Alabama being on the receiving end of the largest contingents. The largest numbers of them are leaving the states of Virginia, Mississippi, North Carolina, Kentucky, Maryland, South Carolina, Georgia, Tennessee, and Arkansas, in the order named. Aged Negroes also are migrating in substantial numbers from the farms to rural-nonfarm and urban districts.*

618. Smith, T. Lynn. 1966. The Redistribution of the Negro Population of the United States, 1910-1960. Jr. of Negro History 51 (3): 155-173.

The 1910-1960 period has witnessed a great redistribution of the black population in the United States. In this paper Smith examines and presents his major findings relative to the major changes in the distribution of the black population in the United States. His analyses are based on the data from decennial censuses.*

619.   Stewart, Douglas E. 1971. Population, Environment, and Minority
Groups. In: Population, Environment and People. Noel Hinrichs (ed.).
New York: McGraw Hill Book Company. Pp. 104-112.

Population control is in the interests of black people and will not
lead to further subjugation. Stewart suggests that by limiting family
size blacks should be able to better afford advanced training beyond
high school and, thereby, be able to acquire economic power.*

620.   Sullivan, Teresa A. 1978. Racial-Ethnic Differences in Labor Force
Participation: An Ethnic Stratification Perspective. In: The
Demography of Racial and Ethnic Groups. Frank D. Bean and W.P.
Frisbie (eds.). New York: Academic Press. Pp. 165-187.

Taken by itself, the labor force participation rate is difficult to
interpret for even one minority group, let alone several. Set within
a conceptual framework that defines minority groups by access to
resources and by the type of income those resources generate, the
labor force participation rate becomes part of a set of variables
that can describe the ethnic stratification system and changes within
it. The unemployment rate, a component of the participation rate,
becomes one important indicator, and a measure of entrepreneurship
becomes another. The ethnic stratification perspective helps define
minority groups, define what is problematic about them, and identify
the ecological niches in which minority groups may flourish. Economic
activity varies by position in the stratification hierarchy, as does
one measure of fertility. Other demographic consequences can also be
expected.*

621.   Taeuber, Irene B. 1968. Change and Transition in the Black Population
of the United States. Population Index 34 (April-June): 121-151.

Transformations within the metropolitan areas cannot be divorced from
transformations in areas of origin. The dynamics of the black population of the United States involve all groups of that population,
whether in the rural areas of the Deep South or the central cities of
the Northeast, the Midcontinent, or the West. The moving youth
transmit the heritage and the retardation of the areas where they
were reared to the areas where they live and seek to work. Social and
economic change, altered marriage and family norms, and reduced birth
rates in the South are essential in national transformation.
Resolution of the demographic difficulties requires that convergence
in the metropolitan North and West to the base of origin in the South
be replaced by convergence in the South to an evolving base in
metropolitan North and West.*

622.   Taeuber, Karl E. 1969. Negro Population and Housing: Demographic
Aspects of a Social Accounting Scheme. In: Race and the Social
Sciences. Irwin Katz and Patricia Gurin (eds.). New York: Basic

Books. Pp. 145-193.

Taeuber discusses black fertility, family patterns, population health, housing, migration, and black population. He calls for extensive and substantive research relative to black population, especially the policy-related issues. The author surmises that using the carrot approach young and capable researchers must be encouraged and/or recruited to do more research about black population, for merely waiting for research proposals to come in will not suffice.★

623. Thomlinson, R. 1975. The Structure of Population. In: Demographic Problems: Controversy Over Population Control, by R. Thomlinson. Encino, California: Dikenson. Pp. 192-214.

The structure of a population, i.e., various aspects of its compositon or characteristics, is discussed. Sex roles and ratios and age composition of a population are the most important variables in this regard. The U.S. and world population are aging, and, at the same time, adding more numbers at the lowest age levels of the population, due to the post-World-War II fertility rise. This combined situation creates a rising dependency ratio. The variations in population composition according to states and regions in the U.S. are pictured in a series of tables. The American marriage rate of over 95% is among the highest in the world; the American divorce rate is also among the highest. Educational achievement in the U.S. is reviewed. Employment and income in the U.S. is discussed and tabulated by states. Female participation in the labor force in various countries is discussed.★

624. Thompson, Charles H. (ed.). 1953. The Relative Status of the Negro Population in the United States. Journal of Negro Education 22 (3): 221-451. The Yearbook Number 22.

This is a special issue of the Jouranl of Negro Education devoted to the study of black population. The articles included in this issue are as follow: (1) Burgess, Robert W. Census data: summary of types available, limitations, and possibility of extension. Pp. 232-241; (2) Valien, Preston. The growth and distribution of the Negro population in the United States. Pp. 242-249; (3) Lorimer, Frank, and Jones, Dorothy S. The demographic characteristics of the Negro population in the United States. Pp. 250-254; (4) Siegel, Jacob S. Natality, mortality, and growth prospects of the Negro population of the United States. Pp. 255-279; (5) Edwards, G. Franklin. Marital status and general family characteristics of the nonwhite population of the United States. Pp. 280-296; (6) Bailer, Lloyd H. The Negro in the labor force of the United States. Pp. 297-306; (7) Hope, John, II. The employment of Negroes in the United States by major occupation and industry. Pp. 307-321; (8) Jones, Lewis W. The Negro farmer. Pp. 322-332; (9) Sheldon, Henry D. A comparative study of the nonwhite and white institutional population in the United States. Pp. 355-362; (10) Miller, Carroll L. The relative educational attainment of the Negro population in the United States. Pp. 388-404; (11) Houchins, Joseph R. The Negro in professional occupations in the United States. Pp. 405-415; (12) DeCosta, Frank A. The relative enrollment of Negroes in the common schools in the United States. Pp. 416-431; (13) Thompson, Charles F. The relative enrollment of Negroes in higher educational institutions in the United States. Pp. 432-441; and (14) Reid, Ira De A. The relative status of the Negro in the United States. A Critical Summary. Pp. 442-451. Summaries of some of these papers are given in appropriate chapters in this volume.★

625.   Tsong, Peter Z. 1974. Changing Patterns of Labor Force Participation Rates of Nonwhites in the South. Phylon 35 (3): 301-312.

The purpose of this paper is to examine one facet of the redistri- bution of the black population, that associated with changes in population of labor force age and in the labor force participation in the South as compared with the non-South or the nation as a whole.*

626.   Tucker, Charles J. 1974. Changes in Age Composition of the Rural Black Population of the South 1950 to 1970. Phylon 35 (3): 268-275.

Of a decline of 1.5 million persons in the South's rural black population between 1950 and 1970, a net minimum of 1.9 million blacks moved to cities within the region or moved outside the region altogether therefore accounting for all the decrease. Had it not been for relatively high fertility among those who remained declines would have been greater still. The estimates of migration presented in this paper are based on the application of 1950-1970 cohort ratios for the total U.S. black population during the period and do not include estimates of migration among those persons born after 1950. These ratios were applied to the age structure of the black rural popula- tion of the South in 1950. For total losses, the heaviest were obviously found among the farm segment of the rural population. The farm population declined by no less than 86 percent over the twenty years. Within this population, losses were heaviest among farm youth who were younger than 20 years of age in 1950, most of whom must have migrated to urban places. For older persons who had already become established in farm occupations by 1950, migration was not as heavy and when it occurred, was probably directed to nonfarm areas or entailed a shift in occupation from farm to other activities without a movement to urban places and jobs. Shifts in occupation or residence on the part of many farm blacks of older ages had the effect of increasing the number of nonfarm blacks by more than 50 percent over the twenty year period. Young adult age groups barely increased in number at all. There is little wonder, then, that the dependency ratio of nonfarm blacks increased drastically due to the shortage of young adults. The growth of the rural nonfarm population is therefore somewhat illusory. Most of its growth was simply due to occupational shifts of the older farm population or its movement from farm to nonfarm areas. As the population base of farm blacks is now so low, it is quite unlikely that in the immediate future the nonfarm

population will experience the massive gains that it did in the
fifties and sixties. Many nonfarm youth are leaving the rural South
for cities as is shown in their low survival ratios. This implies
that even if employment opportunities are available, they are not
commensurate with levels of educational training being obtained by
youth or their aspirations, nor are they as renumerative as jobs in
cities. What can be envisioned is continuing aging of the farm
population due to heavy outmigration of youth and possibly declining
patterns of fertility. The same will be true for the nonfarm
population but not to the same extent found in the farm segment. A
word of caution needs to be issued in the interpretation of phenomena
associated with the rural population which is not a homogeneous
geographic or residence category. Many counties which have substantial rural populations are found in close proximity to the
South's developing metropolitan areas and cities. Insofar as they may
be closely integrated both economically and demographically with the
metropolitan complex, these counties may well reap the benefits of
the suburbanization of retail and wholesale trade, the suburbanization of industry, and a wide array of essentially urban jobs and
services. This will certainly be true for the rural population found
within metropolitan counties which constitute a major portion of the
metro "ring." In such instances, jobs become available not only for
males but females as well with the result of increasing family
income. Counties which contain high proportions of rural blacks,
possess few urban centers, and are isolated from metropolitan areas,
constitute areas in which employment opportunities are scarce and
when they do exist, usually entail only unskilled or seasonal labor.
There is little chance for upward mobility for the young. These are
the areas which are losing population and are increasingly bearing
the burden of unemployment, poverty, and care for the elderly and
infirm.*

627. U.S. Bureau of the Census. 1965. **Distribution of the Negro
      Population.** 1960 Census of Population, Supplementary Reports, PC
      (S1)-49. Washington, D.C.: Government Printing Office. 2 pp., plus 3
      maps.

      This report consists of three maps and one table, showing the
      distribution of the black population in the U.S. for 1950 and 1960.
      Map 1 depicts the distribution of urban and rural population for the
      country as a whole. Map 2 depicts the distributions of increases and
      decreases between 1950 and 1960. And, map 3 shows the percent change
      in the black population during the 1950-60 period. The one table in
      this report, shows the number of black population by regions,
      divisions, and states for 1950-60 period and the percent change
      between 1950 and 1960. ★

628. U.S. Bureau of the Census. 1966. **Negro Population: March 1965.**
      Current Population Reports, Series P-20, No. 155. Washington, D.C.:
      Government Printing Office. 30 pp.

This report is a demographic, social and economic profile of the black population in 1965. The statistics presented in this report are based on a national sample collected by the Bureau of the Census in the Current Population Survey. In addition to some 11 pages of introductory definitions of terms and analysis, this report consists of five text and twenty detailed tables. Topics covered include: regional distribution and farm-nonfarm residence, age, mobility status, school enrollment, educational attainment, marital status, families, occupation, and income in 1964.★

629.   U.S. Bureau of the Census. 1968. **Negro Population: March 1967.** Current Population Reports, Population Characteristics, Series P-20, No. 175. 7 pp.

This report consists of seven tables (Table A, and Tables 1-6) depicting the social and economic characteristics of black population by place of residence in 1967. Data are from the Census Bureau's Current Population Survey of March 1967, and is based on a national sample of about 50,000 households. Black-white comparisons are also made. ★

630.   U.S. Bureau of the Census. 1971. **Distribution of the Negro Population, by County.** 1970 Census of Population, Supplementary Report, Series PC (S1)-1. 4 pp., plus two maps.

This report consists of two maps and three tables showing the geographic distribution of the black population in the United States in 1970.★

631.   U.S. Bureau of the Census. 1971. **Negro Population in Selected Places and Selected Counties.** Supplementary Report, Series PC (S1)-2. Washington, D.C.: Government Printing Office. 17 pp.

This report consists of a compilation of seven tables from the 1970 census showing the distribution of the black population in selected places and selected counties in the United States. Data shown relate only to places with a population of at least 25,000 and a black population of 10,000 or more.★

632.   U.S. Bureau of the Census. 1973. **Negro Population.** 1970 Census of Population, Subject Reports, PC (2)-1B. Washington, D.C.: Government Printing Office. 207 pp., plus 24 pages of appendix.

This report presents statistics on the Negro population, cross-classified by various social and economic characteristics for the United States, regions, selected States, standard metropolitan statistical areas, and cities. Selected housing character stics are also given.*

633.   U.S. Bureau of the Census. 1973. **The Social and Economic Status of the Black Population in the United States.** Current Population

Reports, Special Studies, Series P-23, No. 48. Washington, D.C.: Government Printing Office. 146 pp.

This report provides data on population growth, composition, and distribution, income, labor force participation, occupational distribution, unemployment, family composition and nature, housing and health conditions, voting behavior, and elected officials with a special section on low-income areas in selected cities.*

634. U.S. Bureau of the Census. 1976. Population Profile of the United States, 1975. Current Population Reports, Series P-20, No. 292. 40 pp.

The 1975 birth rate was 14.9/1000, as in 1974, but the fertility rate fell from 1857 in 1974 to an all-time low of 1800/1000 in 1975, representing a 27% decline since 1970. A 2120 rate is required for net replacement of the population, but the present age structure postpones attainment of zero population growth. The 1975 net civilian immigration rate was 2.3/1000, largely due to the influx of Vietnamese refugees. Ever-married women age 40-44 in 1975 have had an average of 3.3 children and will finish their childbearing years with the highest fertility rates of any cohort since the 1880s, while married women under age 25 are expected to show all-time low rates, intending to have 2.2 children on the average. The dependency ratio (population under 18 and 65 and over/100 population 18-64) dropped from 78.2 in 1970 to 71 in 1975 as the number of children declined. The annual number of divorces passed 1 million in 1975 for the 1st time in history. There is a trend toward marriage postponement, with 60% of men and 40% of women ages 20-24 having never been married. Female-headed households increased by 30% between 1970-1975. About 25% of those 25-34 have completed 4 or more years of college. Metropolitan areas are now growing less rapidly than nonmetropolitan ones, and fewer blacks are leaving the South. Women's labor force participation rate rose from 37.7% in 1960 to 46.3% in 1975. The number unemployed increased 54.3% between 1974 and 1975, with the rate highest for teenagers. Average family income (in constant dollars) declined 4% in 1974. 1974 median income was $13,360 for white families, $7810 for black families, and $9560 for those of Spanish origin. The lowest income category was families headed by a female ($4465/year). Blacks and Spanish-origin persons comprised 11% and 5%, respectively, of the population in 1975.*

635. U.S. Bureau of the Census. 1979. The Social and Economic Status of the Black Population in the United States: An Historical View, 1790-1978. Current Population Reports: Special Studies, Series P-20, No. 80. Washington, D.C.: Government Printing Office. 271 pp., Tables and Charts.

This report presents an historical review of changes in the demographic, social, and economic characteristics of the U.S black population. The historical profile is the distinguishing feature of this report. The focus of the study is on changes that have occurred in population growth, distribution, composition, mortality and fertility rates, income, labor force participation, education, employment, family composition, voting behavior, and black Armed Forces personnel. Data for this report are primarily from the decennial censuses and current population surveys. This report assembles under one cover data that have been published previously in several different reports, some of which are also cited in this bibliography.*

636. U.S. Bureau of the Census. 1980. **Population Profile of the United States, 1979.** Current Population Reports: Population Characteristics (350): 1-52.

This document provides a profile of the U.S. population in 1979 in terms of: 1) population, size, growth, and distribution, and 2) the social, economic, and racial characteristics of the population. Trends during the 1970s are also noted. The total estimated population of the U.S. in 1979 was 221,719,000. The population increased by 0.9% in 1979 and this increase was slightly larger than the increase in 1978. The increase was due to a slight increase in immigration and a slightly higher birth rate. The birth rate increased from 15.3/1000 population in 1978 to 15.8/1000 population in 1979. The total fertility rate increased from 1800 to 1840/1000 women of childbearing age from 1978-1979. During the 1970s, the total fertility rate decreased 26% and the fertility rate for both blacks and whites declined. Between 1970-1979 the population under 14 years of age declined by 14%, the population 65 years of age or older increased by 24%, and the cohort of 25-34-year-olds increased by 39%. In 1979, 49% of the women, aged 20-24, were never married. In 1960 the respective proportion was 28%. From 1970-1979, the proportion of children under the age of 18 who lived with a single parent increased from 12% to 19%. 91% lived with their mothers in 1979; however, the proportion of those living with their fathers increased over the past year. During the 1970s nursery school attendance increased 71% and about 85% of all young adults completed 12 years of education. In 1979 college enrollment was higher for women than for men due primarily to the high enrollment of older women. The annual rate of population growth in non-metropolitan areas was 1.18% and in metropolitan areas it was 0.73% during 1970-1978. Central cities experienced an annual decline of 0.4% during the 1970s due primarily to out-migration of whites. Northeast and north central regions experienced out-migration and the southern and western regions experienced in-migration. During the 1970s the labor force grew by 24% while the population of 16-year-olds grew by 18%. In 1979, 42% of the labor force was made up by women and 10% by teenagers. Median family income was $17,640 in 1978. The median income for full time workers was $9640 for women and $16,000 for men. 9% of the whites, 31% of the blacks, and 22% of persons of Spanish origin lived at or below the poverty level in 1978. In 1979 the proportion of blacks and of persons of Spanish origin in the noninstitutionalized civilian population was respectively 11.6% and 5.6%. Numerous tables provide information on the U.S. population for 1970-1979.☆

637. U.S. Bureau of the Census and U.S. Bureau of the Labor Statistics. 1967. Social and Economic Conditions of Negroes in the United States. BLS Report No. 332. Current Population Reports, Series P-23, No. 24. Washington, D.C.: Government Printing Office. 97 pp.

This is a statistical report about the social and economic conditions of the Negro population of the United States. It shows the changes that have taken place during recent years in income, employment, education, housing, health and other major aspects of life.... The aim throughout has been to assemble data to be used by government agencies at all levels, and by the general public, to help develop informed judgments on how the Negro is faring in this country.*

638. U.S. Bureau of the Census and U.S. Bureau of Labor Statistics. 1968. Recent Trends in Social and Economic Conditions of Negroes in the United States. Current Population Reports, Series P-23, No. 26. BLS Report No. 337. Washington, D.C.: Government Printing Office. 28 pp.

This report is a demographic, social, and economic profile of the black population in the United States. The analysis is based on the March 1968 Current Population Survey. Poverty and income, residence and migration, jobs and unemployment, education, family composition, life expectancy, maternal and infant mortality rates, 1940, 1950, and 1960-1966, are among the topics discussed.*

639. U.S. Bureau of the Census and U.S. Bureau of Labor Statistics. 1969. The Social and Economic Status of Negroes in the United States, 1969. BLS Report No. 375. Current Population Reports, Series P-23, No. 29. Washington, D.C.: Government Printing Office. 96 pp.

The progress of the Negro toward full social and economic equality with other Americans has been one of the major issues of the 1960's. Impressive progress has been made, but wide discrepancies remain. This report, prepared jointly by the Bureau of the Census and the Bureau of Labor Statistics, is the third in a series of statistical reports about the social and economic conditions of the Negro population of the United States. Current data are presented in tables showing the changes that have taken place in income, employment, education, housing, health, and other major aspects of life.*

640. U.S. Bureau of the Census and U.S. Bureau of Labor Statistics. 1971. The Social and Economic Status of Negroes in the United States, 1970. BLS Report No. 394. Current Population Reports, Series P-23, No. 38. Washington, D.C.: Government Printing Office. 156 pp.

This report is a demographic, social, and economic profile of the black population in 1970. In addition to four pages of introductory remarks, section headings include: I, Population Distribution; II, Income; III, Employment; IV, Education; V, Housing; VI, Living Conditions and Health; VII, The Family; VIII, Women; and IX, Military and Voting, followed by an appendix.★

641.   Valien, Preston. 1953. The Growth and Distribution of Negro Population in the United States. Journal of Negro Education 22 (3): 242-249.

Valien examines the rate of growth, geographic distribution, urban-rural distribution, and black migration. He then discusses the demographic, political, and socioeconomic significance and implications of the changes in the growth and distribution of the black population in the United States.★

642.   Valien, Preston. 1970. Overview of Demographic Trends and Characteristics by Color. Milbank Memorial Fund Quarterly 48 (2, Part 2): 21-37.

The growth and changing distribution of the Negro population have important social implications for the Nation. The percentage of Negroes in the total population has changed little since 1890, when it was 11.9 per cent. For several decades after 1890, the Negro population declined as a proportion of the total population until 1930, when it was 9.7 per cent. Since 1930, however, lower Negro mortality, relatively higher Negro birth rates and the restriction of European immigration in the 1920's combined to reverse the declining trend. In 1960, the Negro population was 10.5 per cent of the total population and in 1970 it is estimated to be slightly above 11 percent. The great change in Negro population has not been in numbers or in relative proportion, but in regional and urban distribution. The movement of Negroes away from the South has reduced the percentage of the Negro population living in the South from 90 percent in 1910 to slightly over 50 percent in the late 1960's. The movement of Negroes has been to the cities and especially to the central cities of metropolitan areas. In 1960, the six cities with the largest Negro population were all outside the South (New York, Chicago, Philadelphia, Detroit, Washington and Los Angeles). These six cities, with Negro populations ranging from over one million in New York City to over 300,000 in Los Angeles, has almost a fifth of all Negroes in the United States. It is the concentration of Negroes in the central cities that heightens the visibility of Negroes in the cities and creates housing problems and pressures on urban resources and services. The metropolitan distribution of the Negro population has implications for other social and economic characteristics. Negroes in metropolitan areas exceed those in nonmetropolitan areas in educational attainment and occupy better-paying and higher-status jobs. It is also well established that the nonwhite to white fertility ratio decreases with increasing income and with urbanization. Finally, voter participation of Negroes in the North and West has been greater than that of whites in the South. As

pointed out, Negroes in the North and West voted at a rate seven
percentage points higher than that of Southern whites. Where voting
participation is combined with the spatial segregation of Negroes in
central cities, the increasing political power of Negroes in densely
populated urban areas comes as no surprise. This, in turn, will
inevitably have long-range effects on the economic, educational,
health, family and political status and ultimately upon the level of
aspirations of the Negro population.*

643.   Van Arsdol, Maurice D., and Leo A. Schuerman. 1971. Redistribution
and Assimilation of Ethnic Populations: The Los Angeles Case.
Demography 8 (4): 459-480.

Redistribution relative to metropolitan growth of Negro, other
nonwhite and Spanish name populations is examined in Los Angeles
County from 1940 to 1960 for a comparable grid of subareas. The
subareas are defined relative to their maturity at different time
points in order to partially control for population redistribution
effects of neighborhood life histories, the spread of older subareas,
and the persistence of neighborhood patterns. Shifts in ethnic
concentration are shown for both older and newer subareas. Concurrent
changes in neighborhood social structures and ethnic populations are
described. Findings are categorized under three themes: First, ethnic
population increments and redistribution were generally restricted to
expanding older subareas. Ethnic populations did not spatially expand
at a rate equal to the spread of the metropolis or of older subareas.
Second, segregation is greater in both older and newer neighborhoods
for Negroes than for other ethnic populations. Negroes experienced
the largest proportional increments in both older and newer subareas,
as well as the greatest stability in subarea occupancy. Finally, the
spatial separation of ethnic population impedes assimilation in that
unique patterns of neighborhood structure come to characterize
different ethnic populations, and changes in ethnic composition are
reflected in changes in neighborhood social structures.*

644.   Walters, Ronald. 1974. Population Control and the Black Community.
The Black Scholars 5 (8): 45-51.

This is part one of a two parts article by Walters, Professor of
Political Science at Howard University. In this paper, Walters begins
with reviewing a 1973 statement issued by the World Population
Society (WPS) calling for the necessity of population control among
the poor who constitute the majority of the world's population.
Walters takes issue with the WPS's statement. Turning his attention
to the poor and powerless blacks in the United States, Walters
examines the reasons blacks do not (or perhaps should not) trust the
family planning and population policies designed by the dominant
group in the American society. Walters concludes this part of his
article by asserting that no doubts a portion of population problem
can be attributed to the unplanned reproductive behavior among the
poor and the powerless, but it is not certain whether the cause of

the problem must be expended against the poor or those responsible for their plight.★

645.   Walters, Ronald. 1974. Population Control and the Black Community. The Black Scholar 5 (9): 25-31.

Part one of this article is cited in the previous item. In this part Walters addresses "the major questions of white controlled population programs by an assessment of the impact of family planning upon the black community. It should be noted at this point that it has not been asserted that family planning is genocidal, or that there is a plot, or that black families do not want fewer children, or that the revolution needs unlimited births, nor do I defend any of the other widely held views among blacks surrounding this complex problem. Rather this article raises questions related to the rationale for black fears as a basis for black control and questions the efficacy of a movement directed toward an overall population limiting strategy visited upon poor and black people in America and in the Third World."★

646.   Watson, Franklin J. 1968. A Comparison of Negro and White Populations, Connecticut: 1940-1960. Phylon 29 (Summer): 142-155.

In this study, Watson describes and assesses the black-white differentials in socioeconomic and demographic variables such as educational attainment, occupational status, age structure, fertility, and infant mortality in the State of Connecticut during the 1940-1960 period.★

647.   Weisbord, R.G. 1975. The Black Debate Begins: Quality vs. Quantity. In: Genocide? Birth Control and the Black American, by R.G. Weisbord. Westport, Connecticut: Greenwood Press. Pp. 41-55.

The history of the movement to provide family planning services among the black community in the U.S. is traced. Opinion concerning the practice of birth control has varied among blacks. Black nationalist opposition to birth control is based on the belief that in numbers there is strength.★

648.   Williams, Dorothy Slade. 1961. Ecology of Negro Communities in Los Angeles County: 1940-1959. Unpublished Ph.D. Dissertation. 200 pp.

One of the major changes in Los Angeles County has been its rapid population growth. An important source of the population influx has been the Negro in-migrant whose rate of increase has surpassed all expected forecasts. Changes in the size, growth, and distribution of the Negro population in Los Angeles County have far-reaching political, social, and economical effects. The general purposes of this study were (1) to investigate the origin and location of the major Negro communities in Los Angeles County, (2) to examine the social and ecological factors affecting their location and internal structure, (3) to analyze the social, economic, and ecological changes of the Negro population, and (4) to analyze the impact of the increasing Negro population upon the nature and distribution of Negro communitiies. Two major hypotheses relating to the proportional distribution of the Negro population were set forth: (1) that areas inhabited by a substantial number or proportion of Negroes tend to increase their Negro proportions, whether rapidly or slowly, whereas a decrease seldom occurs once an area has reached a proportion of 10 per cent Negroes, (2) for communities with the highest proportions of Negroes there is a progressive decrease in proportion of Negroes with increasing distance from the center of the city outward. The   principal source of data for testing the above hypotheses was census material. Using the concept of succession as an analytical tool, 110 census tracts were classified on the basis of the proportion of nonwhite residents to the total population. According to the succession scheme, the tracts were grouped into five stages of invasion, early consolidation, consolidation, late consolidation, and piling-up. Changes in racial composition, educational level, home ownership, age comparison, and overcrowding were analyzed. Negro communities were identified by stages of succession. Findings: The findings were analyzed under two categories: (1) those relating to the hypotheses of the study, and (2) those relating to stages of succession. The first hypothesis which stated generally that the proportion of Negroes in an area will continue to increase after the 10 per cent level is reached was supported by the empirical findings of the study. The second hypothesis which attempted to verify the existence of a spatial gradient in the proportional distribution of the Negro population from the center of the city outward was not substantiated. Data analyzed on the stages of succession showed: (1) In each stage of succession the Negro population increased during the 1940-1950 decade. (2) In the consolidation, late consolidation, and piling-up tracts the Negro population decreased from 1950 to 1956. (3) The proportion of Negroes continued to increase in all stages of succession for the entire period under investigation. (4) The Negro population increased more rapidly than the increase in occupied dwelling units in each stage. (5) The increase of nonwhite owner-occupied dwelling units exceeded the increase in succession. (6) The rate of increase in room crowding was greater for the nonwhites than for the total population in the consolidation, late consolidation, and piling-up stages. (7) The median number of school grades completed for the nonwhite population declined slightly in the piling-up and thirty-eight of the consolidation tracts but the total educational attainment of the tracts remained stable. (8) The age compositoin of nonwhites showed a distinct concentration of persons in ages 15-49 in the consolidation, late consolidation, and piling-up tracts for the ten-year period. (9) The major Negro communities included in this study were in the consolidation category in 1956, except the West Jefferson and Central Avenue communities which were in the late consolidation or piling-up stage. Conclusion: Certain tentative conclusions relating to Negro communities in Los Angeles County may be drawn from these findings: (1) The original Negro

community has served as the core for the establishment of other major
Negro communities. (2) New communities are usually formed by
centrifugal expansion. (3) Within Los Angeles County, the major Negro
communities are concentrated in Los Angeles City. (4) Communities
with 10 per cent Negro proportion tend to increase in their Negro
proportion. (5) Communities invaded by nonwhites have a more rapid
increase in owner-occupancy and room crowding among nonwhites than
among the total population. (6) The educational level of communities
invaded by nonwhites remains stable or improved. (7) The majority of
nonwhites in census tracts with highest concentration of Negroes are
in the age group 15-49. (8) The succession concept is a useful tool
for the analysis of population trends among nonwhites. On a whole the
entire study seemed to point to the continued concentration and
segregation of the Negro population in Los Angeles County.*

649.   Willie, C.V. 1971. Perspectives from the Black Community: A Position
Paper (Presented to the Commission on Population Growth and the
American Future). Population Reference Bureau Selection No. 37: 1-4.

Willie discusses the United States' population policy and growth as
they relate to the black community. He, himself a black sociologist,
explains the reasons why blacks consider the U.S. population policy
as genocide against blacks. He points out that the major problem
facing the population planners is the task of achieving their goal
without causing deep-rooted suspicion in the hearts and minds of
those they are trying to reach. He concludes his position by stating
that: "...a national population policy which would serve the best
interest of the blacks as well as the other citizens of this nation
should focus not on family planning, family size or family stability,
but on enhancing the health and wealth of every household in
America." ★

650.   Woofter, T.J., Jr. 1935. Southern Population and Social Planning.
Social Forces 14 (October): 16-22.

Contending that the nation as a whole is adjusting to a population
which is becoming stationary, but the rural South continues to
contribute vigorous increases, Woofter tries to examine possible ways
to deal with this increase. "This excess of population is reared in
an area where agriculture has declined rather than advanced." Several
reasons for the decline of agriculture are discussed. The study deals
with the situation before and after 1930. The author discovers
significant differences in the trends before 1930 as compared with
that after 1930. Woofter suggests the reconstruction of an agrarian
culture of expanding numbers, the rehabilitation of rural institutions and rural families, and the integration of this development
with that of the other major regions of the nation. Some of the far
reaching implications of the expanding population is discussed.★

651.   Word, David L., et al. 1978. Population Estimates by Race, for

States: July 1, 1973 and 1975. U.S. Bureau of the Census, Current Population Reports, Series P-23, No. 67. Washington, D.C.: Government Printing Office. 15 pp.

This report presents the results of research directed toward the preparation of population estimates by race. The method investigated is an extension of the Administrative Records technique used in preparing estimates of total population for States and local jurisdictions. The basic approach and procedures of the Administrative Records method are retained, but rely upon background data compiled by race to develop independent parallel series of estimates for each racial group.*

652. Zelnik, Melvin. 1965. An Evaluation of New Estimates of the Negro Population. Demography 2: 630-639.

After a short summary of the general assumptions and methods employed in the work by Donald J. Bogue, et al. (A New Estimate of the Negro Population and Negro Vital Rates in the United States, 1930-1960. Demography 1 (1): 339-358, 1964), this paper considers the specific steps Bogue, et al. took in arriving at their various sets of estimates, examines the actual census data they used, and discusses some of the results they obtained. Zelnik presents some new estimates of the size and age composition of the black population, and points out that his estimates are consistent with all the bits and pieces of information currently available.★

------O⊕O⊕O⊕O⊕O------

Author Index

Author	*Item*
Westlake, W.	388
Westney, L.	403
Westoff, C. F.	078, 092, 235, 256
Westoff, Charles F.	079, 305
Westoff, L. A.	092
Whitaker, K.	119
White, R.	584
Wienker, Curtis Wakefiled	528
Wilkie, Jane Riblett	529
Wilkinson, C. A.	586
Wilkinson, Doris Y.	151
Williams, Barbara A.	257
Williams, Dorothy Slade	648
Williamson, J. G.	526
Willie, C. V.	649
Willie, Charles V.	424
Willie, Charles Vert	530
Wingate	388
Wolf, S.	291
Wolfe, S. R.	258
Wood, Charles H.	004
Woodside, Moya	331
Woodson, C. Godwin	531
Woofter, T. J., Jr.	650
Woofter, Thomas Jackson	532
Word, David L., et al.	651
Wright, Gerald C., Jr.	260
Wright, N. H.	259
Wynder, E. L.	425
Yancy, W. L.	465
Yang, C. C.	299
Yetman, N. R.	213
Zelnik, M.	035, 095, 123, 137, 152, 153, 154, 155, 214, 261
Zelnik, Melvin	093, 094, 652
Zodgekar, A. V.	533

About the Author

JAMSHID A. MOMENI is Associate Professor in the department of sociology and anthropology at Howard University. He has previously published *Population of Iran: A Dynamic Analysis* and *The Population of Iran: A Selection of Readings.*